O9-AIG-871

R U S S I A

KAZAKHSTAN

GEORGIA
Tbilisi
AZERBAIJAN Baku
Yerevan
ARMENIA
Caspian
Sea

UZBEKISTAN
Tashkent

Bishkek (Frunze)   Almaty

KYRGYZSTAN

TURKMENISTAN

TAJIKISTAN
Ashkhabad   Dushanbe

CHINA

Tehran

Kabul

Bagdad   AFGHANISTAN   Islamabad

IRAQ   I R A N

KUWAIT

PAKISTAN

Delhi

NEPAL

Persian Gulf

UDI ARABIA

Riyadh
UNITED ARAB
EMIRATES   Gulf of Oman

INDIA

OMAN

Indian Ocean

YEMEN

Sanaa

DJIBOUTI

0	500	1000 km
0	250	500 miles

Studio Gideon Dan, 02-6520464

From Survival to Revival

From Survival to Revival

A Memoir of Six Decades in a Changing Jewish World

Stanley Abramovitch

gefen גפן

publishing house בית הוצאה לאור

JERUSALEM • NEW YORK

Layout: Marzel A.S. — Jerusalem

Cover Design: S. Kim Glassman

ISBN: 978-965-229-361-9

Edition   1 3 5 7 9 8 6 4 2

Gefen Publishing House Ltd.
6 Hatzvi St.
Jerusalem 94386, Israel
972–2–538–0247
orders@gefenpublishing.com

Gefen Books
600 Broadway
Lynbrook, NY 11563, USA
1–516–593–1234
orders@gefenpublishing.com

www.israelbooks.com

Printed in Israel

Send for our free catalogue

In memory of

My parents, Moshe and Adela Abramovitch

My late brothers Boruch and Herschel
who perished in the war

My late brothers Sam and Mick

My late son, Moshe

With love for

My wife, Noemi

My daughter, Edna, and her husband, Shaike

My son, Yossi, and his wife, Tammy

My grandchildren and great-grandchildren

Contents

Acknowledgements ix

Preface xi

The War Ends — A New Calling Awaits 1

From London to Tehran 31

Back to Europe 79

North Africa and Beyond 109

Israel and the Yeshiva Program 163

The Former Soviet Union — Reconnecting Communities 189

Epilogue: Reflections on a Lifetime 251

Glossary 257

Maps 261

Index 267

~ Acknowledgements

A number of years ago I was recuperating after having heart surgery. Time was heavy on my hands as there was not much I was permitted to do. At the suggestion of an old and dear colleague, Herbert Katzki, I started to dictate some of my recollections into a small tape recorder.

From those beginnings the present memoir grew. The original recordings went through many changes. They had to be shaped, put into proper sequence, supplemented with facts that I did not recall during my initial dictation, and trimmed of unnecessary and unsuitable details.

Unfortunately, Herb Katzki and other former colleagues who could have confirmed or corrected information are no longer with us. As much of the memoir has been compiled from memory many years after the fact, it could be that some details are inaccurate. I shall be happy to be corrected should any misinformation or mistakes be found.

I could never have completed this complicated task without the encouragement and assistance of colleagues and friends to whom I owe a great debt. Since this memoir is also the story of the American Jewish Joint Distribution Committee during more than sixty years, I had to have not only the consent of JDC headquarters, but also its support. That was readily given, especially by JDC's Chief Executive Officer Steve Schwager, its chief operating officer Eugene Philips, and assistant executive vice president Amir Shaviv. I am grateful for JDC's encouragement and generosity.

As a member of JDC's former Soviet Union senior staff team, I work closely with our regional director, Asher Ostrin. He more than encouraged me in this endeavor. He pushed me, he nagged me to continue in this effort, which turned out to be much longer than originally estimated. To him I would like to say thank you, friend, for your kind words and your interest not only in this memoir but also in the many short stories I have written over the years about people I have met and events I have witnessed.

This project could never have been completed without the unstinting, generous help of Antony Korenstein, a colleague at the JDC in Jerusalem. He reviewed every chapter. His advice and criticism were always relevant and constructive. He guided me step by step to the work's successful conclusion. I want to acknowledge his great contribution and express my heartfelt gratitude to him.

Naftali Greenwood helped me to prepare the first draft of the manuscript and Rachel Feldman reworked and shaped it. I am grateful to both of them for their patience in preparing the many drafts until we reached this final text.

Needless to say, my wife and children were and are my permanent support in all my activities. Their love, admiration, and advice have served me well throughout many years. I hope that this book will compensate them in some measure for the many hours I devoted to it instead of spending with them. I am fortunate to be part of such a warm family of children, grandchildren, and great-grandchildren.

~ Preface

Man proposes, God disposes, it is said. The account that follows proves the truth of that truism, as it tracks a Jewish boy from Poland to Great Britain and then over six decades of assignments on behalf of his people in dozens of countries on three continents.

I was born in Kalisz, Poland, on Pesach in 1920, as Yehoshua Abramowicz. I was the fourth of seven sons whom my parents, Moshe and Adela Abramowicz, brought into the world. Shlomo (Sam) Zalman, Avraham Mordechai (Mick), and my twin, Boruch, preceded me. Five years later, triplets were born. One of them, Herschel, survived; the others died at nine months and eighteen months respectively, of pneumonia, an incurable disease at the time.

We lived in a three-room apartment on the second floor of a three-story tenement building so infested with rats that even our dog was afraid of them. One large room served as kitchen and dining room, another for children and guests, and the third for my parents.

Conditions were primitive by today's standards. There was no running water, so everyone in the building made do with a common toilet in the courtyard. Drinking water was hauled upstairs from a well in the courtyard by a deliveryman who wore a special yoke to carry the buckets. Across the street was a large house, owned by wealthy Poles of German origin, that had a pump in its courtyard that produced very clean water. Occasionally we would go there and fill a bucket. We thought this would anger the owners, but they were very nice about it.

We regularly shared our apartment with at least one or two cousins who came from small towns in search of work. Since we were five children and the house had only a cot and two beds, we slept two or three to a bed, cousins and all, male and female.

These were considered reasonable accommodations in Polish terms; they sufficed for our family — and for our guests. Hotels were not ubiquitous in towns like Kalisz a century ago, so out-of-towners, especially Jewish ones, were directed to people's homes. I often woke up at night to find, sleeping next to me, a stranger whom my father had brought home from the synagogue. Our family was by no means rich, but it was leagues ahead of the genuinely poor, of whom there were many. We, at least, had beds to share. Three cousins of mine, who lived in a village not far from Kalisz, slept on the floor.

Hundreds of Jews in Kalisz were even worse off. They circulated from door to door, collecting coins, some supporting families in this fashion. They would enter our house and say, for example, "Good morning, five" — shorthand for, "I represent five other needy people; give me five *grush*." Once, an older person climbed the stairs to our apartment in severe winter weather. Mother gave him hot coffee and some bread and butter. Then my older siblings treated his frostbitten toes by smearing kerosene on them.

When I was ten, we had a regular guest at meals, a yeshiva student whom we treated to *essen teg*, a weekly "eating day" that householders provided to yeshiva students to help them stave off starvation. In addition, most Fridays it was my job to deliver a basket of groceries to a maternal uncle who had settled in town and owned absolutely nothing.

My parents never told us children that by sharing our beds we would emulate the Abrahamic code of hospitality. They never cited the chapter and verse of the admonition to help the downtrodden. They never told us that yeshivot and their students were the pillars of our people and that we had better support them. Nor did they expound on the moral value of distributing one's groceries among the worse-off. They just did it. And hundreds of thousands of Jews in Poland and elsewhere did the same.

Kalisz was not a shtetl but a substantial town whose 16,000 Jews comprised a third of the total population in 1921. The Ger Hasidim were dominant in Jewish affairs; the head of the *kehilla* — the Jewish community administration in Kalisz — belonged to the Ger court.

Even though there was a Hasidic synagogue on the ground floor of our tenement building and another group of Hasidim occasionally met on a higher floor, my family belonged to the non-Hasidic minority. The town had a Great Synagogue with a *beit midrash* (study center) next door. We attended this synagogue on Friday nights, primarily to listen to the magnificent cantor. The rest of the week, we attended a *shtibl*, a small and somewhat informal synagogue, which had been rented by men hailing from my father's home town, Sieradz. It was one of about thirty small prayer houses in the town.

All Jewish political parties were active in Kalisz; several published their own local newspapers and periodicals. Jewish trade unions enlisted both Jewish and Polish workers. As many as eleven Jews served on the thirty-four-member town council. There was a Jewish secondary school, the Gymnasium, and a Jewish primary school called Tachkemoni. There was a central place in the Jewish section of town where the kosher butchers practiced their trade and where there was a Jewish theater.

What Jews in Kalisz and Poland lacked, however, was a future. As the 1920s transitioned into the 1930s, the government enacted laws that increasingly crimped Jews' economic possibilities. In response, Jews sought ways to leave the country — something the Polish authorities both encouraged and perversely seeded with difficulties. Be this as it may, none of those who left planned to return.

I became aware of the process in 1928, when my father left to join his mother, three brothers, and three sisters in London. He went there on a tourist visa and stayed on once it expired. His plan was to obtain entry visas to England for the rest of the family. Until that could be arranged, he sent us money and clothing into which he sewed watches and other items that we could sell. Thus, the five Abramowicz boys grew up with an absentee father.

Despite it all, ours was a wonderful, happy family that lived decently with very little. Our parents struggled to raise children who had no options for the future. As teenagers, my brothers Sam and Mick were apprenticed to tailors in a career path typical of Jewish households. Neither of them, however, found work at the end of their training. Like hundreds, if not thousands, of young Jewish men, they were unwillingly idle.

Never, though, did the harsh conditions force us to compromise on our dignity. My mother was an unusual woman. She had the courage to handle all the problems, crises, difficulties, and unforeseeable obstacles of Jewish life in Poland alone.

Father tried hard to obtain immigration papers for the rest of the family but did not know exactly how to go about it. Furthermore, as an illegal alien, he was fearful of missteps that could jeopardize his own stay in England and therefore scuttle the entire plan to reunite the family there.

As a result, our family did not so much emigrate (at least in any orderly sense) as disperse. Some time in 1933, after Hitler had come to power in Germany, Sam was smuggled from Poland through Germany into France, the destination of many Polish Jews. He made it to Paris, found work, and endured severe hardships to build himself a future. Mick was to be sent to France in the same way at the ripe age of sixteen. On the first try, his smuggler defrauded him, pocketed his fee, and disappeared. On the second occasion, the smuggler led Mick and four others across the border, left them in some German town, and returned to Poland. German police captured four of the five the next day. Mick eluded them by hiding under a haystack, but while crossing back into Poland he was caught by Polish border police and imprisoned for a week in the company of hardened criminals. Upon his release, he unexpectedly showed up at home. One can only imagine my mother's anxiety. Still, conditions for Jews in Poland were such that young people had no choice but to try and try again. On his third attempt, Mick reached Paris safely.

For Jewish refugees from Poland, Paris was a haven but no paradise. Police often cordoned off streets or raided residences in search of undocumented persons. Those who could not produce papers went to prison. Work was hard to find. My brothers lived in attic rooms under terrible conditions and often verged on starvation.

I was too young to give thought to my future at that time. I was a good student, so my mother enrolled me in the prestigious Jewish Gymnasium of Kalisz. Since we spoke Yiddish at home, she hired private tutors to bring my Polish up to par. Due to our financial difficulties at home, my paternal Uncle Abraham, a very successful tailor and a bachelor, paid my tuition for the first three months or so. My mother covered all expenses after that. After two years at the Gymnasium, my father, applying connections in London, sent me a visa for study at the Etz Chaim Yeshiva in the East End of London.

At fourteen, I could not fathom the value of this document. Fortunate indeed, compared with the refugees and those who had no way to leave, were people like me who received a legitimate entry visa to any country other than Poland. Later on, Polish Jews who obtained such visas would live, and those who did not would die. It was that simple.

To my mind, however, the greatest challenges were my total lack of familiarity with either the English language or the Talmud that I would be studying. Dedicated as always, my mother sent me for tutoring in the latter subject.

These, however, were just the first steps toward emigration. To leave the country I next had to procure a Polish passport. The Polish authorities in Kalisz were loath to issue Jews with passports and in my case refused to come through until a schoolmate's father used his connections. Then I had to go to Warsaw to take physical possession of the British visa. I rode alone for an entire night on a truck that was traveling to my destination. When the vehicle stopped at Nalewki Street in Warsaw, I alighted. But not knowing where the British Embassy was, I stayed around the truck until it was ready to return to Kalisz, boarded it again, and went back home. We sent a friend to fetch the visa some time later.

Before my departure, Mother took me to her home town, Wieruszow, to pray at her parents' grave and to visit her family. They were much like our own family — poor, modest, and dignified people who led religious lives and shared what little they had with each other and their guests.

Returning to Kalisz, I left school and said goodbye to my friends. One night in March 1935, my mother, my brothers Boruch and Herschel, and several friends drove me to the railway station, where I bade them all farewell. My mother's final words to me as she held me close were, "Be a good Jew."

Mother remained behind with Boruch and little Herschel. I would never see them again. During the war they went together to the Warsaw ghetto and perished either there or in Auschwitz. On one occasion, we received a desperate letter from Mother, through the Red Cross, stating that Boruch was ill with typhus and needed oranges — as if a Jew in wartime Britain could simply pick up some oranges in the supermarket and send them on to Nazi-occupied Poland. It was merely her way of letting us know that my twin brother was very, very ill.

Had I remained in Poland, I probably would have shared their fate. Had I been spared, I doubt that I would have maintained my Orthodox orientation, though neither would I have "assimilated," since neither Jews nor Poles were receptive to that idea. Instead, I would probably have blended into the gray mass of nonobservant Polish Jews. The Gymnasium would have deserved the "credit" for this. Its teachers were great scholars; its stress on Hebrew was such that Israel's renowned "national poet," Chaim Nachman Bialik, paid it a visit. However, its Jewish education flowed from a purely secular point of view. Generally speaking, those associated with the Gymnasium regarded the Hasidic majority with some derision, labeling them uneducated, backwards, and medieval.

I boarded the train in a state of emotional exhaustion. I crossed Poland and Germany, eventually reaching Brussels, where a distant cousin's son, Zygmunt, greeted me. Zygmunt took me to his home, where the family had prepared a bed for me. Next to the bed they placed a large bowl of fresh grapes, a rarity in Poland that I had not eaten for quite some time. As soon as the light was turned off, I devoured as many grapes as I could.

The next day, Zygmunt sent me on by train and boat to England. Disembarking in Dover, I was greeted by Zygmunt's sister-in-law, Fanny, who took me by train to London. There, we went to my father's apartment at 46 Basset Road, North Kensington, which he shared with two bachelor brothers, Mendel and Leon, and my grandmother, Rose (Reisel).

Living elsewhere in London were Uncle Isaac, Auntie Feige, and Aunt Tzirel and her husband Luzer. These relatives had come to England before World War I and were quite Anglicized. It was Zygmunt's sister-in-law who furnished me with the name Stanley.

Sam reached London at about this time too. He had obtained a visa for Ireland and then, without documentation, took a boat to Liverpool and moved on to London by train. Mick stayed behind in Paris, alone, waiting for an opportunity to join us in London. We were very anxious for him. Whenever we saw anyone resembling Mick on the underground train, we stared in hope and then turned away in disappointment. He eventually made it to England when a sailor agreed to hide him in a boat, dress him in sailors' attire, and escort him out of the port.

Settling into Life in England

I found it all very strange, but settled into my new life quickly. First I visited Rabbi Eliyahu Lopian, Rosh Yeshiva (dean) of Etz Chaim Yeshiva, to be tested for placement. I approached the matter confidently; after all, I had learned a bit of Bible in school and had been tutored in Talmud. After I failed to answer any of Rabbi Lopian's questions, I was enrolled in the lowest class of the yeshiva, a class meant for ten-year-olds. I took my studies seriously and was promoted to the next class within six months. I found a good *havruta* (study partner) who helped me prepare for each day's lesson. Additional promotions followed over the next few years.

The Etz Chaim Yeshiva followed the Lithuanian Jewish tradition in scholasticism and piety. Rabbi Lopian himself was an important disciple of the *musar* movement, which preached and practiced an especially demanding version of Jewish ethics that focused on the perfection of individual virtues. The need to avoid wasting time on trivialities was only one of the *musar* teachings that I assimilated. Rabbi Lopian was assisted by Rabbi Nahman

Greenspan, who embodied the characteristics of scholarship, saintliness, and kindness, and projected the desired moral traits in innumerable small ways. Their actions gave me the fringe benefit of yeshiva life: the lifelong impact of the sacred teachings that transcended the contents of the texts per se.

My aptitudes and upbringing, however, ruled out religious scholasticism as an exclusive lifetime vocation. So, I began to study English in evening classes in order to be able to continue with my secular studies and go on to university. As soon as I felt I had enough English to begin studying for matriculation, I enrolled in additional evening classes at a preparatory school, choosing subjects that I thought I could pass easily, such as Hebrew, Latin, and German, as well as English and math.

The days were long. They began at Bayswater Synagogue, where I was a "*minyan* man," a regular, paid participant in the weekday morning services. After that, I spent the day learning at the yeshiva.

At age sixteen I took on a new responsibility: at 6:00 p.m. each day I reported to the Talmud Torah (boys' religious school) to teach. I was given this posting without preparation, let alone formal credentials. At first I did not know how to handle the class and the students took advantage of me until I learned the ropes. My salary for this work (two pounds per week), plus what I earned as a *minyan* man, sufficed for pocket money and transportation expenses. By the time I got home, after the evening classes, it was nearly 11:00 p.m. Father had dinner waiting for me. As a teenager, I could take it all in stride.

I recall this period as a relatively carefree time spent in the company of relatives. Sam and Mick held jobs in London and lived at home. My father dealt in furs, ran the household, and did the cooking for all of us. In the meantime, Nazi Germany steadily gathered strength. Father never stopped trying to obtain immigration papers for the rest of the family, but he never succeeded. To this day, I feel that had we been more energetic, daring, and assertive, we could have succeeded. When war finally broke out, it was too late for everybody. I did make an effort during the war to obtain a visa to Tangiers for Mother, but this attempt failed as well, possibly because I was too young, inexperienced, and ignorant of procedure.

In the summer of 1939, Father got a job as a kashruth supervisor at a summer camp of Torah V'Avodah (a religious Zionist movement) and I spent an enjoyable summer with him there. During that time, I received news that I had passed my matriculation exams. We returned to London in time for

Germany's invasion of Poland on September 1 and Britain's declaration of war on Germany two days later. A new chapter had begun, the consequences of which none of us foresaw.

Polish Jewry was trapped by the German and Soviet forces that partitioned the country. The Germans removed the Jews of Kalisz to the ghetto in Warsaw, which in due course was emptied into the furnaces of Auschwitz. The few Jews who survived did so by fleeing to the Russian occupation zone in the early going or outlasting the atrocities of the Nazis' camps. Mother, Boruch, and Herschel were not among them.

And there I was in England, beginning a fifth year at the Etz Chaim Yeshiva and, having earned matriculation, exploring possibilities of higher secular studies in the academic year to follow. At first I considered studying medicine, but the tuition fees for medical school were beyond my reach. My only realistic option was Jews' College, which offered undergraduate programs in rabbinics and teaching. I had by then ruled out a career in the rabbinate but had no idea what profession I might wish to pursue, except that it should be exciting, interesting, and challenging. After being accepted by the College, I embarked on a BA program in Semitic studies, in conjunction with the University of London.

It was a different life than I had known. I maintained friendly terms with Rabbi Lopian, who years later officiated and spoke at my wedding. However, I now moved in different social, religious, and academic circles. I adjusted to college life well enough to become chairman of the Students' Union. I continued to tutor and teach children, sharpening my pedagogical skills on the job. At the same time, I became involved in two Jewish youth movements. The first, Bachad (Religious Pioneer Alliance), offered an appropriate social setting for people of my age and outlook. In one of its weekly Shabbat encounters, I met a group of young people, aged thirteen to fifteen, from the Bnei Akiva[1] movement with whom I spent an enjoyable afternoon of study, song, and prayer. In subsequent weeks, I followed up with the group and became its counselor. In the movement, I used my given name, Yehoshua, and its diminutive, Shia. I continued to render my surname in its Polish spelling, Abramowicz.

September 1940 to May 1941 was a difficult period as London and other

---

1.   Bnei Akiva is a religious Zionist youth movement established in Palestine in 1929. Its ideology focuses on religious commitment and work on the land of Israel.

British cities endured nightly German aerial bombardments. Sometimes Father, Mick, Sam, and I descended to the Underground (subway) for the night, as did thousands of other Londoners; on other occasions we sat with our neighbors under the staircase of the building, which we considered the safest place above ground. I managed to go through the entire five volumes of Meyer Waxman's *History of Jewish Literature* under those stairs. Eventually, Sam and I habituated ourselves to the nightly bombings well enough that we simply stayed in bed.

During that time Mick and Sam enlisted in the Polish army, joining Polish formations that regrouped in Britain and took part in various Allied operations. In the very last large raid on London, on May 10, 1941, a German bomb blew out some windows in our house. I was thrown against the door by the blast, suffering a cut forehead, a broken finger, and shock. Several days in the hospital restored my health. However, in the inhabitants' rush to get out of the building, Father was evidently struck by the front door. He died of liver failure in March 1943. We could only speculate whether the blow inflicted by the door had led to his death.

My years in yeshiva and Jews' College had instilled me with knowledge of my Jewish background, a religious approach to life, and a strong sense of belonging to the Jewish people. I had begun to view Jewish life in its broad aspects. However, I still lacked the stroke of fortune, or the act of Divine providence (as my yeshiva training had taught me to regard it), that would create a personal connection with my people and its life.

Reaching Out

Most of my activities between Father's death and the end of the war remain somewhat murky in my mind. The war continued. Sam and Mick were away and we had no news of Mother, Boruch, and Herschel. In June 1943, after several months of cramming, I passed the BA Honors exams and received an upper second-class honors in Semitics. Then, more due to inertia than out of a sense of mission, I applied for doctoral studies and began research on the twelfth-century work *Sefer ha-Hasidim*. I pledged less than full efforts to my doctorate, which seemed to be leading me in an undesired direction — the rabbinate. As a PhD candidate, I received a small stipend that I augmented by teaching Hebrew and conducting morning services on Rosh Hashanah and Yom Kippur, even though I do not have a cantorial voice. More fulfilling were my activities in informal education. I became increasingly active in Bnei Akiva, running a large and successful camp in the summer of 1943, and counseling a Bnei Akiva group in subsequent months.

The galvanizing event for my future was a session of Parliament in 1942, at which the MPs commemorated the victims of Germany's crimes by rising to their feet. That spectacle, coupled with leaked reports about events in Germany and the German-occupied areas, elicited a stampede of volunteers for relief and reconstruction work in the postliberation era.

The agency that involved itself in this cause was the Central British Fund for Jewish Relief (CBF), through its Jewish Relief Unit (JRU). The organization had labored on behalf of German Jewry from the dawn of Nazi rule. It had helped German Jews emigrate and/or acquire vocational training, aided and lobbied on behalf of German Jewish refugees in the United Kingdom, and played a key role in the Kindertransport, in which more than 10,000 unescorted refugee children, nearly all of them Jewish, reached Great Britain from Central Europe.

In 1942–1943, the JRU began to form task forces that it intended to dispatch to Germany after the liberation of that country, to help Jewish survivors. The JRU urged all young people to volunteer, and anyone who identified strongly with Jewry felt duty-bound to respond in the affirmative. In fact, the main organizer of this venture, Janet Siebold, chief executive secretary of the CBF — a wonderful woman — was not Jewish. The volunteers came from across the spectrum of Jewish youth movements that operated in Britain, and I, as an activist in Bnei Akiva, was among the first in my circles to enlist. My reasons for doing so, apart from my Jewish connection per se, stemmed from gratitude: I had avoided the Nazis' clutches by coming to England and felt indebted to the survivors. Subconsciously, too, I may have hoped to find surviving members of my family.

From then until the liberation, I and other volunteers trained to rehabilitate the Jewish survivors whom we hoped to find in Germany. The training had a sense of vagueness. It was irregular, held on weekends and evenings in diverse locations. Both the trainers and the hundreds of trainees were volunteers. Oblivious to the actual developments in Europe, no one knew for what to train. All we could do was to simulate and role-play various situations that we imagined might be, such as states of emergency and encounters with ill and hungry survivors in camps.

As the Allied forces gradually liberated Europe, the JRU sent task forces to two locations — the Netherlands (which was liberated in phases starting in the summer of 1944) and Bergen-Belsen (liberated on April 15, 1945, and situated in the British occupation zone). The organizers overlooked me for these missions, instead choosing the most experienced and trained professionals (rabbis, community functionaries, social workers, nurses) available to them. I assumed that the JRU, which continued to form additional teams, would employ me when my strengths — experience in running Bnei Akiva camps and working with youth generally — would come in demand.

When Germany finally surrendered on May 8, 1945, I briefly joined the general revelry in the West End of London. I considered the significance of the victory. Since 1942, I had known — like everyone who kept even slightly abreast of developments — that the Jews had experienced a tragedy. We would only learn the full extent of the horror once the post-victory news reports would emerge. I had no idea then that my mother and youngest brother had died in Auschwitz. I could not know that my twin brother had probably died in the Warsaw ghetto. All I had known of Boruch's fate was that he had "needed oranges" — that he had been seriously ill.

Several weeks after the final liberation of Germany, an organization of which I had never heard — the American Jewish Joint Distribution Committee (AJJDC, JDC, or the "Joint") — contacted the CBF and the JRU. JDC, which had co-funded some activities with CBF over the years, had reopened its office in a liberated Paris in 1944, and in early 1945 launched a program to assist displaced persons (DPs) in Germany and Austria. Short of social workers and other staff members, JDC asked the JRU to recommend candidates for its work in Germany. Those chosen would report to JDC-Paris, whence they would be sent on to Germany for six months' volunteer service in establishing an education camp for displaced Jewish youth.

The JRU furnished JDC-Paris with a list of ten candidates and their curriculum vitae. JDC selected two of them. One was Mrs. Miriam Warburg (no relation to the founder of JDC, Felix M. Warburg). As the director of Youth Aliyah in the United Kingdom, Mrs. Warburg had a track record in rescuing children and youth. I was the second to be chosen. Here began my life's work with JDC. We left for Paris in June 1945.

JDC's Background

JDC was founded in 1914 to meet the Jewish welfare emergencies that World

War I had occasioned in Turkish-ruled Palestine and in Eastern Europe. After visiting Jerusalem in 1914, Henry Morgenthau, who was then United States Ambassador to Turkey, sent a telegram to Louis Marshall and Jacob H. Schiff of the American Jewish Committee in New York to ask for $50,000 to save the Palestinian Jews from starvation. The funds were raised and three American-Jewish organizations came together in a "joint distribution committee" to disburse them.

After the conflict and the calamities that befell the Jews of Eastern Europe in its wake, JDC embarked on a vast enterprise of "Rescue, Relief, and Rehabilitation" — the three goals that would direct JDC's endeavors in most locations around the world. The soup kitchens, workshops, cooperatives, and credit unions that it established, mostly in the 1919–1923 period, enhanced the welfare of nearly every Jewish community in Eastern Europe and helped strengthen the economic and social service foundation of the *Yishuv*, the Jewish community in pre-state Palestine.

There was also a fourth, implicit *R* that has informed JDC's work since the organization's earliest days. It is the *R* of "Retreat": the idea that JDC's assistance is temporary and that our interventions be designed to enable us to phase out our involvement when the work is done or when local Jewish organizations gain or regain the capacity to undertake it themselves.

Although JDC's mandate originally excluded education and culture, the new organization noticed that recipient communities were themselves setting aside some of their JDC welfare allocations for those purposes. The community leaders told a JDC commission that explored the matter in 1919 that they valued education and culture as highly as welfare. JDC acquiesced to the communities' wishes and supplemented its welfare activities with assistance in Jewish day schools, heders, and yeshivot, in teaching aids, teacher training, and cultural activities.

The devastation of European Jewry during World War II surpassed even the calamity that befell the Jews of Eastern Europe during and after World War I. JDC contributed immensely to aiding Jews during this Holocaust. Before the United States' entry into the war, it worked openly in the ghettos to provide vital relief. Then and later, its opertatives helped hundreds of thousands to escape Hitler's clutches.

Nevertheless, during the war, the Jewish population of Europe, including the Soviet Union, had plummeted from nearly 10 million to about 4 million. After V-E (Victory in Europe) Day, JDC engaged almost exclusively in feeding the hungry, clothing the naked, healing the sick, finding new homes for the homeless, and meeting one emergency after another as they arose to threaten the vestiges of European Jewry. I was grateful to join the laudable endeavor of this organization at such a crucial time.

The number of people assisted by JDC worldwide reached a peak at nearly 1 million in 1946. By 1953, however, their numbers had declined to 162,700. This reflected not the "solution" of most Jews' problems but mass emigration to Israel, the end of the rescue era in Europe, and the descent of the Iron Curtain, which deprived JDC of access to Jewish communities in all Eastern European countries save Yugoslavia. The human and financial resources that JDC had once invested in Poland, Hungary, Czechoslovakia, and Romania now began flowing with greater intensity to Israel, where most former DPs, as well as tens of thousands of refugees from the Muslim world, were settling.

The newly founded State of Israel was a refuge for these battered Jewish masses. For many, aliyah — the "ascent" as an immigrant to the Jewish homeland — was and is the ultimate and best answer for those who cherish Jewish identity. Recognizing Israel's unique value in the Jewish world, JDC has encouraged those who need or wish to do so to relocate there, while honoring and supporting the ability of those who wish to remain in other countries to live in functional Jewish communities. As an expression of the commitment that Jews everywhere have to the Jewish state, JDC has worked tirelessly on behalf of its American Jewish constituency to help strengthen Israel's own capacity to address the social challenges it faces.[2]

I myself long nursed the hope of making aliyah. But it would be decades before my work would allow my relocation to Israel — by then with my wife and children. Now, though, we are well into our fourth generation at home.

JDC takes both *J*s in its name — "Jewish" and "Joint" — seriously. It represents all Jews and serves all Jews, especially when they are in need. A Talmudic dictum illustrates the basis of JDC's philosophy: "*Kol Yisrael 'areivim ze l'zeh*" ("All Israel is responsible one for the other").[3] "All" includes Jews who harbor

---

2. At first, JDC's Israel offices were based in Tel Aviv. When JDC-Israel was established in 1976, its headquarters were opened in Jerusalem. In 2007, JDC-Israel won the Israel Prize for Lifetime Achievement and Special Contribution to Society and the State of Israel.

3. Babylonian Talmud, *Shavuot* 39a.

almost any attitude toward Israel — "Israel" in the broad sense of the Jewish people, as well as in the narrower sense of the state — and have any feeling of Jewish belonging. Adopting this approach, JDC rules out any trace of paternalism in distributing aid to others. It also eschews insularity and encourages action among and for non-Jews as well. Indeed, JDC has a substantial "non-sectarian" program, funded by Jewish and non-Jewish supporters.

As for me, I have been blessed with an uninterrupted tenure of over sixty years of active service with JDC, two-thirds of JDC's history thus far. Even though I was entitled to be pensioned at sixty, I felt it inappropriate to retire as long as I could make a contribution and my health permitted it. I am thankful that JDC concurred — a decision entirely consistent for an organization that respects history and those who have lived it. It was out of this respect, indeed, that I was encouraged to write this professional memoir.

The account in this book is arrayed geographically and sometimes reads like a travelogue. In fact, I enjoy all kinds of travel. That is fortunate: only a person who does can endure many years of constant flying, long trips along poorly maintained roads, and overnights in Second and Third World towns and villages. However, the many destinations described are truly one: a world where Jews have lived in severe distress; a world where Jewish communities have faced disarray if not devastation; a world where our brothers and sisters have needed help.

I hope to continue serving these Jews as long as I am able. JDC will continue to do so for as long as Jews are united by the spirit of "*Kol Yisrael 'areivim ze l'zeh*" — the bond of each Jew's responsibility for his fellow.

The War Ends — A New Calling Awaits

Our stay in Paris lasted all summer. Although our time there was intended to be brief, we could not be transferred to Germany sooner because of the chaotic state of transportation in Europe. The US Army was reluctant to share transport with meddlesome civilians, and JDC had a policy of operating wholly within American law.

For me, this first stay abroad was a pleasant, exciting interlude. Unlike London, Paris had not suffered significant war damage. I explored the city up and down. I visited every place of interest, and enjoyed a great deal of good food. I cherished my first banana in years, this fruit having long vanished from England.

On September 8, 1945, I attended Rosh Hashanah services in a Paris synagogue with a Rabbi Schneerson, a member of the Lubavitch dynasty. Later, I heard that he and the Lubavitcher Rebbe[1] in New York had had a falling-out of such severity that he had become estranged from the Lubavitch mainstream. I also heard that he had saved many Jewish children and adults during the war.

During this time, Miriam Warburg and I attended briefings and training sessions. These were meant to prepare us for a Germany that had been reduced to rubble. I also became acquainted with Dr. Joseph J. Schwartz, director-general of JDC and director of JDC programs in Europe. Identifying himself simply as "Joe," at first impression he gave no hint of his greatness. Within a short time, I would observe how his words were always well chosen and showed deep understanding. He had a clear vision of what had to be done

---

1. Rabbi Menachem Mendel Schneerson (1902–1994), "the Rebbe," leader of the Chabad-Lubavitch movement from 1950.

for the survivors of the Holocaust and he had the ability to persuade the JDC board to accept and support his vision.

"Joe" Schwartz received us warmly and delivered a concise but inspiring briefing. He told us that we would encounter harsh conditions. He did not burden us with a grand mission statement or finely detailed guidelines. He simply sketched out the stages of our mission in Germany. First, we would restore the survivors to normalcy. Second, we would attempt to reconstruct Jewish life. Third, we would prepare survivors for resettlement in other countries — foremost Palestine or, failing that, the United States, South America, or South Africa. We, Dr. Schwartz's emissaries, were to "go there and help." We were to boost the aid that other agencies were providing, give matters a Jewish slant, think on our feet.

As I would discover later, JDC did have a grand mission, one that would eventually give rise to a vast program of assistance among the DPs.

JDC had made its first appearance in a Displaced Persons (DP) camp — Buchenwald — on June 15, 1945, but it did not deploy relief teams systematically until it formalized its status with UNRRA (United Nations Relief and Rehabilitation Administration) on July 31.

Several days after Rosh Hashanah, we were flown to Munich by US Army air transport. From there, we visited various facilities in the area to complete our training and preparation. We spent Yom Kippur — September 17, 1945 — at the large DP camp in Landsberg, about twenty miles west of Munich. We took the opportunity to visit a few synagogues in Landsberg proper. At one of them, I witnessed a marvelous spectacle.

We saw people walking from one synagogue to another. As they walked, they encountered a young Jewish girl. The very sight of this lovely apparition agitated them greatly. For one, they had not seen a Jewish child in years. Second, it was Yom Kippur, one of the four days in the Jewish calendar on which *yizkor*, the memorial prayer for the deceased, is recited. However infrequent the *yizkor* service is, these Jews in Landsberg needed no prayer book for the occasion.

To solemnize this amazing sight — a living Jewish girl — they stopped and recited a silent *yizkor* for their own children and young siblings who had perished at the hands of the arch-murderers. As these people gaped at her, the girl smiled, not realizing what the fuss was about. She had survived the mass extermination, but some 1.5 million did not.

We left Landsberg to make a short visit at the DP camp in Feldafing, and from there we were driven to our destination, Camp Föhrenwald. It was less than two miles outside a small town called Wolfrathshausen, and about twenty-two miles from Munich.

Camp Föhrenwald

My training in Paris had prepared me to witness dire conditions and horrific deprivation. I was to experience something of an anticlimax. Appalling scenes, such as rotting corpses and skeletal survivors (many of whom perished soon afterward of disease and overeating) had greeted the first Allied observers in the liberated concentration camps. These observers ranged from General Dwight David ("Ike") Eisenhower, supreme commander of the Allied forces, down to rank-and-file soldiers and journalists. By the time I arrived, the area was several months removed from that. The physical conditions in Föhrenwald were such that I had no need for the spade that I had brought for use in maintaining basic sanitation.

The camp was made up of small houses that had been requisitioned by the US Army, a central mess and dining hall, a small hospital, and other facilities. It had been built for employees of a nearby munitions plant that had served the Wehrmacht;[2] it may have been meant for their families as well. In all, it could accommodate about 2,500 people. A team of eight Hungarian doctors staffed the camp hospital, brought in by the Germans to care for the munitions workers.

The camp was run by an UNRRA team. JDC and UNRRA were by that time well acquainted at the highest levels. The UNRRA director in the camp, a Canadian named Jean Henshaw, greeted me amiably. We kept up a friendly relationship during the time we worked together. She was an effective administrator — although her short stature almost masked this attribute.

DPs of fourteen European nationalities were gathered in the camp. Our goal was to have the American Army and UNRRA move the non-Jewish residents out and replace them with Jewish youth from Feldafing and Landsberg. It was for this purpose that JDC decided to post a representative to Camp Föhrenwald in particular. At this stage, most camps had no JDC representative at all.

---

2.   Wehrmacht: The armed forces of Nazi Germany.

The DPs in Germany

At first, most of the Jewish DPs in Germany were survivors liberated from concentration camps on German soil. They were soon joined by those who had been haphazardly marched or transported by the Nazis from extermination and labor camps in Poland, the Baltic states, and the occupied areas of the USSR, as the Red Army gradually liberated those areas.

At the time of liberation, as many as 100,000 Jews, out of an estimated 1.5 million survivors on the continent, shared camps with even larger numbers of unwanted neighbors. In some cases, these neighbors included Nazi collaborators and other anti-Semites from the Jews' "home" countries!

That Jewish DPs should have their own camps represented an important policy shift on the authorities' part. It became obvious that in the initial DP period, UNRRA and the US Army — which had liberated the area and retained it after Nazi Germany's surrender (as did the British, the French, and the Soviets elsewhere in Germany and in Berlin) — did not quite appreciate the uniqueness of the Jewish condition. I was told of how Germans were once brought in to guard a DP camp. Needless to say, that led to violent friction between Jews and Germans. At JDC's insistence, the Germans were removed from the camp, for their own good.

The US Army initially perceived surviving Jews through an American prism. This meant that they considered the Jews as members of their respective non-Jewish nationalities — Polish Jews as Poles, Hungarian Jews as Hungarians, and so on. As a result, the US Army also expected the Jews to accept, if not to desire, repatriation to their countries of origin.

Back in those countries, however, Jews largely perceived themselves, and were perceived, as members of their own distinct nationality. And that nationality had just taken the most hideous beating in history — partly at the hands of members of their non-Jewish former compatriots.

At the time of Germany's surrender, the number of displaced Europeans came to more than 13 million. This figure quickly diminished as non-Jews were returned to their countries of origin or emigrated under the laws of various host countries, foremost the US quota system.

For most Jews, though, the prospect of returning to their countries of origin was almost as repugnant as that of remaining in DP camps in Germany or Austria. Some who did return received a welcome reminiscent of the wartime atrocities. Thousands of Jews returned to postwar Poland, but found their homes now in hands of their former non-Jewish neighbors who refused to return the properties to their Jewish owners and often acted violently against the claimants. In July 1946, a pogrom in Kielce massacred forty-three Jews.

Moreover, the Jews still had no nation-state of their own. Zionism, the movement that aspired to correct the Jewish predicament, had managed by the time of liberation to create a proto-state in faraway Palestine. A majority of Jewish DPs wished to emigrate to that state-to-be. Even those who had not subscribed to Zionism before the war understood its necessity now.

The gates of Palestine, however, were carefully guarded by a British government that opposed nearly all Jewish immigration. Consequently, the distress suffered by Jews in DP camps was more compounded than that experienced by any other group. They grieved the loss of loved ones and the obliteration of communities. Dislocation and statelessness left them in despair.

Germany's own fate was undecided too. The country was in ruins and the victorious Allies had partitioned it into four occupation zones — American, British, French, and Soviet. The eventual disposition of each zone remained uncertain. Moreover, Germany was as opposed to serving as a refuge for displaced Eastern European Jews as these Jews were to accepting such a solution.

Thus, liberation day set a chaotic flux in motion. Borders and zone frontiers were unstable, to put it mildly. Survivors moved from camp to camp, from one zone to another. They hoped to better their personal circumstances. For many, this meant the hope of finding relatives.

Many Jews would have departed for Palestine — by braving the British blockade if necessary — had they not harbored hopes of finding surviving family members in Europe. Lists of names were posted in all possible locations. They advertised scores of survivors who desperately scoured the area for one another and for any clue of lost relatives. The center of this and other Jewish activity in the American zone was at the headquarters of the Central Committee of the Liberated Jews in Bavaria, located in Munich. This committee compiled the lists, to which DPs would add their own names. Most of the quests ended with painful disappointment.

The Population of Camp Föhrenwald

American Army policy had been somewhat perplexed with regard to handling foreign DPs in Germany. To sort things out, President Harry S Truman sent

Earl Harrison, the US representative to the Intergovernmental Committee on Refugees (IGCR),[3] to visit the DP camps and examine the overall situation in Germany. Harrison's recommendations, including the establishment of specifically Jewish camps, were accepted and then carried out by General Eisenhower.

The camps were placed under UNRRA auspices, and several organizations obtained UNRRA authorization to operate in them. JDC had had experience with distressed Jewish communities before and during the war, and so was considered the best suited to meet urgent needs in Jewish DP camps, such as the establishment of schools and the distribution of its own supplementary supplies.

The plan for Föhrenwald, then, was to make the camp all-Jewish and I, as JDC's representative, was to help implement this policy.

To gather young survivors in Föhrenwald, I was to visit other camps along with Eli Rock, who was the JDC director in Munich, and persuade young Jews to make the move to what, at the time, was conceived as a camp for Jewish youth.

Once this was accomplished, I was to work hand in hand with the other organizations that operated in the camp. There was UNRRA, the US Army at a later stage, the Jewish Agency for Palestine,[4] various Jewish movements, and groupings formed by the DPs themselves. Our shared goal would be to reinstate the most basic of Jewish needs: education for youth, in all its senses.

The very notion thrilled me. This undertaking would put my training to service in the highest calling. I would be taking part in the rescue of Jews. I would have a hand in the reconstruction of European Jewry.

Almost as soon as we began working on this mission, though, we were forced to abandon it. The reason was simple: The Nazis had left so few young survivors that the mission as we had conceived it could not be accomplished. Instead, we found ourselves negotiating with older people. Among them was Rabbi Jekutiel Judah Halberstam, the Klausenberger Rebbe.

---

3.   The Intergovernmental Committee on Refugees (IGCR) was established at the Evian Conference in 1938. Its goal was to assist in the resettlement of refugees from Europe.

4.   The Jewish Agency for Palestine was the government-in-waiting of the Jewish community — the *Yishuv* — in pre-state Palestine. In 1948, it became the Provisional Government of Israel under the leadership of David Ben-Gurion.

Rabbi Halberstam, a descendent of the Hasidic Sanz dynasty, was living with his surviving Hasidim in Feldafing. JDC promised to help him and his followers to relocate to Föhrenwald.

The rabbi balked at the conditions that he and his flock would receive in Föhrenwald. Nutrition was his main concern, as it was for administrators and inhabitants of DP camps throughout Germany, Austria, and Italy. In fact, this concern reflected survivors' recent deprivation. Having been starved by the Nazis, they now concerned themselves with every detail of their diet. Various camps offered different levels of diet, precisely measured in calories. By the end of 1945, daily rations provided by the Army and UNRRA in DP camps were approximately 2,500 calories. Some Jews living outside the DP camps were even worse off: the military treated them as Germans, who received a meager 1,300 calories a day.

A typical target allowance, such as that requested by the Klausenberger Rebbe, was 4,000 calories per day — almost twice the official ration. It was not an unreasonable request, and JDC agreed to it.

Rabbi Halberstam was also concerned about the accommodations that he and his Hasidim were being offered. He sent his own people to inspect the camp, to assess its potential. Only once the rebbe was satisfied that Föhrenwald had much more to offer than Feldafing did he agree to relocate. He moved there with nearly all his Hasidim, using transport provided by the US Army and UNRRA, their arrival occurring at a time when non-Jewish nationals were gradually leaving the camp.

Other Jews were also arriving in Föhrenwald, taking advantage of the porous borders of postwar Europe. One of these new arrivals was another rabbi from Hungary, a younger man named Nathan Zvi Friedman. I discovered that he was a great Talmudic scholar, and that he, his wife, daughter, and a son had somehow escaped during the war and survived by disguising themselves as non-Jews.

In Föhrenwald, Rabbi Friedman and the Klausenberger Rebbe became rivals. Their personalities and outlooks were very different. The rebbe influenced people by sheer Hasidic charisma. Rabbi Friedman did so by force of scholarship. Rabbi Friedman, believing that some people would prefer to stay out of the Hasidic rebbe's orbit, established a congregation in one of the houses. The rebbe did the same in the large hall of one of the central buildings. Rabbi Friedman's synagogue held services daily. The Hasidim convened in the large synagogue mainly on Shabbat.

Although I did not take sides, I often attended services at the Klausenberger Rebbe's synagogue. As part of its efforts to help the DPs resume normal Jewish life, JDC provided the synagogue with a Torah scroll, from which the rebbe himself would read.

Jean Henshaw, the UNRRA director, was particularly awed by the rebbe. In fact, she would summon me to her office whenever she heard that he was about to visit — ostensibly to translate for them, but as much, I suspected, to help her feel that the conversation would take place on near-equal terms.

As for Rabbi Friedman, I encountered him regularly in the camp. JDC helped him too, furnishing a truck to gather water from natural sources — snow in this case — for the ritual bath (*mikve*) that he built in the basement of a small building.

I also gave him something that became a cherished gift. While exploring the attic of my requisitioned house, I had found a photocopy of a substantial portion of the famous Munich manuscript of the Talmud. After making the discovery, I took it to the camp and lent it to Rabbi Friedman at his request. He kept it for the rest of his life — an outcome that, truth to tell, had not been my intention, but which nonetheless represented a small example of how our efforts contributed to the rebuilding of Jewish practice among the survivors!

Years later, I met Rabbi Friedman several times in Israel, where he settled in Bnei Brak. In 1957, he and Rabbi Lopian, my former yeshiva principal from London, officiated at my wedding in Tel Aviv.

Another personality who left a favorable impression on me — and on many others — was an American Army chaplain named Abraham (Abe) Klausner. A Reform rabbi, Klausner was also unorthodox in his actions. He was a dynamic man who wore fixity of purpose on his sleeve. He worked with the US Army on the Jews' behalf and, when necessary, employed his authoritative, sometimes abrasive, manner to bend Army and UNRRA officials to his will. Klausner accomplished much for the Jews in the camp.

Members of the Jewish Brigade were also active in the camp. These were Jewish soldiers from Palestine who had fought in the service of the British and remained in Europe, sometimes clandestinely, after the war. One of my closest coworkers belonged to the Brigade. He was Menachem Gemorman, a wonderful human being: quiet but dynamic. He was a member of a kibbutz south of the Sea of Galilee. He brought supreme devotion to his task in the camp, helping wherever help was needed. He became an informal address for people who had problems or grievances, and would often bring these to my attention when special handling was necessary.

Conditions and Supplies

Although my formal status was JDC volunteer under the supervision of Eli Rock, the JDC director in Munich, in practice I was closer to being my own boss. I received an allowance of two pounds per week from JDC and, after being annexed to the UNRRA team, I gained several amenities. I shared a private house with the UNRRA people several miles from the camp, a house that had been requisitioned from the Germans for UNRRA use. From there I commuted to the camp by UNRRA transportation.

Like all members of the JDC staff, I wore an American Army uniform. This policy was of the Army's making and was advantageous to both sides. It enabled the Army to control access to its facilities, allowing its guards to admit its own and affiliated personnel, and to exclude others, specifically German workers. For those of us who wore it, the uniform provided access to the PX (the Army canteen). The JDC jeep even carried American license plates, allowing me to go wherever American travel authorizations permitted.

The Army and UNRRA provided the DPs of Föhrenwald with the standard, basic foodstuffs and other commodities, but many were not satisfied with them. Most people made breakfast for themselves at home; others visited the central kitchen. They received enough food at lunchtime to suffice for dinner as well, but supplemental rations were always needed.

The first supplements from JDC came in the form of clothing. Extra food, such as chocolate and canned preserves, began to arrive somewhat later. We made parcels out of the food supplements and used them as wedding presents. In due course, the value of in-kind provisions that JDC sent for DPs in Germany amounted to many millions of dollars.

None of the food provided by the Army and UNRRA was kosher and therefore was not acceptable to those who adhered to the kashruth laws — myself included. The authorities gave this no thought at that point.

In the first weeks after the liberation, some DP camps were almost as tightly quarantined as concentration camps had been. By the time of my arrival, though, DPs were mobile and those in Föhrenwald traveled about quite a bit, giving them the opportunity to find commodities they needed. They were remarkably self-sufficient and resilient.

Munich was the closest major town, but some people went farther afield. A few began to do business with Germans, who were willing to barter valuables for food, coffee, or cigarettes. Some of these goods were contraband, part of a trade known to the authorities as the black market and to the Jews as the "free market."

This "free market" was an important source of supplementary foodstuffs, and virtually the only source of kosher food — specifically meat. The camp had its own kosher butcher, who would buy chickens and the occasional cow from the local German farmers, which he would slaughter and prepare according to dietary laws, and then sell to observant camp residents.

Since I didn't have a kitchen of any kind, I wasn't able to take direct advantage of the butcher's services. I generally ate whatever was inherently kosher in the UNRRA canteen — bread, butter and jam, peanut butter, fruit, and vegetables. On a fairly regular basis, though, camp families would invite me for a meat meal, particularly on Shabbat.

Food and lost family members were not the only things DPs sought outside the camp. They were eager to exercise their freedom to wander in and out of the open borders. They would travel extensively by train, visit friends or family in other camps, or simply roam for days with no particular aim. They were, indeed, amazingly mobile, despite the paucity of available transportation.

Working on a Personal Level

In a typical day in Föhrenwald, I drove to the camp with the UNRRA staffers in time to reach my office at 9:00 a.m. As self-sufficient as the DPs were, when I arrived in my office in the morning, I often found people waiting for me with personal problems.

Some would want me to help track down relatives in the United States. Others would ask for supplies for the workshops. Couples came to present notes from rabbis confirming that they were about to get married, an event that under JDC policy entitled them to supplemental provisions. People wanted to move to different quarters. Relatives of the sick required my help in arranging a stay in a convalescent home. Members of the detail that felled trees for fuel in the winter required extra rations. Rabbis needed a tractate of Talmud to study.

I had two sources of supplies: JDC, or UNRRA in coordination with JDC. The nature of the supplies was "whatever was available at the time of shipment." Occasionally, people made requests that I could not honor. Visa applicants, for example, often asked me to sign character references. I refused to be anyone's rubber stamp, and would agree to sign only for those I knew and considered worthy.

A Safe Place to Be

The camp had its own resident-run police force — headed by a rather disreputable young man who did a lot of illegal business. It also had its own prison. Sometimes Jews were imprisoned for their own protection. In one such case, someone in the camp had accused a fellow resident of having been a Kapo — a Jew whom the Nazis had placed in charge of a residential barracks for a group of prison laborers, or the like. Many Kapos, thinking they could save themselves from the other Jews' fate by doing the Germans' bidding, had been cruel and zealous in their duties, although one occasionally heard exculpating stories — of a Kapo who merely pretended to brutalize his charges, for example.

When the inhabitant of Föhrenwald recognized the alleged former Kapo, he announced the discovery in public. This attracted a furious mob. To avoid being lynched, the suspect allowed himself to be incarcerated in the camp prison. In other cases, Kapos fled from the camp in hopes of starting over somewhere else, where they would not be recognized.

Focus on Education

Although my colleagues and I realized that the notion of transforming Föhrenwald into a center for Jewish youth was unrealistic, education was nevertheless a priority for the youngsters who were in the camp. As such, my first major task in the camp was to set up a Jewish school. Today, such a school would be termed a "day school." We recruited teachers from among the DPs and were allocated a house in the camp as the school premises. JDC provided some books and teaching materials. We left the curriculum to the teachers. The school functioned.

My next mission came out of nowhere. One day, a man walked into my office in the camp and identified himself as Gad Goldman of Kalisz — my hometown. Gad said he would like to work for me. He turned out to be a decent and pleasant person. What is more, he had the organizational talent to arrange matters that I could not handle myself. I agreed to use him, although in what capacity I did not yet know.

From the start, he proved invaluable. Gathering a group of people, Gad sent them to a nearby German munitions factory, where they dismantled a large number of machines and brought the parts back to the camp. In this fashion we created a vocational school in the camp — in addition to the day school — something I could never have done alone.

Once this was accomplished, I invited Yaakov Oleisky, a former ORT[5] official in Lithuania who was then living in Landsberg, and others to see the vocational school. Oleisky took the floor and delivered a speech: "I am here today to open the ORT school," he began. This affiliation was news to me, but I was too flabbergasted to react. As a matter of fact, it was better to leave the school in the hands of ORT, with its superior resources and experience, than in the care of a JDC volunteer.

Lasting Relationships

Shortly after becoming my indispensable assistant, Gad Goldman met Sylvia, a young Jewish woman from Romania. She was a wonderful, wise, and warm human being. They soon married. As time passed, Gad and Sylvia accompanied me wherever I worked, moving with me from camp to camp. They later emigrated to Honduras and, subsequently, to the United States, but remained my lifelong friends.

In the meantime, my relationship with Rabbi Halberstam improved steadily. As we became more friendly, I began visiting him at his home in the camp and took part in some celebrations of his Hasidim.

On an occasional evening, Rabbi Halberstam would ask me to drive him to places where some of his Hasidim had settled. He wanted to give them moral support and offer whatever assistance he could provide. By doing so, he kept up a large and strongly attached following among survivors who originally came from Transylvania, where the rabbi had resided before the war.

So it was with one young couple who visited me to obtain one of our JDC wedding-present parcels. To obtain this, the groom presented a rabbi's note confirming that they had registered for marriage. I could tell from their origins and behavior that the bride and groom were bona fide Klausenberger

---

5.　Organization for Rehabilitation in Training, founded in 1880.

Hasidim. However, the note bore the signature of Rabbi Friedman, indicating that he would perform the ceremony. I asked the woman why she had not given Rabbi Halberstam this honor. She explained that the Klausenberger Rebbe insisted that she wear a wig after the wedding. She told me that she and her future husband did not plan to practice this custom.

I wondered if this couple was among the many who had strictly observed the religious commandments before the war but had lost their faith in the cataclysm. In the wake of the Holocaust, some young people from strong Hasidic families abandoned religious practice. Many also brushed aside the social principles that had guided them. Their former world was gone. They had watched their families go "up the chimney," in DP jargon.

To my great surprise, several days before the wedding the bride told me that she had decided to ask Rabbi Halberstam to officiate after all. She felt that she belonged to his "crowd." Thus was the rebbe's profound impact on his followers.

Lasting Duties

In the course of our nocturnal outings, Rabbi Halberstam and I discussed many topics. He told me of his ordeal during the war. When the Germans occupied his area of residence in Transylvania, intellectuals, leaders, and rabbis were the first targets for extermination. For this reason, he shaved his beard to blend in with the Jewish masses. He was sent from one labor camp to another until the end of the war; his last stop was a camp near Dachau where he hauled cement bags. Whenever the Allies bombed the area — which they did frequently — he and the other men in his detail seized the opportunity to take a break from their backbreaking work. They were so exhausted that they would fall asleep in the woods, undisturbed by the bombs that thundered to earth around them.

Rabbi Halberstam's wife and eleven children were all murdered. He survived to reorganize the lives of many thousands of followers. Years later — by which time he had become famous in much wider circles and had built a town-sized neighborhood called Kiryat Sanz in Netanya, Israel, for his followers — I paid him a visit. He remembered me well. The rebbe asked me what I was doing and I explained that I was doing the same as I had done in Germany, that I was working for JDC. To which the Klausenberger Rebbe replied, "I, too, am doing the same as I did in Germany."

Miriam Warburg was another early associate who went on to do "the same as in Germany." She went about her labors in Föhrenwald in a methodical manner that revealed her German upbringing. She always kept copious notes and a diary. Unfortunately, her accomplishments in Germany were cut short. In the fall of 1945, she contracted pneumonia and tuberculosis and went to Switzerland for treatment. After her recuperation, she resumed her activities with Youth Aliyah in London.

I also fell ill in the winter of 1945/46. My affliction, diphtheria, landed me in the camp hospital, where I spent some time in quarantine. I felt it ironic that part of my work was to make sure that DPs who fell ill in the camp were visited by doctors. JDC made sure I received excellent care, and as I recovered, I was sent to convalesce at a mountain retreat where Jewish DPs were also recuperating from various illnesses.

My first replacement in the camp during my absence was a young American woman who was so overwhelmed by the daily problems that needed attention that after only one day she sent a jeep to bring me back. I clearly could not return at that moment — it took me a full two weeks to recuperate. So another assistant from JDC took over and handled my duties until I returned.

The Residents' Committee

In Föhrenwald, as in other camps, Jews with "strong elbows" took over various functions — a reflection of the residents' burning desire to reclaim control over their own lives. In Föhrenwald, a three-member residents' committee managed internal camp affairs.

The members of this committee had evidently obtained these positions through appointments from the US Army. But they lacked what might be called popular support. The camp residents accused all three of pilfering, profiteering, and abusing their posts.

On one occasion, one of the committee members drove to Munich to bring a truckload of clothing from JDC for camp inmates. He returned suspiciously late, explaining that the truck had broken down on the way. No one in the camp believed the story. They were convinced that he had detoured to some other location to sell some of the clothing. All three appointees were eventually deposed and replaced by an elected and much more representative panel.

Stories of Survival

My frequent evening visits in the homes of families in the camp, with whom I often ate my evening meal, gave me an understanding of their former lives and how they survived. A lawyer named Oldak lived with his wife and baby in the camp. Oldak was a pleasant and cultured person who had managed to survive the Warsaw Ghetto. He told me about himself and some stories of his survival. The Oldaks were a nice family and they eventually made their home in Israel.

I encountered Oldak in a hotel sometime in the early 1960s, when I was visiting Israel before I moved there. The lawyer and his wife asked if they could join my mother-in-law and me at our table. I recognized the Oldaks at once, but I noticed that they did not recognize me. I invited them to seat themselves — their daughter, by then in her early twenties, joined them a short time later — and I played a little game with them.

I claimed that I remembered them from Warsaw. I then retold a story that Oldak had told me years back about hiding in a dark sewer in Warsaw. He was there searching for food and sensed someone approaching in the absolute darkness. Was it friend or foe?

I shared additional recollections. Finally, I asserted, "Your name is Oldak." The family had adopted a Hebrew name in the intervening years; he was practically unknown by his former name. He was amazed! I finally disclosed my own identity, and together we shared stories of the past.

Visiting residents' homes, I also learned about the irregular structure of survivor households. One person I met in the camp shared a flat with his wife, her two sisters, the husband of one of the sisters, and the husband's mother. It seemed peculiar, but this kind of arrangement was typical of the time.

Some survivors assumed that their spouses had perished during the war. They yearned for love and companionship. They moved in with new partners, either for human warmth or with the intention of eventually marrying. Sometimes, though, men and women suddenly materialized in search of their spouses, only to discover that they had taken up residence with others.

One man, a huge and unruly specimen, had heard that his wife was in the camp. He traced her to her apartment, and found her living with another man — whom he promptly tossed out the window. Wives generally returned to their husbands in such cases, and certainly in this one.

Years later, I heard the circumstances of one couple's much more complicated story, which typified countless similar experiences from that time. This story involved an old classmate of mine from Kalisz.

Besides the lists posted outside public buildings in the hope of locating surviving relatives, there were also books of survivors. These books were kept at the Munich headquarters of the Central Committee of the Liberated Jews in Bavaria. In one such book, I noticed the name of this former classmate, Selig Ginsburg. I recalled how Selig's parents had made a bare living in Kalisz. His sister, Channa, augmented their income by tutoring me in Polish.

I decided to leave messages for Selig in various places, inviting him to visit Camp Föhrenwald and look me up. One day, Selig Ginsburg opened the door of my office and peered in. He saw a uniformed man behind the desk and quickly withdrew. Selig gathered up courage, opened the door again, and explained that he had been asked to look for someone named Abramowicz. Could I help him?

I understood Selig's reserved behavior. There was the fear of uniformed persons that gripped many survivors. There was the dread of disappointment — the searches for lost families and friends that went on at that time were so tentative. I had already encountered a man from Italy who had come to Föhrenwald to search for an Abramowicz and assumed that I was a relative of his; I had to disappoint him. As for Selig, I explained that an Abramowicz in the camp had attended the gymnasium in Kalisz with him and had studied Polish with his sister. Surprised, he replied that this Abramowicz had emigrated to England and could not be in the camp. Then I identified myself. He stared at me for some time and finally realized that we had both changed over the years.

Selig Ginsburg spent a day or two in the camp. Then he returned to his rented room in Munich and to the German girlfriend with whom he shared it. Incredibly, not a few Jewish men set up common residences with women of the nation that had nearly exterminated their people. (Interestingly enough, however, I did not come across any cases of Jewish women with German men.)

But Selig's touching Holocaust story and its aftermath came to my knowledge later on. He, his wife, and their child had escaped from Poland to Lithuania at the beginning of the war. When the Nazis occupied Lithuania in late June 1941, the child was taken from Selig and his wife and they were banished to a ghetto. From there Selig was transported to an extermination camp. He survived by hiding under a heap of corpses and running away at night. He eventually landed in Auschwitz and managed to survive.

His wife was also placed aboard a transport to extermination. The train stopped in the Polish countryside on the way and the women were allowed off to drink some water. Selig's wife strayed into a farmhouse, where she asked the farmer's wife for water. After the woman had given her some water, Selig's wife thanked her and prepared to leave. The farmer's wife asked her where she was headed.

"Back to the train," she said.

"Do you know where the train is going and what will happen to you?" the Polish woman asked in response. "Don't go back. I'll hide you here."

"Whatever you say," Selig's wife answered indifferently.

Thus she remained in the farmer's house and survived. Eventually, she became involved with the farmer's son and planned to marry him. Having gone through hell, she was unwilling to pick up the torn threads of her former life.

After liberation, Selig heard of his wife's survival through the grapevine. He was unable to sit back and let it be. He asked a cousin to return to Poland and bring his wife to Germany. Since DPs were then still able to move about freely, the cousin traveled to Warsaw and sent Selig's wife a message that on a certain day, someone would be waiting for her at the Warsaw railroad depot; that she should go there and receive good news.

At first she hesitated. Then she did as instructed. She met the cousin, who told her that Selig was alive in Germany and quickly boarded a train with her. They reached Munich in the middle of the night.

Selig asked his German girlfriend to leave. The reunited couple subsequently settled in Israel and had a son and daughter.

Another visitor in Camp Föhrenwald was Ignacy Zelkowicz. He was also a former classmate. Ignacy, too, was caught by the Nazis and sent to Auschwitz.

In the concentration camp, Ignacy had been a member of the Sonderkommando, a group of prisoners tasked with loading Jews' corpses onto carts and hauling them to the burial pits. He came to Föhrenwald with an uncle, Jakob Ingwir, who had helped me obtain the Polish passport that I needed to travel to England.

Ingwir, his wife, and three sons had escaped from Poland to Russia at the beginning of the war. With great enterprise he had furnished his children with false identity papers and documents that showed that one was a doctor and another a dentist. Ingwir's wife died during the war. Subsequently, when several hundred thousand Polish Jews were allowed to repatriate, he returned to Poland with his sons.

But the family's ordeal was not yet at an end. Angry Poles, resentful of Jews who returned, shot and killed his eldest son. Ingwir and his two remaining sons fled to the American occupation zone in Germany, where they later obtained American immigration papers. In the United States, Jakob Ingwir became a rabbi, his youngest son really did become a dentist, and his other son became a doctor's assistant.

Unbeknownst to him, my school friend Zelkowicz's wife survived and ended up in Paris. Over time, they had each found new spouses — without official and religious sanction, of course. Ignacy's newly betrothed was a young Auschwitz survivor whose name also happened to be Zelkowicz. With their respective new spouses and establishing new lives, Zelkowicz and his first wife chose not to reunite.

Family reunification had yet another aspect in those years. It concerned Jewish children who had survived the Holocaust with the assistance of non-Jews, "Righteous Gentiles." It was not easy to reclaim these children. It was hard to show proof of parentage, and foster parents were often reluctant to relinquish the children they had raised for so many years.

In late 1945 or early 1946, a man arrived in Föhrenwald from Poland, along with a young girl whom he had removed from the home of a Polish family who had sheltered her during the war. Two days later, a second man from the same town, with the same name, came to the camp. He claimed that this was his child.

The camp population broke into two factions, each favoring a different man's claim. The camp officials, including myself, were at a loss as to how to resolve the conflict, until the camp doctors suggested that the girl's age be ascertained by taking an X-ray of the wrist. The girl was sent to a medical institute in Munich for the procedure. The X-ray showed that she could not be any older than five. Since the second man claimed that she was eight years old, the paternity problem was solved.

Evolving Roles

In early 1946, the camp acquired yet another set of officials. The US Army had allowed about 100 Jewish Agency workers into Germany. Three of them arrived in Föhrenwald. These new representatives informed me that henceforth the day school I had set up would belong to the Jewish Agency. I had been taken by surprise a few months earlier with the ORT arrangement. Now I was shocked a second time. But again, it was for the best. Again the school would benefit from the full-time attention of a reasonably well-provisioned organization.

The Jewish Agency representatives refrained from propagandizing in the camp and I appreciated their immense practical contributions. They taught in the schools, gave public lectures in the camp, helped the DPs to organize themselves into functional administrative committees, and sometimes they would approach UNRRA officials as spokesmen on behalf of the Jewish DPs.

In time JDC had found a niche in Föhrenwald. It augmented the Army's food rations and provided supplements, such as extra clothing, wedding parcels, and newspapers. In addition to initiating the camp's Jewish day school and its vocational training program, we also encouraged and supported a wide range of informal cultural activities such as theater, lectures, and study groups.

With time, the roles of other agencies also became clearer. The Jewish Agency had taken over formal Jewish education, for example, while ORT had become responsible for vocational training.

These developments coincided with the change in the direction of the UNRRA team: Mrs. Henshaw ended her tenure in April 1946 and was replaced as head of Föhrenwald's UNRRA team by Henry Cohen.[6] After his arrival, Cohen helped "democratize" the camp committee. He organized elections that led to a more representative group of members who worked to ensure that the camp's internal affairs were managed to the benefit of all residents.

---

6.   Henry Cohen subsequently became a lecturer in sociology at Queens College, New York. We met once or twice in later years.

Visitors to Camp Föhrenwald — Making a Difference

During my term in Föhrenwald I met a number of outstanding people who came to visit the camp. There had been visitors such as Zerach Warhaftig, later to become a government minister in Israel; Isaac Herzog, chief rabbi of Palestine; and General Eisenhower.

There had been much criticism about Army neglect and mistreatment of Jewish DPs in the camps. When this became known, General Eisenhower made a point of visiting my camp and others in the American zone. Our relations with the US Army were generally useful and good, but the reports contained some truth. I had overheard occasional anti-Semitic wisecracks from American Army personnel. Eisenhower's visit alerted him to matters in need of correction. Things improved after that.

The American-British Commission on Palestine also visited Föhrenwald. Hundreds of residents had expressed a strong desire to relocate to Palestine. The commission was to gauge the sincerity and depth of their eagerness. I knew that the vast majority indeed saw Palestine as their only destination, some for ideological reasons, some for lack of anywhere else to go. A minority of DPs set their sights elsewhere, usually because relatives in other countries offered to support them. Indeed, small numbers of DPs left for Australia, South Africa, and the United States with promises of support; some of those just imagined that such was available.

At the end of its work, the Commission recommended the immediate admission to Palestine of 100,000 Jewish survivors. This proposal was thwarted by British opposition and my work continued unaffected.

The JDC director for the Middle East, an American Jew named Harry Viteles, made a visit to Camp Föhrenwald. He lived in Palestine — one of the few American Jews who had made this revolutionary move in the pre-state era. Golda Meir and Judah Magnes are others who come to mind. From the narrow perspective of my personal future, his visit was to be the most important event in the camp.

Viteles was an expert on cooperatives. He later published *History of the Cooperative Movement in Israel*, a three-volume definitive work. In the camp, he spoke with me about the cooperatives that I was helping to establish and support as part of the JDC program for adults. I was pleased that he seemed to be quite impressed with what we had accomplished.

I wondered, though, exactly what had impressed him. I can only assume that we exhibited the kind of qualities — concern, commitment to effectiveness, and fixity of purpose — that he expected of JDC representatives. Besides that, I was also almost obsessive in hating to leave any task undone. And I was a painstaking report writer.

At that time, I still had no career intentions vis-à-vis JDC and JDC had none toward me. Within a few years, Harry Viteles would change that.

From Föhrenwald to Windsheim

In the spring of 1946, I felt that the time had come for me to move on, my original six-month term of volunteer service having long-since expired. But in view of the immense needs in the camps, JDC's Munich office asked me to stay on. Believing that I had done well in Föhrenwald, the organization wanted me to repeat the performance in additional camps.

I signed on for another six months. Instead of going home for good in March 1946, I took a brief furlough in Britain.

I headed for London in my American Army officer's uniform — not that I was actually entitled to wear it outside Germany! Before reaching my destination, I made a brief, but modestly eventful, stopover in Brussels.

There, I followed up on a request from a Föhrenwald camp resident to search for his mother's name. He had known that she had reached the Belgian city, but had no idea if she had remained there, or if she had survived the events of the war. I combed through various lists, located her, and even visited her in Brussels. When I later reported the encounter to her son, he was astounded and, of course, elated at the prospect of being reunited with his mother.

I also enjoyed two personal encounters that brought back my past. At the Brussels airport, I came across several members of the Jewish Brigade who were stationed in Antwerp, including an old friend, Yehuda Datner.

Finally, I met up with Zygmunt Biegeleisen, my distant cousin who had survived the war with his wife and daughter. I had not seen him since his family had hosted me in Brussels a decade earlier, on my way from Poland to England.

When I returned to Föhrenwald in March 1946 — after just two weeks in England — I received instructions from JDC to prepare to transfer to another camp. We had succeeded in making our work in Föhrenwald more and more systematic. I was now to take that system and replicate it in a new location.

Before leaving Föhrenwald, I drew up a report and handed my duties to the assistant who had substituted for me during my absence. I had gained much experience during my stay in Föhrenwald, experience that would see me through my next posting: Camp Windsheim, near Nuremberg.

Camp Windsheim was in the town of Bad Windsheim (we called it simply "Windsheim") and was made up of three-story apartment buildings and several residences that the Army had requisitioned. Gad and Sylvia Goldman moved together with me, Gad having become a "second-degree" UNRRA official (this was the term for a DP with limited privileges as a uniformed UNRRA official).

I was housed, as in Föhrenwald, in quarters that the Army had reserved for the UNRRA people. The general state of affairs there was little different from Föhrenwald's. My new tasks also resembled past ones — at least at first.

My assistants and I carved out JDC's niche as a facilitating agency in this camp that had only recently been set up. We organized a vocational training program in tailoring, shoemaking, and carpentry. We gave support for training initiatives put forward by DPs themselves, such as a beauticians' course. We provided various kinds of provisions for Jewish schools. And here, as in Föhrenwald, we provided food to supplement the still-limited official rations, clothing, and a range of cultural and religious materials.

In was at this stage that JDC's mass distribution of Bibles began. By the time the DP camp era ended, JDC had distributed hundreds of thousands of Bibles and other religious books in the American zone. In 1949, JDC and the US Army funded the printing of a special edition of the Talmud. The Army considered it an instrument in its rehabilitation projects. In all, 600 sets of the Talmud reached communities, chief rabbis, and others. It was a remarkable project, but my only part in it would be in distribution. (Vaad Hatzala of the United States[7] also printed basic religious books in hundreds of thousands of copies soon after the war.)

I was soon assigned a new duty: to train a newly posted JDC social worker. Such were the conditions at the time, that I — a young man, with no training in applied social work and only a year's experience in Germany — was asked to instruct a qualified social worker.

---

7.   Vaad Hatzala, or Rescue Committee, was established in New York in 1939. Its goal was to provide religious and material assistance for Jewish survivors of the Holocaust in Eastern Europe.

My trainee was a man from the United States. He had arrived in the camp shortly after I did. He was to receive training by example, namely by following me around. He did just that but eventually received a posting elsewhere and I received an additional trainee. I repeated the procedure and was, once again, followed around Camp Windsheim.

Shaken Values

In Windsheim, as in Föhrenwald, I saw what effects the war, the Holocaust, the deprivation, and the DP environment had had on human behavior. There were two groups of Orthodox DPs in the camp. One was a group of teenagers living not far from the UNRRA residence; they called themselves a kibbutz.[8] The other was made up of a number of older people. It became clear that these Orthodox chose adherence to tradition and the optimistic principles of their faith as their mechanism for self-rehabilitation.

On the opposite side of the board, I witnessed relationships that settled societies would hardly tolerate. UNRRA men often became romantically involved with women on the staff or with local German girls, for purposes that ranged from wife hunting to convenience or sheer caprice. A Dutch woman who had worked with me in Föhrenwald became friendly with the UNRRA director in Windsheim. She eventually married him. The UNRRA warehouseman in the camp conducted affairs with two German women and impregnated one. An alcoholic American nutritionist shared her life with the alcoholic mess officer who prepared her recipes. It was clear that these dubious relationships were also closely connected to the recent past and present conditions.

DP Committees

Supplies for my distribution work generally came from the JDC warehouse in Schleissheim, outside Munich. This was a very large facility that contained millions of dollars worth of goods. The supplies, once checked out, were

---

8. Although we associate this term with farming collectives in Israel, Jewish movements had used it before the war to denote various collective enterprises. DPs adopted it for their cooperative ventures or simply to indicate that they were living together. This group in Windsheim did eventually settle collectively in the north of Israel.

trucked to individual locations — Camp Windsheim among them — where committees of Jewish DPs distributed them.

Since JDC had as many as 250,000 DPs to provide for, it drew upon competent DP committees to administer various matters, such as parcel distribution. The DPs involved in this enterprise developed a terminology of their own. JDC was "the Americans"; the DP committees were "the locals."

As time passed, however, the DP committees became increasingly restive. This became particularly evident to me in my sessions with the committees of Camp Windsheim, when they would declare their capability of better management of DP affairs and of distribution of supplies in the camp.

In Munich, a Central Committee of Jews of the American Zone took shape. It was made up of people from various camps. All were capable people who wished to run their own affairs, including distribution of supplies. To do this they lacked only a stocked warehouse — and JDC had such a facility. Some time after I had left Windsheim, they asked JDC for the keys.

JDC refused and the decision had to be explained to the committee. Sam Haber was the administrative director of JDC-Munich by that time. He made two facets of JDC policy clear to the committee members. First, he explained, JDC did not object to co-opting DPs in its activities. In fact, a large majority of its operatives were chosen from the DP population. What is more, JDC worked well with the committee in Munich. If it had not been formed, JDC would have had to invent it. But second, Sam admitted, turning over the keys to a multimillion-dollar facility would amount to outright abdication of responsibility for programs that JDC funded.

What Sam might not have mentioned, but knew, was that turning over the keys might also have offended three other parties. Those who supported JDC in the US would frown upon JDC's giving up control. So would the US Army, under whose auspices JDC worked. And the German government would not have taken such a shift very well; the German government greatly feared anarchy.

On one occasion, the German government and US military were given reason to continue their trust in JDC's management of the warehouse and distribution. JDC generally ordered large quantities of supplies from Switzerland and elsewhere. The goods were hauled to its warehouses by train. One of these trains pulled in at the Schleissheim warehouse with two extra cars packed with contraband cigarettes — prized merchandise in Europe at the time. The smugglers who had hitched the cars to the train had intended to uncouple them along the way but failed to do so because of some mishap.

The smugglers were obviously dismayed. They sent someone to the warehouse office and offered JDC $50,000 to reclaim the loot. This was a sizable sum in 1946, and the purchasing power of hard American currency in post-liberation Europe was especially great. JDC spurned the smugglers' offer.

JDC then transferred the unwanted goods to the authorities, and enhanced its reputation as a responsible and accountable partner. The smugglers took a heavy loss.

Youngsters Join Camp Windsheim

During my tenure in Windsheim, the population at the camp — and the general DP population — was being significantly transformed by the Bricha. This was an organized, JDC-supported escape movement of Jews from Eastern Europe that gained momentum and became a large-scale phenomenon after the Kielce pogrom of July 1946. It referred large numbers of survivors to DP camps, particularly to those in the American zone of Germany, from where many of these Jews would attempt to join the Aliyah Bet "illegal" emigration to Palestine.

Bad Windsheim absorbed considerable numbers of children and young people who were delivered by the Bricha organization from Eastern Europe to the camp. This shift in the camp's population could have brought me back to my original mission in Germany. It could have led to establishing an education camp for displaced Jewish youth. But that did not happen. The schools at Bad Windsheim, while funded by JDC, were run mainly by the Jewish Agency. The emissaries of the Jewish Agency kept "their" youngsters under control as future citizens of the Jewish state. My role, and that of JDC at large, remained one of facilitation, its scope increasing steadily as the young Jewish DPs filled the camp.

Extending My Commitment to the DPs

By early 1947, I had completed almost two years of a volunteer stint that had originally been intended to last only six months. I spoke again of ending my relationship with JDC and of returning to England to complete my PhD.

The JDC personnel officer would not hear of it. The expansion of JDC's programs in the camps had created demand for significant numbers of qualified personnel that the organization was having increasing difficulty in meeting.

I realized that although my personal obligation had been completed, the need to help the DPs in Germany was still great. So I re-enlisted once again as one of several hundred members of the JDC overseas staff. My position in Bad Windsheim was extended for another three months.

Toward the end of the third month, I was placed on the JDC payroll and renewed my contract for yet another six months. Oddly, I was paid less than my American colleagues. JDC, I heard, had a different wage scale for non-Americans. I also began to anticipate a new posting, even though career service with JDC was still far from my mind. If I entertained career thoughts at all, they concerned England and a life in Jewish community service.

Naturalization Papers

Up to that point, I had been traveling on my Polish passport, the only one I possessed. I felt no personal ties to that country. In fact, I understandably harbored unfavorable feelings toward it. During a home leave in England in early 1947, I considered applying for naturalization as a British subject. This, though, was a cumbersome process that often ended in rejection.

I mentioned this to Janet Siebold, the astounding, righteous Gentile, chief executive secretary of CBF (Central British Fund for Jewish Relief, forerunner of today's World Jewish Relief). She encouraged me to apply, so I did — in the name of Stanley Abramovitch. Shia Abramowicz would be no more, at least not on paper.

Then, evidently, Janet Siebold pulled some strings. I received my naturalization papers within a week. My British passport arrived a day later. Unheard-of efficiency!

A Year in Frankfurt: Education and Vocational Training

Concurrently with my joining the JDC payroll, I was given a new appointment at the initiative of JDC-Munich. Unlike the previous posting, this was a promotion. I was assigned to the JDC office in Frankfurt, where I would remain until I finally left Germany a year later. There I would be in charge of education and vocational workshop programs from Heidelberg in the south to Kassel in the north. My responsibilities would cover a radius of about sixty miles from Frankfurt.

I was assigned quarters in the Americans' residential compound. As previously, I bought provisions at the PX and used the central mess hall, where all uniformed persons could eat to their hearts' content. As an observer of the Jewish dietary laws, I limited myself to dairy foods, bread, butter, canned fish, and the like. I always found something to eat, without having to resort to acquaintances for a kosher meal — as I sometimes had had to do in Föhrenwald.

The loyal Goldmans followed me to Frankfurt and rented an apartment there. Gad Goldman continued working with me. I spent almost every Shabbat with them. Sylvia Goldman prepared our Shabbat meals from whatever rations they had on hand.

Again my responsibilities were to facilitate. At first, JDC had regarded the vocational training workshops as welfare projects — a way of rehabilitating the DPs involved. But beginning in early 1947, JDC started considering them as a springboard toward genuine employment.

The necessary conditions were provided. Raw materials and components were supplied. JDC cooperated with the Jewish Agency, which was preparing future citizens of Palestine, and agreed that cadres of skilled workers for Palestine would be trained in the JDC workshops.

My routine in Frankfurt was now much different from that in Föhrenwald and Bad Windsheim. My work covered a large area, and my responsibilities were much broader. I planned out each day's itinerary of visits to schools and vocational workshops. I had a driver and a car, which I usually shared with Gad Goldman.

The itinerary for one day could begin with a drive up to Kassel to meet with the field-level personnel there. We would discuss their work and assess their supply needs. A requisition list would be drawn up. It would be forwarded to Munich with a report on the output of Kassel's workshops. Questions of quality would be left for JDC experts in Munich to judge. I would carry out similar procedures for all the JDC schools in my area of jurisdiction.

Later in the day, DPs would visit me in Frankfurt, just as they had visited me in my previous postings. Only now they came in greater numbers, since the city was a major intersection. There was always someone waiting for me when I reached my office. Their requests were different too. I no longer distributed food, and I had no money to distribute. When DPs asked for those things, I gave them the nearest equivalent: American cigarettes.

I was allowed to buy two cartons per week. As a nonsmoker, I allowed deserving DPs to use them as people all over Germany did, as ersatz currency. Some DPs offered to involve me in black-market transactions. They would offer me a fine pair of boots or perhaps a stopwatch in return for extra cigarettes. I wanted nothing to do with it. I have no aptitude for business, but I understood that once one engages with the black market, one cannot disengage.

Although I now traveled extensively and had broader responsibilities, my work in Frankfurt was less taxing than that in Föhrenwald and Windsheim. The JDC program at large was run from Munich. Education itself was in the hands of the Jewish Agency and vocational training was directed by ORT. It was my duty to provide these two organizations with supplementary aid, from JDC supplies. It included school provisions, books, anything we had on hand for distribution.

By this time, many of the DPs' personal initiatives were also gaining in importance. More than two years after the liberation, the Jews found it truly demeaning to remain dependent on rations, adequate or not. Furthermore, hoping or expecting to move on soon, they needed hard currency. They traded in all manner of goods, from cigarettes to silverware, furs, and leather goods — and even provided brokerage services. One could find almost anything one wanted in a DP camp by then. In Zeilsheim, a suburb of Frankfurt, the Jews had expanded a large camp into a veritable shtetl and business center.

I often visited the Zeilsheim camp in the course of my work. On one occasion, I delivered a Torah scroll to the camp synagogue and there met one of the camp residents. Soon after our meeting, I discovered how he set a small piece of Jewish history in motion.

His name was Rabbi Gershon Liebman and he was a charismatic, brilliant personality, one of the great surviving members of the *musar* (Jewish ethics) movement. I was told that he organized a group of yeshiva men in the camp and made it his goal to somehow keep them together until the DP camp system disintegrated — as it eventually did.

One idea that Liebman came up with was to resettle the group in Palestine. Liebman negotiated with Dr. Judah Shapiro, head of education and culture at JDC's European headquarters in Paris to effect this transfer. But he evidently changed his mind. His yeshiva eventually moved to a location outside Paris and named itself Le Refuge. It attracted large numbers of students — including many French citizens.

The yeshiva took advantage of a provision in French law that allowed a one percent tax deduction from total salary costs for continuing education. With the help of that one percent, Rabbi Liebman was eventually able to open many schools. These schools included religious academies and vocational institutions for boys and girls. Some continue to function to this day. Rabbi Liebman deserves credit for helping to revitalize Jewish education in post-Holocaust France, for a Jewry left badly mauled by the horrors of the Nazi occupation. Rabbi Liebman's efforts resulted in a genuine upfront contribution toward rescue and revival of Jews.

But my efforts were pulling me in what I considered the opposite direction. It had been thrilling to enter the camps in Föhrenwald and Windsheim. It had been greatly satisfying to play a hands-on role in facilitating the DPs' daily survival. But now, the excitement of the early days was abating. Instead, I found myself settling into a different — more "routine" — assignment. Simply put, my promotion left me dissatisfied, because it removed me from front-line work.

A New Era — Time to Move On

During 1946–1947, my two full years of service in Germany, JDC carried out the largest task ever undertaken by a voluntary nongovernmental agency. It had provided supplemental relief and — perhaps more importantly — spiritual, communal, and educational sustenance to hundreds of thousands of Jewish survivors of the worst calamity man had ever inflicted on man. JDC, indeed, had been a critical factor in the rehabilitation of innumerable Jewish lives. I was privileged to be part of that great enterprise.

As 1947 drew to a close, it was clear that the DP era itself was beginning to wane, even though the last DP camp (which, ironically, was Föhrenwald) would not close until 1957. On November 29, 1947, the United Nations passed a resolution ending the British Mandate in Palestine and approving the wondrous, miraculous establishment of a Jewish state there. For DPs across Europe, a chance to begin their lives anew was finally at hand.

Characteristically, JDC, too, was preparing for the next great challenge: that of Jewish statehood. The shift of focus away from Germany was reflected in the rapid turnover of the administrative directors at JDC's Munich headquarters.

Eli Rock, my first JDC boss when I was posted in Föhrenwald, returned to the US. He was succeeded by Lavy Becker, who in turn soon returned to Canada, settling in Montreal. He was succeeded by Leo Schwartz, the author of anthologies of Jewish stories and Jewish literature. Schwartz stayed for a while and was later replaced by Charles Passman and Herbert Katzki. Their terms were temporary and brief. Katzki's successor, Sam Haber, took over in early 1947. He stayed on for several years, by which time the Jewish DP period was largely over.

By early 1948, I began to consider returning to England and resuming my studies. I had vague thoughts of making aliyah — settling in Israel. The head of the Jewish Agency mission in Germany, Chaim Hoffman (who later changed his family name to Yahil and became director-general of the Israeli Foreign Ministry) had handed me a letter assuring me that I would be able to receive a legal immigration visa to Palestine.

I appreciated the gesture — I still have the letter to this day. But aliyah would have to wait until after completing my studies. When I did move to Israel in 1972, it was not on the basis of a visa issued by a foreign power, but by birthright, as a Jew, returning to my Jewish homeland.

Still, it was time for me to move on. I talked it over with the JDC regional headquarters in Munich and by the end of May 1948 I was back in England.

ᴄ From London to Tehran

A Busy and Boring Interlude Ends

I returned to England at loose ends. My father had died more than five years earlier. My mother had perished. I had two brothers and several uncles and aunts in England but, while we were by no means estranged, each of us lived quite independently of the other. I shared an apartment in the west of London with a bachelor uncle.

With my academic and rabbinic qualifications, I could easily have turned to spiritual leadership of a congregation. The JDC episode, however, had interrupted this career direction and I now found myself with qualifications but no clear professional orientation.

I immersed myself in stopgap activities that made use of the skills I had acquired. Friends found me a job as a part-time representative in Youth Aliyah, working with Jewish children who had reached Britain from Europe with the Kindertransport[1] or in other ways, to prepare them to settle in Israel. I resumed my voluntary involvement in Bnei Akiva, running weekend activities, organizing summer and winter camps, and serving on its five-member administration. I also did some tutoring.

At the same time, I renewed work on my PhD in Jewish philosophy, comparing the teachings in the twelfth-century *Sefer Hasidim* with those of St. Francis of Assisi, in relation to the thirteenth-century ascetic movement and its influence on the Jews. But as busy as I seemed, I could not find my place after my exciting mission in Germany. I slowly dropped the whole idea of becoming a Doctor of Philosophy — soon to learn that one often never

---

1. The Kindertransport was the British rescue mission that evacuated some 10,000 children from Nazi-occupied areas of Eastern Europe in 1938 and 1939. The children were brought to British soil and adopted by foster families.

finishes what one postpones.[2] Instead, I resolved to wind things up and emigrate to Israel.

In January 1949, as I was planning my aliyah, the JDC office in Paris informed me that Harry Viteles, the JDC director for the Middle East whom I had met in Germany, would be visiting London and would like to meet with me. Viteles was generally considered a difficult person to work with, possibly because he was so highly principled. Somehow, though, we had taken to each other, so I was pleased to have a chance to renew the acquaintance.

When we met a few days later, Viteles made an intriguing proposition. Operation Magic Carpet, the airlift of Yemenite Jewry to Israel, was under way. JDC had established and was supporting a camp called Hashid near Aden, the British-controlled port at the southern tip of the Arabian Peninsula. Yemenite Jews had begun arriving at the camp from all over the country, and JDC expected the flow to attain mass proportions. Viteles proposed that I go to Aden and take charge of the camp.

The idea excited me. And with nothing of substance to keep me in England, I gave my assent.

It took JDC some time to furnish me with the necessary papers, although I already had the most important of them — a British passport. On March 1, 1949, after a break of only eight months, I again became a JDC employee.

Just as I was to leave for Aden, the British closed the camp.[3] But JDC gave me no time for disappointment. Instead, it came up with a new proposition: that I head for Tehran and become JDC country director for Iran.

A New Focus on Iran

After the Holocaust obliterated the Eastern European Jewish masses, Jews in the West began to pay new attention to communities in Muslim countries, including Iran. Their motives ranged from sheer Jewish altruism to the creation of an alternative population base for the Jewish state-in-the-making.

---

2.   Fifty years later, I did, finally, receive a PhD — an honorary one from Bar-Ilan University.

3.   Operation Magic Carpet (also known as "On Eagle's Wings") later resumed from the camp near Aden and became the largest civilian airlift undertaken to that time. Between December 1948 and September 19, 1950, when the last JDC-chartered plane took off for Israel, it brought nearly 50,000 Yemenite Jews to Israel.

A group of prominent Syrian Jewish philanthropists in New York set up an organization called The Forgotten Million, referring to the number of Jews in Muslim countries who had lost touch with European and American Jewry. Its founder and head was an outstanding, self-made philanthropist, Isaac Shalom, who throughout his life was also the organization's main benefactor. The Forgotten Million sought to help these Jews in every sense. Above all, it was their goal to provide them with schooling that would create an eastern version of Rabbi Shimshon Raphael Hirsch's[4] famous hybrid philosophy of *Torah im derekh eretz* — religious and secular studies.

The Forgotten Million, soon to be called Ozar Hatorah[5] and to become the Middle East's Jewish school agency, asked JDC to help it establish full-time schools in Iran, Morocco, Tunisia, Lebanon, and other areas. JDC gave grants for these countries, including a one-time grant of $100,000 for the development of Jewish schools in Iran.

The director of Ozar Hatorah in Iran at this time was a Galician Jew, Rabbi Isaac Meir Lewi. A man in his forties, he had escaped to Palestine during the war and contacted the Vaad Hatzala (Rescue Committee) in New York, which dispatched him to Tehran. From there he was to send parcels and other forms of assistance to Polish rabbis who had become refugees in the neighboring Soviet Union.

A dynamic, imaginative, and well-meaning person, Rabbi Lewi soon realized that the Jews of Iran also needed his attention, lest liberalization trends there lead to their assimilation. In 1944, he opened Ozar Hatorah schools not only in Tehran and other cities with large Jewish populations, but in villages as well. His schools created a thirst for knowledge of Hebrew and Jewish history and tradition.

Amidst his educational whirlwind, Rabbi Lewi had the extreme good fortune of locating his wife, his son, and his daughter, who had all survived Bergen-Belsen. He traveled to settle them in Palestine, returned to Iran alone, and once again immersed himself in his goals. Rabbi Lewi even assumed

---

4. Rabbi Shimshon Raphael Hirsch (1808–1888) lived in Germany and Austria, where he served a number of communities as their chief rabbi, and where he implemented his dictum *Torah im derekh eretz* — that a Jew should have knowledge of the religious and the secular world.

5. Its full name is Middle East Jewish School Agency, Ozar Hatorah, Inc.

local customs and had his rabbinic coat embroidered in the fashion of the Sephardic chief rabbi.

From 1947 on, JDC considered Ozar Hatorah an integral part of its program in Iran and gave it small monthly subventions plus occasional special grants. However, JDC found Ozar Hatorah lacking in accountability and difficult to audit. In November 1948, Harry Viteles visited Tehran, reviewed the program, assessed what had become of JDC's $100,000 grant, and reported less than favorably on its disposition. In fact, Viteles considered no local Iranian agency capable of using JDC funding effectively. Unless JDC sent a qualified educator-administrator to Tehran as country director, he concluded, its investment would not be used effectively. I, it seemed, had the background he was looking for.

My Mission

Iran? The name meant nothing to me. I even had to check its location on a map. However, my friends again encouraged me to accept the offer. In addition to believing it would help Israel, my sense of adventure called me forward. Though the high-sounding title of "country director" was somewhat daunting, my time in Germany had given me a self-confidence that, together with the natural buoyancy of youth, made me feel that I could do the job. I did not know yet what the task would really involve. But I seized the opportunity.

I traveled to Iran as I had to Germany four years earlier, via Paris. There, in June 1949, I re-encountered Joseph Schwartz, along with his deputy and staff members Moses (Moe) Beckelman and Herbert Katzki. They provided me with an outline of my assignment: to assess children's poverty and needs and meet them by starting programs in nutrition, medical care, clothing, and education. The latter was to be developed in conjunction with Ozar Hatorah and Alliance Israelite Universelle (the French-Jewish educational organization) and include training for local teachers. Dr. Schwartz apprised me of JDC's concern over the management of its funds. Besides that, and as with Germany, I received no specific training and very little background material.

I learned from that meeting that Iran was not high on JDC's priorities. In Europe, the needs of the DPs persisted, while Israel had been founded barely a year earlier, had endured a difficult war of independence, and was being inundated by destitute immigrants. Many of these were arriving from a Muslim world that was in an uproar after its defeat in that war; some — such as Jews in Iraq, Morocco, Tunisia, and Libya in particular — were clamoring to reach Israel before emigration deadlines imposed by those countries' governments sealed them in. JDC strained its resources to help them. Additional areas of the world, from China to Latin America, competed for aid funds. Iran, by contrast, was considered an island of stability and the region's friendliest country toward Jews. A modest mission would do for the time being.

Finally, Dr. Schwartz told me that my budget for the first year would be $150,000.

"So little?" I asked, thinking on the German scale.

"Stanley," Dr. Schwartz replied, "you will see that it is not easy to spend $150,000 constructively."

He was right. Joe Schwartz was indeed a man of few words, but each word was measured and important. Once again, I was impressed with his exceptional vision, foresight, and great heart. Years later, I would describe him as a Jew who left an indelible mark on Jewish history and who did for world Jewry what David Ben-Gurion did for the State of Israel. I am proud to have had the privilege of working with him.

Making First Acquaintances

Landing at the Tehran airport on June 24, 1949, I was welcomed by Rabbi Lewi. As he drove me into town, I saw that he was trembling and wondered whether it was with excitement or fear. I settled on the latter. He must have known about Harry Viteles's report and suspected that I had been brought in to terminate his work in Iran. I told him at once that he should not feel threatened by me. I had not come to Iran to punish, oppose, or diminish him. I would treat him like a friend and brother, avoid prejudice, and do my very best to cooperate with him. Relieved and surprised, he promised to help me in every possible way. He would be true to his word.

As soon as I had unpacked at the Park Hotel — the only decent establishment in town — I began to meet additional Jewish personalities with whom I would need to interact. That very day I was visited — probably at Rabbi Lewi's instigation — by the Elghanayan brothers, David and Habib. The Elghanayans, businesspeople and recognized leaders of the Jewish community, welcomed me and offered me all possible assistance. Indeed, during my thirty-eight months in Tehran they were always available and helpful.

Another visitor that day was Joshua (Yehoshua) Pollack, a German Jew who had settled in Tehran with his wife, their baby, and his mother-in-law. Pollack was a businessman who had planned to export Persian lambs to Israel for breeding purposes. The authorities torpedoed this by allowing him to export ewes but not rams. However, his initiative led him to other fields — exports of dried fruit, rubber, and leather — that evidently did well. He invited me to spend my first Shabbat with him. The Pollacks' home became my de facto home during my stay in Tehran, as I became a frequent Shabbat guest and consulted with Mr. Pollack on many issues.

As he had promised, Rabbi Lewi began to help me in every possible way. Although we were very different in personality, approach, and focus, we managed to cooperate and to become friends. Together we would crisscross the country, visit almost every Jewish community of consequence, and find ways to help most communities in limited but beneficial ways.

I took care, of course, to dispel any impression that he was my guide, mentor, or superior, and to avoid becoming absorbed into his program. I did so by educating local people about the difference between Ozar Hatorah, an educational organization, and JDC, which had broader interests, including health and welfare.

One of the first things that Rabbi Lewi assisted me with was to begin building a staff. My budget was not itemized; JDC had no idea how to itemize it. Neither did I, at first. However, Dr. Schwartz's guideline — spend what one must, but constructively — and the low wage levels in Iran kept staff expenses modest.

My first hire was a secretary, "Lova" Lewine, a bright young man of Russian-Jewish origin. Lova typed my copious letters and reports, filed all my paperwork, and interpreted for me until I became more conversant in Farsi. Lova eventually emigrated to Israel, obtained a position with the Israeli Foreign Ministry, changing his name to Aryeh "Lova" Eliav, and later became Israel's first ambassador in Moscow in 1991. In fact, I would re-encounter him in Moscow in 1990, in the dying days of the USSR.

After settling in, I presented myself at the American embassy with a letter of introduction from Moe Beckelman. The ambassador, John C. Wiley, received me very warmly. He knew JDC from its work in Eastern Europe at the beginning of the war, and he took this opportunity to tell his staff what a great organization JDC was. During my stay, Ambassador Wiley helped me in every way possible.

Early on (and incredibly generously), he arranged an audience for me with Iran's ruler, the thirty-year-old Mohammad Reza Shah Pahlevi. The Shah had succeeded his father, Reza Shah Pahlevi, the founder of the country's first modern dynasty. I would be the first official representative of a foreign Jewish organization to meet with him since the establishment of Israel.

To prepare me for the occasion, Mr. Wiley briefed me on the Shah's favorable attitude toward Israel and the Jews. His protocol officer coached me in how to dress, what to say, and how to address the Iranian potentate ("His Imperial Majesty"). I rented a morning suit and went to the palace.

The Shah was very pleasant and warm. He spoke about Cyrus, the Persian emperor of the sixth century B.C.E. who allowed the Jews whom Nebuchadnezzar of Babylon had exiled to return to their homeland and re-establish their statehood. He spoke about Queen Esther and stressed the centuries-old Persian tradition of treating the Jewish minority liberally and considerately. This policy, he assured me, would not lapse in the future.

I found the visit useful and certainly satisfying. I knew that public knowledge of the meeting could help me in my relations with the authorities. Indeed, it was followed by exposure in the Iranian press, giving me confidence that government ministers would become more willing to provide assistance for the Jews if approached in the future.

The golden age in Iran-Israel relations was under way. Over the coming years, the Shah's government proved most liberal in allowing Jews to move from the countryside to Tehran for eventual emigration to Israel. Among Muslim countries, only Iran allowed such emigration without penalty to the emigrant. Furthermore, Iran did not turn back Jewish refugees from Iraq at its frontiers. The Shah's government defined Jews as one of three minority groups — the others being the Armenians and the Zoroastrians — that had equal rights de jure. Each of these minority groups had a representative in the Majlis, the Iranian parliament. Jews there were not subject to official discrimination and they did not pay the *dhimmi* head tax that many Islamic countries imposed in the past on non-Muslims. Anti-Jewish violence in Iran seemed to fall into the realm of historical oddity. Finally, as best as I could gather, Iran was a generally stable and up-and-coming country, where the importance of oil, and British influence related to it, was growing.

Discovering Iranian Jewry

Having made my introductions, I now had to learn about Iranian Jewry and devise programs that would benefit it. To make my work efficient, I rented an office and adjoining living quarters near the center of town and paid three months' rent up front.

At the time, the Jewish population of Iran was approximately 120,000 — some 45,000 in Tehran, 15,000–20,000 in Shiraz, about 10,000 in Isfahan, several thousand in Hamadan and Kermanshah, and smaller numbers else-where, in about thirty identifiable communities. About one-fifth of Iranian Jews were school-age children.

The Jews of Iran spoke Farsi. They had no general "Judeo-Persian," akin to Yiddish or Ladino, although various Jewish communities did have their own local dialects, incomprehensible to their neighbors.

Iranian Jewry had a central committee that posted a delegate to the Majlis. The committee had little influence, however, and few Jews concerned them-selves with it. It did little to coordinate its work with the communities; and the communities did little to coordinate their own activities. Although Iranian Jews were uniformly hospitable and often personally generous, they generally — with a few notable exceptions — did little to contribute to local needs and to care for poor fellow Jews.

The most religious Jewish subcommunity in Iran were the Mashhadi Jews in Tehran, named for their town of origin, the Muslim holy city of Mashhad. In 1839, a Jew in Mashhad had been accused during a Muslim religious festival of blaspheming a holy saint by giving his name to a dog. After the resulting pogrom, the Jews were given the option of death or forced conversion. They chose the latter but, like the Spanish Conversos before them, continued to practice Jewish customs in secret. After several generations, opportunities to emigrate became available, and many Mashhadi Jews emigrated and imme-diately reverted to full Jewish practice. Mashhadi Jews who came to Tehran did the same.

I also became acquainted with members of an Iraqi-Jewish community in Tehran. This community had arrived there some twenty years earlier and had formed an impressive colony of some seventy-five or eighty families. Better educated than other Iranian Jews, the Iraqis did well in various lines of business. Some intended to move to Israel, but most did not have any such intention. They maintained a separate community structure and considered themselves of higher class.

At the time of my arrival, some 40,000 Iranian Jews were largely unemployed and lived in poverty. Typical households in this group packed six to ten persons into one room. In the summer, many slept in courtyards or on roofs to avoid the suffocating heat indoors. Another 50,000 Jews earned a paltry living at unskilled labor, and lacked many basic necessities. Only 30,000 Jews had sufficient education and wealth to live comfortably. In larger towns, Jews had entered some occupational niches, such as gold, silver, and rug dealing. Some had entered the government administration, and a few merchants established contact with counterparts abroad. Perhaps 2–3 percent of Iranian Jews could be considered wealthy.

Comfort in Iran was a relative concept. Tehran, the capital of a viable state in central Asia, was without a modern water system. Until 1952, when the Shah modernized it, water was channeled into town from springs in the mountains twenty-five or thirty miles away. The town's inhabitants would take water from the ditches in the town to fill cisterns under each house. Westerners found the water only clean enough for gardening and showering (insofar as their quarters were so equipped in a country where Western-style sanitary fixtures were rare). To cook and drink, they paid people to deliver buckets of water from a well at the British embassy. Even that water needed boiling and filtration.

If such were the conditions in the capital, one can appreciate the poverty of the Iranian rural masses. Of children born in these areas — most of the country — 80 percent died before the age of five. A mother would give birth to ten children so that two would survive to adulthood. Most survivors had serious eye infections, mainly trachoma. Parents took the loss of their children's vision as a fact of life. Also rampant were smallpox, tuberculosis, malaria, disfiguring boils, and a scalp ringworm that left children bald.

Nothing, however, verged on the Jews' poverty. Poverty, in fact, was synonymous with Jewishness in Iran. For centuries, Jews had been *dhimmi*, a circumscribed and ritually-defiled underclass in Muslim society. Even though the incumbent Shah's father had abolished the *dhimmi* laws in the 1920s, the old ways persisted in many locations. Even large towns in Shiite areas had no Jewish artisans, because non-Jews refused to take on Jewish apprentices. At best, one might find an occasional Jewish cobbler or tailor. Itinerant Jewish peddlers risked life and limb on the roads and at the entrances to villages. Jews were also barred from public baths. In some places, they were not even allowed to sell or touch food in the market, because they were considered ritually unclean.

Most Jews lived in open self-formed ghettos, known in Farsi as *mahaleh*, where they could have the benefit of mutual support and maintain their Jewishness as a community. The poor Jewish children wore rags, went barefoot, and suffered chronic malnutrition.

Jews received medical care so rarely that I could not obtain reliable information concerning their health. Only a few could afford hospital care. God helped the others, I was told. He helped mothers at childbirth, since there were few proper midwives. He helped boys at circumcision to survive the circumciser's dirty fingernails and tools. He helped children and adults to survive typhus epidemics in a country where sanitation was unknown. In the capital, the only Jewish polyclinic in Iran — Kanoune Kheyr Khah — had just been built near the *mahaleh*. Yet the facility was still largely an empty shell, there being no money for beds, sheets, or medical instruments.

Although, at this early stage, I was not quite ready to establish JDC's medical and welfare programs in Iran, I made a strategic decision to base these programs in schools, rather than in community institutions. I had three reasons for this. First, medical programs could hardly take place elsewhere, since the only Jewish polyclinic in the country was evidently unable to meet many basic needs of children. Second, most Jewish children who attended school at all, went to Jewish schools. This self-imposed educational segregation would ease JDC's access to schoolchildren. Third, by basing feeding and clothing programs in schools, I would be able to create leverage for education programs. The availability of a decent lunch and the distribution of clothing could induce a youngster to stay in school instead of dropping out to pursue more petty opportunities such as peddling, shoe polishing, and the like.

I observed how Jewishness was a relative concept in Iran. My religious studies in Britain had introduced me to several Persian rabbinical scholars. But generations of Muslim intolerance, forced conversions, and grinding poverty had eroded Jewish practice among most Jews.

Some traditions survived nevertheless. The main Jewish holidays were upheld, as were traditional marriage, divorce, and burial rites. There were also some local practices. After Pesach or on the holiday's last day, for example,

Jews in Tehran mimicked a Muslim new year's day observance by going out of their homes to picnic and celebrate the arrival of spring. This resembled the Mimouna celebrations in Morocco.

The Jews called the rabbi the *hakham* (sage), the term common among Jewish communities in Muslim countries, or the *mullah*, the Iranian term for a Muslim religious authority. These community rabbis were neither ordained nor well versed in Jewish law at the level one takes for granted in the West. Only in the late 1950s, after my departure, did the Chief Rabbinate of Israel help to correct this situation by posting emissaries to Iran, primarily to teach the laws and practices of Jewish divorce.

In religious instruction, the barely schooled *hakhamim* who served as teachers indiscriminately mixed authentic Biblical material with miscellaneous parables. To the extent they could understand the material at all, the children could not tell the two apart, and few knew what the Bible had to offer beyond Genesis. In some of the outlying towns and villages, the Jewish schools peddled teachings that, to me, seemed to border on superstition.

Toward the end of my tenure, in 1951–52, as oil revenues created wealth, people were able to become prosperous virtually overnight. At that time, Iran's infrastructure underwent vast improvements; roads and houses were built at modern standards, piped water was brought into homes. Tehran expanded and the value of real estate rose.

Many Jews, too, gained much wealth. As they became wealthier, they became even less observant. For the well-to-do, Shabbat was a business day, even if they attended services in the morning. Observance also waned then due to a generation gap. Graduates of Ozar Hatorah and Alliance schools surpassed the previous generation in Jewish knowledge, but as education made them worldlier and more sophisticated than their parents, many of them left little room in their lives for interest in Jewish tradition.

Into the Countryside

Since most Iranian Jews lived outside Tehran, I embarked on a long tour to familiarize myself with them. I spent much of summer 1949 traversing the vastnesses of Iran with Rabbi Lewi and, sometimes, with the director of the Alliance schools in Iran, Andre Cuenca. We traveled over the dusty dirt roads that linked the Jewish communities of the major cities. One never knew whether Rabbi Lewi's old Ford would survive its punctured tires, fallen springs, brake failure, or ruptured oil pan, but our excellent driver, a young man named Ali Ibrahim, made skillful impromptu repairs and unfailingly revived the ailing vehicle.

We would travel from one place to the next at night to avoid the heat of the day. But roads in some areas were beset by bandits after dark, and at times, gendarmes or military police would warn or order us to spend the night in whatever village we were passing through at that time. Should we continue, we were cautioned, we might become victims of these plundering outlaws.

I internalized these warnings and always took them seriously — so much so that when a driver hired for a one-day excursion south of Tehran ran out of gas in the mountains, I was close to panicking. With not a soul to be seen for miles, I actually feared for my life. Thankfully, my fears proved unfounded and before long the driver of a passing truck gave us enough fuel to make it back to base.

Our only intentional stops between our destinations were for prayers and for tea at caravanserais — way stations that took their name from camel caravans but that were now used mainly by truck drivers. Each caravanserai had a central tea room in the middle of which was a small pool, its water flowing slowly in and out by narrow channels. In small side rooms, drivers and other visitors smoked opium. Western notions of hygiene in the handling of food and water were a far cry from the conditions of these places.

I took three separate routes to the outlying communities, which I would repeat each summer during my tenure. The first took me directly south from Tehran to Isfahan and Shiraz. A second route was south to Kashan and then southeast to Yazd and Kerman. The third was to the southwestern provinces, to Hamadan and Kermanshah.

At each destination, we first headed for our accommodations. In Isfahan and Shiraz, we used hotels. In Hamadan, we stayed at the Alliance school. In smaller locations, we stayed with local Jews, whose poverty never, but never, diminished their hospitality. They would serve us enormous dishes of rice, cucumbers prepared in a dozen different ways, sour milk, butter, and fruit. Wealthier hosts offered to slaughter a sheep for us. Since we avoided meat due to concerns about its ritual preparation, we turned down this sincere generosity.

We would stay in each village or town for a night or two; enough time to meet the people and initiate JDC programs, at least on paper. I would take my notes back to Tehran, where my staff and I would then continue our contact, ensure that the most responsible people in each place would oversee JDC's programs, and transfer money to the communities' accounts as necessary. This money would be sent at intervals as programs developed. Communication was mostly by telegram; occasionally, telephones worked too.

Isfahan and Shiraz

Air service from Tehran to Isfahan was available, but we made the trip by car — a grueling seven-hour journey over dirt roads — because Rabbi Lewi was afraid of flying. I shared his feeling in Iran, and for good reason.

Jubareh, the Jewish *mahaleh* in Isfahan, was rivaled for poverty only by parts of its counterpart in Shiraz. The main industry of Jews in Jubareh was the spinning of cotton and wool, practiced by several hundred Jewish men and women in huge cellars. These were the well-off inhabitants of the *mahaleh*; the others wore the most wretched collection of rags I had ever encountered.

I realized at once that JDC could not cure all this misery. But I would do whatever I could to help. My first move was to open a clinic there and appoint one of the two Jewish doctors in the city to run it. We gave the doctor a salary, various forms of assistance, and a twofold mission: to inoculate children and treat the needy, free of charge.

We visited the Ozar Hatorah kindergarten in the *mahaleh*, which enrolled close to 300 children. One would never confuse this institution with a Western-style kindergarten, but it did teach songs, the Hebrew alphabet, and a few other skills that prepared its children for school. We arranged for the women running the kindergarten to receive the guidance of a JDC daycare consultant from the Paris headquarters.

My next project was to expand our aid for at least some of the neediest Jews in Isfahan. To achieve this, I attempted to co-opt Jews outside the *mahaleh* in sponsoring a feeding program and distribution of clothing and footwear in Isfahan's Alliance school, and also used the kindergarten as a setting for welfare and medical programs for the preschoolers. In seeking local partners, I mainly targeted the local Jewish committee, as well as the three famous Saadya brothers (smiths and vendors of silver goods), and an insurance agent named Gabbai. My efforts to bring them together failed. In the end, in a rare departure from standard procedure, JDC provided the funds and arranged the program itself.

We traveled from Isfahan toward Shiraz, which had the largest Jewish community outside Tehran. It was a very colorful community. Many of its members worked as porters.

There were two Jewish schools in Shiraz at that point. (At a later stage, an ORT school was also opened there.) One was a government-run girls' school in the *mahaleh* that had a government-appointed Jewish principal. The second, named Kowsar, was in a spacious building near the *mahaleh* that Rabbi Lewi had acquired before my arrival. As one of the first schools instituted for Ozar Hatorah outside of Israel, he had obtained the first $25,000 toward the purchase from that organization. A similar amount had to be raised locally.

Rabbi Lewi pulled off this daunting task by going from Jew to Jew, door to door, and soliciting donations in return for blessings that his hosts asked him to recite over their food and drink. He then invested all his energy in setting up the school, which would serve the Jewish community for many years to come. Both schools were in immediate need of teacher training, but until early 1951, we had no one who could provide it.

It became clear to me that this community would need the full package of welfare programs that were taking shape in my mind. This would include providing food, shoes, and clothing for the schoolchildren. JDC created a clinic in the *mahaleh* for the adult population, again supervised by an Iranian Jewish doctor.

Our contact in Shiraz was the richest and most important Jew in town: Aziz Cohanim, a rubber dealer and an exporter of dried fruit. Cohanim had his own synagogue in the Jewish ghetto, and managed the community's accounts. Rabbi Lewi registered his new school building in Aziz Cohanim's name. I sat with Cohanim at length and reviewed the accounts line by line. He must have considered my behavior rude and insulting, yet he patiently answered all my questions with the understanding that JDC's support for the community depended on his trustworthiness.

Kashan, Yazd, and Kerman

Our travels toward the east first brought us to Kashan, a six-hour drive southward from Tehran and a place so infested with scorpions that in the summer people placed their beds in pools of water. Jews in Kashan were rug dealers.

Here I carried out JDC's first intervention in Jewish education. Visiting the local school, run by Alliance, I asked the teacher (there was only one) to augment the government curriculum with Jewish and Hebrew studies. He agreed, although only later would we able to bolster these studies with a curriculum and textbooks of our own.

Kashan was probably the only place in Iran where women — a group of girls aged fifteen or sixteen — studied Jewish and general subjects, and even had some knowledge of the *Shulhan Arukh*.[6]

From Kashan the road led to Yazd, a fascinating city and the center of Zoroastrianism — a religion once ubiquitous in Iran and practiced by a minority today. Jews in Yazd proudly called their community the "Jerusalem of the East," in deference to the scholars who had once hailed from the city and of the community's general adherence to tradition. Indeed, the head of the community was a learned man by local standards. The Jews in Yazd wove silk until a modern factory drove them out of business.

We spent three days in Yazd, our main stop being the Jewish school. It was run by Alliance and housed in a particularly spacious building.

From Yazd we continued southeast to Kerman. We were already relatively close to the border with Pakistan and thought that we must have arrived at the most remote community in Iran. The Jews of Kerman told us that there were in fact a few Jews who lived even farther east from there. Unfortunately, I could not reach them.

In this city, a center of the Persian rug industry, my search for someone to run a feeding program had a positive but unexpected outcome. Kerman had a substantial community, several thousand in number. The main community leaders were the Zrubavlis, rug merchants. When I asked them for advice about the feeding program, they referred me to a Dr. Bachrach, who worked for an English mission in Kerman.

When I met with Bachrach to discuss the kinds of food the children should be given, he recommended a menu that corresponded perfectly to the Polish-Jewish fare that I knew from childhood. As we became friendlier,

---

6. The *Shulhan Arukh* was redacted by Rabbi Joseph Caro in the sixteenth century and became accepted as an authoritative code of Jewish law.

I discovered that he was an Ashkenazi Jew from Riga who had converted to Christianity in London, married a non-Jewish woman, and joined her in Kerman in the service of the missionary group that had converted him. Since he did not impress me as a zealous proselytizer, I asked him to visit the school occasionally to keep an eye on the feeding program. Bachrach took on the responsibility with utmost sincerity.

Hamadan and Kermanshah

The third route, which went west from Tehran to Hamadan and thence to Kermanshah, held much historical interest for me. In Hamadan, the summer city of the Persian rulers, we visited the tombs reputed to be those of Queen Esther and her uncle Mordechai, and the mausoleum of the Islamic philosopher and scientist Avicenna.

High up in the mountains between Hamadan and Kermanshah is an engraved stone with inscriptions in Elamite, ancient Persian, and Akkadian. As the Rosetta Stone did for Egyptian hieroglyphics, this stone provided the key to deciphering these ancient languages and was of particular interest to me given my past studies of Semitic languages. But it would have taken many hours to reach and I had to move on to become acquainted with the next community.

In Kermanshah, I discovered an oil and opium center that, by Iranian standards, was relatively modern. To form a local committee to run programs in the school, we located a pharmacist who would head it and also oversee the welfare programs, in this case focusing on feeding and clothing.

Small Villages — Small Communities

As we traveled from one place to the next, we visited small villages where I was told there were Jews scraping out a living. These primitive outlying localities, with their dried-brick huts, were the most exciting part of my work in Iran. I found them exotic and reminiscent of how Jews elsewhere must have lived centuries ago.

Jews in most such localities lived together in one small area. Some of these communities were impoverished to an extent that defies at least this Westerner's capacity for words. Irrespective of the Shah's emancipatory measures, Jews there were still distained as *dhimmi*.

In these villages, as in the larger towns, we would stay for one or two days, would meet with the local committees or community representatives, discuss where JDC could help, and try to get the communities' participation in feeding and clothing programs that we wished to initiate and support. Where they existed, we would visit the communities' schools, almost all of which were run by Ozar Hatorah.

Such a community in Iran might have a *hakham* and a small volunteer committee headed by a chairman or president. Other than the school teacher, only the rabbi was modestly paid, for his services as *shohet* (ritual slaughterer).

The most prevalent vocation among Jews in the hinterland was itinerant peddling. The most sophisticated peddlers exploited their mobility to serve Muslims as brokers. Only in a few localities did Jews work the land.

Most outlying communities had a Jewish doctor (known there as the *hakim*). Although deficient in equipment, the *hakims* did have rudimentary medical knowledge and skill. And since they treated Muslims too, they were relatively well off.

To escape their harsh conditions, Jews from such poverty stricken villages had begun trekking to towns and thence to cities and finally to the capital, Tehran. In 1950–51, entire communities moved to Tehran, from where many left for Israel.

Between Yazd and Kerman, I visited the small community of Rafsanjan. The head of the community was a dentist and opium addict who refused to leave Iran for Israel because he did not know how he could satisfy his habit there. Eventually, however, the dentist, his two wives, and their children left for Israel — to find or not to find opium in the Promised Land.

I visited two villages in the Isfahan province, south of Tehran: Golpayegan, where the Jews dealt mainly in agriculture, and Khonsar. The head of the Khonsar community was a goodhearted physician who invited me to refresh myself in the small pool in his garden after the long journey.

Sensing that the physician could not possibly have studied his profession in any medical school, I asked him, "How on earth did you become a doctor?"

Astonished at my question, he explained, "Look, my grandfather was a doctor; my father was a doctor; so I am a doctor and I hope my son will be a doctor."

This was how most of the village *hakim*s learned their trade. This physician was responsible for 10,000 people in the region.

Eventually the Jews of Khonsar also moved to Tehran.

In Budan, a town in the Isfahan province, Jews hid their identity for years, practicing their faith surreptitiously, pretending to be Muslims. Legend has it that one day, an itinerant merchant who happened to approach the community for sheepskins used a Hebrew word during the conversation.

"Are you a Jew?" the sheep owners asked in amazement. "Are there really Hebrews in the world?"

They had long been convinced that they were the last Jews on earth.

Farther south, just north of Shiraz and near Persepolis, was the village of Zargan, which had a Jewish population of 400. Of these, a few Jews — mainly women — spun wool for a pittance, but the overwhelming majority derived most of their "income" from gleaning Muslims' cornfields. It was fortunate for those Jews that the Muslim harvesting practices resemble those in the Jewish tradition: leaving uncollected and forgotten grain for the poor and one corner of each field unharvested. Between harvests, many Jews survived by begging.

I found that the Jewish children of Zargan did not attend school. In fact, the small village, struggling in extreme poverty, had no school at all.

When I described to the Jewish committee the sorts of programs JDC could offer, its members feigned deafness. Only an evacuation program would do, they claimed. Better still would be emigration.

If the children of Zargan knew only one word in Hebrew, it was "Jerusalem."

"Take us to Jerusalem," the committee members shouted at me.

At that point, I could respond to these pleas with no more than vague promises.

Roads southwest of Tehran also led to the Lorestan province, where I visited a few small communities and the larger communities of Khorramabad and Borujerd. The Jewish community of Khorramabad was particularly interesting, being the only one I encountered in Iran where women ruled the roost.

Our visit began with the generous hospitality that never failed to make an impression on me. Sitting cross-legged on a dusty rug in the courtyard of the biggest house in the *mahaleh*, Rabbi Lewi and I discussed the community's affairs with the all-male Jewish committee of Khorramabad. Suddenly, the courtyard door sailed open and in strode a retinue of tough, wild-looking women wearing headbands. The men fell silent as one of the women issued a string of demands — for food, clothing, education, medical care — in a tone that implied we would never get out of town without complying.

I responded to their requests to the best of my ability and deflected the rest with extreme diplomacy. To this day, I doubt that JDC could ever have found enough money to keep all the promises I made that day. However, with our help, those women were soon running a wonderful feeding center, keeping the village children properly dressed, and setting new scholastic and hygienic standards for their school. I never had to visit Khorramabad again.

Our route from Tehran westward took us to Nehavand, home to 800 Jews and where the slaughterer's workload was a mere one sheep a day. Members of the community wished to show us the nearby burial place of Habakkuk the prophet, to which we made our way on horseback. I had no idea how to stay astride, let alone how to control a horse. Before I knew it, my horse began to gallop wildly in all directions until our guides restrained and calmed the animal.

On our first summer tour, we extended our western route so that from Kermanshah we headed northwest into Iranian Kurdistan to the provincial capital, Sanandaj and from there to visit the old communities of Kurdish mountain Jews in Saqqez, Miandoab, and Rezayeh. All told, these westernmost towns, where I witnessed how Kurdish Jews had lived for many centuries, may have been the most exotic localities I visited during my tenure in Iran.

Kurdish Jews estimated their total population at 20,000, but no one really knew. Jews in Kurdistan, like their non-Jewish neighbors, wore a *rishta* (a cloth turban with fringes that dangled over the forehead), wide trousers that tapered at the ankles, a tight black tunic, and a broad, long sash around the waist. They spoke Jebali, a dialect similar to Aramaic. Some members of the community traced their collective origins to the Ten Lost Tribes.

Sanandaj had a substantial Jewish community — about 2,000 strong — headed by the patriarch of the most prosperous Jewish family in town. Rare among Iranian Jews outside of Tehran and Shiraz, he evidently owned extensive properties.

We spent a Shabbat in his home and on Friday night before kiddush,[7] all kinds of fruits and appetizers were placed on the table so that those seated could recite a range of blessings. Only men were present; the women who prepared the food were not allowed in. Our host's sons served the food from the kitchen. From my seat on the carpet, I could see a woman or girl peering at us from under the curtain that separated the dining room from the next room. She must have been lying flat on the floor.

The scene reflected women's status in Iranian society. Generally, women were unwelcome at birth, unheeded during life, and not missed at death — except for housework, cooking, and producing offspring, all of which they began in their teens. Knowing no other lifestyle and accepting their husbands' and children's love, and such pittances as they earned, the women did not protest this.

This was not the Jewish way as I knew it, but 1,000 years of anti-Jewish abuse had insinuated such Iranian attitudes among Iran's Jews. Observing these, I resolved to contribute wherever I could to elevate the status of Iran's Jewish women. In my capacity as JDC representative, though, all I could do in this respect in Iran was to give the women's committee that was active in Tehran my support and enable its members to assist in the JDC programs.

The next stop on this route was Saqqez, a mountain stronghold where some 5,000 Kurdish Jews engaged mainly in the wholesale and retail trade of textiles and lumber products. Most were poor, although our hosts, the young community leader Shalom Khomani and his family, were not.

Khomani greeted us and led us into town and through the streets, where excitement reigned. Most men in the community came out to greet us, and women and children hung their heads out of their windows to get a glimpse of us. Indeed, the presence of a European guest was such a rarity that the local authorities assigned a soldier or policeman to watch and protect us from the crowds wherever we went.

Finally, we were ushered into Khomani's house. There, his mother had taken two measures to ward off the evil eye: she invited a *shohet*, to slaughter a sheep as a sacrifice, and she burned incense. The meat was given to the poor. We were escorted into the salon, followed by a horde of men.

On entering the room, the men seated themselves along the walls and

---

7.   A blessing over wine, sanctifying Shabbat or a Jewish holiday.

carried out an elaborate ritual. As each one entered, all those present greeted him by standing up as a sign of respect. The newcomer would then gesture to indicate that he did not deserve the honor, sit down, and rise once again to pay respect to all persons present. This went on until the room filled to overflowing. The women stood on the roofs of neighboring houses — a rare spectacle in Iran — attempting to get a glimpse of the goings on.

Rabbi Lewi said a few words to the gathering in Farsi, which I strained to follow. I was able, though, to understand enough to know that the conversation revolved around how many Jews lived in the town. Estimates varied widely, depending on which surrounding communities were included in the tally. The discussion continued late into the night.

We eventually crawled into our beds — wooden platforms covered with blankets, to be precise — that were set up outdoors. At daybreak, Rabbi Lewi and I opened our eyes to quite a sight. We were in the midst of a yard full of goats, sheep, cows, geese, and hens.

Rabbi Lewi, still half asleep, asked me, "Where am I?"

"In Noah's Ark," I chuckled.

After we washed and recited morning prayers, we shared a sumptuous breakfast of eggs, milk, tea, and fresh bread with our host, during which we discussed community business. Then, after giving our promise to provide support for the community, we picked up to continue our journey farther north.

Our northernmost stop was Rezayeh, where another substantial Jewish community existed. Our concern in Rezayeh was the school, where displeasure with the principal was harming the educational work proper. We mediated between him and the community and helped straighten out their relationship, facilitating his future management of the school.

We spent one night in Rezayeh — at the home of the community president — and then set out on our long journey back to Tehran. Soon after our departure, we passed by Lake Urmia. The water looked so blue and beckoning that we decided to take a dip. No one had informed us that the lake was in fact a salt sea! As we emerged from the water, our eyes were stinging and we found ourselves covered with a layer of salt. We stood scorching in the sun while Ali, our driver, fetched buckets of fresh water for us to rinse ourselves off.

Heading back on our route southeastward, we visited the small village of Miandoab. One local Jew there approached us asking for a blessing to find his lost cow. We spent a night in that village on a rooftop, as was the custom in the hot summer months, when sleeping indoors or even on the ground was almost unbearable. In the middle of the night, we were shaken from our slumber by shrill screams followed by a stampede of people jumping over us. When morning came we discovered that thieves had come to the house, one of whom jumped on the roof to cause a stir so that the other could plunder the empty house below undisturbed. This, we found out, was a common practice!

Although nearing its end, the excitement of that trip did not end there. Farther along the route back to Tehran, we were chased by non-Jewish Kurdish bandits who, on horseback, outran our car in the mountainous terrain. Holding onto our seats with fear, we eventually came to a straightaway and made the narrowest of escapes. Finally, we reached Tehran, exhausted — and greatly relieved to be "home."

Initial Conclusions and Shaping a Modus Operandi

That first fact-finding trip left me with no doubt: the small outlying communities needed every sort of program that JDC could offer. They knew it, greeting me in many places like God's personal emissary on earth.

However, I could not apply my DP-camp experience at random. For one thing, it would take until the following spring to activate programs in many localities due to the lengthy and rough winter. Second, these programs would be new to them; I would have to explain them in detail and at length.

I reported my findings to JDC in September 1949 and listed our aims: food and clothing for needy children; medical aid for schoolchildren and adults; Hebrew and secular education for schoolchildren and vocational training for young adults; and finally, facilitating emigration through the Jewish Agency.

I was given the opportunity to emphasize my conclusions at a JDC country directors' conference that took place in Paris the following month. I described the situation of Jews in Iran as the worst in the world. I presented an envisaged breakdown of my $150,000 annual budget over four areas of activity. Priority would go to feeding (about one-quarter of the budget) and clothing, followed by medical care, education, and vocational training. A minimal amount would have to be allotted to administration and miscellaneous. By that time, the Jewish Agency was the sole financing body for emigration, so JDC's assistance in that area would primarily be informative — getting the word out concerning the urgency of emigration to JDC's representatives in Israel. It was my hope that they, in turn, could pull some governmental strings to speed up the aliyah of Iranian Jews.

Each of these aims had several prerequisites. Medical aid had to be based on, or preceded by, instruction in elementary hygiene. To provide effective school education, it would be necessary to train teachers, to import and/or write textbooks and curricula, and, in some places, to build schools. To feed and clothe needy children, it would be necessary to establish relations with local school committees and artisans. Economic improvement for youth would require far-reaching vocational training.

To accomplish these goals, I spent about five months a year visiting provincial towns up to 900 miles from the capital. Each year I repeated the three main routes of my first tour of 1949. This way I revisited many communities to help maintain and improve the programs that I had initiated on my first round. We would develop these programs further over time, with each subsequent visit and from our office in Tehran.

While even the poorest village had a charity box, the philanthropic record of Iranian Jewry's affluent class was not strong. I made it clear everywhere that JDC would not begin projects unless some local help was forthcoming and that responsibility for direct management of the programs would be local.

By now, I also understood the limitations of my initial strategy of basing programs in schools: clearly, this approach was only possible in towns and villages where schools existed. Elsewhere, I would have to appoint a local person or someone from a larger town to run things. Whom could I trust? I tended to focus on the local doctor, the *hakim*, and other members of the local Jewish committee.

Our modus operandi, used in almost every case, was to locate or create a committee for each project, to which JDC funds and local money would be allocated. Sometimes negotiations to set up this mechanism took a long time and would include haggling over how much the local committee would contribute. Until the bargaining stage was over, I had to contemplate and sometimes witness barefoot children shivering in rags in unheated classrooms during the harsh winter months. If I was on site, I would not leave until I could be sure that these children would be taken care of. If negotiations were being carried out from our base in Tehran, I would not rest until they had been resolved for the good of these children.

Even once agreement was reached, implementation was sometimes far from smooth. I once had to get our local partners to pay the tailor in order to provide a clothing program; I found that at times it was easier to exert pressure on the local committees to pay the tradesmen directly than to have them issue their participation to JDC.

My successor, Abe Loskove, preferred a different tactic to achieving local participation in funding. He would bring a delegation of affluent figures of the Iranian Jewry into the *mahaleh* to shock them into awareness of their fellow Jews' living conditions. Abe reported an equally successful response.

The methods that I employed helped to bolster the Jews' charitable instinct by providing systematic outlets for it. Sometimes the JDC program was the only reason for forming a committee in a given town. Our mechanism opened Iranian Jews' eyes to a Jewish world that was willing to feed and clothe their children, pay for their education, and help in every way possible — but only with their participation.

By April 1951, I was able to report to JDC that local Jewish businesspeople were supporting JDC work among refugees (Jews from outlying villages who had arrived in Tehran) and schoolchildren. Over time, the local committees assumed additional community functions and tasks. The committee in Kerman, for example, undertook to relieve the Jews' dependence on the filthy water that flowed into a ditch in the town by digging a well and channeling water to the school and synagogue. JDC supplied a hand pump and the necessary piping.

Based in Tehran

Once the first programs had been shaped and the various communities were assisting in their maintenance, I could become more settled in Tehran, from where I could continue to initiate and develop programs. I moved to new accommodations that could facilitate a more active JDC office. This was a two-story house, with a kitchen, dining room, two offices, and two bedrooms. It had an indoor bathroom and toilet — impressive features in those days — even though water for the shower had to be pumped from the kitchen.

Many of the basic furnishings were bought with the help of Iraqi Jews. I was brought a straw-filled mattress, which lasted my entire tenure in Iran, though by the time I left it had become rather flat and long! Since, in Iran, any respectable house had to have carpets, without my even requesting it, a Jewish Iraqi rug merchant turned up one day with a pile of outstanding rugs to place in the house. He spread them all over the house at no charge, and when my tenure was up returned to take them all back.

In order to carry out the programs initiated in the provinces, I needed to begin filling out the small JDC staff. Lova, the excellent secretary Rabbi Lewi had recommended to me, soon left for Israel and was replaced by a book-keeper who also helped me with correspondence. He was a local Jew named Frouzan who also worked for the American embassy and later emigrated to the United States. Ambassador Wiley assisted in acquiring an entry visa for a medical doctor, Dr. Maurice Brown, to join us from Israel. The doctor arrived in April 1950 and eagerly joined our staff. To help me develop the medical pro-gram, JDC sent me an American public-health nurse named Sylvia Hurwitz, who had served in Germany and Aden. I also kept on Ali Ibrahim as the JDC driver. At one point, I bought a Chevrolet for daily errands and travel to the provinces, instead of using Rabbi Lewi's Ford that he had so kindly shared with us. For my personal needs, I hired a cook and a general handyman and errand-runner.

As JDC's country director, I found I was expected to develop a representa-tive role among Tehran's community of non-resident Jews. We hosted Jewish Agency and ORT representatives, as well as Israeli, American, and other Jews who were visiting the city on business. Friday nights were open house to these visitors. All this required skills that I had never developed, and I was fortunate that Sylvia Hurwitz's flair for management also extended to ensuring that we were appropriately hospitable.

As I became more and more familiar with my immediate surroundings, I mastered an additional form of efficiency. I learned how to get the most for each JDC dollar without resorting to the black market. The official dollar exchange rate was thirty-two rials; the black market would deliver fifty to fifty-five. JDC bridged the difference legally by mailing me duty-exempt British gold sovereigns, which I would sell on the open market. When this became too complicated, I imported gold bars and the same Iraqi Jew who had brought his rugs into the JDC office also handled all my money changing from his office in the bazaar, with utmost reliability and honesty.

During this time, I was able to learn more about the heterogeneous Tehran community and their different origins. There were various synagogues in Tehran, serving the different groups. The Mashhadi Jews had two, situated in one building. There was a synagogue in the Kuresh school (an independent community school administered by Alliance), where the de facto chief rabbi of Tehran led the services. A small community of Ashkenazi Jews from Russia attended the Haji Aziz synagogue. Iranian Jews worshipped in a larger building next door. The Iraqi Jews had their own synagogue. Toward the end of my tenure, in 1952, the newly affluent class of Jews of Tehran would build new synagogues that competed with each other as an expression of Iran's newfound wealth, boasting chandeliers, marble floors, and decorative gold lettering.

Jewish Education in Iran

I now also delved more deeply into the Jewish educational network in Iran. During our travels that summer of 1949, Andre Cuenca had already given me a rundown of the operations of Alliance Israelite of Iran. Alliance had been running schools there since the late nineteenth century. At the time of my arrival, it had ten schools in Iran. Two of these schools were located in Tehran — one, École Populaire, just outside the *mahaleh*, and the other, Jaleh, within town. All the Alliance schools offered a French-Jewish curriculum, which qualified their students for higher studies in France. Their total enrollment was approximately 8,000 — more than half of the total attendance of Iran's Jewish schools.

Alliance, created by French Jews, tasked itself with imparting French schooling and culture to Jews in Muslim countries. At its peak, it operated in Morocco, Egypt, Lebanon, Syria, Turkey, and Iran, and had an important cultural impact on Jewish populations in all these countries. Some Muslim regimes viewed Alliance with suspicion as an agent of foreign culture, but France appreciated Alliance for that very reason and provided Alliance with a large subvention. JDC supported Alliance's work in Muslim countries through a central budget from JDC's New York headquarters.

My inquiries satisfied me that, by and large, the Alliance schools did a good and constructive job. In educational terms, they surpassed almost all other schools in Iran. They were also crucial in the nascent Jewish emancipation that the Shah's father had set in motion. Alliance trained many if not most of Iran's first Jewish professionals, teachers, and public figures.

Nevertheless, the schools were severely deficient in several respects. Due to their staff's lengthy tenure, progressive educational techniques seemed to have passed them by. Alliance headquarters in Paris never in the past sent a qualified educator to inspect the schools. The funding from Alliance headquarters, intended to cover the payroll and the schools' maintenance, sufficed only for the principals and a few teachers of French. The average class size verged on fifty. Furthermore, the curriculum was weak in Jewish education, even though it was implemented in a traditional atmosphere.

Jewish education was, on the other hand, the forte of Ozar Hatorah, especially in respect to the Hebrew that was much in demand after Israel's establishment. Ozar Hatorah enrolled some 4,000 children in its own schools (in Shiraz and Kerman and other provincial communities, where Alliance did not operate), which stressed the Jewish connection and promoted it in a religious atmosphere.

On the side (in social terms) was the Iraqi school, so named because it served Tehran's community of Iraqi Jews. The curriculum was geared to the British matriculation system, which qualified the youngsters for higher studies in England and the United States. The Iraqi school had been built by a man known as Haji Abdallah of that community and was run by an Iranian Jew named Beruchim.

Finally, English and American missionary schools also catered to Iranian Jews. The missionaries never made big inroads in Iran, but their work in training and education was an important factor of enlightenment.

All of these schools were also under Iranian government supervision. The Ministry of Education provided them with its required general education, for which it supplied the schools with its own teachers, curriculum, and textbooks.

One of the challenges I faced, as JDC country director, was the friction that existed between Alliance and Ozar Hatorah, due to Ozar Hatorah's plans to open additional schools. To help overcome this conflict, I brokered an unwritten agreement between them that assigned responsibility for Jewish education in Alliance schools to Ozar Hatorah. Each organization came out ahead. Alliance cut its expenses and Ozar Hatorah gained influence over Jewish education at the Alliance schools and access to thousands of children.

The agreement we reached held together throughout my tenure, albeit sometimes precariously. It was never formalized, as it would have had to be pushed through the bureaucracy of Alliance Paris headquarters. That, of course, would have been a time-consuming process, and time was precious as far as these children were concerned. The mutual trust and successful

cooperation enabled us to move ahead together swiftly, enabling the children
to receive education and welfare almost immediately.

With this development in hand, Ozar Hatorah facilitated our work greatly
by opening the way to many small communities. As such, I decided to do all
our Jewish education work through Ozar Hatorah. Furthermore, I sincerely
believed that Ozar Hatorah, with its greater commitment to Jewish education,
would do a better job in that respect than Alliance would have done on its
own.

That said, during my tour of the outlying areas, I had found that the teachers employed by Ozar Hatorah were such largely in name only. Despite their
lack of teaching qualifications, however, these teachers were able to attract
children off the streets and provide initial education for youngsters who
would otherwise have been totally illiterate.

As for the Alliance system, I quickly grew to appreciate its foreign-service
staff. Where, at first, I had considered them an outmoded bunch who held
their posts too long, I came to the conclusion that despite this drawback, they
were devoted and under-compensated servants of the Jewish people.

It became clear to me that JDC's efforts in the realm of Jewish education
in Iran should focus on systematizing the schools countrywide, improving
the syllabus, and guiding the Hebrew teachers in their subject matter and in
the art of teaching. In Tehran, I visited some form of educational institution
almost every day to see what was needed, what was being done, and what
could be done further.

First and foremost, however, I found that teachers and principals were in
such short supply as to endanger the mere existence of the Jewish schools.
Some classes were taught by young girls. Our education budget would not
suffice to open new schools and improve all existing schools countrywide.
Thus, we decided to concentrate on fewer schools. With limited resources and
few qualified local instructors, we placed those available in ordinary teaching
positions and had them concurrently train some of their colleagues.

By early 1950, the Hebrew education program with JDC's support was
well under way. More children had already been enrolled in Jewish schools —
now more than 12,000 Jewish children in Alliance and Ozar Hatorah schools
learned the standard Iranian curriculum, supplemented with Jewish studies.

In July 1950, JDC brought in two Hebrew teachers from Israel, Israel Szyf and Avraham Shoshani, to train the existing and additional local teachers. Shoshani brought his wife with him and they rented an apartment in Tehran and focused his efforts there. I posted Szyf to Shiraz to establish a teacher training program for several young men. He spent the next two years there, under poor conditions, teaching these men and supervising Rabbi Lewi's Kowsar school. The graduates of Szyf's "seminary" became teachers for Ozar Hatorah throughout Iran.

As it turned out, Israel Szyf made Iran a career posting. He stayed in Iran with JDC until 1968 and then went to work for Ozar Hatorah, first in Iran and later in Paris and New York. In later years, between 1992 and 2002, we would work together again as part of the JDC-Former Soviet Union team.

Books were of great importance to our work in Iran. We printed a set of primers — reprints of Israeli-American texts, to be precise — in about 30,000 copies. We also photocopied the Five Books of Moses until we had enough for all the children. Szyf and Shoshani oversaw the preparation of two new textbooks for study of the Hebrew language, as well as special booklets for Jewish festivals.

Medical, Feeding, and Clothing Programs

One of the biggest challenges was to prevent parents from pulling their children out of school at age nine or ten to go to "work." This was where my idea of basing JDC's feeding, clothing, and health care programs in schools could help. By implementing these welfare programs in the schools, we managed to alleviate the problem. The children did not have to go out to earn their basic needs, since their food, clothing, and medical care was now provided free of charge.

The schools in Iran did not run through the summer months. Therefore, in order to enable schoolchildren continued Jewish education and welfare, I gradually supplemented the regular countrywide programs with summer programs. These programs would provide morning summer classes for schoolchildren, when they would also receive basic foodstuffs, such as dairy products, eggs, bread, and butter.

In medical care, our office took its quickest and largest strides in Tehran. The Alliance schools in the capital were especially poor. Surveys carried out by our new staff physician, Dr. Brown, found that 50 percent of children in these schools were undernourished and that even more were anemic. Many children reported to first grade with distended stomachs. Dr. Brown promptly established Iran's first school clinic in the Jaleh school, with the authorities' appreciative approval. In time, JDC's initial medical programs were run in all of the Jewish schools in the country, mostly supporting the local physicians' day-to-day work, providing them with supplies, and taking care of inoculations.

Within weeks of running the medical program, the Iranian minister of education and his physician-general wrote to us to communicate their satisfaction with our work in the Jewish schools. Furthermore, the physician-general authorized our nurse, Sylvia Hurwitz, to inoculate schoolchildren against typhoid, smallpox, and diphtheria. All the schoolchildren were given TB patch tests — a first in Iran. At our request, a World Health Organization team chose the Alliance Populaire school in Tehran for a Mantoux (TB) test, and those found positive were administered the BCG vaccine — again the first schoolchildren in Iran to receive it. At that time, too, the ministers of finance, national economy, and health gave JDC a customs exemption for medical supplies and equipment.

Besides the establishment of a clinic, the medical work in Tehran began with the installation of extra water taps in the school buildings, distribution of towels and soap to the children, and a special financial bonus for teachers who would make sure the children used them before eating. The American embassy helped out by lending us films on various health topics.

The school clinic kept records on schoolchildren's care and arranged ophthalmic care by a doctor who made various visits to the Tehran schools four times a week. The clinic attacked trachoma and other illnesses, but only had the capacity to treat the Tehran children, and was inadequate even for them. Unfortunately, besides Isfahan and Shiraz, there were no similar, encompassing facilities in provincial cities. In 1950–51, we helped to improve the existing polyclinic that served the general Jewish population of Tehran by expanding its outpatient clinics, hiring additional local doctors and district nurses — a new notion in Iran — to give preventive and promotive, rather than therapeutic care, providing some assistance in prenatal and postnatal care, establishing a milk-distribution center for expectant mothers, nursing mothers, and children, and setting up a medical laboratory.

Later, before the end of my tenure, JDC established and equipped a pediatric hospital in the polyclinic for the Jewish children of Tehran. With thirty-four beds and a turnover of sixty to seventy patients per month, it tackled the most acute cases.

By now, the feeding program had been initiated in Tehran and various communities around the country. The programs were mostly based on supplies of rice and meat; children who were especially underfed received a range of supplements. As time went by, I could sometimes see youngsters blossoming — not from miracle drugs but from things that Western mothers take for granted, such as milk and school lunches.

Most of the children had rarely seen milk and initially balked at drinking it. To entice them, we would mix the milk powder with cocoa to make a chocolate-flavored drink. They were soon begging for more.

The clothing program was also fast taking shape. In the Iranian context, this referred to the issue of one garment and one pair of shoes to each child, once or twice a year. They would serve for two or four seasons, summer and winter. In some locations, we also clothed the teachers. As I had intended, this program was also run through the schools across Iran, again by local committees and appointees whom we considered trustworthy. The program entailed measuring each and every child's shoe size, employing local artisans to sew the clothes and make sturdy shoes, and coordinating organized distribution.

I took great pleasure in observing how, with JDC's help, many youngsters thrived at acquiring new cultural experiences. At a Hanukkah party that JDC held for the children in one of the schools in Tehran, we gave the children modest presents. At the end of the party, they lined up to give them back. It was difficult for us to make them understand that they could keep the presents, since none of them had ever received a gift before.

Contacts and Friendships in Iran

In the late summer of 1950, we acquired a new colleague: Abraham Blass, who had come to Tehran for ORT to establish vocational schools for Iranian Jewish youth. A former Israeli naval officer, Blass was a rough-mannered, tough-talking person but also a good and very capable Jew. He set up one school in a beautiful building in a vacant area of Tehran's old Jewish cemetery — the only Jewish-owned property in Iran that had available land — and another in Shiraz. Blass did a fine job.

ORT received JDC funding from the central budget in New York, but on a professional level, ORT was highly independent, and as such, I had no need to maintain involvement in the Jewish vocational training in Iran. Nevertheless, I maintained a friendship with Blass.

Among my Iranian Jewish contacts, I kept up a loose relationship with the Elghanayans. I also interacted with several members of the Tehran community's clinic committee, foremost a pharmacist named Mr. Frouzan (of no relation to the bookkeeper employed in the JDC office).

Mr. and Mrs. Kashfi were recognized as important figures in the Tehran community and they too were frequent visitors in my office. Mrs. Kashfi had initiated a remarkable thing in a Muslim country: a women's committee. Unlike many Jewish committees that we helped to form to sustain JDC programs, this one, comprising about a dozen women, predated my arrival, and met regularly to help others, mainly women, in various ways. In fact, I found them more active than the men's committee. Their ability to lend a hand to others was not based on personal wealth — for most had little — but on their ability to assert themselves.

Mrs. Kashfi, who possessed a combination of financial resources (from her family) and warm-heartedness, was uniquely paired in leading the committee with Mrs. Hekmat, who projected strength. In Western countries today, such women serve in cabinets and head corporations. In Iran, during my tenure, these outgoing women raised funds and organized various functions involving additional women. Mrs. Kashfi frequently discussed her undertakings with me, and I was able to help her and the women's committee — but most surely did not lead them.

Their main achievements were in the establishment of an independent Jewish kindergarten and the development of the Kanoune Kheyr Khah Jewish clinic in Tehran in 1948.

Mrs. Kashfi's family was the prime benefactor for the clinic, which was named after Mrs. Kashfi's late brother. As under-equipped as it was, the fact remains that local efforts had brought it into being.

All said, this was one of the few families that played a significant philanthropic role in Iran.

Perhaps the most helpful sector of the Tehran community as far as my work was concerned were the Iraqi Jews. Among them, I developed close relations with the Kuku family and with Nahman Namurdi, the very fine Jew who had lent rugs to the JDC office and who served as my money changer. (After settling in Israel, some members of the Namurdi family renamed themselves Nimrodi and amassed large real estate and media holdings.)

The Iraqis were quite generous, especially toward each other but also beyond. For example, the member of this community known as Haji Abdallah, who had built the Iraqi school in Tehran, pledged some of his wealth to the construction of the Iraqi synagogue and a wedding hall adjacent to it. He also donated a building to the Jaleh Alliance school, even though it served Iranian Jews in the main.

Without rights to Iranian citizenship, the Iraqis' position in Iran was precarious. In December 1949, the Iranian government gave them fifteen days to evacuate, probably in retaliation for Iraq's expulsion of some Iranian citizens. In New York, various Jewish organizations — including JDC — interceded with the Shah to cancel the decree, which he did without giving clear permission for them to stay indefinitely. At that time, the UN representative in Tehran informed me that Iraqis who applied for Iranian citizenship would not be expelled. Many did acquire Iranian nationality over time, and although the threat of expulsion recurred several times, nothing came of it.

Social life for me in Tehran was scanty, but I did manage to form friendships. One was with Alliance's Andre Cuenca, who would drop by in the evening or meet me after work for a beer and an hour or two of conversation. Cuenca was a Sephardic Jew from Salonika who had come to Iran over twenty years earlier, at age twenty, to serve as principal of a school in Yazd. After visiting Yazd myself, I regarded his acceptance of that post — a career position in a harsh place of exile, with no family or friends — as an act of courage and self-sacrifice. His devotion in taking the job in fact saved his life: the Jewish community of his hometown was obliterated by the Nazis in the Holocaust.

Cuenca eventually married into an Ashkenazi family that had a lengthy tradition of Jewish life in Tehran and, with his wife and children, moved to Tehran to direct the Alliance program at large. They lived comfortably but not luxuriously and toiled around the clock.

Andre's wife, Batya, was wholly dedicated to her husband's cause. She was her husband's right hand, a very wise and patient woman. In fact, without her, Andre could not have managed to run the Alliance programs to such an extent. They were full partners. They had four daughters, then between the ages of ten and twenty.

The family's fate in later years is typical of that of Iranian Jewry. The Cuencas sent their oldest daughter to Paris to study, where, to her parents' anguish, she married a Gentile. Their second daughter became a sewing teacher and married a nephew of David Elghanayan. This couple fled when Ayatollah Khomeini came to power in 1979. The third daughter emigrated to Israel, married an Israeli, and settled in Rehovot. The youngest married Habib Elghanayan's youngest son.

Andre and Batya pledged their lives to Jewish education in Iran. In addition to being educators, they had to be politicians who could stay on the good side of the government authorities, on whom they depended for many of their permits. I did not realize at the time just how much they were doing for Iranian Jewry.

Hands-on Involvement — All over Iran

My efforts to develop JDC programs from Tehran were limited. Telephones were sometimes available but were not useful for doing business in Iran. Besides, nothing could replace hands-on attention. I consolidated this necessity into the annual tours that I took of the Jewish communities, mostly accompanied by Rabbi Lewi and/or Andre Cuenca. As I repeated the three main routes of my first trip of summer 1949, I was able to review, maintain, and develop the programs that we had initiated and supported at the outset.

As with our first trip, others typically began with several car breakdowns, which Ali Ibrahim tackled as I slept on the backseat. At each destination we were, as always, greeted with various forms of hospitality — all sincere. I would meet the committees and representatives who were supervising the JDC programs to discuss any problems, visit schools, and assess the children's educational and medical progress. At each location, reports would be drawn up for continued follow-up work in Tehran.

In some locations, new facilities were initiated. In Hamadan, Yazd, Kerman, and Kashan, for example, first steps were taken to open medical clinics for adults, in addition to the medical programs running in the Jewish schools there. In July 1951, Dr. A. Vynnikov, a Russian Jewish doctor in Isfahan, also opened an eye clinic for adults in that city, on JDC's behalf.

Since most Jews of the Iranian Kurdistan region moved to Tehran in the winter of 1949/50, their hearts set on emigration to the Holy Land, there was no reason to visit the region again. Being of the Sunni tradition, the Muslim Kurds shared the same religion as the Palestinian Arabs that the newly established State of Israel had recently defeated. Their sympathy for the Palestinian Arabs led them to attack the Kurdish Jews the previous winter, killing twelve and causing much property damage. This created the "push" factor for emigration to Israel, along with the "pull" factor of messianism and the awareness that the Jews had established a state in Jerusalem or Zion (the name "Israel" was not yet often heard).

Emigration Fever

From the moment I arrived in Iran, I noticed the yearnings of many Iranian Jews to emigrate and took note of their messianic and material motives. In remote Kurdistan, children wished to learn Hebrew, having heard that the Redemption had begun and that Jews were returning to the Holy Land, where King Chaim Weizmann and Commander-in-Chief David Ben-Gurion reigned. No briefings before my arrival had prepared me for this.

I did not realize that within months all the Jews of Saqqez and Sanandaj, and some of those we saw in Rezayeh, would abandon their centuries-old homes and come to Tehran for what they believed would be their return to the Land of Israel.

But it happened. Entire villages emptied of Jews as families sold everything they had in order to make the trip to Tehran. Empty patches in the *mahaleh*s of Saqqez, Sanandaj, and Rezayeh in Kurdistan soon marked the sites of former Jewish houses. The Jews had ground their mud houses into dust, mixed the dust with water and straw or dung, and sold the end product as fertilizer for opium fields. With this they managed to raise the few rials necessary for the trip. These Kurdish Jews joined the thousands from ethnic Iranian regions whose desire to emigrate began decimating outlying communities in the middle of 1950.

Despite the Jewish Agency's efforts to stanch the influx of Jewish refugees, who were overwhelming the Tehran community's sparse resources, by the winter of 1949/50 the thousands of Jews from Kurdistan had already descended upon the capital. The refugees formed a camp in Tehran's new Jewish cemetery, pitching improvised tents between the tombstones. They were later transferred to the old cemetery, where they built a primitive building to serve as a clinic, the Jewish Agency providing doctors, nurses, and basic medical care.

Aliyah was handled by the Jewish Agency, but admission to Israel depended on the Israeli authorities, which, under severe financial and social stress, gave priority to communities that were being threatened with liquidation or physical peril.

The first round of prospective emigrants were Iraqi Jews who had crossed into Iran in 1949–50 and were set up in a refugee camp in Tehran's old cemetery. The efforts to deal with them delayed the processing of Jews who wished to emigrate from Iran proper. For this reason, large numbers of Iranian Jews wishing to make aliyah became stranded in Tehran. During 1950 Iraq finally allowed mass emigration of its Jews and their influx into Iran came to a standstill. Those refugees in the old cemetery of Tehran were slowly airlifted to Israel, while other Iranian refugees joined the camp.

JDC became involved in the matter by providing temporary emergency assistance as the population of the Jewish refugee camps — in the old and new cemeteries of Tehran — climbed to as many as 10,000 and overwhelmed the Jewish Agency's capacity. The refugees, encamped amid graves in the cemeteries, were awaiting a miracle. Some were passive, others dying, most undernourished, a few violent.

After I apprised JDC of the situation, JDC, at Dr. Schwartz's initiative, made a special allocation for emergency relief and medical and sanitation supplies. In May 1950, Dr. Schwartz himself came to Tehran. At first, we visited the refugee camps and discussed the situation with the Jewish Agency aliyah emissary and a group of local Jews who had formed a relief committee. Dr. Schwartz offered to contribute one million rials (nearly $20,000) for refugee relief programs if the central Jewish committee matched it. After some negotiations, the committee agreed.

Dr. Schwartz also had time to visit the Jewish *mahaleh*s of Isfahan and Shiraz to inspect JDC programs. He concluded — as I had — that the situation of Jews in the *mahaleh*s was the worst in the world. He left for Israel on the morning of May 15 with more than ninety Kurdish Jews on a private plane.

That May, hundreds more Jews arrived in Tehran from the far south of

Iran, from the vicinity of Bushehr, on the Persian Gulf, where Jewish communities had been devastated by an earthquake. All were ill with trachoma, scalp ringworm, and other communicable diseases. In their present state, few could be sent on to Israel. I arranged provisional assistance for them.

I set to raising funds for the Jewish refugee camps of Tehran, working at it harder than I ever had to raise funds. Eventually, I obtained close to 80 percent of the $20,000 sum that the central Jewish committee had guaranteed. They had promised it, but when push came to shove, I had to find it! To put the money to use, the Jewish Agency erected a spacious dining hall, a 140-meter-long housing facility, a thirty-bed infirmary, latrines, and a water system, all in an open space in the old Jewish cemetery.

JDC's Dr. Brown and Sylvia Hurwitz oversaw the hygienic improvements, arranged medical care for the ill, and inoculated the entire refugee population against typhoid, until the Jewish Agency brought their own doctor and nurses. The Iranian Health Ministry also contributed personnel, DDT, and a provisional public bath.

These relief efforts for the refugees made the camps attractive to other destitute Iranian Jews, who besieged the gates in thousands and occasionally broke in. I decided to extend some of our services to them.

It took until the spring of 1951 for the Jewish Agency and the Israel immigration office to impose order and expedite the emigration of those who were free of contagious disease. As the refugee population declined, the Jewish Agency rearranged priorities and cut back on services.

Later in 1951, the Jewish Agency formulated a plan for evacuating small communities that had become nonviable as a result of emigration. I persuaded the Agency to pilot the program in Zargan, one of the poorest places in the country. I reasoned that under the current selective-aliyah policy, only the fittest Jews in Zargan would be allowed to emigrate, and the others would remain behind in helpless conditions. The Agency agreed and subsequently transferred the Zargan community to Tehran. JDC thereupon terminated its feeding and clothing programs in that village. Similar relocations, at the communities' initiative, took place from villages such as Golpayegan and Khonsar in the Isfahan province, and Khomein in the Markazi province.

At one point in 1951, the entire Jewish community of Afghanistan also came to Tehran and settled in a synagogue courtyard, surviving in terrible conditions. These poor Jews were helped by the Mashhadi community of Tehran, their former neighbors. JDC did not maintain this camp of refugees.

Informing American Jewry

In March 1951, at the time of the massive emigration from the Tehran refugee camps, Dr. Joseph Schwartz invited me to the United States on a speaking tour about the refugee situation in Iran. By that time, Dr. Schwartz had left JDC, where he was overseas director, and had taken on the position of director-general of the United Jewish Appeal. He wished to inform American Jewry, UJA supporters in particular, of the harsh conditions and the needs of their Iranian brothers. Mine, he knew, would be a clear, first-hand report on the situation in Iran that would open the hearts — and hopefully the pockets — of American Jews for this cause.

I flew out to New York as he requested. I participated in a number of parlor and public meetings, at first feeling that little was achieved from my discourse. However, with some added guidance from Dr. Schwartz and his associates on how to present my experiences in the Iranian *mahaleh*s and refugee camps to the audiences, these meetings brought much success to the intentions of the tour.

Ferment and Change

Throughout the refugee crisis, I made every effort to continue my regular work. Yet at the same time, domestic strife in Iran — a precursor of the events that would, in 1979, transform the country into a virulently anti-Western Islamic Republic — began to affect my work.

The tension had to do with long-simmering domestic resentment of British-American oil influence, and the level and proper use of oil revenues. The end result was a coup in August 1953 by xenophobic and Islamic forces under Prime Minister Dr. Muhammad Mossadeq, shortly after which the Shah fled to Rome, only to be returned to power shortly after by a counter-coup staged by the Iranian army.

As xenophobia surged, I noticed changes in Iranian attitudes toward Jews and Israelis. In my area of activity, the finances of the schools were being monitored closely by Iranian authorities — a process of which I actually approved, since it helped prevent waste and theft.

As 1951 progressed, some Israeli personnel were recalled by their home offices. Other non-Iranian Jews who left Iran temporarily found return visas hard to obtain. My trusty companion, Rabbi Lewi, was among them. Hakham Netanel took his place as director of the Ozar Hatorah schools.

That summer, the government began requiring nonresidents to obtain special permits for each provincial town they wished to visit and some towns, mainly those near oil centers, were declared off-limits. Visa applications for foreign passport holders now required police clearance, making it difficult for me to arrange visits by colleagues from Paris. The threat of expelling Iraqi citizens, including Jews, arose again and caused some tension until it receded after UN intervention.

Pressure also mounted on those of us who remained. Local media linked the Israeli and ORT activities in Iran with espionage for Israel and against the USSR and its satellites. The Soviet authorities extended this suspicion in an unexpected direction. In late 1951, according to people who tuned into its Farsi broadcasts, Radio Moscow devoted air time to "the capitalist activities of the American Joint Distribution Committee[8] and its director in Iran, Stanley Abramovitch, who on the pretext of bringing relief and assistance to the poor, have built themselves a network of contacts throughout Iran for the American capitalists." I never found out exactly when that broadcast took place, and I had no idea where Radio Moscow obtained my name and title. I reported the matter to Paris headquarters and carried on.

The internal crisis ebbed in the autumn. By that time, the Iranian climate seemed less edgy to me than the foreign press was reporting.

Over the winter of 1951–52, however, the situation was again deteriorating. Some old hands assured me that "nothing bad ever happens here." But in January 1952, local Jewish leaders who only a few months earlier had laughed at my anxiety spoke earnestly and seriously about being willing to cooperate in any plan that would assist their communities should they be targeted as scapegoats. Jews in Kermanshah, for example, were under threat because the Jewish pharmacist had wrapped some medicines in a page of the Koran that had found its way into a package of scrap paper.

---

8. The American Jewish Joint Distribution Committee (JDC) often omitted its first *J*, for "Jewish," in its work in sensitive parts of the world.

Large-scale anti-Jewish riots, though, did not seem imminent, but we recommended emergency evacuation for Jews if such were to occur. JDC and the Jewish Agency also worked out a plan to be implemented if ordered to close down on short notice. This included immediate provision of funds to local Jewish committees and large emigration efforts for the transfer of threatened provincial communities to Israel.

By February 1952, Iran's xenophobic unrest was affecting all aspects of my work. I found each day burdensome. A trial of young Jews in Baghdad heightened anti-Jewish sentiments in Iraq and prompted the Iranian Foreign Office to launch an inquiry on all Israelis and members of Jewish organizations in its country.

The red tape that had accompanied every official contact now took a hostile turn. Iranian officials judged JDC's work not on its merits but on the nationalities of its personnel. As a British national, I belonged to the second most disfavored group of foreigners after Israelis.

As 1952 progressed, the situation seemed to stabilize, at least in the sense that the same rumors, fears, and hopes continued to circulate and no new ones arose. By summer 1952, I signaled to JDC-Paris my wish to conclude my tenure in Iran. I had done what I could in my posting, I was tired, and I wanted to do something new.

I considered JDC's future in Iran and sent my recommendations to the Paris headquarters. A non-British and non-Israeli JDC representative would best fill my post, so that even if the Jewish Agency and ORT were expelled, it would be likely that JDC could continue operating.

A Final Tour

In June 1952, I prepared for a final visit to the provincial communities, in the company of Dr. Meyer Herman (who had replaced Dr. Brown as director of the JDC medical programs in October 1951) and Israel Szyf, our education consultant. Andre Cuenca of Alliance and Mr. Cohen Sedeq, chief of office of Ozar Hatorah (under Hakham Netanel) joined us for part of the tour.

My focus on this tour was educational progress and the maintenance of JDC's welfare programs in each location. I generally observed that despite significant progress, the schoolteachers in most communities still had much to learn, so I invited them — about thirty in all — to Tehran for a teacher's training seminar later that summer.

We found the Isfahan community at loggerheads with the Alliance system over personality issues and noticed that the feeding program there, which had taken me eighteen months to set up, had broken down due to community-generated red tape. We put on our mediators' caps and helped work out solutions that would enable the program to continue smoothly.

Most of the Jews of Shiraz, we discovered, had given up on the notion of emigrating to Israel in large numbers. Like other Iranian Jews, they had become aware of the hardships in Israel's *ma'abarot* (immigrant transit camps) and of food shortages there. There were even reports that 1,000 Iranian *olim* (immigrants to Israel) sought to return to Iran. Moreover, conditions in Iran had eased in the meantime. JDC long-term programs in the city again became important.

The Shiraz community was fortunate to have Mr. Aziz Cohanim in charge. We could not have worked in Shiraz without him. Alongside him, Israel Szyf had endured nearly two years in this remote town, where he had toiled with limitless devotion and where he was sorely missed when he returned to Tehran.

We had a large relief program there that focused on the Kowsar school and the government-run school. Our clothing program also included the ORT school.

I examined the schoolchildren at Kowsar thoroughly and noted their progress in both Jewish and secular subjects. One exceptional group there studied separately on weekends, evenings, and holidays, with the local *hakham*. These youngsters, staunchly religious, had mastered the Pentateuch, the early Prophets, some Mishnah, and even some Talmud.

With its limited resources, the Jewish school in Shiraz could not cater to girls. There being no mixed schooling in Iran, Jewish girls could only attend the government girls' school, for which there were no suitable Hebrew teachers. At this point, I considered their consequent ignorance in religious subjects a shameful blight on our work. Even a government inspector remarked negatively about it. To remedy the situation, we made arrangements to begin a training program that would qualify several women for work in the government school. As with our other programs, this program was followed up by the JDC office in Tehran, ensuring that it would be a worthwhile and successful endeavor.

Since the Jews in Shiraz spoke a ghetto Farsi, I also made sure that the

curriculum of the summer program included standard Farsi. Soon after this
visit, JDC also opened clinics at the three schools.

We arrived in Yazd on a Friday. The community educators had prepared a
public examination of the children's scholastic achievements. The entire community turned out. Parents and extended families hovered over their children
to "help." I asked everyone but the children to leave. At first, the congregation
thought I was kidding. But I insisted, and the Jewish committee members
evicted them, leaving the children defenseless.

The examination then went surprisingly well. I judged the children not
in comparison with counterparts in Western countries but against their own
performance three years earlier. In early 1951, we had placed three new teachers in Yazd, graduates of Israel Szyf's seminary in Shiraz, and ousted — with
considerable difficulty — several old-time *hakhamim*. The new teachers did
what they were capable of, as did the students.

There was one peculiar difficulty. One Hebrew teacher there was toothless,
so as his pupils read, they pronounced the Hebrew as if they too had no teeth.
The man seemed quite unaware or undisturbed by this drawback. He needed
some extra money and assured us that if we raised his pay, he would teach all
the boys to read Hebrew just as well as — and in the way that — he read it!

Since it was a Friday, we remained in the school for Shabbat, spending
the night on shaky beds on a shaky roof. Israel Szyf, Dr. Herman, and I had
ordered rice and sour milk for our Friday night meal from the school cook.
The rice arrived covered with sand and the sour milk with a layer of dust.
"Don't touch it," Dr. Herman advised us. By now much less fastidious, I ate it
anyway. I had experienced bouts of dysentery but kept them from disabling
me by keeping a special antidote with me at all times — a sack of dry toast
that I would bolster with tea.

We left before dawn on Sunday morning so as to manage a visit in
Rafsanjan en route to Kerman. By the time we reached Rafsanjan, it was Dr.
Herman — who had eaten nothing in Yazd — who came down with dysentery.
Instead of medical care, however, he and the rest of us received a hard-learned
"lesson" in healthcare in Iran's outlying towns.

Early in the morning, we knocked on the door of the head of the community, the opium-addicted dentist, to invite ourselves for breakfast. After
greeting us warmly and serving us food and drinks, he told us about his small
daughter of six, who had severely scalded her arm. Dr. Herman took one

My family in 1928, just before my father's departure to England. Left to right standing: my older brothers, Sam and Mick; Left to right seated: my father, Moshe; my youngest brother, Tzvi Herschel; myself; my twin brother, Boruch; and my mother, Adela.

Officiating at one of the first weddings in Föhrenwald. The newlyweds were concentration camp survivors.

Admiring one of the first babies born in Föhrenwald DP camp, 1946.

General Dwight David ("Ike") Eisenhower, supreme commander of the Allied forces (left), visiting Föhrenwald DP Camp; accompanied by UNRRA camp director, Jean Henshaw (center).

With Jean Henshaw, UNRRA camp director of Föhrenwald.

Unloading matzoth and supplies for DPs in Germany at one of the warehouses that JDC maintained.

Food distribution in a DP camp.

Carrying a Torah scroll into Zeilsheim DP camp, near Frankfurt, 1947; attended by DPs and the camp's rabbi.

Displaced Persons in Germany leaving for Israel, escorted by AJDC staff to the train that would take them to the port at Hamburg.

A lunch break at the Ozar Hatorah school in Shiraz in 1949 — before JDC opened a feeding center there.

A JDC-supported feeding program at the Alliance school in Hamadan.

JDC milk distribution at the Jewish clinic in Tehran.

Mr. Cohen Sedeq of Ozar Hatorah (right) examining a schoolboy in Shiraz, 1949.

Visiting Nehavand, a mountain town in Iran, 1949, accompanied by Andre Cuenca, director of Alliance schools in Iran.

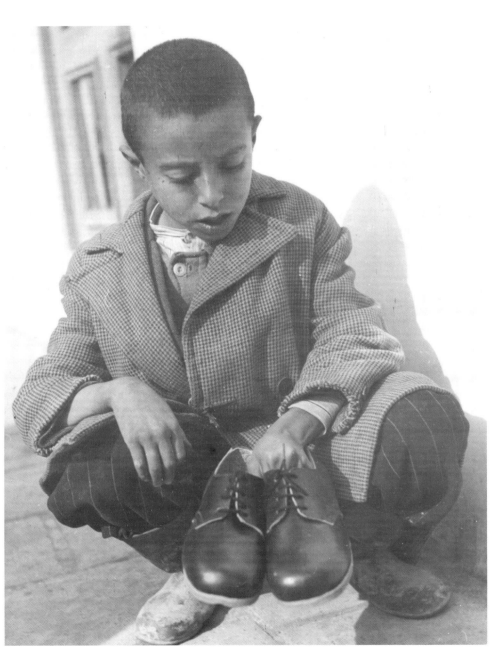

A schoolboy admiring the new shoes he received from JDC.

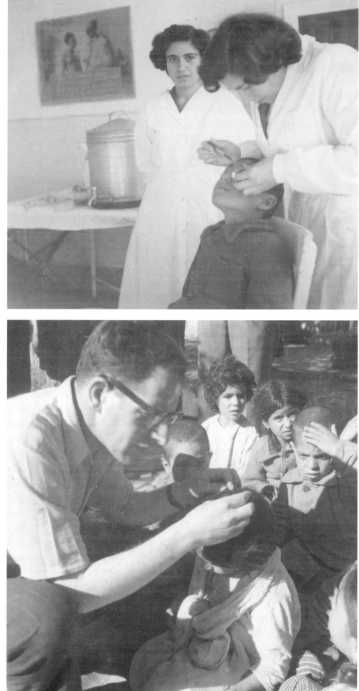

Sylvia Hurwitz, JDC's nurse from the United States, treating a boy's eyes at the Alliance Jaleh school clinic in Tehran, 1950. Sylvia is assisted here by Hilda David, an Iraqi Jewish volunteer in Tehran.

Dr. Meyer Herman, JDC's physician in Iran from October 1951.

The Jewish dentist and head of community in Rafsanjan. See pages 72-73.

Paris, 1948. This rare photograph captures two of the central figures in JDC history. On the left is Paul Baerwald, a founder of JDC, who gave his name to the School of Social Work in Versailles and its successor, the Paul Baerwald School of Social Work at the Hebrew University of Jerusalem; Joseph Schwartz, JDC overseas director general during the war period and until 1950, is on the right.

Addressing a meeting of country directors in Paris, 1949. Seated beside me is Herb Katzki, then overseas deputy director general. We remained very close over the decades and it was Herb who first urged me to record my memoirs.

Kindergarten children of the Polacco school in Rome, in the early 1950s, confidently singing the Hebrew songs that they have just learned. Chief Rabbi Elio Toaff reopened the school after the war and received assistance from JDC and the Claims Conference.

Jewish Education Conference at the grand Hotel de Crillon in Paris, 1957. Front row seated, from left to right: myself; Dr. Azriel Eisenberg, conference organizer, Rabbi Dr. Leo Jung, JDC board member, Edward Warburg, JDC president, and Moe Leavitt, JDC executive vice-president. Speaking is Charlie Jordan, general of JDC's Overseas Program. Jordan was tragically murdered in Prague in 1967.

A boy works diligently at the Sally Mayer Jewish school in Milan, one of the many schools across Europe that received advice and assistance from JDC during the postwar reconstruction period. Early 1960s.

look at the child's arm and diagnosed infection and gangrene. Disregarding his own ill-health, Dr. Herman went into town with the dentist and bought penicillin and syringes. He gave the child an injection, then another a few hours later, and showed the dentist how to disinfect the needles and carry on the girl's treatment. The father followed the instructions diligently.

Weeks later, we received a letter from the dentist with a photograph of his daughter clutching flowers in the hand Dr. Herman had saved. On the back was an inscription of deep gratitude for our ministrations. In encounters such as these, I sensed that Divine Providence was at work and that Dr. Herman was God's angel.

By the time we reached Kerman, Dr. Herman's dysentery had completely incapacitated him. Szyf and I left him to rest, and headed out to the Ozar Hatorah school, where I examined the children's scholastic progress, and again came away impressed. Such a visit compensated for all the hardships of our work.

As for JDC's feeding program, our medical man in Kerman — Dr. Bachrach of the British mission — who was supervising the provision of the schoolchildren's lunch, morning milk, and afternoon snacks, was in the process of shutting down his mission's clinic due to political pressure and prejudice. His was the best such infirmary in the country. Apostate Jew or not, we were sorry to be losing him. At his suggestion, we arranged with a Dr. Azim, a Zoroastrian, to continue supervising our care programs. We could be relatively confident that being a Persian, Azim's activities would not be threatened by the authorities.

Our trip back to Tehran crossed the desert on a trail that fell short even of Iranian standards. Frequent punctured tires, constant dust in the car's engine that caused it to stall, and a lack of facilities for refreshment rendered us quite exhausted by the time we reached our destination.

Summing Up

While JDC had never envisaged Iran as a main arena of activity, by the time I took leave of the country, the enormity of the need had resulted in its being a location for one of the largest JDC welfare and education programs outside of Israel and western Europe.

By 1952, JDC was subsidizing welfare and medical programs for more than

12,000 boys and girls in the Jewish schools. Feeding programs served about 2,500 children daily, while 4,500 in the fourteen communities that had Jewish schools received clothing.

The schools themselves had improved over the three short years. In primary schools, we labored to introduce order, systematic reporting and inspection, and educational values. Our two professional instructors, Israel Szyf and Avraham Shoshani, were working full-time to retrain local teachers and train new ones.

Immense challenges remained, however. Since we focused on the primary level, secondary schooling was, regretfully, somewhat neglected. And despite all our efforts, in 1952 thousands of Jewish children, including about 1,500 of those remaining in the Tehran *mahaleh*, still attended a non-Jewish school or no school at all.

JDC's medical programs operated in all Jewish schools in Iran and had administered close to 60,000 treatments annually by the time I left. In some locations, hygiene programs that provided baths of clean water, soap, and clean towels for schoolchildren were running efficiently.

In Tehran, we were giving full support for the Jewish school clinic and for the polyclinic. The latter was treating 5,000 outpatients each month.

Nevertheless, the extremely harsh conditions of the Iranian *mahaleh*s and refugee camps made the outcome of all our efforts seem minimal. In fact, my successor, Abe Loskove's first impression of the Tehran ghetto was not markedly different from mine in 1949. He wrote:

> When I served in Tripoli, [Libya,] I considered the *hara* [ghetto] of that city a hell compared to the DP camps. But after I reached Iran, it seemed to me that the Tripoli *hara* was Paradise by comparison with the *mahaleh* of Tehran.

Despite our feeding and medical programs, there were still children suffering from malnutrition and other medical problems. By 1952, we had not yet succeeded in initiating wider medical and dental care programs. Projects like the establishment of a maternity hospital, a training program for nurses' aides, polyclinics in outlying towns, dental aid, bathing programs in most localities, and daycare programs would largely be my successors' accomplishments.

The *mahaleh* of Tehran continued to experience seasonal epidemics: dysentery in the summer, typhoid in the autumn, respiratory diseases in the winter. Child patients were taken to the pediatric hospital in the polyclinic, whose reputation helped the hospital committee raise funds for the facility, which was still lacking an x-ray unit. Indeed, the hospital in Tehran benefited from the most generous regular philanthropy in Iranian Jewish history. As I left, land for a new hospital building had been acquired, allowing a maternity clinic to open in the old building.

My efforts to consolidate JDC work in Iran through local committees had paid off. Our small contingent of JDC foreign-service personnel started with five in 1950 and remained at five at the end of my tenure. The local committees sustained our programs and understood the necessity of regular local — albeit modest — contributions toward their projects. The annual JDC budget for Iran had grown from $150,000 in 1949 to $400,000 in 1952, with the increase invested in cosponsored programs that resulted in still more income from the local community.

As I prepared to leave Iran, I scheduled a trip to Afghanistan for September 1952. I obtained a visa and persuaded the Afghan ambassador to Iran to furnish me with letters of reference to the governors of the areas I wished to visit. From Paris, Moe Beckelman approved the trip: I had developed contacts with the Jewish communities of Kabul and Herat due to their close relations with those in Mashhad. JDC would be delighted to receive a first-hand report on conditions there.

I never made it. On a visit to Tehran, Herbert Katzki, Beckelman's deputy, talked me out of it due to concern for my safety. To this day, I regret the lost opportunity.

Gone but Not Forgotten

Shortly before Rosh Hashanah 1952, I flew to Paris and reported to the JDC headquarters there. I left JDC's Iranian operation in the very capable hands of the forty-year-old Abe Loskove. An American, his training included rabbinical ordination and seven years as a JDC overseas representative, most recently as country director for Libya and Italy. In Libya, he had done much of what I had been doing in Iran, including arranging for the Libyan community to emigrate to Israel. He was probably the warmest, kindest, and most sincere person I knew in JDC service. As the years went by, I became closer and closer to Abe and his wonderful wife, Ruth.

In December 1952, Abe Loskove reported that most Iranian Jews no longer wished to emigrate to Israel. Preferring to consolidate their own communities, they looked to JDC as the organization to help them. The refugee camp in Tehran's new cemetery existed until mid-1956, when the Jewish Agency finally shut it down.

The segment of the Iranian Jewish community that had moved to Israel gave rise to parliamentarians, manufacturers, senior army officers, and even a president. Some of the Jews who remained in Iran amassed wealth and status due to the oil-based transformation of the economy and the encouragement of Western tendencies by the Shah's regime. The JDC program never lacked for clients but now, with many fewer cases of severe distress, it could concentrate on educational, vocational, and general medical and welfare programs.

I occasionally visited Iran in subsequent years, staying in touch with many friends and acquaintances. And on January 1, 1978, I began an eight-month tour in Iran as interim country director. It was a sequel of sorts. Our country director had departed two weeks earlier, and his intended replacement, Michael Schneider (JDC's future chief executive), was delayed for several months by bureaucratic complications in taking up his post.

I found an Iranian community that was wealthier, more demanding and more outspoken than the one I had known. Local committees had become more independent minded and, in some cases, critical and argumentative. Community philanthropy was still insufficient; the rich had become richer, the poor stayed poor. We were viewed in some quarters as rubber-stamp financiers, or were expected to serve as such.

My mandate this time was much less sweeping than it had been thirty years earlier. JDC had developed a large program by then. I was to sustain JDC's activities while playing the role of mediator to draw alienated Iranian Jews who had previously been active back to participating in the programs. Even Ozar Hatorah and Alliance were at odds again; I was to help even matters out.

This second tour of duty was short lived, as was JDC's program itself. Once Michael Schneider arrived in Tehran in August 1978, I stayed on for one more week to hand over the reins, and then bade farewell to Iran again — for good, as it now seems.

A powerful Islamic backlash to the Shah's Westernization was already underway. While riots escalated, JDC brought in an American expert to show our Iran staff how to pack up the files that we had accumulated. The idea was to ship everything to Israel either by air or by sea. Toward the end of 1978, as JDC negotiated with carriers, the Islamic Revolution of Ayatollah Khomeini erupted in full force, and the Iran that we had known collapsed. The foreign staff was forced to burn all the files and make a rapid departure from the country. Soon after us, on January 16, 1979, the Shah fled Iran. Two weeks later, on February 1, Khomeini arrived and anti-Western sentiment escalated drastically.

During those months, Jewish life was severely disrupted. In May, Habib Elghanayan, head of the community, was arrested and executed for his relations with the Shah. Accused of a variety of crimes, the rest of the Elghanayan family spent a fortune to smuggle themselves out of Iran, abandoning their factories and homes, and emigrating to the United States. At least a dozen other Jewish notables were also executed at that time, mostly because of their ties to the Shah.

On November 4, 1979, Khomeini supporters seized the US embassy in Tehran, taking tens of American citizens hostage. The upheaval led to another exodus of Iranian Jews — those most closely associated with the Shah's era — and left the rump Jewish community in a precarious state. The Jews who left Iran at that time made their way to Vienna via Turkey and Pakistan. The new regime treated American and international Jewish organizations, including JDC, as profoundly unwelcome.

Since then, of course, no JDC staff member has set foot in what has, regrettably, become a hostile country.

⌒ Back to Europe

Leaving behind the *mahaleh*s of Iran and the great responsibilities I held for the Jewish community there, I returned to Paris in September 1952. I reported to JDC's European headquarters to discuss my next posting. I met with the director of the JDC Education Department, Dr. Judah Shapiro; that I would remain with JDC was implicit — neither of us mentioned any other possibility.

I no longer wished to return to my pursuits in England. My experiences in Iran had left me feeling that I had at last found my vocation and that JDC offered me a rare opportunity to make a meaningful contribution to the Jewish people. I was thankful that JDC seemed to take the same view of my potential.

Dr. Shapiro had three alternatives in mind for me.

The greatest European centers of Jewish learning had been virtually erased by the Nazis, and now JDC felt it was necessary to run a program for the reconstruction of yeshivot (rabbinical academies) in Israel. With my capabilities in education, this, Dr. Shapiro felt, would be a program that I could head.

In North Africa, JDC had already established a large welfare program and financially aided Jewish educational agencies to run Jewish schools. However, JDC was in need of an education director there. I knew that with my experience from Iran, I could also perform this job very well.

Lastly, Dr. Shapiro required assistance in JDC's Education Department in Paris.

I considered all three and concluded that even though the yeshivot program had the distinct advantage of allowing me to fulfill my desire to make aliyah, at this stage I did not feel quite ready to make the move to Israel. The North Africa program also had strong appeal. Its large scope — geographically speaking and in terms of the Jewish population and its needs — would be another welcome challenge. Yet it was the third alternative that I accepted. The Paris-based option allowed me to spend time in the familiar European environment, something I felt I needed after three years of living a very different life in Iran.

It also appealed to me on a professional level, since it would enable me to expand on the work I had done in my previous JDC postings. Whereas my DP service had involved me in the immediate aftermath of the Holocaust, I would now be involved in the longer-term effort to reconstruct Western Europe's Jewish communities.

That said, I was reluctant to give up entirely on the challenge and appeal of education directorship of JDC-North Africa. So in addition to my duties in Europe, we concluded that I would spend considerable time across the Mediterranean.

Based at JDC headquarters in Paris, I embarked on what would turn out to be a thirty-year career in Jewish education in Europe, alongside missions of many kinds in the countries of northern Africa.

JDC's Place in the Reconstruction of Communities

My work in the reconstruction of Jewish life in Europe was part of a vast and daunting enterprise in which JDC was prominent — no less than a "Jewish Marshall Plan"[1] for our people's remnant on the Continent. However, like the United States' massive reconstruction initiative, our efforts were geographically restricted. By 1953, the Iron Curtain was firmly in place and the Cold War was intensifying. The Jews of the Soviet Union and its Eastern European satellites were all off-limits to us, and except for Romania, JDC's representatives had been expelled from these Communist-dominated countries.

With other Jewish relief organizations far away and with shipping in short supply, JDC, with its on-site presence, was uniquely positioned to step up its activities for the Jews of free Continental Europe. Thus, it became JDC's main theater of activity outside of Israel.

---

1. The Marshall Plan (later known as the European Recovery Program — ERP) was the US program to aid in the reconstruction of Europe in the aftermath of World War II. The program provided both financial and technical assistance to sixteen European countries between 1948 and 1951.

Before the war, Poland alone had a Jewish population of some 3.3 million. Now, in the early 1950s, France had the largest community in free Continental Europe, with a Jewish population of about 250,000, which was more than could be found in the rest of the region combined.[2]

At that point in the 1950s, some 45,000 Jews on the Continent — survivors who had returned to their places of residence and languished with neither families nor livelihoods — still required and received JDC support. Another 15,000, mostly former DPs and those who had managed to flee the Eastern bloc into Western Europe, remained refugees and were dispersed across the Continent from Scandinavia to Italy, and from Austria to Portugal. Several thousand even remained in DP camps in Germany, Austria, and Italy. JDC obtained a small number of visas for DPs each year, mainly to Scandinavia and South America. Others slowly found ways to integrate in their localities, frequently with JDC's help. There was also a minority group of survivors who had already moved to Israel during or after the war, but returned to Germany to resettle (called "returnees") and possibly become eligible for visas to America. They, too, received whatever assistance JDC could offer.

Of the Western European countries only Great Britain and Switzerland did not need our assistance. These countries had their own Jewish Welfare agencies, all of which had risen to the challenge of aiding the thousands of Jewish refugees who had reached British or Swiss soil before, during, and after the war.

Even so, the war had exhausted Britain, its empire, and its Jewish community. So while British Jewry was always able to cope with its own needs and those of the thousands of Jewish refugees living in Britain, it was in no position during this time of postwar shortages and rationing to provide more than the most limited assistance to communities on the Continent.

Switzerland, on the other hand, was still able to lend a helping hand to other European communities, even while supporting its own Jewish infrastructure and development after the war.

In 1954, a typical year in that decade, JDC spent only $4.5 million or so in Europe out of a global budget of some $26 million. But the financial scale of JDC's involvement in Europe cannot give adequate indication of the

---

2.   There were about 400,000 Jews in Great Britain in the early 1950s.

immensity of its endeavors, which focused on institutional reconstruction, leveraging of community projects, and investment in human capital rather than cash handouts.

JDC's main long-term task — the revitalization of the shattered Jewish communal array — meant phasing out short-term programs such as those we had implemented in the DP camps (soup kitchens, cash relief, feeding, medical programs) and replacing them with more specialized and professional services that would last for years. It meant rebuilding institutions, reclaiming confiscated buildings, and recruiting and training new communal leaders, lay and professional.

The ultimate goal of these programs was the restoration of West European Jewry's capacity for self-sufficient community life. Beyond the dramatic rescue and relief operations for which JDC is known, it is this strategy of restoring communities' ability to meet their own needs — whether in serving their poor and elderly or in educating their children — that sets the organization apart.

The DP-camp period had been a time of urgent needs that required creativity and spontaneity more than deliberate, systematic responses. JDC rose to the occasion then with the best of its resources. By now, though, free Europe had become a relatively more settled place, where JDC could apply normal reconstruction strategies.

The initial steps to implement these reconstruction strategies had already been taken when I took up my new position in 1952. In France, JDC, in cooperation with the local Jewish community had set up a central fundraising mechanism, the Fonds Social Juif Unifié, also known in short as Fonds Social or FSJU. By 1954, the Fonds Social received more than 60 percent of its budget from JDC, the remaining 40 percent coming from local community donations. The organization used the money for cash relief and to support childcare, full-time and part-time schools, canteens, dispensaries, and cultural and educational activities. In France, JDC provided medical aid through the OSE (Children's Aid Society)[3] and in other European cities it was provided through similar local organizations.

To help rebuild Europe's decimated cadre of Jewish communal professionals,

---

3. The Oeuvre de Secours aux Enfants (OSE) was founded in Russia in 1912 and head-quartered in Paris from 1933 on.

JDC had established the Paul Baerwald School of Social Work in Versailles, near Paris in October 1949. The Baerwald School initially enrolled students to study social work. By the time of my arrival, it had become an in-service institution that admitted professionals from various countries and upgraded their skills so they could return to their communities and provide better aid. The school's areas of study were gradually widened too, and included training for other communal needs, such as administration, youth work, and management of old-age homes. Many of the school's students acquired training on JDC scholarships. Having also channeled many of its resources to the training of social workers from Eastern Europe, the school's ability to continue was weakened drastically with the drop of the Iron Curtain, and in August 1953 the school was closed down.[4]

In other areas of Europe, JDC had become equally active in training community center directors, health-care workers, and other professionals whose numbers had been drastically reduced during the war. The organization selected highly regarded training institutions in different cities and sent them potential community staff to train for service in their respective communities.

JDC and communal leaders adopted a plan for the establishment of loan institutions in four German cities. JDC also strengthened the survivors and DPs of German Jewry by helping create a central fundraising organization for them in Frankfurt. In Vienna, apart from a direct welfare program, JDC supported the Israelitische Kultusgemeinde (IKG), which provided social and religious services for that community. JDC played a similar role in Scandinavia, although there the work was carried out by Scandinavian Jews.

In most Western European countries, JDC had begun to put up funds for distribution to resettled refugees and augmented individual communities' welfare arrangements for them. JDC subsidized apartments and hostels for penniless survivors of the war, and it was the prime initiator, although not the direct builder, of community-based old-age homes throughout Europe. It invested almost as much in informal education, mainly through youth and community centers, as it did in schools.

---

4. In 1958, JDC resurrected the successful Baerwald training program in Israel by setting up the Paul Baerwald School of Social Work at the Hebrew University of Jerusalem.

Finding My Place in the Works

From my corner of the enterprise, I would observe the scope of JDC's work in Europe and marvel at its enormity. I was part of a team at the wide-reaching JDC executive headquarters that included, apart from my department, an accounting department, medical personnel, welfare workers, vocational training specialists, a daycare consultant, and a procurements officer who arranged worldwide shipments. It was quite staggering to compare this operation with the five-member staff of my Tehran office.

My duties, too, proved to be immense. That said, Dr. Shapiro's task was even broader — Jewish education in Europe, Israel, Northern Africa, and Iran — but then, he was an exceptionally capable individual.

No longer a country director, I had less latitude in Europe than in Iran. However, I did not feel crimped. First, I was able to focus on education — an aspect that JDC had come to recognize as crucial. Furthermore, it was and remains JDC's approach to give staff members a great deal of leeway in fulfilling their assignments and to ask only for results. Thus from the outset of my tenure in Europe, although everything I did was in consultation with Dr. Shapiro, I made my own decisions.

One of my first was to develop contacts throughout Europe and acquaint myself with all Jewish schools and their principals. As I had done in Iran, I began with a set of fact-finding trips.

On my initial tours of Europe in late 1952 and early 1953, I visited communities from Scandinavia down to Spain, Italy, and Greece — wherever Jewish education programs were initiated. I found German and Austrian Jewry particularly interesting. These were reconstructed communities made up of individuals who had survived in hiding and of former DPs.

I found European Jewry still in shambles. The plight of the Jews bore no resemblance to what I had witnessed in the DP camps or the Iranian *mahaleh*s, but the ravages of the war were still painfully evident, even though almost eight years had elapsed since the war's end. Most communities were not yet organized; the Jewish schools were not yet reestablished. Jews were still migrating frequently from town to town and from country to country — mostly from Eastern Europe to Belgium and France — in search of a place where they could feel comfortable and make a living. Many refugees remained highly dependent on JDC help.

A particularly painful visit at the outset of my tenure in Europe was to the

Jews of Amsterdam. They were mostly survivors who had returned to their homes only to find them ravaged by non-Jewish locals — walls and floors completely pulled apart — in search of diamonds and other treasures. The survivors were disheartened and were finding it difficult to overcome the shock and disbelief, even as they slowly picked up the remains of their lives and homes.

One such survivor was Mr. Mundschtuk. He had left his native Warsaw before it was turned to ruins and moved to Amsterdam, where he established an afternoon Talmud Torah.[5] He was highly respected by the community, and those who enrolled their children in his school did so with great admiration and pride. Mundschtuk somehow survived a Nazi concentration camp and after the war returned to what had become the ruins of Amsterdam. To him the Talmud Torah was a precious home that needed restoration, and he dedicated himself to restarting the afternoon school that he had so proudly directed before the war.

In most of the larger European towns, Jewish day schools had been established by local communities right after the war. For example, in Spain, the Jewish Moroccan immigrants of the 1950s (who had left their country of origin due to anti-Jewish attacks at the time of impending Moroccan independence) opened their own day schools in Madrid and Barcelona. This community was enhanced by later waves of Moroccan Jewish immigrants in the 1960s. In Italy, Rabbi Elio Toaff, then chief rabbi of Rome, saw his primary trust as reopening the Polacco school in the capital. In Milan, Astorre Mayer, a great Jewish leader, built a dynamic Jewish day school in that city in memory of his late father.

I learned from Dr. Shapiro of the religious and vocational schools for young adults that had been established in France in the aftermath of the Holocaust by Rabbi Gershon Liebman, whom I had met a few years earlier at the Zeilsheim DP camp in Germany. Also in France, four full-time Jewish day schools had emerged after the war. The principals of these schools had been trained in hiding during the war by the chief rabbi of Strasbourg, the late Rabbi Abraham Deutsch.

Rabbi Deutsch had escaped the German occupation of his city and went into hiding in a mountain village, where a peasant family gave him asylum.

---

5. An Orthodox primary school for boys that provided religious instruction only, also known as a heder.

More than anything, Rabbi Deutsch missed his former students. After discussing the matter with the local police chief, the village elder, and his host, he decided to invite at least some of his former students to the village. He sent a messenger to his hometown and asked the young men to come to him. Many of his former students had left for other hiding places. One or two had been deported. Six showed up. Rabbi Deutsch was convinced that when the war ended, his students would be the key people in rebuilding the broken Jewish communities.

His small school of six young men studied daily; Rabbi Deutsch took care of all their needs. The village police would inform him ahead of time when German or other French police were about to visit the village, whereupon the rabbi and his students would take cover in well-prepared hiding places. When the war finally came to an end, it did not take long before Rabbi Deutsch's students formed the new Jewish day schools in Paris, Strasbourg, Marseille, and Lyon.

The devotion Rabbi Liebman and Rabbi Deutsch displayed in building pillars of cultural reconstruction in the very midst and aftermath of the Holocaust astonishes me to this day. Even with the Nazis breathing down their necks, they had the foresight to invest in molding tomorrow's educators.

Despite such altruism and commitment, I found the communities' reestablished schools to be ragged around the edges — housed in poor conditions, weak in staff, short on administrative skills, and lacking in up-to-date equipment, curricula, teaching aids, and textbooks. In particular, the schools' Jewish studies were affected by these conditions, so it was clear to me that JDC's assistance was most needed precisely in my field, Jewish education.

Visiting the European communities turned out to be the work that I found the most constructive, apart from which I always found human interaction stimulating and pleasant. The reconstruction of Jewish education in Europe was led by no more than 100 selfless educators across the Continent, several in each community, none of whom were liberally rewarded in any sense other than seeing the development of their charges. Everywhere I went, I found that cooperation was easy to achieve. Community leaders and educators were enthusiastic for any assistance and advice they could get in the redevelopment of their communities' educational infrastructure. There was no disagreement about the essence of the task at hand.

I was able to establish fruitful, professional relationships with the principals of nearly all Jewish schools in Europe. There were two reasons for their willing-ness to work with me: their urgent need for JDC's financial and professional assistance; and JDC's — and my own — conviction that recipients of aid though they may be, they were not supplicants, but colleagues and partners.

I also developed close working relations with others concerned with Jewish education — Dr. Schauman, the school principal in Milan; Mr. Bamberger, the principal of the Jewish day school in Brussels; Chief Rabbi Melchior of Copenhagen and his son (later to follow his father into the office of chief rabbi); David Kopnivsky, secretary of the Jewish community in Stockholm; chief rabbi of Rome, Rabbi Toaff, who directed Jewish education there; and miscellaneous intellectuals and scholars.

At a time when the struggle of Jewish families was to reestablish them-selves economically, these Jews chose Jewish education as their vocation, knowing full well that it was poorly rewarded. I was greatly impressed with these modest heroes of Jewish life.

Other Players in the Reconstruction of Europe's Jewish Education, 1952–1972

JDC was not the only player in the reconstruction of Jewish education during the three decades of my tenure. I encountered familiar organizations in this area of activity, such as ORT, Chabad-Lubavitch, Ozar Hatorah, the Jewish Agency for Israel (JAFI), and Alliance Israelite Universelle.

ORT stressed vocational training in France, Germany, and other countries in Europe, and our financial headquarters in New York supported it substan-tially. Indeed, the ORT connection was JDC's main activity in the vocational field. Even though I felt that the ORT curriculum underemphasized Jewish studies, I appreciated the organization for doing its mission well. Enrolling thousands of idle young Jews and equipping them with trades is no simple matter, and ORT has done it to this very day.

The Chabad-Lubavitch educators I encountered were originally from the Soviet Union. They had made their way to France after the war by changing their names, obtaining Polish documents, and joining Polish citizens who were repatriated after spending the war in the Soviet heartland. Once in

Poland, these Hasidim went on to France while the borders remained porous. Penniless, they settled in a suburb of Paris and, using the JDC financial aid that they received as refugees, began building institutions: first a yeshiva, then a girls' school, afterwards a seminary. Today, they are a force to reckon with in the French Jewish community and, indeed, throughout the world.

Alliance Israelite served the general Jewish mainstream in ways and along lines that reflected the shifting Jewish demography. Alliance had lost or discontinued many of its schools in the Middle East and Turkey over the years and had been evicted from Iraq and Syria. During my tenure in Europe, France again became a major arena of operations for Alliance.

It was in the 1950s, as the French empire began to decline, that a substantial portion of North Africa's Jewish population relocated to France. Later — during and at the end of the strife that preceded Algeria's independence in 1962 — nearly all of that country's 120,000 Jews moved to France, which, as French citizens, they were entitled to do. Most Moroccan Jews did not hold French citizenship, and many moved to Israel in the mid-1960s, but a substantial minority — the more educated, generally speaking — chose France and were allowed to enter under relatively liberal immigration laws. Smaller numbers of Moroccan Jews, mainly from Spanish Morocco, resettled in Spain. It was natural then that Alliance felt an obligation to the school-aged Jewish immigrants in both countries, especially in France, where it had its roots and headquarters.

In 1867, Alliance had established a central teachers' college in Paris, the École Normale Israélite Orientale (ENIO), and about a century later it founded two Jewish day schools there. In Spain, Alliance supported schools that agreed to hire its educators. During my years in Europe, it was my pleasure to interact with the headmaster of the ENIO, the Lithuanian-born Emmanuel Levinas, whose formidable credentials included a premier status among French philosophers.

Ozar Hatorah began to operate in France in 1961, when it opened a school in Lyon. Being an organization dedicated to the education of Sephardic communities, it responded to the immigration of North African Jews by opening additional schools in Sarcelles, Strasbourg, and Marseille. By 1972, the chain of Ozar schools in France was in need of additional support to meet the needs of the increasing numbers of North African Jewish immigrants who were enrolling in those schools. Observing that the local communities were not able to cover the extra costs of maintaining these larger schools, JDC responded with financial assistance.

JDC played an important role alongside Alliance and Ozar Hatorah in helping the existing French Jewish community to cope with the newly arrived masses, for whom they were not prepared. Besides financial assistance for their schools, we provided funds that these communities could not possibly have raised from their own resources for welfare, communal organizations, and additional teacher training seminars.

As the number of Jewish schools in France climbed rapidly, so did their material needs. The schools were now predominantly Sephardic at all levels — students, teachers, and principals. We provided teaching aids and text books to the schools, and in an effort to understand the differences between the various North African communities, we tailored the material to their respective conditions. Some of the communities required more strengthening in Jewish subjects, while others were already quite strong in that field and needed encouragement in general studies. Likewise, we provided counseling for the teaching and administrative staff in building appropriate curricula for the schools' educational programs.

Jewish Agency emissaries, representing Israel, were ubiquitous at the beginning of my term of service, especially in formal and informal education. The Jewish Agency still attempted at this time to implement the classical Zionist "negation of the Diaspora" philosophy, i.e., to liquidate Jewish communities and transfer them to Israel. This approach did not succeed in Europe. Although some Jews did move to Israel under JAFI patronage, others stayed on in the hope of recovering businesses and properties. These circumstances became clear when additional Jews came to Western Europe from Eastern Europe and when many North African Jews who had financial resources considered Europe, not Israel, the place to reestablish themselves.

JAFI and JDC had different overarching goals in Europe — emigration to Israel and reconstruction in Europe, respectively. Nevertheless, in our educational activity, my associates and I would collaborate intensively with emissaries from JAFI's Torah and general education departments. I worked mostly with the former because the schools at issue, like most Diaspora schools, were traditional to one extent or another, and many clearly needed more backing in the area of religious study.

Funding Education

In France in 1960, the government set up a contract arrangement by which independent schools would receive government financial support and still be allowed to remain independent, provided that they taught the government curriculum. The organizationally independent Jewish schools joined this arrangement over time, happy to receive whatever financial backing was being offered. As the Alliance schools and several Ozar Hatorah schools enlisted, they accorded more time to the government curriculum and less to Jewish studies. Lubavitch avoided the contract relationship but still received some government funding for seminars and training.

Jewish schools in most other Western European countries received government funding under similar terms, as did various Jewish communal organizations that had been established to provide for the general needs of their communities. Governments of this region — unfettered by concerns over church-state separation — were supportive of community organizations, and particularly of schools. We helped these schools and organizations to become sufficiently established, by means of initial funding and hands-on involvement, so as to enable them to receive this government backing.

Thus, by and large, JDC did not continuously provide for schools' expenses and was able to concentrate its efforts on upgrading skills and producing and distributing materials.

As important as education was in the JDC scheme, it was JDC's highest priority only in the immediate aftermath of the war, when it used schools as channels for welfare. As soon as the communities separated their welfare and education systems, welfare took primacy, and education retreated to second place in JDC's funding priorities. As such, less was made available for my work.

Whatever budget there was for education in Europe, no JDC budget was "mine," as the operations budget in Iran had been, since I was no longer involved in budget management. However, JDC's education personnel were able to access it along with regular JDC funds and used it to sponsor our teacher training activities, print textbooks and other materials, write curricula, provide technical assistance, and carry out teachers' seminars.

A Library in Paris

One of my first uses of the finances available to me was to set up a library in Paris, of textbooks and teaching aids from the United States and Israel. The library could be consulted by school principals and teachers. This service, I believed, would provide a good start in upgrading the schools' advancement in Jewish studies. I would recommend suitable material to users, but I believed that the principals and teachers directly responsible for the programs should select those books that would be most appropriate to their country and children.

JDC also invested heavily in the production and distribution of books and other teaching aids, covering the most rudimentary of Jewish materials. They included beginners' Hebrew books, Bibles, basic commentaries, and history books, most of which came from Israel and the United States. The schools adapted these education materials to their needs, and translated what was required by them. (We had less involvement in the general studies program, which had to follow government requirements.) Tangential to this, JDC assisted in the printing of an offset reproduction of the Talmud in Germany for distribution to Jewish communities across the Continent. I took it upon myself to make sure these books, and many others, were made available to educators through the JDC library and by making recommendations during my visits to schools across Europe.

By the 1970s, the pedagogical and Jewish library had amassed an enormous collection, turned out numerous books and pamphlets, and offered consulting services on the availability of materials.

The Claims Conference

In 1954, Dr. Shapiro left our organization — he was the sort of person who felt most fulfilled by changing positions frequently — and became the director of the education department of the newly formed Conference on Jewish Material Claims Against Germany, also known as the "Claims Conference."

I regretted Dr. Shapiro's departure, having come to admire this articulate, brilliant man. To my delight, however, I continued to cross paths with him.

The Claims Conference worked very closely with JDC, and I was promoted to the post of consultant to the American Joint Distribution Committee (AJDC) on Jewish education in Europe and North Africa, in which capacity I interacted with Dr. Shapiro.

No account of postwar Jewish reconstruction can overlook the endeavors of the Claims Conference. An amalgam of twenty-three Jewish organizations, including JDC, it had been founded in October 1951 to receive and distribute the reparations proceeds that were about to be provided by the West German government. In September 1952, the Germans concluded two agreements: one with the Claims Conference and the other with Israel.

The agreement with the Claims Conference provided $110 million for distribution beginning in 1953/54. A large percentage of these annual allocations were transferred to JDC for use in meeting the welfare needs of Jewish communities and individual Jews in Europe, which JDC augmented with contributions it received from America's Jewish Federations through the United Jewish Appeal.

The Claims Conference's funding became the fulcrum on which the entire physical reconstruction enterprise was leveraged. Its capital grants aided in the construction, expansion, furnishing, and repair of community institutions: kindergartens, schools, community and youth centers, children's homes, summer camps, old-age homes, religious institutions, hospitals, and clinics. JDC soon developed an effective partnership with the Claims.

Part of the Conference's budget has been dedicated to Holocaust research, documentation, and education. The Claims Conference leadership in New York has consulted with JDC before investing money in many education-related activities that the Claims undertook on its own and has carried out cultural activities in coordination with JDC.

In the mid-1960s, when the original funds from Germany had been allocated,[6] the late Nahum Goldmann negotiated funding from Germany to establish the Memorial Foundation for Jewish Culture which would assist in rebuilding the cultural foundation of Jewish life in Europe. The Memorial Foundation was to provide grants and scholarships to aid Jewish education

6.   The Claims Conference continued with other activities, which expanded enormously when East Germany was reunified with West Germany in 1990.

and culture. As it had with the Claims Conference, JDC maintained close cooperation with the Memorial Foundation.

In my new capacity as an education consultant for AJDC, my advice to the Claims Conference included construction and capital investments in schools — fields in which JDC did not engage. The function of JDC liaison with the Claims Conference — working closely with Dr. Shapiro and his successors — became an explicit part of my job and an increasingly important one as time passed.

The Claims also financed training and related aspects of the education reconstruction enterprise. This included scholarships, fellowships, rabbinical research grants, and publication of books of Jewish scholarship and literature. We at JDC often received Claims funding for textbook and program development.

In conjunction with other JDC experts, I made special visits to schools that the Claims Conference wished to expand or rebuild. I would escort Claims executives during their visits to these institutions, inspect various projects during their development, and represent the Claims vis-à-vis communal organizations.

After less than a year in his position there, Dr. Shapiro decided to move on once again. I frequently traveled with his successor, Mark Uveeler, to review funding applications that the Conference had received. Mr. Uveeler made his recommendations based on background material and opinions that I provided, on our discussions as we traveled, on his talent for working with lay leaders, and on his own careful judgment.

Through this association, I watched the physical infrastructure of Jewish education take shape. In Antwerp, for example, two day schools — Jesode-Hatora and Tachkemoni — developed, added new wings, and increased their enrollment. Jesode-Hatora, the more Orthodox of the two, had a wonderful principal, Rabbi Shmuel Ostersetzer who bought up all the houses around his school with Claims and local funding, took in about 1,000 students, and developed what eventually became one of the finest Jewish schools in Europe.

In Milan, the Sally Mayer day school, opened by the Mayer family, grew with aid from the Claims Conference. It eventually attracted almost all Jewish children in that city. In Rome, the Polacco school used Claims Conference funds to expand its premises and boost its enrollment to about 600. In Strasbourg, the Akiva school grew and developed in the same way. What is more, these schools became capable of continued development with resources drawn from government support, school fees, and community contributions.

For JDC, however, the schools' physical facilities were but the first important phase. Our main concern was how Jewish subjects were taught within their walls.

Teacher Training and Seminars

Many teachers around Europe were yeshiva graduates who had taught before the war but were not qualified. A yeshiva-trained teacher was well versed in Bible, its major commentaries, and the procedures and liturgies of prayer. However, my concern — and theirs, since we had the same goals — was how to teach these subjects. Almost all needed additional training, especially in methodology and pedagogy.

I took this on as a personal cause. At each school I visited, I began by sitting in on lessons — entire lessons — and followed up by meeting with the principal and teachers, giving an evaluation, and noting the shortcomings that needed to be addressed. I also brought Professor Hanoch Enoch, professor of education at Tel Aviv University, and Professor Moshe Arendt of Bar Ilan University to Paris to train staff at day schools.

One of the first programmatic steps I took to make advancements in the field of teacher training was to organize — together with the JAFI emissaries — professional liaison activities, in the form of summer seminars for teachers in Switzerland. Qualified professionals from Israel were invited to offer training and help design school programs, and we provided the seminars' schedules and materials. JDC split the costs with the participating teachers, but also made efforts to recoup the JDC subventions from the communities being represented.

The Israeli educators led discussions that addressed limitations and deficiencies in education, and the teachers would bring case studies for analysis (e.g., how to teach different aspects of Jewish study, be it in Bible, prayers, or Jewish history). The dynamic exchanges usually led to practical and realistic solutions.

The German and Austrian Jews were the most eager participants in our seminars. Their involvement with other Jews helped them create links with the rest of European Jewry and, I imagine, helped ease their misgivings over having reestablished themselves in the countries that so recently had been the core of massive Jewish persecution. They were able to achieve a heightened sense of belonging and assurance.

After running some of these seminars, JAFI and JDC worked out a long-term program to hold them annually — sometimes semiannually — and arranged for those completing the training to receive teacher certification by the Israeli Ministry of Education's Department for Jewish Education in the Diaspora. With this certification in hand, teachers who later chose to emigrate to Israel were exempt from some of the Israeli government's re-qualification procedures. In this fashion, JAFI and JDC made a contribution to Jewish education both in Europe and in Israel.

The teachers' seminar initiative had been a first attempt to remedy the lack of qualified teachers. It became clear by 1955, however, that JDC had to do much more.

As a step toward further corrective action, I recommended that we carry out a survey of Jewish education in Europe. The director of the JDC Paris office invited Dr. Azriel Eisenberg, head of the Committee for Jewish Education in New York, to conduct it. Dr. Eisenberg arrived in 1956, and together we visited and observed nearly all the Jewish schools in Europe, attended the seminars in Switzerland, and met with rabbis, educators, and anyone involved in Jewish education in any way.

On the basis of these visits, JDC, with Dr. Eisenberg's help, organized a conference on Jewish education at the Hotel de Crillon in Paris in early 1957. The foremost educators, rabbis, and community leaders in Europe of that time participated. I was impressed by the interest and eagerness of these community leaders to give so much of their time for Jewish education.

The problem of intercommunity communication and cooperation between far-flung Jewish schools was addressed at length. It was clear to all participants that the reconstructed communities lacked an educational infrastructure that would link individual schools and enable them to learn from one another.

Many decisions were made at the conference — for greater cooperation between communities, for giving Jewish education priority in communal funding, for enabling Jewish educators to come together on a regular basis, for improving the financial status of educators, for providing conditions that would attract suitable young adults to teaching, for upgrading teaching standards, and more. JDC made a moral commitment to help carry out some of the concluding recommendations.

Personal and Professional Developments

The grand encounter in Paris gave me my first experience in what would nowadays be called "networking." I would make much use of this technique later, in putting together a continent-wide association of school principals.

The gathering also had very important personal outcomes. First, Dr. Eisenberg and I struck up a friendship that would last a lifetime; his widow is still a good family friend. And second, at the end of the conference, as the delegates made their recommendations, Dr. Eisenberg proposed two of his own.

First, he recommended that an American Jewish educator be invited to Europe to help carry out the conference's projects and decisions and strengthen JDC's Education Department. I was familiar with and appreciated the fact that the Americans already had a structured Jewish education program suitable to the Diaspora, and that a representative of the American program would surely be highly constructive in the development of a similar program in Europe. A short time later, Dr. Elijah (Eli) Bortniker, a leading Jewish American educator, joined the staff in Paris for this purpose.

Then Dr. Eisenberg suggested to Charlie Jordan, at that time director-general of the JDC Overseas Program, that I be given a sabbatical, during which I would earn a master's degree in education at the Teachers College of Columbia University in New York.

There was no question in my mind that I would accept this opportunity. I knew of no activity more pleasurable and fruitful than study. I also recognized JDC's adoption of Dr. Eisenberg's recommendation as a personal vote of confidence.

In August 1956, I had met Noemi in Switzerland. Her family had moved to Israel from Czechoslovakia at the beginning of World War II, when she was only four years old. After graduating high school in Israel, Noemi traveled to England for a year of study there, and it was on her way back home from England that she had visited the teachers' summer seminar in Switzerland. My mysterious and highly uncharacteristic absence from some of the meetings that summer of 1956 greatly puzzled some of my colleagues! Noemi and I married in Israel in April 1957, returned to Paris, and then sailed to New York together in August to begin my sabbatical.

While in New York, I was able to observe the Jewish educational system that I had heard so much about from Dr. Eisenberg. Each community had an educational board made up of a number of full-time educators, most of whom were highly qualified university graduates. Indeed, I found that many young people happily made Jewish education their career.

In comparison, Europe was just beginning its Jewish education reconstruction and development: it had a long way to go after having just lost the vast majority of its learned intelligentsia, its educators, and its physical educational infrastructure.

It proved to be quite an intensive year. The university credit system was "indexed" to how much reading one accomplished, with a target of approximately 150 pages per week for each course. My American classmates had been taught to scan, and applied this skill to the required reading. My yeshiva studies had taught me to analyze every word. I spent many white nights at study for that reason. But unlike in the past, at least I was not spending them alone.

During our year in New York, I completed my degree and Noemi took courses at the Jewish Theological Seminary and at Hunter College. We lived on JDC financial support in a university apartment near the Theological Seminary. On June 21, 1958, the day I finished my last course, our daughter Edna was born.

US Consultants in Europe

Later that summer, I returned to the JDC executive headquarters, but not to Paris. During my absence, the headquarters had relocated to Rue du Stand in Geneva, to join the many international agencies that had been gathering in the city. Since we had no apartment set up yet in Geneva, Noemi and Edna traveled to Israel to be with my parents-in-law. We were reunited only after I found a suitable home for us in the city — a time-consuming process as it turned out.

Following my return to work in Europe, I familiarized myself with my new JDC colleagues. One was Ted Feder, then deputy director of the headquarters, later to become director of the European and overseas programs. He had served for a number of years in Austria and Germany, almost until the liquidation of the DP camps. Hence, we had already crossed paths during my post in Germany, and now it was a pleasure to be working alongside him again.

My closest associate at first was Dr. Bortniker, who had been responsible for the education program during my stay in New York. He was an active and dynamic educator with a firm command of Hebrew, yet he was less familiar with Jewish religious education and, like some other educators from the United States, found it difficult to establish a common language with Jewish educators and communities in Europe.

A most significant and enduring contribution made by Dr. Bortniker was the founding of the quarterly French-language Jewish teachers' journal *Hamoré* (the French transliteration of the Hebrew word for "The Teacher") in 1958. Very shortly after my return, Dr. Bortniker decided, for personal reasons, to terminate his term — a year earlier than planned — and it became my job to find a replacement for him.

While in New York, I had met Dr. Ezra Shereshevsky, a lecturer of Jewish texts, Hebrew language, and philosophy at Temple University and Graetz College in Philadelphia. I recommended and JDC hired Ezra, who was tasked with the development of Europe's largest education program: that in Paris.

I paired him with Louis Cohn, whom Bortniker had hired as assistant while I was away. Louis, the son of a historian and teacher from Breslav, had spent more than two and a half years in internment by the Vichy regime and then served five brutal years with the French Foreign Legion in Algeria in order to avoid Nazi deportation. Having survived that — not without scars on his body and soul — he returned to France, where he taught Greek and Latin at the Yavne School in Paris. His skills and his devotion to his work brought him to the attention of the Central Committee of Jews in France, and from there he made his way to this service with JDC. Although unfamiliar with Jewish education, and despite having never been an observant Jew himself, Louis was an able professional who did his best to adjust to the needs of the Orthodox and traditional Jewish schools in Europe.

My relationship with Louis was close and problem-free. When he left JDC later in 1958, Louis became director of the Education Department of the Fonds Social in Paris, where he worked until his retirement. Despite our different lifestyles, we remain close friends to this day.

Eventually, Dr. Shereshevsky left too. Like many of those JDC brought to Europe, he was employed on a short-term contract and had never viewed himself as a JDC careerist; in fact, to take the assignment with JDC he had taken a leave of absence from his own career post in the United States. Such arrangements were characteristic of JDC, which did not then — and still does not — offer career positions; a long-term relationship with the organization jells informally, if at all.

After Dr. Shereshevsky's return to the United States, I assumed full and sole responsibility for JDC's education program.

Invested in the Job

I was emotionally engaged in my work and colleagues learned that I did not give up easily. On one occasion — unrelated to professional development — my pressure led to an internal reform over the initial objections of the director-general: the closing of the Geneva office on the second day of Pesach. Logic was on his side: most staff members were not Jewish, and none of the Jews on the staff apart from me was observant.

To me, though, the issue was not one of practicality but one of principle, that a Jewish organization should not work on a Jewish holiday.

I pressed my case until my superior, director-general Charlie Jordan, replied, "You're a bulldog. Have it your way and leave me alone!"

Hamoré

In late 1958, after the first issue of *Hamoré* was printed and its founder, Dr. Bortniker, returned to the United States, I took over as editor and was assisted at first by Lucien Lazare, an educator in Strasbourg. When Lazare left for Israel, he was replaced by Madame Gugenheim, wife of the late Rabbi Ernest Gugenheim, professor of Talmud at (and later director of) the Rabbinical Seminary in Paris.

Hamoré — to this day Continental Europe's only Jewish pedagogical quarterly — was a bootstrap initiative. I recruited volunteer contributing editors and worked on a minimal JDC budget for printing and distribution. The material published in the journal was of a very practical nature. The contributors wrote articles on a wide range of topics, such as teaching skills, the teaching of specific topics, and lesson planning. Teachers sent their own lesson plans and described their experiences so that others could learn from them. Case studies were analyzed as practical illustrations of how to handle educational and classroom situations. Some basic subjects in Jewish education, such as Bible, Jewish history, and the prayer book were given great prominence. Once in a while, sections of *Hamoré* provided source materials that were then taught in classrooms, such as articles on historical personalities and events, and basic religious concepts.

To further assist our readers' teaching capabilities, we also issued a dozen pedagogical supplements. These included a book-length manual by Dr. Eisenberg on how to teach history and a shorter publication on teaching the Jewish prayers. Another supplement, *Learning and Teaching*, was written by Professor Hanoch Enoch, our teachers' consultant in Paris.

Hamoré also reviewed, in French, materials that other organizations published. It was a distressingly scanty collection at first, but it developed and grew over the years. As the number of reviews increased, we gathered them into a comprehensive list of available materials, itemized by subject and target age group. Finally, we published a book of case studies for classroom teaching.

At one time, we published a German edition of the journal for the Swiss, German, and Austrian communities, and a separate North African edition from which all references to Israel were expunged.

Hamoré became a platform for discussion among Jewish teachers in their day-to-day pedagogical problems. The teachers were able to benefit from much of the material by applying it to their personal teaching skills and curricula. Some wrote to *Hamoré* about the values or shortcomings of the material provided in the quarterly, feedback that was evaluated and drawn upon for future issues.

The journal was the right vehicle at the right time. Its impact may be hard to grasp from the perspective of today's hyper-connected, information-rich age. Yet in Europe of the late 1950s and early 1960s, the developing, relatively inexperienced, and resource-strapped community of educators who were struggling to rebuild their communities' Jewish education, thirsted for the regular professional and practical information *Hamoré* brought them. Our subscribers were not just readers — they were users of the know-how that the publication brought them.

The Association of Jewish Day School Principals

My second educational achievement of consequence in Europe was the establishment of the Association of Jewish Day School Principals, a systematization and outgrowth of my random meetings with individuals and school visits in Western Europe.

I chose the term "association" carefully. I intended to create a professional forum, not a trade union that would concern itself with rights and benefits. Moreover, I kept politics, including Jewish politics, out. Non-politicization was and remains a principle of JDC's work and of my own, and this aspect of the venture required no small measure of vigilance. Because of it, however, we were able to bring together principals of all backgrounds and outlooks, from Lubavitch to Modern Orthodox, non-Orthodox, and even one Gentile principal from Scandinavia.

As with the contents of *Hamoré*, our JDC department laid down the agendas of meetings and limited them to topics in education. How to teach a given chapter of Isaiah was a relevant topic; French and Algerian politics was not. The most successful aspect of this policy was the participants' willingness to accept these rules with grace and without feeling threatened.

Our first meeting took place in March 1960 in Paris. Then JDC covered participants' travel and lodging expenses, but it wasn't long before the principals assumed the financial responsibility themselves and continued to meet regularly, initially twice a year and then once yearly. The meetings took place in a different community each time, so that apart from basic lectures on Jewish education, all participants could observe many schools firsthand. Principals in England joined the association at a later date.

Before long, the European Association of Jewish Day School Principals gave rise to a subsidiary, the Association of Jewish School Principals in France. This reflected the explosive growth in the number of French schools, from four when I first took up my European post, to over fifty today.

Supporting Jewish Education within the Community

Hamoré and the Principals Association were two prongs of my efforts in Europe. A third — the mainstay, in fact — was the strengthening and supporting of Jewish education within the communities.

My days were concentric swirls of simultaneous activities. For three decades I crisscrossed the Continent (up to the Iron Curtain, that is), mainly to visit schools. I usually set up these day-long visits in advance, not wishing to play the surprise-inspector role. At each school I would offer encouragement, provide sample textbooks and recommend others, make suggestions, and discuss local problems.

Over the years, I was pleased to see the practical impact of *Hamoré* on the day-to-day work in the classroom. The questions raised during discussions with the educators helped me determine future subjects for the teachers' seminars in Switzerland and for discussion in *Hamoré*. I observed how the level of teaching improved with teachers' experience and with the help of the other educational tools that JDC provided for the teachers. All this was reflected in the results achieved by students in the end-of-year examinations, proudly presented to me by the principals and staff.

Merely meeting with teachers, as a representative of JDC, increased their value in the eyes of the lay leadership, leading to increased support from the latter. I made a point of meeting with the communities' lay leaderships too. By doing so, I was able to encourage them to support their schools financially and help increase the schools' prestige.

In the office, I fielded vast quantities of correspondence from schools. Typically, teachers and principals asked me to furnish them with particular books or to recommend sources that they could use. When my storage facility and library lacked requested materials, I made inquiries with others, such as JAFI, to secure the required material.

The educators surely needed money, too, but were aware that this did not belong to my purview. At most, I could ask the director-general to provide financial support for a year's training in Israel for an educator whom I considered deserving, or to award a teacher a sabbatical so that he or she could obtain a degree. Some of these requests were answered in the affirmative; others were not. The Claims Conference could provide one-time grants where it deemed worthy and with my recommendation.

I was a central address for Jewish educators in search of suitable training activities. Whenever a new school opened, its administrators dispatched a staff member to my office for guidance.

Many would seek counseling in teaching first-grade Hebrew. In this subject, schools had a problem with the language of instruction. A "Hebrew in Hebrew" system, which many schools would have preferred, could hardly be used during the 1950s, until new teachers became proficient in the Hebrew language themselves. Neither could Yiddish be used, seeing as the few Yiddish speakers, mainly in Belgium, were gradually aging and retired from teaching. Moreover, the student body, particularly in France, was increasingly of Sephardic origin and had neither knowledge of nor affinity for the language of the East European Ashkenazim.

The decline in spoken Yiddish (my mother tongue) was much to my personal dismay; I had a short-lived hobby at that time — reading fine literature and essays in Yiddish — that perhaps can be traced to the atmosphere of reconstruction that pervaded my work. (That said, I also found Agnon's Hebrew prose, with its skillful use of Talmudic and Midrashic roots, especially enjoyable.)

The younger generation of teachers, therefore, yielded to teaching in local languages for all topics of study. Thankfully, though, within a number of years, many European schools did manage to hire teachers who had a good command of Hebrew and who could teach "Hebrew in Hebrew," a system that is successfully utilized in some European schools to this day.

JDC Scholarship Fund

My fourth main function in Europe was with the JDC Scholarship Fund — an initiative of New York headquarters that was launched in July 1959. I began to participate in the fund's meetings in May 1960 and later chaired the scholarship committee, composed of my professional colleagues, for a number of years.

Since the late 1940s, JDC had been giving occasional scholarships and stipends to people who were actively engaged in some aspect of JDC-supported work in different countries. When Jews who had no such connection applied to JDC for support in their studies — as they often did — JDC referred them to outside agencies, such as the International Council of Jewish Women, the Council of Jewish Federations and Welfare Funds, the Claims Conference Cultural Department, and JDC's separate Warburg Scholarship Fund. In some cases, JDC sent these applicants brochures and forms and helped them to apply.

As the 1950s were drawing to a close, however, JDC moved to invest more extensively in the training of "Jewish civil servants," appreciating that these individuals formed the basis for the ongoing development of Jewish communities. The Scholarship Fund was an important vehicle by which to make such an investment.

For several years, we had fewer applicants than money available and accepted people on a first come, first served basis. Forty-nine scholarships were granted by May 1963 — twenty-one of them related to Jewish education — for the training of teachers, youth leaders, kindergarten directors, and school supervisors.

The committee gradually widened the eligibility criteria for Scholarship Fund support and accepted people as young as eighteen for post-high school professional studies. In view of the paucity of candidates (economic developments in Europe attracted Jews to more profitable areas than education), I backed and welcomed this change in approach.

Since Jewish education was my field, I reviewed applications that pertained to it and argued the applicants' cases before the committee. I watched proudly as the number of scholarships for Jewish education grew. Over the two decades of the fund's existence, we awarded more than 400 education-related scholarships.

Once the students were admitted to the program, I monitored their progress and reported it to the committee. But my tasks did not end there. As the students completed their studies, I made great efforts to place them in jobs. I approached communities to ensure that they lived up to their commitments to employ these graduates.

In the big picture of Europe's postwar Jewish community reconstruction, the comparatively humble dimensions of the JDC scholarship program mask the significance of its accomplishments. The program provided seed money that revived the shrunken Jewish "civil service" in Europe and elsewhere. Hundreds of young men and women who participated in the program became teachers who filled important functions in Jewish schools around the globe. Clearly, the impressive growth in the number of Jewish schools would have been impossible without the availability of these new and well-qualified teachers. I still have the personal satisfaction of encountering them here and there, and remain proud of having played a role in enabling the program to have such widespread and enduring impact.

The Reconstruction Phase Winds Down

The community reconstruction phase ended gradually, at different junctures in different locations. Finland was the first — followed by Sweden, Norway, and Denmark — to relinquish JDC funding in the late 1950s. Belgium, Holland, Italy, and Greece followed suit. As the communities gathered strength, JDC phased out its subventions and handed some of its programs to local players. The numbers of Jews receiving JDC support also declined over time due to aliyah and emigration to the United States, Australia, and other countries, and due to economic progress, which made many Jews, individually, more independent.

France, coping with the large influx of North African Jews until well into the 1970s, was the last community to reclaim financial self-sufficiency. Eventually, the FSJU (Fonds Social) assumed full professional and financial responsibilities there that had initially been JDC's. This included school inspections, seminar activities, and the JDC feeding programs. In time, *Hamoré* was also taken over by the Fonds Social.

A milestone in the general changeover was the end of routine funding from the Claims Conference in 1968. This eliminated a major source of funding for physical infrastructure work. By this time, however, most of the communities were sufficiently organized to tap into other sources — their own or philanthropic.

The JDC Scholarship Fund survived until the late 1970s; JDC's individual country directors assumed responsibility at that point for sponsoring training from their own budgets where they felt it was necessary.

JDC gladly relinquished these roles to the Jewish communities. This, after all, indicated its success in achieving its ultimate goal: restoration of the communities' capacity for self-sufficient community life.

While the entire period of my tenure was marked by gradual but generally consistent progress toward this goal across Western Europe, developments occasionally required increased, localized JDC assistance for limited periods of time.

In 1956, for example, JDC resumed its role in large-scale refugee aid when the attempted uprising in Communist Hungary and the violence that followed it prompted approximately 20,000 Hungarian Jews to escape into Austria. JDC set up reception facilities for these Hungarian Jewish refugees in Austria and helped those who wished to move on to emigrate to Israel, the United States, Belgium, France, and other Western European countries.

Increased assistance from JDC was also required with the development of the East/West détente of the early 1970s. At that time, a stream of Soviet Jews wishing to emigrate to Israel traveled via Vienna to their destination. Thousands of other Jews left their homes in Russia on a pretext of going to Israel, and upon arrival in Vienna opted to go to the United States. They traveled to Italy and waited there for US immigration papers. They were concentrated in Ladispoli, a small coastal town near Rome. JDC provided for the welfare needs of these Russian Jews in Austria and Italy and arranged education programs for the adults and school-aged children.

In Israel — At Last

The International School of Geneva was possibly the best school on earth. It taught a combined English and French program that opened doors to universities all over the globe. What it did not teach, however, was a Jewish way of life. My sons and daughter were studying in the school, and as the years rolled by, my concerns regarding their Jewish education grew.

On the face of it, my children had it made in Switzerland. We lived in a spacious apartment and had a live-in maid. They loved their school, despite my concerns for their Jewish education, and had good friends. Every winter we spent time skiing in the mountains. Every summer we would enjoy a long vacation in Israel — an exciting experience for the children, and an opportunity to intensify their Jewish education and make them fluent in Hebrew.

It was largely the material element of their upbringing that was rapidly becoming a struggle, as the children, backed by their surrounding society, were exposed to values and experiences that conflicted with the Jewish education that their parents would have liked them to have. As he neared bar mitzvah age, our son began to experience this discomfort in Switzerland. He was unable to partake in the school lunches because of kashruth, and had to eat his homemade sandwiches on his own. Many of his school friends threw birthday parties on Shabbat, rendering him unable to participate. And of the hardest things to bear, he would complain of being ridiculed for wearing a skullcap.

By the early 1970s, with JDC's downscaling of its activities in Western Europe, I ceased to view the region as my career home and, in fact, as my home in any sense. To spare the youngsters the need to swim against the tide, we pulled up stakes. They were powerful stakes for the parents, too.

In 1971, I enrolled my daughter in an Israeli post-primary program. The facility she attended in Israel was rudimentary compared with the school she had attended in Geneva, and the experience only strained her ability to live so far away from us. In 1972, we finally moved to Israel and settled in the Tel Aviv suburb Ramat Gan.

The relocation took place with the consent of JDC Executive Vice President Sam Haber. JDC assumed that my career would continue unabated. Thus, instead of receiving an official assignment in Israel, I carried on as education consultant for Europe and made occasional trips via Geneva to Morocco and Tunisia. For a decade, I was away from home for up to two months at a time, living in hotels. This belonged to the sacrifice side of the balance sheet. The gains side was more important.

My involvement in Europe during that time was focused on the publication of *Hamoré*, the Association of Principals, and the Scholarship Fund. Making the most of my presence in Israel, I visited schools there and examined educational material to see how it could be helpful for schools in Europe and North Africa.

In Summary

Looking back on my tenure in Europe, I am now and was then, aware that my role centered on process and facilitation, not command and control. No individual (and no individual organization), however committed, could have single-handedly orchestrated the reconstruction of European Jewry. Instead, capable people in the communities — teachers, community leaders — came forward and offered their services, and the JDC staff, of which I was member, helped them to maximize their contributions. In subsequent decades, it was my privilege to continue interacting with the selfless community representatives who had set the system on its feet.

Still, without losing sight of the collective and cooperative nature of my work, my duties had allowed me to play a significant role in restoring Jewish education in Europe, itself a key element in JDC's grand mission of revitalizing Jewish life on the Continent. I had played a substantial part in the reconstruction of schools, the growth of education programs, and the development of European Jewish communities. We laid the foundations for what would eventually become a broad network of Jewish schools and an important Jewish education system that continues to thrive without JDC involvement.

While my thirty-year stint as its director has long since ended, *Hamoré* still exists and has now reached over 180 issues, in its 50th year of publication. The European Association of Jewish Day School Principals continues to operate some fifty years after its establishment, now completely independent of JDC and a fixture in the Jewish education scene in Europe. The teachers' seminars continued after my tenure in Europe and alongside the JDC scholarship program ensured continued Jewish education at high standards all over the world. These teachers became highly skilled, their biggest qualification being their devotion. The Claims Conference phased its program out decades ago, but the successful outcome of its funding, including the Memorial Foundation for Jewish Culture, endures.

Today, indeed, there are few overt reminders of JDC's role in the mammoth reconstruction endeavor that was the "Jewish Marshall Plan." With the possible exception of Germany, which has recently strained to respond to the massive influx of Jews from the former Soviet Union, JDC's support for internal communal activities in Western Europe is no longer needed. JDC does, though, continue to promote inter-communal professional development and relations: among its current initiatives is the European Council of Jewish Communities, an organization whose work in fostering stronger ties among its members is reminiscent of the work we did decades earlier in creating the European Association of Jewish Day School Principals. Since the 1980s, JDC has also worked to help regenerate Jewish life behind what was the Iron Curtain.

The absence of reminders of our immense intervention of only a few decades ago is perhaps the truest measure of its success. For this absence reflects the fact that the communities indeed steadily gained in strength, assertiveness, and autonomy. This outcome was JDC's greatest accomplishment in Europe.

I came away with a clear sense of having made a contribution in this vast effort to reconstruct organized Jewish life in post-Holocaust Europe. It is a sense that has remained with me to this day.

☞ North Africa and Beyond

Jews in Europe corresponded with their fellows in North Africa for two millennia. Such contacts, though, were few and rare. It was the end of World War II and the creation of the State of Israel that brought increased interest in North African Jewry among European and American communities. At that point, American Jewry recognized the need to help North African Jewry, just as it helped the communities in Europe. JDC, as the overseas arm of American Jewry, took up this challenge.

When I began my decades of service in the reconstruction of Western Europe's Jewish communities in 1952, JDC had already targeted countries of northern Africa for far-reaching efforts in all its fields of activity. While based in Paris and Geneva, I was to participate in these efforts and devote most of my time to northern Africa. I would witness the colorful, traditional lives of its Jews. I would play a part in strengthening its communities and, with the future of its children topping my priorities, in its Jewish education.

Today, with Morocco and Tunisia maintaining small Jewish communities and other North African countries upholding even smaller vestiges — or none at all — the once rich Jewish life in the region has all but vanished. Most of the children who benefited from JDC's assistance in education and welfare are now leading Jewish lives in Israel, Canada, France, Spain, and other Western countries.

Morocco

A Great Jewish Community

In the eighteenth and nineteenth centuries, Jews living in Muslim countries had been subject to various restrictions. They had been prohibited to ride donkeys (then the primary form of transportation) and were bound to other *dhimmi* laws intended to keep a tight rein on non-Muslim residents. Despite these restrictions, the Moroccan Jewish collective had turned out renowned rabbis, poets, Talmudists, and legal authorities who presided over strong communities.

In 1912, France established protectorate rule in 90 percent of Morocco, with Spain doing the same over the remainder in the country's northern and southern extremes. Tangier, at the northern tip of the country, was an international zone — an open city for all commercial, duty-free import and export — a status imposed by the French and Spanish authorities to facilitate business activities for local residents.

Under the protectorates, Jews enjoyed complete freedom of religion, occupation, and movement for the first time in many centuries, even though they were left under the sultan's protection as opposed to being made French or Spanish subjects.

Moroccan Jewry was able to practice its religion openly within well-organized communities with powerful lay leaders and committees that exercised some political influence. Above all, the Jewish masses in Morocco were noted for religiosity. Rabbinical scholarship and study were common in many educated circles. Rabbinical courts adjudicated legacies, marital status, and monetary issues.

Following World War II, the grip of the colonial powers slipped and their respective colonies pressed for independence in a complex political struggle that would affect the Jewish community of Morocco. Some of the ferment in the last pre-independence years — the early 1950s — spilled into pan-Arab turbulence as many Muslims identified with the Arabs who had been defeated by the new State of Israel. This nationalist incitement prompted ferocious attacks on Moroccan Jews, strengthening the allure of Israel ("Jerusalem," as they termed it) and leading growing numbers of Jews to emigrate to the Jewish state.

Thus the Jewish population of approximately 265,000 in 1948 dropped significantly. By 1953, some 30,000 Moroccan Jews had relocated to Israel and another 15,000 to France, Canada (mostly Montreal), and elsewhere.

It was during this period, when the community had begun its fitful decline, that JDC began its vast service for the Jews of Morocco.

The attainment of independence itself in March-April 1956 actually did no harm to the Jews' domestic circumstances. But on May 13, 1956, the new regime issued an order forbidding any of its (by then) 200,000 Jews to depart for Israel. Still, the government did not actively prevent individual Jews from leaving and sometimes turned a blind eye to large-scale emigration. Thus about 47,000 Jews were still able to move from Morocco to Israel between 1956 and 1960.

As time passed, Zionist activity was banned and many Jewish organizations had to close their doors. All Jewish Agency personnel had to leave and their excellent work was halted. Some time later, though, Israel sent clandestine Jewish Agency immigration emissaries to villages and the Berber areas in the mountains to assist the Jews remaining there with emigration to Israel. Although they entered on French passports and worked with great caution, several of these Jewish Agency representatives were caught, imprisoned, and beaten. Each of these dedicated individuals made a significant contribution to aliyah from Morocco.

In 1961, the accession of King Hassan II ushered in a more tolerant era and emigration to Israel was again permitted. As of early 1964, JDC believed that the outflow would subside and that the community's numbers would stabilize at around 85,000. Circumstances intervened, however. Domestic economic woes later in the 1960s sparked further large-scale emigration that included Jewish businesspeople. Then, the 1967 Six-Day War heightened the Jews' sense of insecurity, prompting still more to leave, whether to Israel or to France. By 1970, only 35,000 Jews remained in the country.

The Development of JDC's Activities in Morocco

JDC's first involvement in Morocco had nothing to do with Moroccan Jews, but with American servicemen who had reached the country during World War II to whom the organization provided Pesach *Haggadas*.

By Passover 1947, however, JDC had begun distributing matzoth in various Moroccan communities and took the opportunity to perform a rudimentary census. It did not have any overseas representatives there or anywhere in northern Africa until 1949. Between 1948 and 1949, JDC operations in Morocco were directed from headquarters in France and inaugurated locally by Madame Hélène Cazes-Bénatar, a dynamic Moroccan Jewish lawyer, who ran the program unassisted for a full year. She arranged the distribution of welfare and first aid, as well as collecting information on the Moroccan Jews

and their overall living conditions. Between 1949 and 1952, a country director and a small staff of about a dozen members managed to build up a network of JDC programs to address the various needs of the Moroccan Jewish community.

These needs were significant. In the *mellah*, the self-imposed ghetto where most Jews lived, malnutrition coupled with poor sanitary conditions and housing congestion — up to ten people inhabiting one room — made disease and infant mortality rampant. Hence, JDC's first goal was to boost nutrition by arranging food supplies from surpluses of the United States Department of Agriculture (USDA). As time passed, JDC-Morocco initiated and/or supported the full range of programs that it had already facilitated in places as diverse as the European DP camps, Iran, and Shanghai — education, nutrition, health care, clothing, and old-age support.

Importantly, Morocco had viable local organizations with which JDC could work — a central committee, a rabbi or chief rabbi, and an education establishment in each community. JDC's programs for the elderly built on the community's *hiluq* distributions, the longstanding — and still-existing — tradition in which the community provides weekly or monthly allowances to the needy. JDC supplemented these handouts, and in larger communities opened a network of old-age homes.

My job in Morocco began in November 1952, very soon after leaving Iran and resettling in Paris. There was then a Jewish population of approximately 220,000 (about one-third living in Casablanca), almost as large as that of France at the time.

As with my previous postings, headquarters provided little by way of background briefing. By now, though, I understood that no briefing of any detail could possibly present the true background to the situation; only on-the-ground exposure could provide the necessary knowledge.

As in Europe, it was clear to me that my work would count for little but for the immense JDC efforts that surrounded me. I was to go about my work in education while other specialists, such as social workers, employment counselors, nutritionists, and medical staff, focused on other aspects in each important community and many smaller ones. We would report our findings to the staff in Casablanca and thence to headquarters.

The medical staff carried out a trachoma survey in Casablanca. They found 75 percent of 2,169 persons affected and in need of treatment. Being a relatively modern city with the largest and best-organized Jewish community in the country clearly did not render its Jewish inhabitants immune to the affliction.

With the survey results in hand, JDC initiated a trachoma treatment program in Casablanca, and within a short time trachoma was virtually eradicated among the children and in most of the homes. JDC later expanded the program to elsewhere in Morocco, a step that saved the eyesight of literally tens of thousands of children. Overall, it was an astounding achievement in a country where inhabitants blinded by trachoma were ubiquitous.

JDC treated children for many other diseases too, such as scalp ringworm and tuberculosis, and thereby helped slash infant mortality.

It being felt that children were JDC's best investment, welfare and medical activities remained largely focused on schools. Most government schools in Morocco had health programs that included basic inoculations. However, the JDC-supported OSE (Children's Aid Society) headquarters in Paris provided children in the Jewish schools of Casablanca and the provinces with complete health care as part of an integrated JDC program that also included education and nutrition. Eventually, the network of OSE health centers expanded into a vast enterprise covering entire Jewish communities in all the major cities and schools in Morocco.

Since proper nutrition was the best preventive medicine, thousands of meals were provided daily in schools and kindergartens. In June 1953, JDC dedicated a milk-bottling plant for children in the Casablanca *mellah* and turned it over to the OSE. The plant's capacity began at 2,000 bottles per day but climbed to 4,000 by the end of its first year, making the milk from powder donated to JDC by the USDA.

Generally speaking, JDC's services in schools were conditioned on co-funding from the local community. At times, though, securing this local funding proved challenging. Moroccan Jewry, like the country at large, was composed of a wealthy upper crust and impoverished masses. Begging was an organized activity in some locations, its practitioners regularly visiting the wealthy for alms. The wealthy helped the poor in this fashion but, having done so, often declined to contribute to community institutions in the belief that they had already fulfilled their duty.

Tangier is an example of JDC's work in the country. In 1953, Tangier had a Jewish population of about 5,000. It had a larger Ashkenazi community than other Moroccan areas, many of its members having arrived there from Hungary with visas that were granted to a limited number of Hungarian Jews in 1941. As an international zone, Tangier was less affected by the nationalist upheaval that was rising in other Moroccan areas. Nevertheless, average Jewish breadwinners in the city earned a pittance. Most Jewish children were ragged and barefoot; some were ill and underfed.

JDC supplemented the local community's efforts. In 1950, JDC gave a group of public-spirited Jewish women in the city equipment for a small TB dispensary that they had established. JDC funded antibiotic treatments in the *mellah* and, for children, powdered milk. The spectacular results of this activity prompted well-placed and affluent Jewish benefactors in the city to donate $25,000 for land outside of the *mellah* for a new health center that JDC helped to equip.

The development of JDC activities indirectly encouraged Jews to move from outlying villages to towns, seeking to improve their standards of living. The JDC staff members had some qualms about this, it not being JDC's brief to foment a population transfer. It also opposed the kind of uncontrolled migration from villages to cities in advance of emigration that we had witnessed in Iran. However, neither JDC nor anyone else was able to stem this urbanization of Morocco's rural Jews. We were left to cope with it as best we could.

As a matter of fact, as this trend strengthened in the late 1950s, it enabled JDC to extend its assistance more efficiently to those wishing to emigrate. JDC provided clothing and medical help for those whose emigration to Israel was being facilitated by the Jewish Agency.

An Introduction to Moroccan Jewry

For my first fact-finding sweep of Moroccan Jewry in 1952, I arranged to be escorted by Rabbi Shlomo Matusof, the coordinator of Lubavitch activities in Morocco, who had opened many schools and heders (Jewish boys' elementary schools for Torah study, also called Talmud Torahs) in peripheral areas. Predictably, the itinerary had a strong Lubavitch emphasis and did not include a visit to the relatively significant communities of Rabat and Fez, where there were no Lubavitch schools. I would visit and assist these communities later.

From our base in Casablanca, we traveled directly to Meknes and a visit with Rabbi Michael Lipsker, who had founded the Lubavitch program in

Morocco. Like many other Lubavitchers, he had emigrated from the Soviet Union to Poland after the war by declaring himself of Polish origin and joining masses of Poles who were being repatriated to their homeland under a special agreement with the USSR. From Poland, he joined thousands of other Lubavitcher refugees in France.

In his last days, the former Lubavitcher Rebbe, Yosef Yitzchak Schneerson had instructed Rabbi Lipsker to go to Morocco. By chance (although no Lubavitcher would construe it as such), Rabbi Lipsker encountered Rabbi Baruch Toledano of Meknes in Marseille and asked him to issue him an official invitation, as the protectorate regime required. The invitation was sent, and Rabbi Lipsker, who could communicate only in Russian or Yiddish, set out for Casablanca and from there to Meknes, where he presented himself one evening at the door of an astonished Rabbi Toledano.

While in Meknes I also learned of the powerful Jewish lay leaders who held a role in shaping that community. The community's president, Joseph Berdugo, for example, had great influence in the city and vied with the strong-willed Rabbi Toledano for final authority in the disposition of community resources. I later learned that for years neither leader yielded to the other until, when both were advanced in age, Berdugo called the rabbi to his bedside, expressed regret for their long-standing dispute, and asked him for forgiveness so that he might leave this world with a clear conscience.

From Meknes, Rabbi Matusof and I went on to pay a visit to the Ozar Hatorah community Talmud Torah in Sefrou. Named Em Habanim ("Mother of the Boys," from Psalms 113), the school had been founded at the initiative of Rabbi Zev Halperin, an Ashkenazi rabbi who, for some unknown motive, spent 1914–1922 in Morocco. Unable to marshal support for the venture among the men, he established a women's committee; hence the name of the school. Rabbi Halperin based himself in Meknes, where he taught Talmud to Rabbi Baruch Toledano, Rabbi Shalom Messas (subsequently a chief rabbi of Jerusalem), and other young men who later became rabbis of their communities. Modern Talmud study in Morocco traces to the efforts of this man, who devoted his time in the country to teaching in various Moroccan communities until he left Morocco one day, as mysteriously as he had come.

From Sefrou we set out southward on a tour of smaller communities, including Erfoud in the southeast (home of Rabbi Meir Abuhatzeira — son of the revered Baba Sali, Rabbi Israel Abuhatzeira[1]) and Tafilalet, a goat-raising area. Farther south, we reached Rissani, the seat of the Baba Sali himself before he moved to the development town of Netivot in Israel. I met with the Baba Sali and found his reputation for charisma fully deserved. I visited the Talmud Torah in Rissani and found that all the boys there had trachoma. It was tragically common to see them with djellaba hoods pulled down over their faces to conceal their blindness.

In early 1952, Rabbi Benyamin Gorodetsky, Rabbi Schneerson's emissary for Lubavitch overseas programs, had visited the country and encouraged Rabbi Matusof to establish heders in the Atlas Mountain areas, south of Marrakesh, in order to provide education for youngsters who had no other schools in their villages. As we were leaving Rissani, Rabbi Matusof gave me an account of his own initial excursion to these Berber villages and gave me a first inkling of part of the community that JDC was to serve.

So, from Rissani we retraced Rabbi Matusof's earlier trek across the Atlas Mountains to visit some of the poorest, most disease-ridden Jewish communities in the world. JDC promptly initiated a welfare and medical program for these Jews, but it was not long after my visit that they all left for Israel.

From there we traveled west and then north, passing through more small communities, and finally reached Marrakesh. This city, the capital of Berber Morocco, is characterized by its red clay structures. It had a large Jewish community that resided in a *mellah* on the outskirts of which an Alliance school had been established for its children. Many Jews were merchants who owned shops in and around the famous Marrakesh marketplace, Djemaa el-Fna, where thousands of Berbers gather daily to buy and sell their wares, to take in enchanting stories from storytellers, or to learn from mystics and snake charmers. After visiting Marrakesh's community and absorbing some of the city's color, we returned to Casablanca.

Now it was time to visit those towns that Rabbi Matusof had not included in his guided tour. I traveled again from Casablanca and headed for Rabat and Fez. Rabat was home to some 8,000 Jews at that time. Some lived in the small *mellah*, but most had moved to a new section of the city. A large Jewish

---

1.   Rabbi Israel Abuhatzeira (1890–1984), the Baba Sali (the "Praying Father"), was born to a family of leading scholars in Morocco. He became a highly revered rabbi and kabbalist both in Morocco and later in Israel.

community building in Rabat included a Talmud Torah-primary school. I arranged for JDC to provide meals for the few hundred students at the Ozar Hatorah-directed school, as well as welfare and medical aid for the senior Jewish population of this capital city.

Fez had some 10,000 Jews at the time of my first visit there. The *mellah* was very old and at one time was home to Maimonides. There is an ancient house that still stands in the *mellah* that — according to local tradition — was the residence of the Jewish philosopher-physician. I visited the communal building in the *mellah* that housed a large Talmud Torah called Em Habanim, which was also directed by Ozar Hatorah. I was able to initiate JDC's support for the school, daily meals for its students, and help for the aged population of the city.

Unique Customs and Traditions

During this trip around Morocco, I was able to glimpse into a Jewish world that would soon disappear. In the *mellah*s, I witnessed impoverished Jews enduring conditions similar to those I had encountered in the *mahaleh*s of Iran. The community lay leadership had by now passed to Jews who had been Westernized (and, to varying degrees, secularized) by French influence. Nevertheless, Moroccan Jewish life continued to revolve around the synagogue.

Religious life in Morocco had a casual ambience. Almost everyone — including the Westernized community leadership — attended services on Shabbat morning, but some disregarded some of the Shabbat restrictions for the rest of the day. Life-cycle events, such as weddings, circumcisions, and bar mitzvahs, followed tradition. On the Shabbat prior to or following such an occasion, a sumptuous kiddush[2] was provided for the community after Shabbat worship, followed by hours of festivities held at a celebrant's home. Some more affluent households would erect an enormous tent in the garden of their homes and invite hundreds of guests to a sit-down meal of local delicacies, ending with *tefina* or *skhina*, the Moroccan equivalent of the Ashkenazi *cholent*. As elsewhere in the Jewish world, but with a distinctive local character, more modest kiddush spreads were also held for lesser affairs,

---

2.   It is a custom to provide refreshments following the kiddush (sanctification) over wine on Shabbat and Jewish holidays after the morning synagogue service.

to honor a person who had a *yahrzeit* (the anniversary of a close relative's passing), or even for no special occasion.

Night-time prayers, also known as *Tikkun Hatzot* (Midnight Service), have long been practiced to mourn the destruction of the Temple and to pray for the ingathering of the exiles. The Moroccan communities modified this *Tikkun* into a tradition of visiting their synagogues at 2:00 a.m. on Shabbat for some three months in the winter to hear *paytanim*, performers of traditional and more recently written *piyyutim*, liturgical songs. Some *paytanim* became famous for their performances.

Most synagogues held classes on Shabbat afternoons, and as night fell, Psalms 16 and 144 were chanted with beautiful melodies, followed by the evening service and the havdalah with which the Sabbath is concluded. Before havdalah, young boys passed around a plate of mint leaves for each person to smell when the blessing over *isvei besamim* (aromatic leaves) was recited. After havdalah, a cup of wine was passed around, and people either sipped from it or dipped their fingers in it and then touched their eyes, as they recited the verse *Mitzvat Hashem me'irat 'einayim* — "God's commandment lights up the eyes." This manner of bringing Shabbat to an end never failed to exhilarate me. Until Rabbi Shalom Messas left Morocco in the 1980s, I often went to his home to hear his havdalah and the centuries-old Andalusian tunes that he sang.

Every home was proud to have guests. Rabbi Yaakov Bouskila of Taznakht, near Marrakesh, raised the hospitality traditions of southern Morocco to a fine art. A scholar and father of fourteen children, he made a living as a textile merchant but reserved his love for Jewish study. Whenever I was in town, he invited me to his home for a "lunch" that lasted from midday until 5:00 or 6:00 p.m. He invited all local rabbis to join us and slaughtered a calf himself. Rabbi Bouskila's wife and daughters made all manner of delicacies from the calf, and whisky flowed without limit. The most beautiful part of his celebration was the stream of rabbinical wisdom and Talmud discussions that lasted all afternoon as Rabbi Bouskila posed questions he had prepared for the invited scholars and then debated the answers with them.

Although fundraising in the European or American fashion was difficult to accomplish, people often made large donations in memory of a parent or on the occasion of a family celebration. This tradition ensured that as much as $30,000 would be raised at the local annual Lubavitch dinner. At such an affair, several items from the Lubavitcher Rebbe that were considered holy were auctioned, and the winning bidder received a congratulatory blessing.

Rabbi Aaron Monsonego, the principal of the Ozar Hatorah boys' school in Casablanca and deeply involved in the Ozar Hatorah activities all around Morocco, rarely called public gatherings to collect money for his organization. Nevertheless, he had admirers who donated substantial sums, and some even bequeathed their estates to him to be used at his discretion.

As I circulated in Morocco on my business for JDC, I found large numbers of Moroccan Jews traveling around for a different purpose: to visit the tombs of Jewish saints that abound in the country. It is Moroccan tradition to hold a festive commemoration, known as a *hilula*, on the anniversary of the death of a revered rabbi. The best known in Morocco is that of the revered Rabbi Amram Divan, who died in 1782 and is buried near Ouezzane, on the road from Tangier to Casablanca. During the French protectorate, as many as 20,000 people would gather from all parts of Morocco on Lag b'Omer, a minor festival on the thirty-third day of the count between Pesach and Shavuot, to celebrate Rabbi Divan's *hilula*.

The *hilula* for Rabbi Divan lasted an entire week. Families would arrive with all necessities, such as beds, food, and stoves. Some rented small rooms that had been built for them in the vicinity; others camped in large tents. I, too, joined this *hilula* more than once, sleeping in a tent on-site.

It was customary to bring sheep or calves to such an occasion, and a *shohet* (ritual slaughterer) was available to slaughter them. The families roasted the kosher meat in a large oven in the field and prepared a feast.

Arranged by a local committee, the evening of Lag b'Omer at Rabbi Divan's tomb was devoted to prayer and to supplications of all kinds. Mitzvoth and honors, such as the recitation of evening prayers and psalms and the lighting of memorial candles, were also "sold," the proceeds going to charity: the poor thronged to the *hilula* to solicit alms from their fellow Jews, who would donate generously.

The festivities continued with the lighting of large candles on the rabbi's tomb until hundreds of candles converged in a large fire into which people sometimes hurled full boxes of candles. A large tree that loomed over the grave never caught fire, even though the blaze climbed to alarming heights. This was considered a miracle.

Another such tomb that I once visited is that of Rabbi Shlomo ben Hensh in Ourika Valley, just an hour from Marrakesh. I was escorting a group of UJA (United Jewish Appeal) visitors, accompanied by Jewish committee members from Marrakesh. The group's American guide explained the local custom of lighting candles and saying prayers at the revered rabbis' graves. He added that most of this was based on superstition and that it was even doubtful who was buried at these sites. The Marrakesh Jews were deeply offended by these remarks, but were too polite to contradict the guide at the tomb. As we all made our way back to the bus, the American guide slipped and broke his leg. The Marrakesh representatives were saved the need to rebuke him now, convinced that the holy saint had dealt him immediate retribution for his disparaging comments.

Cooperation and Budgets

Following my first tour, which lasted about a month, I made two, and occasionally three visits to Morocco per year, each lasting up to two months. My wife and children stayed behind in Geneva. This grueling schedule eased considerably after 1955, when JDC posted a resident education consultant to Morocco — the first being Israel Szyf, who had worked with me in Iran. Szyf's stay was curtailed a year later by Moroccan independence, which rendered him unwelcome because of his Israeli citizenship. Andre Fraenckel, a French Jew from Strasbourg, replaced him.

Fraenckel's appointment and overall competence decreased my direct role significantly. However, I continued to participate in an annual review of JDC's education program in Morocco, which required that I participate in countrywide visits and meetings with the directors of JDC-supported education organizations. Fraenckel and I would then make recommendations to headquarters as to which programs should be continued, which expanded or curtailed, and which eliminated altogether.

At no point, though, was the education budget for Morocco mine to dispense. Most final budget decisions were made by the JDC director-general in Europe, in consultation with those responsible for the different programs.

Thus, for example, Alliance would present JDC-Morocco with a detailed annual budget request, which JDC-Morocco reviewed and sent to European headquarters for a decision. Upon approval from Europe, JDC funds would then be provided directly to the Alliance office in Paris through the JDC headquarters in New York. If Alliance wanted a larger subvention to expand its school in Fez, for instance, headquarters asked me to visit the institution and prepare a report on its current functions, attendance, and maintenance. If the enlarged grant was approved, I monitored its implementation.

Jewish Education in Morocco — The Cast of Players

JDC involvement in Jewish education in Morocco was less hands-on and intensive than in Iran, expressing itself more in terms of assessing the existing education programs and providing financial subsidies where required. Although there were many Jewish schools, there was no indigenous Jewish school system that provided combined general and Jewish education.

In earlier decades, Moroccan Jewry's strong and deeply rooted Jewish tradition had motivated each community to open small heders or Talmud Torah schools, several of which provided a good Jewish education with no foreign assistance long before the "outside" educational organizations came on the scene.

Each significant Jewish community that I visited still had a locally-run community school in the synagogue. Many communities had a Lubavitch heder in the synagogue, taught by a local teacher whose small wage was paid by Lubavitch. Teaching methods were rudimentary: with no books available, instruction consisted of rote learning of Hebrew words, orchestrated by a teacher who clutched a heavy stick. Children learned prayers, but little more.

By the time of my arrival on the scene, these synagogue-based schools were attended largely by lower-middle-class children. In most central locations, the poorest still did not attend school at all, while more affluent parents preferred to enroll their children in the French government schools, private French institutions, French cultural mission schools for girls, or Alliance schools, where they would learn French and prepare themselves for white-collar careers. However, when enrollment in these schools became increasingly Muslim in the late 1950s, many parents moved their children to the Jewish schools.

I had understood during my initial tour that the provision of books would be an important first step in JDC's efforts in Jewish education in Morocco. JDC headquarters readily provided funds to print and distribute Hebrew books — beginning with the Bible and a series of language primers — in initial runs of over 50,000. The printing was done locally, using an inexpensive photo-offset process.

JDC's firsthand operations in the field revolved particularly around teachers' seminars. Since we did not have the staff needed to run such seminars locally, and since we could not bring the qualified Israelis to Morocco, JDC would send groups of over twenty Moroccan educators to Europe to participate in the seminars there. On a smaller scale, JDC held kindergarten teachers' seminars in Morocco, run by JDC's daycare consultants, to maximize the teachers' capabilities. JDC's efforts to train Moroccan Jewish educational leadership continued in this fashion into the late 1980s. By that time, its clientele had dwindled.

JDC took a secondary role in supporting Hebrew-language courses for adults, run by local Zionist groups and Israeli emissaries until 1956/57. At that point it became illegal to teach Hebrew, but classes were quickly reinstated by local teachers under various camouflages.

Informal activities for youth were another area of JDC involvement. These activities were developed by local agencies in all the larger towns and appealed to two different groups. The Jewish Scouts movement became very popular among children from affluent homes. Parallel to the Scouts was the Unite Populaire, which catered to children from the *mellah*s and poor homes. Eventually, with JDC's encouragement, the two organizations merged under a local organization, the Departement Educatif de la Jeunesse Juive au Maroc (DEJJ). In the 1960s, Lubavitch organized additional youth activities of its own.

JDC invested heavily in these youth activities by providing audiovisual and sports equipment, and by supporting summer and winter camps that were organized by DEJJ, Alliance, Ozar Hatorah, and Lubavitch. In the early 1950s, community institutions sent some 8,000 children to summer camps, with JDC covering the major part of the expense.

Amidst the experiences of my initial tour of Morocco, I learned how the array of "outside" education programs and agencies interacted — sometimes meshing, sometimes clashing — with the ebbing efforts of this once large and grand but now waning Jewish community. For JDC to maximize its own contribution, it would have to square a mass of circles.

Alliance Israelite Universelle

Unlike in Algeria, the French protectorate regime in Morocco never viewed its sphere of influence as a virtual extension of the home country. However, the French had long sought to maximize their influence, and this had an impact both on the Jews and on the education agencies that served them.

Alliance was the first, the largest, and the most important Jewish outside organization to operate in Morocco, founding its initial schools in the northern Moroccan town of Tetouan in 1862, fifty years before the French protectorate was even established. By the 1950s, it was a force to be reckoned with: its enrollment in Morocco stood at 21,823 pupils in fifty-two schools in 1948, rising to 33,000 pupils in eighty-three institutions on the eve of Moroccan independence in 1956 — 80 percent of all school-aged Jewish children.

Alliance, which received financial support from the government, had its own teacher training programs. Therefore, its teachers generally did not participate in JDC teacher training seminars. JDC's main support for the network was provided centrally, by our headquarters in New York to theirs in Paris. My roles in working with Alliance in Morocco were mostly to help strengthen the Jewish education component in their schools, and to ensure that our subvention was being well and wisely spent on the ground.

Alliance placed more focus on imparting French schooling and culture to Jews in Muslim countries than it did on the Jewish education portion of its curriculum.

As it had been in our partnership in Iran, inevitably, this was a source of disagreement between JDC and Alliance in Morocco too. Alliance's veteran teachers aimed to turn out Westernized Jews and regarded some religious customs as old fashioned. This impacted on the centuries-old Jewish traditions of Morocco. The Westernization of the new social class — for which Alliance was in no small part responsible — was rapid and often superficial, leading many of these Jews to abandon the tradition to which the bulk of the community still adhered, even as their wealth and sophistication enabled them to take on increasingly important roles in Moroccan Jewish life. Whatever one's opinion of its impact, however, there can be no question that Alliance was a key player in the transformation of Moroccan Jewry.

At the time of Morocco's independence, the general atmosphere of detachment from French rule in the country was so far-reaching that the Jewish community also wished to shift away from the Alliance-Paris administration.

It was ousted by local Jewish lay leaders and replaced by a local organization known as Ittihad-Maroc (Moroccan Alliance). Nevertheless, Ittihad-Maroc continued to receive financial support from Alliance headquarters in Paris.

Ozar Hatorah

Having worked closely with Ozar Hatorah in Iran, I was already familiar with its infrastructure and principles. It was in Morocco, however, that I met with the organization's founder, Isaac Shalom, and learned firsthand of his intriguing background. He told me how he had come to New York from Syria as a penniless young man who spent his first nights in the big city sleeping on a park bench. He started his business career by peddling bric-a-brac until he could purchase a pushcart. In due course, he made a fortune by patterning handkerchiefs and branching from them into tablecloths and other items. Mr. Shalom eventually handed over his business to his three sons.

Well versed in Jewish life but poorly schooled in general subjects, Isaac Shalom saw the need to establish schools that would provide both Jewish and general education in Sephardic communities.

The first of all Ozar Hatorah schools was opened in Morocco in 1947. Following that, Ozar Hatorah opened many schools in Iran and Morocco and supported two others, one in Lebanon and another in Syria.

When my service in Morocco began, Ozar Hatorah still had only one school in the country, in Casablanca, as well as the Talmud Torah in Sefrou. By 1956, however, the Ozar Hatorah system had expanded to over two dozen institutions, and was educating 6,564 students — 16 percent of school-age enrollment.

I was much involved in the Ozar Hatorah program, working closely with Rabbi Monsonego in Casablanca, particularly on teacher training, school book acquisition, and joint budgetary issues. The Ozar Hatorah program stressed Jewish and Hebrew studies in tandem with general learning, and I strongly believed that its approach could accomplish much if the staff were given a free hand.

Such professional latitude, however, was being stifled. At first, the schools were run by local lay committees that assumed plenary responsibility for the schools' curriculum and staff, often dictating how the school principals should administer the schools. This situation was exacerbated by Ozar Hatorah's funding structure: Funds were forwarded from Isaac Shalom to these committees, which decided how to use the money in the schools — not always very wisely.

JDC, however, had some financial leverage of its own. Unlike Alliance and ORT, for which JDC provided global budgets through its New York headquarters, Ozar Hatorah received money from JDC locally, in Morocco.

At one point in the 1960s, I put JDC's leverage to use in an attempt to rectify the situation. I wished to bring about a transfer of management decisions from lay individuals to the professional leadership in Ozar Hatorah schools. At a meeting in the presence of Isaac Shalom, Rabbi Monsonego, and the lay director of Ozar schools, I insisted that directorship of the program be handed over to Rabbi Monsonego then and there. Having already come to know this rabbi well in his capacity as principal of the Casablanca community Talmud Torah, I was aware of his capabilities and considered him a perfect candidate for the position. Mr. Shalom agreed only due to my adamancy.

Ozar Hatorah has operated smoothly under Rabbi Monsonego's professional leadership since then. The transfer of power saved the education program by limiting lay interference in management that must properly remain a professional domain. My part in arranging it may have been one of my more important contributions to Jewish education in Morocco.

Today, Rabbi Monsonego is the central figure in Jewish life in Morocco. After years of declining the role of chief rabbi of that country (a position previously occupied by his late father), believing Jewish education to be more important, he finally accepted the appointment in the late 1990s. Highly respected throughout the country, he is turned to for any problem that arises.

Rabbi Monsonego and I became close friends over the years, and my acquaintance with him has been one of the great rewards of my work in Morocco.

The Ozar Hatorah yeshiva in Tangier deserves special mention. Mr. Samuel Toledano, a well-known Jewish architect in Tangier, built the yeshiva building in 1952 after becoming more religiously observant. The yeshiva was opened in 1953 under Toledano's choice of principal — Rabbi Zushe Waltner, a Hungarian-born, Polish-educated former head of a yeshiva in Sunderland in northern England. Rabbi Waltner was not only a Talmudic scholar, but also a gifted orator, and under his direction the yeshiva grew rapidly to include schooling at the primary and secondary levels, as well as a *kollel* (religious academy for married men).

Rabbi Waltner then initiated a parallel institution for girls, which became a training center for teachers. In fact, the campus in Tangier became a training center for boys and girls, men and women. JDC was a full and substantial partner in the ongoing development of this outstanding school campus.

So important did Rabbi Waltner's institutions become, that hundreds of Moroccan Jewry's educational and religious leadership passed through their doors. Rabbi Waltner should be credited with producing dozens of first-class scholars who have played leading roles in Jewish education wherever they settled. In Israel, for example, one encounters his alumni in prominent positions as heads of educational institutions, rabbis, and rabbinical judges.

The educational achievements of Ozar Hatorah in Morocco crested in the late 1950s and early 1960s. As Jewish emigration accelerated after Moroccan independence, Rabbi Waltner's schools were drained of their students. Eventually, he too decided to settle in Israel and his institutions were closed. In Israel, he spent the last decades of his life studying and teaching in a *kollel* opened by his son.

Ozar Hatorah and Alliance — Partnership with JDC

The ascendancy of Ozar Hatorah in Morocco in the 1950s led to a rivalry between it and the predominant Alliance. When Ozar Hatorah first became active, its representatives and teachers in Morocco (as opposed to the directorate in New York) regarded the Alliance teachers as confirmed secularists who were distancing young Moroccan Jews from their Jewish heritage. Competition was sometimes so intense that both organizations opened schools in locations that would have been adequately served by one.

Jewish parents were of divided opinions. On the one hand, Alliance facilitated the Jews' emancipation from the *mellah*s, thereby making a significant contribution to Jewish life in Morocco and in other Muslim countries where similar processes occurred. But parents also wished to maintain Jewish life through their offspring. Alliance's weakness in Jewish education gave Ozar Hatorah — with its more balanced approach — a fertile field in which to operate.

The rivalry had consequences that revealed themselves beyond the walls of the schools, too. Relations between religious Jews whose children attended

Ozar Hatorah and the less religious Jews at Alliance were visibly tense. Still, JDC continued to provide support to all the agencies involved, since their individual schools made such an important contribution to Morocco's Jewish life.

The answer, in the long run, was to redress Alliance's imbalance in Jewish studies. I made this one of my highest priorities. I used my visits to schools to help them overcome deficiencies in the children's Jewish knowledge, explained these matters to Alliance's officials, and gave my recommendations. In May 1953, Alliance appointed an inspector for Hebrew studies and set up a central department of Jewish education to serve its schools. This made principals more willing to integrate Jewish studies and Hebrew into school life. JDC helped by providing textbooks and Alliance undertook to devote more time to Hebrew instruction within its curriculum.

At first, however, Alliance did not have enough qualified personnel to do its share. The solution came about due to the efforts of Jules Braunschvig, a French Jew in the cereal business who exerted much influence on Alliance after the war and eventually became the organization's foremost lay leader.

During the war, while a prisoner in France in the hands of the Germans, Braunschvig had met another Jew, a teacher named Kohn, who influenced him to become more involved in Jewish learning. After settling in Morocco for business reasons, he became involved in the Alliance schools and noted the shortage of Hebrew teachers available. To solve that problem, he founded the École Normale Hébraïque in a suburb of Casablanca, a Hebrew teachers' training program where the students received more intensive Jewish studies. During 1956, the veteran Hebrew teachers in Alliance were slowly replaced by graduates of École Normale. Some of the graduates moved on to teach at Alliance schools in other countries in the Mediterranean Basin, in Iran, and, in due course, also in Israel, Latin America, Western Europe, and Canada.

Over the years, Mr. Braunschvig and I developed a relationship of friendly competition. He was convinced that my criticism wasn't always justified. Nevertheless, I was a frequent guest in his home, where we spent many hours discussing Alliance's Jewish education. In retrospect, I know that without his influence, Jewish studies in the Alliance program would have been far weaker and might not have progressed at all.

Lubavitch

As I witnessed on my first tour of Morocco, Lubavitch ran yeshivas, schools, and kindergartens in the larger towns of Meknes and Casablanca, but placed its focus on the some fifty heders that catered to poorer populations in the peripheral villages and towns. All told, enrollment in the Lubavitch education system in Morocco was 3,500 in the late 1950s.

The first Lubavitch educational institution in Morocco was a yeshiva in Meknes that Rabbi Lipsker started in a rented garage in 1950. Within a year he had between 80 and 100 students, a large kindergarten, a girls' primary and high school, and a class to train ritual slaughterers. He also organized youth and other educational activities in Meknes.

Rabbi Lipsker worked closely with the city's Rabbi Toledano but not under him, since one of Lubavitch's principles is that the movement's emissaries work on their own. For many years, there was no shortage of students: for the street children of Meknes whom he enrolled, his was the only Jewish education opportunity available.

However, toward the end of the 1960s, mass emigration to Israel left Rabbi Lipsker's yeshiva with fewer than twenty boys. At that point JDC informed him that it could no longer support his sadly dwindling institution. He left for the United States, where he served as a Lubavitch yeshiva supervisor until he passed away a few years ago.

Rabbi Matusof, the coordinator of Lubavitch activities in Morocco and my guide around Morocco, had established a yeshiva and Talmud Torah in the Casablanca *mellah* in the early 1950s. Years later, he moved the yeshiva to a newer section of the city, where he also started a girls' primary school that expanded into a high school that led up to the French baccalaureate, a kindergarten, a boys' primary school, a youth movement, and other programs that contributed significantly to Moroccan Jewish education.

During my first tour of Morocco, I had the opportunity to hear the astounding life story of Rabbi Matusof. He was not born a Lubavitch Hasid but became one in later years in Russia. During the Stalinist era, when it was dangerous to teach Judaism, the Lubavitcher Rebbe sent him to do just that to children in various Soviet communities. Denounced to the authorities, he sent the children away so that he alone would remain to be arrested. He was sentenced to five years' hard labor in Siberia, during which he endured weekly beatings for refusing to work on Shabbat.

One year, when Rosh Hashanah fell on a Thursday and Friday, he sought some way to protect himself from three consecutive daily beatings. He found a hole in the floor of the barracks that led to a small, dank, underground room, and there stashed some dry bread and water to sustain him for the three days. When his absence was noticed, the guards thought he had escaped but assumed he could not get away since the camp was so far from the nearest settlement. At the end of the third day, Rabbi Matusof rejoined the group, only to encounter the guards who, convinced that he had returned after an unsuccessful escape attempt, subjected him to abuse that far surpassed the normal.

When his sentence in Siberia was almost up, Rabbi Matusof was tried again, for no apparent reason, and given another five years. (It was not unusual for the gulag authorities to extend a prisoner's sentence under dubious pretenses. Not only that, but they would incarcerate many thousands of people whenever more workers were required.) By the time of Rabbi Matusof's second internment, World War II had begun and the authorities took him and other prisoners to the front to walk through minefields ahead of the army's tanks. Somehow, Rabbi Matusof survived, only to be sent to another labor camp. There, though, he met some devout Christian peasants who agreed to work for him on Saturdays if he would replace them on Sundays.

After the war, he was released and, like Rabbi Lispker, made his way to France as a Soviet "Polish" refugee. Rabbi Matusof joined the Lubavitch community there before being posted to Morocco by the Rebbe in 1950 and settling in Casablanca.

Rabbi Matusof was one of the very few saintly individuals I have met — a wise, self-taught man who adhered to the highest standards of personal and religious conduct. During my subsequent visits to Morocco, I regularly spent time with him and his family. His wife, raised in Leningrad, was an intelligent woman who became the principal of the Casablanca girls' high school. When she fell ill some thirty years after I first met him, Rabbi Matusof pleaded with the Rebbe for permission to join his children abroad. The Rebbe never relented. After the Rebbe died in 1994, Rabbi Matusof finally moved to join the Lubavitch community of Crown Heights in New York and contented himself with the modest income he received for some teaching that he performed while otherwise filling his time with Torah study.

I encountered several other fascinating Lubavitch emissaries in the course of my work in Morocco. One in particular was Rabbi Sa'adia Liberov, principal of a small village school near Sefrou. He was another refugee from the USSR and he too, like Rabbi Lipsker and Rabbi Matusof, had found his way via France to Morocco. On one of my visits, I found him sitting alone at his table singing Lubavitch tunes, wearing his Shabbat caftan and immersed in a world far removed. He had just received a letter from the Rebbe, his wife explained. To elevate his soul properly before reading it, he had gone to the *mikve* (ritual bath), said his prayers, and ascended to a higher plane. By the time I arrived, he was altogether unreachable. He had not yet opened the letter. Not wishing to disturb him, I went away.

Of particular interest to me on a professional level was the Lubavitch girls' high school in Casablanca, which provided teacher training and encouraged its students to take on positions in Moroccan Jewish schools. Recognizing the importance of this program, JDC provided it with regular financial support and included some of its graduates in the JDC teacher training sessions in Europe and locally.

However, the Lubavitch-JDC relationship was strained in two senses: financial capability and principle. JDC-Europe objected to Lubavitch's desire for what seemed to JDC, as Moses (Moe) Beckelman put it to me, "a program without [financial] limits" and a "duplicative and wasteful" autonomy. Moe Beckelman, JDC director-general in Paris in the early 1950s, was not very enthusiastic of the Lubavitch program because it kept general education in its boys' schools to a minimum and did not believe in general high-school education for boys in Morocco. JDC nevertheless continued to include Lubavitch's Moroccan program in its budget due to the unquestionable value that it held, particularly for the poorer Jewish population whose children were not sufficiently educated to be accepted by Alliance or Ozar Hatorah.

I also took up the issue of secular education on my first visit with the Lubavitcher Rebbe, who remained adamant. He felt that general French education had been overemphasized and Jewish education undervalued for Moroccan Jews. Indeed, on the purely Jewish side of the coin, the Lubavitch institutions spared no effort.

Ultimately, I predicted, Lubavitch would have to close its yeshivas because many students would prefer to attend a school that offered general alongside Jewish education. And, in fact, the Lubavitch yeshiva in Casablanca and all of the Lubavitch boys' schools in Morocco closed down rather early in the mass emigration period.

As a result of our discussions, Lubavitch did introduce some new subjects into the yeshiva program. These included general studies, such as basic arithmetic, and a program to train graduates of its schools as scribes and ritual slaughterers.

I also conditioned JDC's acceptance of Lubavitch requests for budget increases for the village heders on their passing inspections that would confirm improvements in scholastic standards — improvements that Lubavitch had agreed to make. I further urged the Talmud Torah schools to modernize by bringing in textbooks, educational programs, standard furniture, and blackboards. Some local people who ran the Lubavitch boys' schools seemed too set in their ways to accept even these reforms; others were more amenable.

Overall, Lubavitch has made a valuable contribution to Moroccan Jewish education in over half a century of activity there. The Lubavitch emissaries earned a place in the Moroccan Jewish community by respecting local traditions, never trying to impose their ways, and always striving to be pleasant and understanding without compromising their principles.

In addition to training rabbis and ritual slaughterers, Lubavitch influenced many adults to strengthen their religious observance and send their children to Jewish schools. Lubavitch provided kashruth supervision for the wines that the communities prepared, making them acceptable to wine merchants in Europe and the United States. It also supervised kosher bakeries and even wedding celebrations and other events in the prestigious hotels in Casablanca, a service that had not been available in the past.

Jewish life in Morocco today is both richer and more religious due to Lubavitch's efforts. The JDC investment in the Lubavitch program has been constructive and through Lubavitch, JDC, too, made a valuable contribution to Jewish education and Jewish life in Morocco.

ORT

The ORT school system was active in vocational education and received JDC financial support through New York headquarters. Its first school in Morocco was established in 1947, a coeducational facility in a suburb of Casablanca. As the Moroccan Jewish population decreased, ORT sold this property and built a modern school in the city proper.

ORT relied on Alliance to provide general and Jewish education in its single large school. However, the Jewish education component, deficient in Alliance's own schools, was negligible in the program it provided to ORT.

Neither the ORT nor the Alliance principals were troubled by this. ORT made a constructive contribution to Jewish life in Morocco by providing many young men and women with vocational training that they might otherwise not have acquired.

Local Community Schools

Many of the preexisting Talmud Torah institutions for boys that almost every community had established now persevered alongside Alliance, Ozar Hatorah, and Lubavitch institutions. By providing financial backing to some of these community schools, Ozar Hatorah influenced them to improve their curricula, to retrain their teachers, and to strengthen their Jewish education. Lubavitch took over some of the local Talmud Torah schools in villages.

Such was the Em Habanim school in Sefrou under the auspices of Ozar Hatorah. At the similar Em Habanim school in Fez, children from the *mellah* attended classes from the morning and students from the Alliance school would come after school hours for additional Jewish education.

A large and very successful community Talmud Torah existed in Meknes. Most of the Jewish boys in this town attended the Talmud Torah until the age of eleven, when they passed on to the Alliance school. This was an arrangement agreed upon between Rabbi Baruch Toledano and Alliance in Meknes.

Tetouan, where the first Alliance school had been established, had a large community Talmud Torah. Some of the Talmud Torah students gradually drifted over to the Alliance school, as it offered a full general education.

The Denouement

At their peak in the late 1950s, JDC's activities in Morocco touched some 46,000 school children. JDC-supported schools and training centers were attended by practically all Jewish children of school age at that time. JDC provided funds to rent better premises for schools, thereby enabling the liquidation of many of the squalid *mellah* schools. The students were transferred to preschools and Talmud Torah institutions that were well-lit, ventilated, and modernized. Since JDC's support included the provision of textbooks and conditioned financial backing on the improvement of curricula and study tools, it also had significant impact in enabling the education institutions to reduce illiteracy significantly. The nutrition program included 89 canteens and daily hot meals for some 18,000 children — the only decent food that 90 percent of them received all day.

The end result of the welfare programs and educational improvements in the schools, the youth activities of DEJJ, and the summer camps was a high standard of child and youth care and a robust array of Jewish schools.

JDC's main success, and ours as education consultants, was in consolidating and bolstering Moroccan Jewry in its modernization and in preparing its young generation for rounded and productive lives wherever they settled. By supporting and facilitating education agencies that pursued these goals, JDC was able to upgrade the education of Jewish Moroccan students. This enabled the majority to settle and succeed in their eventual places of residence, in Europe, the United States, and Israel.

In Israel, Moroccan Jews were the country's largest Jewish ethnic bloc until the 1990s and remain an important community with many intellectual, economic, spiritual, and political achievements to their credit. The Moroccan Jews who emigrated to France augmented French Jewry significantly. Those who moved to Montreal, Canada, were received, thanks to the Francophone movement there, with special favor by the provincial government.

Inevitably, the declining Jewish population of Morocco had a dramatic impact on the country's Jewish institutions, services, and education. The emigration of teachers caused teaching quality to deteriorate. Professional skills were placed under further pressure by the concurrent influx into the Jewish schools of children less educated in Jewish subjects from general government schools, French cultural mission schools, and other private French institutions.

In the late 1950s, following Morocco's independence, government support of Alliance/Ittihad and affiliated schools diminished due to economic hard times. Many Jewish institutions, including yeshivot, schools, synagogues, charitable organizations, and newspapers, had closed by the 1970s.

JDC kept its annual budget for Morocco nominally steady over many years, with the decline in population and programs offset by inflation and the loss of dollar purchasing power. Most of the disbursements were in the form of direct annual grants for local activities. About half of the budget was dedicated to welfare programs and the other half to education (e.g., grants for Ittihad-Maroc, Ozar Hatorah, Lubavitch, and ORT).

Today, even though the schools have contracted, JDC is still an investor in Moroccan Jewry, albeit on a smaller scale. By the early 1990s, no Jewish schools remained outside Casablanca, but JDC support has remained critical to the ability of the several institutions that do remain in the city to function effectively.

Continued Personal Involvement

After I moved to Israel in 1972, my work in Europe practically ceased. Initially, I continued to visit Morocco frequently, but gradually disengaged from my responsibilities there too. During the 1980s, JDC transferred my remaining Moroccan (and European) duties to Seymour Epstein, who followed me to Israel but remained education director for Europe until he left JDC in 1999.

Nevertheless, my association with the JDC program in Morocco continued into the late 1990s. I visited the country now and then, maintained a number of great personal contacts, and was sometimes asked to run the JDC office there during periods of transition between country directors. In these last years, my wife, Noemi, ran seminars on working with learning-disabled youngsters — her area of expertise — for teachers in the Ozar Hatorah, Alliance, and Lubavitch systems. I continued to find each visit inspiring and instructive.

Today Moroccan Jews lead emancipated lives under the patronage of King Mohammed VI, the successor of Hassan II. Even though aliyah is relatively unrestricted, the 4,000 or 5,000 Jews who remain in the country are mostly content to remain where they are. Businesspeople are doing well and the middle class are able to maintain the jobs they have.

Even today, the attractive customs of Moroccan Jewry are evident, and the synagogues and institutions of religious study fill me with inspiration and satisfaction. Remnants of the original network of community institutions have persisted, and the rabbinical courts retain their jurisdiction and autonomy. Intermarriage is almost unheard of.

JDC still helps the community care for its indigent — particularly elderly — members. But Morocco's Jewish poor are now few in number, and fewer still live in the *mellah*s.

Our education programs, too, have contracted along with the Jewish community, but remain important. The Lubavitch-JDC connection remains quite strong. When Rabbi Matusof left Morocco, the movement's work was carried on by Rabbis Yehuda Raskin and Shalom Eidelman. Rabbi Raskin expanded Lubavitch activities to include summer and winter camps, doing so until his unexpected and untimely death; Mrs. Raskin took over from her late husband and runs a Lubavitch preschool and a high school, both of which continue to function today. Rabbi Shalom Eidelman supervises kashruth and spends his days and nights learning and teaching in Casablanca. Every evening, he runs a *kollel* for teachers and laymen. At one time, JDC subsidized studies for a group of young potential rabbis learning in this *kollel*. Today, almost all holders of rabbinical positions in Morocco are alumni of the program. JDC underwrites the main part of the cost of the Lubavitch programs.

Ittihad-Maroc (Moroccan Alliance) still has a Jewish education program, which has only improved over the years. Ozar Hatorah, under Rabbi Monsenego's guidance, continues to maintain a primary school and evening classes.

There is no ORT school in Morocco today, but a handful of private vocational schools cater to Jewish and non-Jewish students.

This may be the last chapter of Jewish life in Morocco. On the other hand, in 2007, 700 Jewish children were enrolled in Casablanca's Jewish schools. Among these is a new institution, the Rashi High School, a grassroots initiative by parents.

These are hardly the marks of a dying community. But whatever the community's future, our Moroccan program — with its many achievements — will remain as a glorious episode in JDC history, and everyone involved recalls the work there with pleasure and pride.

Tunisia

Tunisia has had a Jewish population for millennia. Some claim that the prophet Jonah left Israel for Carthage (Tarshish in the Bible), which is on the outskirts of Tunis, in order to join the city's Jewish community, who were members of his tribe, the tribe of Naphtali. Over the centuries, Tunisian Jewry turned out religious and lay scholars, merchants, artisans, administrators, and even diplomats.

The French protectorate came earlier to Tunisia than to Morocco. Thus, the Jews had been longer emancipated, had developed a larger affluent class, and were generally better off. Teeming, impoverished *mellah*s did not exist.

The community lived in relative security during the protectorate era and after it, interacting peaceably with the rest of the population.

Tunisian Jewry published an abundance of popular literature in Judeo-Arabic (colloquial Arabic printed in Hebrew characters), which began to appear in the late nineteenth century and continued until the 1960s. Tunisia's island of Djerba, where two old-fashioned Hebrew printing presses functioned, was the center for Jewish publishing in North Africa. The country's chief rabbi in the 1970s and 1980s, Bughid Sadoun, was dedicated to typesetting modern rabbinic works, letter by letter. Between the two world wars, a large French-language, Zionist, and independent Jewish press enjoyed a wide circulation. The Carthage Prize was awarded to Tunisian Jews three times.

Tunisia experienced a brief Nazi occupation between November 1942 and May 1943, during which some 4,000 Jews were mobilized for forced labor, and a few were deported to death camps in Europe. Yet the community rebounded quickly afterward.

Emigration began after the State of Israel was established in 1948. The major outflow came in the early 1950s, as Tunisia prepared for independence from France and the Jewish population suffered from an economic downturn, civil unrest, and relative insecurity. The agitation intensified following Tunisian independence in March 1956. The old Jewish cemetery in the center of Tunis was made into a public park without compensation to the community.[3] In its Arabization and "Tunisification" efforts, the government abolished the rabbinical court on September 27, 1957, and dissolved the Jewish community council on July 11, 1958. Government subsidies to the Jewish community were discontinued.

These steps spurred more emigration. Another wave occurred in the 1960s, amidst another economic crisis, and in the wake of the anti-Jewish violence that erupted after the 1967 Six-Day War.

Between 1948 and 1970, over 40,000 Tunisian Jews settled in Israel and nearly as many in France (most had acquired French citizenship prior to Tunisia's independence), leaving barely 20,000 Jews in Tunisia. Emigration from Tunisia continued thereafter on a smaller scale, Jews from the south leaving primarily for Israel and those from Tunis for France. By the beginning of this century, the Jews remaining in Tunisia did not exceed 2,000.

---

3. Visitors to Belvedere Park today can still find pieces of Jewish tombstones, their Hebrew lettering clearly evident on the paths.

The Communities of Tunisia

When I first encountered Tunisia in late 1952, most of its 100,000 Jews lived in the capital, Tunis. It was considered a modern city, its center built on a model of French cities. In the heart of town was the palace of the bey — the Ottoman-appointed Muslim ruler of Tunisia. Next to it was the administration building of the French governor. This governing infrastructure was changed in 1957, when Tunisia obtained independence and Habib Bourguiba took over the country as prime minister and president; the role of the bey was abolished and the French withdrew.

The majority of the Jewish population of Tunis dwelled in the Hara (the "quarter" or ghetto), but since French occupation many had moved to the new section of the city, the center of town, where the large synagogue on Boulevard de Paris was built.

I found that the Jews of the capital were well represented in liberal professions, including doctors, lawyers, and engineers, and also owned most of the shops in the newer section that they had occupied. Most law clerks and staff in large stores were Jewish. Certain banks and enterprises employed many Jews. Members of the younger generation joined the civil service, particularly in teaching. Many of the Jewish population were craftsmen. There were traditional Jewish occupations: artisans, cobblers, and butchers in the Jewish quarters; merchants in the Arab bazaars; and tailors, goldsmiths, and textile merchants in various locations.

They did not, however, overtly mix with the Muslims. The Muslims of Tunis lived in their own overcrowded area and depended mainly on work provided by the European part of the city.

There were sizable Jewish communities in Sfax and Sousse, each a few hours drive from the capital. Sfax was a center of olive oil industry; Sousse had the largest coliseum outside of Italy. Each had a central section built by the French, which was also inhabited by the Jews, and in which the Jews occupied most of the business sector.

Perhaps most remarkable of all, though, were the 5,000 Jews living in Djerba, an island off the coast in the south that was reachable by ferry. Most Djerban Jews dwelled in the Hara Kabira, the "large quarter," which due to migration to inland areas had become the last outpost of Jewish life in southern Tunisia. A smaller community (about 1,500) lived in the Hara Srira, the "small quarter," four miles away.

Djerba, in fact, was the destination for my first excursion outside the capital. It is a beautiful, flat island in the Mediterranean, famous for its rugs and its fishing industry. The fishermen there use a fascinating system, whereby reeds are stuck into the sea floor in V-shaped forms and to which large nets are attached at the lower, narrow ends. Fish entering between the two walls of reeds continue swimming toward the narrow end and enter the net. The fishermen collect their catch during the early morning hours, when the ebbed sea is shallow enough for them to wade out to the nets. I marveled at the sight of these beautiful designs swaying in the water. In Djerba, irrigation for agriculture (vegetables and grains) was achieved by using rainwater that was drained into cisterns and then hauled out to the fields by camels.

With no hotels in the Hara Kabira at that time, I stayed in the nearby town of Hom-Suk, at the Grand Hotel. It was anything but grand. The beds were clean, but there was no running water and the electricity supply was intermittent. When I arrived, the proprietor, a Frenchman, assured me that I could leave my belongings in the car. No one in Djerba would steal anything, he told me. He was right, although this changed over the years.

The attire of most Jews in Djerba, like traditional Jews throughout Tunisia, was distinguished from Muslims only by a black band worn below the knee to signify their mourning over the destruction of the Temple in Jerusalem. The communities of Djerba were guided by rabbis who maintained very strict discipline in religious matters. Every Jew attended morning, afternoon, and evening prayers. A shofar was blown before Shabbat to announce the advent of the holy day. According to a tradition that is still maintained, boys and girls in Djerba never met, walked together, or spoke to each other until their wedding day.

The Jewish quarters were encompassed by a large *eruv*, an enclosure that distinguishes a private area from a public domain and which enables Jews to carry things from one place to another within its boundaries on Shabbat. The *eruv* omitted the central market, lest Jews be tempted to "borrow" products (no one would really shop) on Shabbat.

The Hara Kabira had fourteen synagogues, each with its own character and community of devotees who maintained their loyalty for generations. So strong were these loyalties, in fact, that they were transplanted to Israel when members of the various synagogues moved there.

Every synagogue had its own rabbi and teacher who taught the young boys Hebrew and Torah until they were sixteen or seventeen when it was time to teach them a trade. The teacher moved from group to group, and the idle groups were expected to review their lessons while they were waiting. More often, they stared out the window or made a noise.

The main synagogue in Djerba is El Ghriba, located near the Hara Srira. A renowned shrine and tourist attraction, El Ghriba's prominence made it the target of terrorist attacks in 1985 and 2002 that killed over twenty people, mainly tourists.

The synagogue is a remarkable place, unlike any other I have ever encountered. Many miraculous stories are told about this synagogue, which is considered so holy that people remove their shoes before entering (a custom presumably traced to Moses' action at the burning bush rather than to the Muslim practice upon entering a mosque). Exiles from the First Temple, people say, brought a stone with them from Solomon's Temple in Jerusalem and placed it in a grotto in the synagogue. The synagogue walls are decorated with gold tablets donated by people who escaped misfortune or who came to pray for a change in their fortunes. So venerated is this place that, in respect for its sanctity, it is the only synagogue in the area of the Hara Srira to have Torah scrolls. On Mondays, Thursdays, Shabbat, and festivals, when the Torah is read, everyone walks to El Ghriba for services.

During one of my visits, I experienced the Djerba version of the Lag b'Omer *hilula*, long attended by Jews from elsewhere in Tunisia and still honored by many expatriate Tunisian Jews who return to celebrate. The Torah scroll at El Ghriba is placed on a stand[4] and people donate money for the privilege of decorating it with kerchiefs and other adornments. The Torah is then led in a procession to make a visit to one of the other synagogues in the Hara Srira.

Many Djerban Jews moved for business reasons to neighboring communities on the mainland, such as Gabes, Zarzis, Foum Tataouine, and Ben Gardane. These Jews became dominant in their new communities, bringing with them the customs and ways of life to which they were accustomed in Djerba. The Jews of Zarzis, for example, were mostly from the Hara Srira and followed its customs and traditions, while the members of the Gabes and Ben

---

4. The parchment is protected by a hinged cylindrical wooden case that can be positioned safely, unlike the Ashkenazi model.

Gardane communities were primarily from the Hara Kabira, and followed its traditions.

JDC and Jewish Education in Tunisia

My work in Tunisia took place against the backdrop of comprehensive JDC welfare programs. One outstanding JDC representative, who ran the program for over ten years from Paris and Geneva, was an admirable lady named Evelyn Peters.

Although JDC's work there was similar to that in Morocco, the Tunisian community was much smaller and more geographically compact, so I visited Tunisia less frequently and was therefore less minutely involved in the community's affairs.

In 1951, a JDC canteen feeding program was providing meals for over 4,700 children and clothing for 470. Some 4,500 were participating in JDC-supported Hebrew courses. JDC's financial support of OSE medical institutions enabled the treatment of 10,000 persons, an effort that — among its other benefits — virtually stamped out tuberculosis by 1954. There being no qualified or Hebrew-speaking kindergarten teachers in Tunisia, the JDC office started an in-service training program to remedy the drawback. JDC helped to establish two old-age homes, one in Tunis and one in Sfax.

JDC promoted Jewish education in Tunisia much as it did in Morocco, using the same methods and in conjunction with some of the same outside organizations, except for Ozar Hatorah. The latter had made an abortive attempt to establish a school in Tunisia, unable to find the appropriate local personnel to staff it. The main Jewish communities in Tunisia also supported their own educational projects, which they took very seriously. In late 1960, for example, the Comite de Gestion (the management committee that replaced the Jewish community council in Tunis that the government had dismantled) opened part-time Talmud Torah schools in Tunis and its suburbs that provided both Hebrew and general education. The Comite admitted all children to these schools and recruited new teachers. JDC provided significant financial support for this activity, as it did for other Comite activities, such as a summer instruction and recreation program for children. It did not, however, need to become more actively involved in the schools' activities, which were run by Lubavitch and the chief rabbinate.

There was a stronger demand for general education in Tunisia than in

Morocco. Generally speaking, although most Tunisian Jews were traditional, the community outside Djerba and the south of the country was not as religious-minded as Moroccan Jewry. In Tunisia, therefore, I was less challenged by the need to strike a balance between religious and general education.

My main contacts in the city of Tunis during those years were Rabbi Nisson Pinson of Lubavitch, the Grand Rabbinate of Tunisia, and the administrators of the Comite de Gestion. Occasionally, JDC served as mediator to ease tensions arising among these parties from competition and a feeling that the local community could take care of all educational needs and train its own religious functionaries. The overall JDC attitude, and mine, was that each entity had a role to play in Jewish education and that Jewish education would be worse off if any of them were to falter for lack of funds.

Since JDC had an education consultant in Tunisia, Mr. Isaac Shebabo, my duties in Tunisia were less comprehensive and time-consuming than they were initially in Morocco before a similar professional was permanently posted there. I assisted the schools by sending sample teaching materials from European headquarters to JDC's Tunis office, where Mr. Shebabo and others presented them to principals. Teachers subscribed to *Hamoré*, the JDC Jewish quarterly pedagogical magazine in the French language, and read it appreciatively. In addition, we sent them supplements to *Hamoré*, some of which were translated locally into Judeo-Arabic and widely distributed. We published a few special editions of the magazine with references to Israel removed.

JDC also helped ease the impact of emigration, which drained the community's pool of qualified teachers. It arranged for several graduates of Ramsgate College (an institution in England founded by Sir Moses Montefiore), who had been recipients of the JDC scholarship program, to accept posts in Tunisian communities that were often the first to be hit by the departure of teachers. Although they were unwilling to stay in such communities for more than two or three years, these Ramsgate graduates filled the gap for a while.

Alliance

Alliance had been active in Tunisia since 1878, sponsoring five government-supported day schools. These schools, like the Alliance schools in Morocco, were weak in Jewish and Hebrew studies. However, JDC did not endeavor to improve them as it had in Morocco, mainly because Alliance in Tunisia was on its last legs even before the country's independence. By that time, the organization had become a victim of the introduction of large-scale free education that prompted many Jewish families to enroll their children in government schools that provided commercial training along with academic education.

After 1958, when the Tunisian government "Arabized" the curriculum in all government-supported schools (including Alliance), Muslim children thronged the Alliance schools, due to their better reputation compared to the Muslim schools. Within a couple of years, the Muslim enrollment accounted for two-thirds of the student body, a proportion that grew as Jewish families began withdrawing their children. By late 1962, the Alliance system had contracted to three schools that enrolled about 3,000 children, of whom only a small minority was Jewish.

Education for Girls in Djerba

For centuries, Jewish girls in Tunisia received no Jewish education at all. The rabbis did not allow men to teach them, and local women, being uneducated, could not do the job themselves. From 1951, there were women teachers and classes for girls, the students achieving high levels of knowledge. Occasionally some Djerba girls wished to earn a baccalaureate and go on to university. Liberal parents honored these wishes; conservative ones did not. Much of this was supported by JDC.

Lubavitch

Lubavitch made first moves toward a program in Tunisia in 1954 by starting a yeshiva in Tunis for a few boys. Rabbi Pinson, who had moved from Casablanca to Tunis to inaugurate the program, ran the yeshiva, taught its Jewish subjects, and even arranged for a program of general studies.

By the early 1960s, the Arabization of Alliance's curriculum and the closure of two Alliance schools left the Jewish community in Tunis without any full-time Jewish school. Rabbi and Rebbetzin Pinson moved to fill the vacuum by opening a boys' and a girls' school in addition to the yeshiva. These schools were important for students from Djerba who had moved with their families to Tunis. These youngsters generally lacked a general education and would not have been accepted to any other schools even if they had been interested in applying.

In time, the Lubavitch schools were developed to include all the primary and secondary grades, leading up to the French baccalaureate. Rabbi Pinson must have persuaded the Lubavitcher Rebbe in New York that without general education, there would be no students willing to attend the schools — something the Rebbe had never been convinced of in Morocco. As Tunis's Jewish population decreased, however, so did their enrollment, leaving only a small group of boys in a combination school/yeshiva, alongside a separate school for girls. Both schools still exist today.

Independent Community Schools

There were also a few part-time, independent Jewish community schools and Talmud Torah institutions in the cities and towns with a higher Jewish concentration. I felt it JDC's duty to support this existing network. Thus, JDC drew up a Jewish education program that could be offered to these schools and provided them with textbooks, audiovisual materials, pictorial aids, and guidance for teachers.

Besides a number of community schools for young boys in Tunis, a group of older students in the capital were learning to become ritual slaughterers in a community rabbinical academy called Hobrat Hatalmud, under the directorship of the chief rabbi.

The Jewish communities of Sfax and Sousse maintained such Jewish part-time schools, but they too closed their doors as their populations decreased. The more southern communities of Gabes, Foum Tataouine, and Ben Gardane had community-run schools that continued to function much longer, until no Jews were left there. In Zarzis, a Talmud Torah continues to function to this day to serve the still active and viable community there.

A number of traditional Jewish schools in Djerba functioned in the different synagogues as small heders, under the instruction of rebbes, each serving its immediate neighborhood. None of these institutions had turned out scholars or rabbis in many years, and had no prospects of doing so in the absence of internal reforms — e.g., the introduction of standard classes, modern teaching methods, and some instruction in general subjects. Indeed, JDC feared that without such reform, these schools would never be able to supply the community with its future religious functionaries.

Thus, JDC intervened, pressed for innovations, and even conditioned future support on the implementation of actions recommended. Our suggestion was to gather all the children of Djerba in one synagogue and then divide them into classes by age. We offered all kinds of enticements to make this reform — at first to no avail. The schools resisted.

Mr. Shebabo, the local JDC education consultant, was caught in the middle, drawing fire from the local religious authorities and community members who saw his "secularist" reforms as an anti-religious crusade. By August 1960, the Grand Rabbinate of Tunisia demanded Shebabo's replacement outright. JDC backed its representative: he was, after all, carrying out organizational policy.

We continued to support these schools throughout the years of dispute, arguing all the while with Djerba's chief rabbi about ways to improve their teaching methods. Time and financial lures had some gradual effects. The children were eventually gathered in one large building (which JDC renovated and repaired) and divided into age groups. Each teacher was given a salaried position and a yeshiva school was established.

When the Djerba yeshiva program was finally initiated, JDC agreed to channel its financial support through Lubavitch, in the hope that the movement could influence the ultraconservative local forces in the direction of change and facilitate more effective teaching methods. Unfortunately, this gambit failed, as Lubavitch was also considered an outside organization by the local rabbis and was therefore rejected by them. Despite much good will finally shown by the local chief rabbi and all our efforts, some of the teachers never mastered useful teaching approaches.

Another community school in Djerba was established in the early 1950s as a continuation of the efforts of the Jewish Agency's Hadassah Shabani. This school, Daber Ivrit ("Speak Hebrew"), had a major impact on Djerba's Jewish girls and boys. It provided classes in Hebrew and general subjects for girls and provided them with the kind of education we could only aspire to in other institutions. Under principal David Kidushin, the girls learned Bible and its commentaries, Jewish history, and Hebrew grammar. Kidushin also stressed secular subjects: whenever he found a book on geography or biology, he copied it, his staff of teachers mastered the material and they in turn expanded the girls' world by teaching it to them.

For boys, who devoted their mornings and afternoons to religious studies, the Daber Ivrit school offered lunchtime instruction in Jewish and general subjects not taught in the central yeshiva-Talmud Torah.

Daber Ivrit was very successful in presenting a group of students each year for examinations for the Jerusalem certificate for the Diaspora. This diploma certified that its recipient had achieved a high level in Hebrew language, literature, and grammar.

JDC encouraged and supported Kidushin's efforts. Beyond their importance to his own students, we had hoped that his success and methods would gradually be emulated by the more traditional Jewish yeshiva school on the island. However, after having achieved the restructuring of the small heder classes of Djerba into the central yeshiva, development there stagnated; nothing changed beyond the original construction of a central open space, blackboards, and clean sanitary facilities insisted upon by JDC.

The Decline

Despite the intervention of JDC, the Lubavitch efforts, and the communities' own admirable labors, it became evident in late 1962 that a significant number of Jewish children in Tunisia still attended French cultural mission and Tunisian government schools where they received no Jewish education at all. This was discouraging for the future of Tunisia's already diminishing Jewry. In time, these children either emigrated or transferred to the Lubavitch school in Tunis.

The aftermath of the Six-Day War further diminished the community, and educational and religious facilities contracted apace. Many synagogues shut their doors and transferred their religious appurtenances to the main synagogue in Tunis. The Lubavitch schools and a small number of community schools were the only institutions that still afforded any form of Jewish education.

Lasting Contacts

My professional work in Tunisia, as elsewhere, led to great friendships. One such friend is David Kidushin, and his wife, Tzvia, who worked with him in Djerba's Daber Ivrit school. Whenever I visited the island, I took my meals at their home in the Hara Kabira and spent many hours discussing education and religion with David, an autodidact who spares no effort in running his school and maximizing his own Jewish learning. Young Jewish women in Djerba owe their knowledge of Jewish subjects primarily to him. The Kidushins remain in Tunisia and help guide the remnants of Tunisia's communities.

I have also long maintained my acquaintance with Rabbi and Rebbetzin

Pinson. He was able to open many doors to Jewish homes in Tunisia due to his skills as a *mohel* (performer of ritual circumcision), a baker of matzoth, a vintner, and an applier of low-key, unobtrusive persuasion. Oddly enough, he landed in hot water with sensitive local rabbis by departing from local tradition in minor ways, such as pronouncing certain Hebrew letters in the Ashkenazi fashion. Still, Rabbi Pinson's gentleness, sincerity, and commitment have earned him much respect and admiration.

In addition to her teaching duties in the Lubavitch girls' school in Tunis, Rebbetzin Pinson organized a women's group that meets in her home on Shabbat to study Bible and imbibe Lubavitcher stories. The pleasure she generates through these activities is another channel of influence that the Pinsons have developed over the years.

In 1982, when Israel drove Yasser Arafat's PLO to leave Lebanon and these forces chose Tunisia as their new headquarters, Rabbi Pinson endured tough times. Due to his stereotypical rabbinic appearance, he was often accosted and spat upon while walking from his home to the school. He was undaunted and saw no reason to leave. The Lubavitcher Rebbe had once assured him that no ill would befall him or his wife.

Several years ago, after a crippling stroke, Rabbi Pinson went to France for medical care and then to Israel for further medical assistance. After making a partial recovery, his wife, a very determined woman, insisted that they return to Tunis to continue their work. The Pinsons' six children today represent the Lubavitch movement in various communities in Europe and America, but the parents are now the sole representatives of Chabad-Lubavitch in Tunis.

The Kidushin and Pinson families are among the people I have learned to appreciate and admire in the course of my work. This is one of the unanticipated rewards of working for JDC.

All that is Left

Less remains of Tunisian Jewry than of Moroccan Jewry, as similar factors — an anti-Jewish environment coupled with the allure of Israel and other Western countries — led to mass emigration at a faster pace and from a narrower population base.

The emigrants left much property behind, including a large synagogue in Tunis and smaller synagogues in Sousse, Gabes, and smaller towns. Most of these smaller synagogues have been expropriated or abandoned. Sfax has a large synagogue building, which was built with German reparation funds following the short Nazi occupation, and an old-age home next door to it. Although the synagogue is no more than fifty years old, it no longer functions and birds fly in and out of its broken windows. The old-age home no longer functions either. The few elderly Jews remaining in Sfax continue to live independently in the town. JDC has offered several times to move them to Tunis and to the old-age home there, but they choose to stay put, preferring to die where they have always lived. The remaining Jews in Djerba have retained their property, but many of those who left sold their homes to Muslims.

Of the fewer than 2,000 Jews still in Tunisia, a small number live in the Sousse-Monastir area, but the bulk are divided almost equally between Tunis and Djerba. Each community is headed by a government-appointed committee. JDC continues to help the needy by maintaining a well-funded welfare program.

In Tunis, the Jewish home for the aged is still supported by JDC, as is the Lubavitch primary school.

In Djerba, there remains one kindergarten for boys and girls, the JDC-initiated yeshiva, and the Daber Ivrit school. The yeshiva still gathers youngsters who in past years would have congregated at the individual synagogues. Nowadays, many of these children also attend a government school located at the entrance to the Hara Kabira, where they receive a general education in the mornings. During the long lunch break they go to Daber Ivrit for instruction in Jewish and other subjects, and from there they go on to the local yeshiva. All these institutions are supported by JDC.

On one of my last visits to Djerba in 1995, I met mothers and grandmothers who remembered my visits forty years earlier, when they were youngsters learning at Daber Ivrit school and accumulating Jewish knowledge that their mothers had had no opportunity to acquire. I also encountered several young women who, following the old tradition, were engaged and had never spoken to their fiancés. They would have plenty of time to talk once they were married, they told me.

Lubavitch continues to work in Tunisia; the Pinson couple will stay as long as Rabbi Pinson's health permits and as long as his wife is able to teach.

JDC will stay as long as Tunisia's Jews need it.

Algeria

The Jewish presence in North Africa was hardly limited to Morocco and Tunisia. Neither was JDC's. For about half a decade, for example, JDC also maintained an office in Tripoli, Libya, which closed after the mass emigration of Libyan Jewry was completed in 1952.

Other communities in Muslim countries — such as Algeria and Egypt — needed and welcomed JDC's involvement, even though they never hosted JDC offices or large-scale programs. My responsibilities, therefore, also brought me to these countries — as well as to others slightly farther afield.

The responsibilities that immersed me in the affairs of Moroccan and Tunisian Jewry led to a lesser involvement with Algerian Jewry, a community that dated from well before the seventh-century Muslim invasion.

A Community Infrastructure

In the early 1950s, the 140,000 Jews in Algeria accounted for 10 percent of the non-Arab population and 1 percent of the total. Half dwelled in Algiers and Oran, and most of the rest in other places along the developed coast. A small percentage lived under benign military rule in the interior and in the south of the country — areas that I never visited. In all, the Algerian Jews were dispersed over some eighty different localities.

The French had been in Algeria since 1830, long before they moved into Tunisia and Morocco, and had declared the country an overseas *departement*, much more "French" than a protectorate. The Cremieux Law, applied in 1870 in Algeria, gave all Jews French citizenship and equalized their status with that of "metropolitan" citizens, giving them an advantage over Muslims.

Thus, the Jews in Algeria, except for those living in the south, considered themselves French. The Muslim masses considered them so too, and regarded the Jews part of the colonial establishment, like the million or more European settlers in the country who were known as *pieds noirs*. It was an alignment that would have fateful consequences in the bitter battle for Algerian independence.

This preferred status, though, had distinct benefits. Unlike their fellows in Morocco, most Algerian Jews did not live in extreme distress and, insofar as they mainly inhabited major cities, they were not concentrated in specific residential areas.

The community also had a rather solid array of institutions. Seventy communities belonged to the Federation of Jewish Communities in Algeria, which supported itself by taxing matzo and wine and by means of general fundraising. The government financed several rabbis' posts. The Federation sponsored an Algerian Jewish Cultural Commission to help in its cultural activities.

Zionist organizations were active too. The community supported the Algerian Zionist Federation; WIZO (Women's International Zionist Organization) had an Algerian section; and the Jewish Agency was active there, posting an emissary to the Alliance-affiliated Talmud Torah in Constantine to function as its principal.

As for education, there was also at least one yeshiva in Constantine, run by Rabbi Zerbib, the chief rabbi. Alliance had a regional committee and ORT ran a school of its own in Algiers.

Despite its relatively strong infrastructure, Algerian Jewry still required assistance. Of the school-age population, 10 percent, mainly in the interior, did not attend school at all. Of those who did, only a few thousand boys received traditional religious schooling. Most of the others marked the beginning and the end of their Jewish education by taking a few days of bar mitzvah training. Professionals were in such short supply that the ORT school, for example, employed a Gentile teacher to teach Jewish history. The Cultural Commission never had sufficient budget for its activities. Part-time school facilities were rundown and inadequate.

Although the community proudly resisted any appearance of penury, its institutions had been asking JDC for subventions since 1948. JDC responded, but in a minor way. Before 1948, Algeria was not high on JDC's priorities since its Jews did not face the kind of widespread poverty prevalent in Morocco or Tunisia. We backed the Dispensaire Polyvalent, a Jewish clinic, despite the fact that it was open on Shabbat and closed on Sundays. It was the only such facility available for the community, and its management was not willing to reverse the arrangement under any circumstances. JDC-supported canteens in Bone (Annaba) and Constantine provided meals to 340 children.

Combating Communism and Assimilation

I first traveled to Algeria in June 1953 and followed up on a few occasions.

My mission, as elsewhere, was education, but as the only representative of headquarters to visit the country at the time, my input on other issues was sought as well.

I visited the major Jewish centers, in Algiers, Oran, Constantine, and Bone, and acquainted myself with the religious and lay leadership. After meeting with the chief rabbi and community officers, I judged the main obstacle to be one of focus and interest, not resources.

Among the most critical problems were Communism and assimilation. These were more than threats; with their potent appeal to the young, they were existential menaces. "The community's conscience is dead," I reported to headquarters, meaning that these trends had blinded much of the community to its Jewishness. "Its Jewish heart is beating feebly, and consequently there is this lack of interest, this deaf ear." To combat this, I recommended to headquarters that we reinforce Jewish consciousness-raising activities in education and help establish a day school-based welfare program that would draw the community in.

Compared to our other activities worldwide, JDC's ensuing activities in Algeria took place on a humble scale. The Algerian Federation of Jewish Communities wished to tackle assimilation by instigating a six-year training program for rabbis and communal workers, a program that JDC agreed to support. We also subsidized the salaries of three specialists from Israel who were given the task of directing education in the main Jewish centers. JDC provided funds to build a high school in Algiers named Maimonides, the cornerstone of which was laid in February 1956. Soon after opening, the school enrolled about 450 students. It also received education materials from JDC.

Escaping Hostility

It was during this period, however, that Algeria became increasingly inhospitable to *pieds-noirs*. Although Algerian Jewry predated the French occupation and was not involved in colonial governance, the Jews' assimilated ways and the Arabs' anti-Israel animus made them targets. In 1956, the Federation of Jewish Communities described Jews in the hinterland as being "in very great physical danger" and recommended that they be moved to coastal towns, to France, or to other countries.

The wake-up call (if one were needed) came in December 1960. Jewish areas were among the targets of anti-French riots, resulting in the desecration of Jewish cemeteries and synagogues including, most prominently and symbolically, the Great Synagogue in Algiers. The riots sparked the beginning of what would soon become the wholesale exodus of Algerian Jews that culminated in 1962, when Charles de Gaulle's government ended French rule and allowed Algeria's Arab majority to declare independence. A million *pieds-noirs* engineered a hasty but controlled relocation to France, with government funding. Among them were some 130,000 Jews, who locked their homes and businesses and fled.

In this process, JDC gave some assistance to those in need through the Fonds Social (the Fonds Social Juif Unifié, a central fundraising organization that JDC had helped establish in France in 1952). Several thousand Jews, mainly those who lived in the south of Algeria, chose Israel as their destination and were helped by the Jewish Agency to make the move.

The severely diminished community rendered JDC's involvement in Algeria even smaller in scale. The Maimonides school in Algiers was closed for lack of students and was then converted into a seniors' residence for the few elderly Jews who stayed behind. A JDC representative from Paris headquarters visited them from time to time to meet their needs. My last visit to Algeria was in 1962, soon after the mass emigration of Jews; assistance with education was no longer needed by those who remained.

Today, Algeria's Jewish population has all but disappeared. JDC's involvement, too, has almost ended: in 2005, it provided supplementary assistance to one elderly woman in Oran, one of the last members of what had been an ancient, thriving community.

Egypt

Post-Exodus Egyptian Jewry is as old as Jeremiah. In its lengthy history, Jews experienced eras of tolerance and intolerance, prosperity and penury, dynamic growth and near-extermination. They made important contributions to the culture of the country at large. They were prominent in Hellenic armies and, during Roman rule, mounted a futile but massive three-year revolt. They thrived under the early Muslim empires, were persecuted by the Mamluks, were reinvigorated by refugees from Spain in the fifteenth and sixteenth centuries, flourished under the Ottomans, sank into poverty under the nineteenth-century monarchy, and seemed to take all sides in the modern national struggle.

A census in 1947 found 65,600 Jews in what was the most urban and best-educated community in North Africa. That year marked the beginning of the end for Egyptian Jewry, however, as Arabist-inspired discriminatory measures were followed by persecution — including the confiscation of some Jewish properties — in response to Israel's defeat of the Arab armies, including Egypt's, in its 1948 War of Independence.

After the creation of the Jewish state, Egypt's Jewish population dwindled so rapidly that by 1957 there were only about 8,500 Jews. Ten years later 3,000 remained, and by 1971, only 400 Jews were left in Egypt. They were, as usual, those who did not wish to forfeit their wealth or could not emigrate for objective reasons such as old age.

Also surviving were community committees in Cairo and Alexandria, one moderately functional synagogue in each of these cities, and one rabbi between them. The rabbi, who had been based in Cairo, left in 1972, and in due course the "committees" amounted to only presidents of committees. Gone were most community properties and institutions, such as a Jewish hospital in Cairo and a chain of old-age homes. Peacemaking between Israel and Egypt in the late 1970s brought relief to the remaining Jews, who were then allowed to reestablish communication with friends and family who were living in Israel and Western countries.

It was for these Jews, living in Alexandria and Cairo, that JDC established a small-scale program in Egypt in the late 1970s. I was appointed as representative there, for which periodic visits sufficed. We provided financial assistance for the lonely and the indigent by means of the community president; brought in festival supplies such as matzo, wine, and kosher-for-Pesach food; and arranged for prayer leaders on the High Holidays.

I visited Egypt once or twice annually in the 1980s to review this activity. I traveled alone, by direct flight from Israel and by Egyptian buses between Cairo and Alexandria. Although no subterfuge was necessary, I took several precautions, such as avoiding the Israeli embassy so as not to identify JDC as an Israeli organization.

It was a dwindling, dying community in the 1980s, however. There had been quite a bit of intermarriage, but we continued to help the widows of the mixed unions. There were irregular prayer quorums in the two synagogues, sustained in part by Israeli diplomats.

I also discovered, to my regret, just how few Jews are necessary for the full-blown practice of Jewish politics. One year, when the president of the Cairo community flew to New York, a woman who opposed him organized several Jews and staged a coup by having herself elected president before his return.

By the mid-1990s, despite or because Jewish communities were no longer harassed by the authorities and enjoyed new freedoms, very few Jews were left in Egypt. The community had dwindled to only a few families — perhaps 100 people in all — mostly in Cairo. The one synagogue there, Sha'ar Hashamayim, continued to function and a second, the Ben Ezra Synagogue, was restored but still did not function. At that time, I became increasingly involved with our rapidly expanding programs in the former Soviet Union, and my duties in Egypt were transferred to a colleague, Ami Bergman, who remains JDC's point person there to this day.

Today, JDC sends few visitors to Egypt. The synagogues no longer function. The remaining Jewish properties have been preserved through the good offices of the Egyptian government.

THE EXTENDED NEIGHBORHOOD

Yemen

At the southern tip of the Arabian Peninsula and far from my other postings in North Africa, the Jewish communities of Yemen trace their origins back to the Second Temple period. The communities grew over the generations, developing unique and colorful traditions that have been persistently preserved.

Yemen was emptied of most of its Jews in two phases during the modern era. The first came in the decades preceding Israeli independence in 1948, during which some 16,000 Yemenite Jews emigrated to Palestine — the highest percentage of any Jewish community to have done so before the State of Israel came into being.

The second exodus occurred after statehood, when more than 40,000 Yemenite Jews moved to Israel in Operation Magic Carpet, one of JDC's largest rescue programs and great success stories. To prepare for that audacious airlift in 1948–1950, Yemenite Jews walked from their villages and towns in the mountainous interior to the Hashid camp near the British-held enclave of Aden, at the southernmost point of the peninsula. They negotiated bandits, local sheikhs, and other power brokers along the way.

JDC could not interact with the dwindling remnant directly, since the Yemenite regimes (the British departure from its territories there resulted in two Yemenite states, North and South, that were only reunited in 1990) were almost as hostile to Americans during those years as they were to Jews.

By the mid-1990s, Yemen's unification had ended the extreme hostility of the South Yemen regime's Marxist rulers and the country's anti-Israel views moderated somewhat. Emigration remained illegal, yet several hundred Yemenite Jews managed to leave for Israel via third countries.

Having followed the emigration of Yemenite Jews with great interest, and out of concern for those who remained in the country, I suggested to JDC's New York headquarters that I make a visit to Yemen.

A Personal Observation of a Complex Community

On June 12, 1996, my wife, Noemi, and I left Israel and traveled via Amman to the Yemenite capital, Sanaa.

Yemenite Jewry at that time consisted of a slender collective of 350–400 people, located mostly in Raida and Saada, two towns north of Sanaa, with others scattered in various villages. There was no longer any Jewish neighborhood in the country; one had to search for Jews family by family.

The narrow road from Sanaa to the two towns and to more outlying localities crossed mountain ranges and obstacles that included not only the detritus of rockslides, but people on the road, vehicles, and domestic animals. Fortunately, a good local driver navigated the treacherous roads and knew exactly where every Jew lived.

The encounter was at once dispiriting and enlightening. Sanaa, the most modern of Yemen's towns, was not as developed as Tunis, Casablanca, Cairo, Amman, and other Muslim cities that I had seen. Streets in the city were never repaired; one had to be an acrobat to steer through them. There was no public transportation in the Western sense. Instead, people moved around in small, open vans whose drivers allowed them to leap on and off and pay for the distance they traveled. There were also taxis and quite a bit of private transportation, including trucks for commercial use. We saw young boys driving vehicles in Yemen — ten-year-olds in my opinion and seven-year-olds according to hearsay.

The cityscape of Sanaa was male. Women rarely left their houses and almost never shopped or circulated alone. When they did emerge, it was with male escorts. The hotel staff was all-male. Even Yemenia, the national airline, used only foreign girls as stewardesses.

Medical care was sporadic in Sanaa and hardly known in the country-side. Many mothers in childbirth, babies, and children succumbed for lack of proper care. The adults wrote this off to fate.

Raida and Saada are small provincial towns that, at the time of my visit, had few paved roads. The towns' Jewish families were scattered among the Muslim population, often quite far from one another, such that only the locals knew which were the Jewish homes.

Overt hostility to Jews in Yemen was not in evidence. I saw how Jews interacted with non-Jews as customers and clients, often shared houses, and lived in full harmony. Jewish girls and women covered their faces in the Muslim manner. However, Jewish men were not allowed to wear the *jambiyya,* the traditional curved dagger that signifies manhood among Yemenite Muslims. Jews were also distinguished from Muslims by various articles of traditional clothing and the *peyot* (sidelocks) ubiquitous among Jewish men and boys.

In Raida, home of the country's largest Jewish population, we found Jews earning their living by making sandals from old tires, doing simple carpentry and silversmithing for the Muslims, and buying or selling farm produce and livestock.

The central square in Raida, as well as in Saada, served as the marketplace. The Jewish silversmiths had their shops around this square. The shops also served as their workshops. Jews and Muslims would visit each other in the marketplace, and they would visit one another's homes too.

Addiction — women to tobacco and men to *qat* — provided the backdrop to this socializing, particularly among men. *Qat* is a plant whose leaves are chewed to deliver a "high" that its users seek as eagerly as do opium addicts, although it falls short of opium in potency. We encountered Jews and others who chewed *qat* every day for hours after lunch. Making my first family visit in Raida, I asked the men, all of whom were chewing *qat* in the main room of the house, how much their habit cost. The expense was staggering.

On one visit to a Jewish family in Saada, I arrived as the head of the family and his friends were taking their postprandial *qat.* They looked upon me with some distrust, obviously doubting my Jewishness because I did not have what they called *simanim* — sidelocks. Thinking of ways to prove it, I eventually pulled out my tzitzit (fringed garment) to establish that I was a bona fide Jew!

I was saddened to find how the distinctive Yemenite version of Judaism, widely practiced and preserved in Israel, was a gutted shell in Yemen of 1996. The community's scholars had left during or shortly after the airlift period, and the remaining rabbis, known as *mori* (teachers), had little Jewish knowledge to offer and could not be trusted to understand basic Hebrew texts. In Kheidar, north of Sanaa, we saw a few Jewish children who were learning to read Hebrew. They were the exceptions; the other children were illiterate. Jewish localities had synagogues but did not have communal prayers because the Jews were either too widely dispersed or too poorly disposed to each other to pray together.

All the Yemenite Jews whom I encountered claimed that they wished to emigrate to Israel but did not indicate when they would actually do so. Most of the impediments revolved around marriages and money. Jewish Yemenite marriages are costly in terms of dowries and flamboyant weddings that must be paid for by the father of the groom. It is common practice, therefore, that a family that cannot afford these practices concludes a marriage by betrothing a daughter and a son to another family's son and daughter, in a barter-like transaction. When misunderstandings, quarrels, or simple incompatibility between one of the couples renders a marriage unworkable, or if a father orders a daughter to return home, the bride returns to her father and the children stay with the husband. The second half of the barter arrangement is then expected to be revoked too, even if it had resulted in a happy marriage. However willing the happy couple may be to continue together, no one on either side can emigrate until a solution is found to the broken marriage, usually in the form of cash, livestock, or a ruling by the local *qadi* (Muslim judge). With only a few hundred Jews in the country, it takes few such incidents to immobilize them all.

The *qadi* is brought in to adjudicate in these cases since no one in these small Jewish communities enjoys the authority to make peace between quarreling families: gone are the days when the *mori* had such standing. The Jews mix with their Muslim neighbors, and therefore, like them, resort to the *qadi*, whose decision is binding on all residents in the village or town.

The Yemenites are an unexpectedly worldly and well-traveled group. Many

I met had been as far afield as Israel, London, and New York, from whence they returned to their villages and carried on their traditional lives. Their "travel agents," as it were, were the Satmar Hasidic courts in New York and London. To further their vehement theological anti-Zionism, Satmar representatives visit Yemen and describe Israeli life in the bleakest terms possible, leading families to refuse to leave for Israel for fear of their children's religious upbringing or of their own economic future.

Satmar would provide funds for Yemenite Jewish men to travel to the United States or England in order to encourage them to study in its yeshivot and tie them to its Hasidic communities. Those Yemenites who took advantage of the travel funds managed to fit in trips to the Holy Land between London and New York.

Unfortunately, the Satmar indoctrination, dissuading emigration to Israel, has served to perpetuate impoverished communities.

Assimilation has been an additional hindrance to emigration. During my visit, I discussed this matter with many families. Despite the headstrong traditions of the Yemenite Jewish families, we had heard of some forty cases of Jews — men and women — who had become Muslim by intermarriage or for other reasons. Such conversion was a one-way street; Yemenite law prohibited Muslims, including those originally Jewish, from practicing Judaism. None of this seemed to matter to our Jewish interlocutors who either ignored or accepted the cases of conversion as the normal price of life among Muslims in Yemen.

A sticky situation I encountered was of a young man who had returned from a Satmar-sponsored trip abroad, and had a quarrel with his wife. That, in itself, was not remarkable. But in this case, the quarrel had prompted the young woman to return to her father.

After some time, the husband had asked her to return and, when she refused, he threatened to take a second wife, polygamy being an accepted practice in Yemen both by Muslims and non-Muslims.[5] When he made good on the threat, the wife returned quickly, fearing that he would take a third wife. At the time of my visit, the second wife was pregnant, the first one was not, and the family carried on as a threesome. Such family dynamics have

5. The prohibition of polygamy instituted by Rabbenu Gershon a millennium ago was never accepted by Sephardic, Yemenite, or Oriental Jews. Israel recognizes cases of polygamy contracted before immigration.

further thwarted possibilities of emigration, since it would involve the consent of the second wife's family too.

Encouragement of emigration from Yemen continued, leaving only a small number of families there in 2006.

A Day in Jordan

Returning to Israel, we had a full day's stopover in Amman. But there was no Jewish community to be spoken of to visit there. We had befriended a Muslim official of Jordanian Airlines who took care of all our needs for the day, from personally seeing us through passport control to treating us to a day in the Jordanian capital.

Arriving there in the small hours of the morning, we arranged to take a hotel room for the day. As we put down our bags, I explained to our escort that I had not yet recited my morning prayers and would like to do so before setting out on a tour of the city. "Ah, neither have I," he responded. While I donned my tallit and tefillin and began to pray, our Muslim friend knelt on the carpeted floor in the same room and began his own morning prayers. It was quite a picture, and the feeling of peace and tolerance left an impression on both of us.

The airline official then took us on a magnificent tour that included the main sights of Amman as well as a visit to his mother's beautiful home and to the relatively new Israeli embassy, established after Israel and Jordan achieved diplomatic relations in November 1994. We flew back to Israel at the day's end and still fondly recall our short visit to Amman.

Lebanon

My only visit to Israel's northern neighbor took place in 1966, when the Muslim-Christian Lebanese experiment[6] seemed to be working and Jews

---

6. In 1943, an agreement was drawn dividing political power between Lebanon's Christians and Muslims. The position of president was to be held by a Christian while a Muslim would serve as prime minister.

could still call the country their home. At the time, a year before the Six-Day War, about 5,000 Jews did just that, and maintained two Jewish primary schools: one in Beirut, operated in conjunction with Ozar Hatorah, and one in Sidon (Saida), which was associated with Alliance. Since JDC gave both schools modest subsidies — in fact, this was the extent of our involvement in the country — an inspection visit by JDC's education consultant was in order.

The trip had no significant effects on our activities in Lebanon, since the schools functioned more or less independently. It did give me a first-hand experience of Lebanon's city lifestyle and of its Jewish communities.

I made the trip from Geneva on my British passport, without an entry visa. I would be issued with one upon arrival, I was told. After the plane landed, a police officer boarded and asked Stanley Abramovitch to follow him. I became very apprehensive at being requested to leave the plane first. I was escorted to the terminal, where a Jewish cinema owner was waiting for me. He told me that the chief of police received two free cinema tickets from him each week, a piece of information whose relevance I soon understood. The cinema proprietor took my passport and led me to the chief of police. Fifteen minutes later, my passport was returned — with the visa.

The Alliance representative, who was based in Beirut, came to meet me and our rounds began: first to the school in Beirut, then to a meeting with the country's chief rabbi. I learned how the Jews in Beirut were living comfortably and unmolested.

They were engaged in business and had connections with other business centers all over the world, and most families were prosperous enough to own vacation homes in the mountains north of the city. In the center of town was a large building where the synagogue, the Jewish school, communal offices, and the chief rabbinate were housed. The school, supported by Mr. Isaac Shalom, the founder of Ozar Hatorah in New York, provided a full general and Jewish education. Chief Rabbi Attie, originally of Syria (also Isaac Shalom's place of birth), took great interest in the school, giving his support to the staff and assisting in any way he could. The Jewish community neither requested nor required JDC financial help.

Touring the city center, I took in the atmosphere of the business district, which offered imports from the Far East and luxury goods from Europe and the United States. The marketplace had a large silver and gold section, with shop after shop offering practically the same goods, while another section was devoted to cloth shops. Jews were very prominent in both the textile and gold businesses. Life in central Beirut seemed to be good and pleasant for its inhabitants — including its Jews.

Later, we set out for Sidon by taxi. To mask our identity, we spoke French in the cab. After meeting with members of the smaller Jewish community of this city and visiting its school, we asked the taxi driver to take us back to Beirut. The driver replied, "For another ten Lebanese pounds I'll drive you to the Israeli border and get you across without problems." We declined the offer and rued the failure of our subterfuge.

On the return trip, along the coastal highway between Sidon and Beirut, we visited a cave reputed to contain the remains of Zebulun, one of Jacob's twelve sons. We were reminded of the patriarch's deathbed blessing to Zebulun: "Zebulun shall dwell by the seashore … and his flank shall rest on Sidon" (Genesis 49:13). When we entered the cave to light a memorial candle, the Palestinian caretaker of the shrine soundlessly presented us with a fresh bottle of oil for the wick. He knew that Jews would not use oil from a container that had been opened by a non-Jew. Again, so much for our disguise.

The 1967 Six-Day War spawned hostility against the Lebanese Jews, and yet another Jewish community in the Muslim world began its rapid decline. As fighting erupted in later years among Lebanon's various groups, the majority of Lebanese Jews left the country for the United States, Israel, France, and other countries, with the assistance of JDC whenever necessary. The chapter of Lebanese Jewry thus came to an end.

❖   ❖   ❖

Finale

Playing a part in the life-saving and historic mission that JDC took upon itself in North Africa was a privilege. I was able to view and guide the communities' distinguished achievements and developments during my tenure in the region. I was given the rare opportunity to know and appreciate North African Jewry, its wonderful qualities and its warm hospitality. My life was enriched immeasurably by my numerous visits throughout North Africa, as well as to Yemen. In particular, the Moroccan community, with which I spent so much time during those many years, left me with the warmest memories.

How much has changed though. The North Africa I first encountered in late 1952 was home to more than 500,000 Jews. They were already fewer than those who had belonged to the vibrant, if often intensely poor, communities that had endured for centuries in every country along the Mediterranean coast from the Atlantic to Suez. They were the communities that remained after the departures sparked by Israel's independence and that continued to wane steadily as the colonial era in the region wound down.

It seems incredible that barely half a century later, only 7,000 Jews live in the entire region. Like the Eastern European communities of my childhood (though, thankfully, for different reasons), the scantest shadow remains of this great Jewry.

⇜ Israel and the Yeshiva Program

JDC in Israel: An Overview

JDC's founding effort to bring relief to Jews in Palestine imperiled by the outbreak of World War I developed after the war to include social, economic, cultural, medical, agricultural, and educational reconstruction programs. It was during the interwar period, indeed, that JDC played a crucial role in laying foundations for the future state.

Following World War II, the Jewish Agency and Government of Israel, dealing with mass immigration from Muslim countries and DP camps, also had to provide for elderly, sick, and disabled immigrants. Since the newborn state had few institutions available for the thousands of blind, ailing, and physically limited newcomers, in 1949, the Government of Israel, the Jewish Agency, and JDC set up an organization called MALBEN (a Hebrew acronym for "Institutions for the Care of Disadvantaged Immigrants") that would provide for the needs of these immigrants. MALBEN set up hospitals, clinics, protected homes, and even a village for the blind. After a short time, JDC was given full responsibility for the MALBEN program. Thousands of handicapped and chronically ill immigrants were accommodated in institutions built or bought by MALBEN.

In 1975, an agreement was reached with the government by which the Ministry of Health and Ministry of Welfare would take over responsibility for the institutions. But JDC's role in Israel did not end. Instead, it transformed its work to become a social service "R & D" organization, working with the Israeli government to develop new and more effective services and thereby strengthen the Israelis' own capacity to meet their citizens' needs.

Israel, indeed, has a special place in JDC's work, just as it does in the life of the Jewish people. It is the only country in which the organization has worked continuously throughout the years since its founding and is the only country from which it has no aspirations of phasing out.

Including Yeshivot in its Responsibilities

In the pre-state years, *Eretz Yisrael* was not yet a major center of yeshiva study. In 1919, when Palestine had a Jewish population of 55,000, there were only several hundred yeshiva students and a handful of teachers and administrators. But already then, JDC saw the importance of sustaining the religious and educational institutions that instilled Jewish cultural heritage in *Eretz Yisrael*.

The oldest yeshiva in Israel, Etz Haim, founded in 1855 in Jerusalem, became a beneficiary of JDC support throughout the pre-state period. The Merkaz Harav Yeshiva, founded in 1924 by Rabbi Avraham Yitzhak Hacohen Kook,[1] likewise received backing from JDC. In 1929, JDC also gave assistance to the Hebron Yeshiva when it moved to Jerusalem after twenty-four of its students were killed in the pogrom in Hebron that year. In the 1930s, as refugees started arriving in Palestine after Hitler's rise to power and many gravitated toward yeshivot, JDC increased its overall funding for these institutions.

The years of World War II and the Holocaust further intensified JDC's commitment to the yeshivot in Palestine. During these years, the Nazis practically obliterated the great religious centers of Europe, along with their communities. JDC tracked and supported the few surviving scholars who made their way to *Eretz Yisrael*, either directly from the towns and DP camps of war-ravaged Europe or by a roundabout route, through Siberia to Japan, on to Shanghai, and then to Palestine.

The Mir yeshiva endured the relocation — from what was then part of Poland (now Belarus), via Shanghai and finally to Palestine — in group form, tens of students arriving together under the leadership of Rabbi Eliezer Finkel.[2] A few other yeshivot also managed to arrive in Palestine as small

---

1. Rabbi Avraham Yitzhak Hacohen Kook (1864–1935) was appointed the first Ashkenazi chief rabbi of Israel in 1921.
2. Once they left Shanghai, the Mir Yeshiva divided into two groups. While one arrived in Israel, the other was reestablished in Brooklyn, New York, headed by Rabbi Avraham Kalmanovitch.

groups, among them the Slobodka (Hebron) yeshiva and the Petah Tikvah (Lomza) yeshiva.

In other cases, survivors of Hasidic dynasties made their way to Palestine independently. Once there, they opened yeshivot for their followers, all of whom were individuals determined to resurrect the Jewish life that had been mercilessly taken from them. Among them were the Ger Hasidim in Jerusalem, Viznitz in Bnei Brak, Belz, and Lubavitch. The Beit Avraham yeshiva was founded in Jerusalem in 1941 by a Slonim Hasid to commemorate the destroyed Torat Hesed yeshiva of Baranovitch, Poland. Some young and previously unaffiliated students arriving in British Mandate Palestine would gravitate toward various yeshivot of their choice.

Non-Hasidic groups such as Ponevez and other "Lithuanians"[3] also opened yeshivot in the country. The Ponevez yeshiva was then the largest in Palestine, started in Bnei Brak by the famous Rabbi Yossef Shlomo Kahaneman. It was in these first years following World War II, indeed, that Bnei Brak became the center for religious Jews and their educational institutions that it remains today.

By JDC's count, a total of thirty-three yeshivot were reestablished in *Eretz Yisrael* during and immediately after the war, and many of them received JDC aid. In their new environment, the yeshivot began to grow again, gradually at first, until some became enormous establishments.

JDC's overseas director general at that time, Dr. Joseph Schwartz, observed the early attempts at rebuilding religious institutions in Israel and proposed a bold step for JDC: to support the reconstruction and rehabilitation of yeshivot in Israel. He considered it JDC's duty to rebuild, particularly in Israel, the tradition and practice of Jewish learning that had been virtually annihilated in Europe.

The Yeshiva Program Takes Shape

Following the JDC board's acceptance of Dr. Schwartz's proposal, JDC's Yeshiva Program became an organized Israel-based activity in 1948. The director of JDC activities in Israel and the Near East in 1948 was Charles

---

3. The "Lithuanian" or "Litvak" stream of Orthodoxy refers to adherents of a more intellectual approach to Judaism and Jewish study, as distinct from the more spiritual or mystical approach of the Hasidim.

Passman, a former American who had settled in Israel in the 1920s. He was assisted in the Yeshiva Program by American-born Rabbi Yaakov Goldman, former secretary to Israel's Chief Rabbi Isaac Herzog. While JDC's support was intended primarily to facilitate and support the growth in Israel of the Torah institutions destroyed in Europe, it also encouraged the opening of vocational yeshivot to provide training for those not suited to full-time study and to prepare personnel for communal services, such as rabbis, ritual slaughterers, and circumcisers.

During the siege of Jerusalem, in the midst of Israel's 1948 War of Independence, JDC subsidized a food distribution center that provided for many needy yeshiva students and rabbis.[4] This distribution center had been established by Vaad Hayeshivot (the Yeshiva Council), an organization originally founded in 1929 in Lithuania by Rabbi Chaim Ozer Grodzinski.[5] It had become the umbrella organization for the yeshivot of Eastern Europe, raising and distributing substantial funds to most of them. In 1945, immediately after the war, Vaad Hayeshivot was reconstituted in Israel by Rabbi Zalman Sorotzkin.[6] All yeshivot in Israel — Lithuanian, Hasidic, even Sephardic — became members of the Vaad, and it was with its help that almost all the larger yeshivot in Israel were inaugurated.[7] JDC's support of yeshivot would continue hand-in-hand with Vaad Hayeshivot, working together to help sustain and strengthen them.

Augmenting JDC's subventions were funds from the JRSO (Jewish Restitution Successor Organization), disbursed mainly in the form of capital-investment grants. The JDC program also extended loans to the institutions for capital investment, in addition to financial support for maintenance.

In 1948, JDC was supporting 41 yeshivot in the new state, with a total enrollment of 2,950 young men. Before long, the program's scope far exceeded

---

4. Dr. Sara Kadosh, "JDC in Jerusalem 1914–2004" (presentation based on archival material in the JDC Archives in Jerusalem, JDC-New York, February 8, 2006).
5. Rabbi Chaim Ozer Grodzinski (1863–1940) was the unofficial and highly revered chief rabbi of Vilna from 1885.
6. Rabbi Zalman Sorotzkin (1881–1966) was the rabbi of Lutsk, Poland, until he fled to Palestine in the midst of World War II.
7. The Vaad, now directed by Rabbi Asher Tannenbaum, maintains lists of all yeshiva students who are exempt from army service. In 2005, this list consisted of about 45,000 students aged seventeen to thirty-five, out of a total yeshiva student population of approximately 80,000.

JDC's earlier support of yeshivot in Eastern Europe and pre-state Palestine, such that by the mid-1950s, the number of institutions receiving JDC subvention exceeded 100.

The program was of immense significance. Without it, this uniquely Jewish form of study might not have reemerged as it did. Although by no means an Orthodox organization, JDC was deeply committed to the growth of Torah study in Israel. Moe Leavitt, executive vice president of JDC headquarters in New York who was not a particularly religious Jew, related to me that he had been asked by Prime Minister David Ben-Gurion to shift the JDC yeshiva budget to secular Zionist causes. "Show me an institution," Mr. Leavitt replied, "that has done as much for the Jewish people's survival as yeshivot, and I'll transfer the money to it." Ben-Gurion fell silent.

Toward a Lasting Contribution

By the mid-1950s, JDC came around to the belief that the emergency phase of its work for yeshivot in Israel had ended and that the time had come for long-term planning and for more professional management of this program. The increase in the number of yeshivot and their enrollment had become a strain on JDC's staff and budget, out of proportion to the board's original intentions for the program.

Judah Shapiro, director of the JDC Education Department at Paris headquarters, sent JDC's religious education consultant in New York, Rabbi Shlomo Tarshansky — a great Talmudic scholar and a former JDC staff member in Warsaw — to Israel to review the Yeshiva Program and submit his recommendations. Rabbi Tarshansky's most controversial recommendation was that JDC should cease to support *kollel* students (married yeshiva students) over the age of twenty-nine, unless they were particularly gifted. JDC accepted Rabbi Tarshansky's recommendations and in 1956 appointed Rabbi Dr. Aaron Greenbaum, a former pulpit rabbi in the United States, to implement them and supervise the program.

Widening Responsibilities

Rabbi Greenbaum proved to be exceedingly capable, establishing and running what was formally called the JDC Education-Religious-Cultural Department in Israel, but that was almost universally known as the Yeshiva Department.

Restructuring the program skillfully and judiciously, he earned the respect of his main "customers," the yeshiva rectors, who spanned the entire Orthodox spectrum. Under Rabbi Greenbaum's tutelage, the program's recipients included institutions as diverse as the Hasidic Yeshivat Sanz, Kollel Hasidei Gur, and Bobov institutions; "Lithuanian" yeshivot such as Brisk, Hebron, Mir, and Ponevez; Merkaz ha'Hinukh ha'Atzma'i (the administration for Ashkenazi non-Zionist religious elementary and secondary schools under the Agudath Israel movement); and independent Haredi yeshivot, such as Yeshivat Toldot Aharon, Yeshivat Meah She'arim, and Satmar institutions. Later years saw the addition of *hesder* yeshivot, which made their debut in the early 1970s and in which students spend three years at study as part of a five-year commitment to the Israel Defense Forces; and yeshivot for ethnic groups, such as a yeshiva for Jews of Afghan extraction (Netiv Binyamin Afghanistan), a yeshiva for Bukharan Jews, and another for Georgian Jews.

Yeshiva high schools were also increasingly included in JDC's Yeshiva Program. Whereas in 1949 three such schools were receiving JDC support, by 1974, the number had reached twenty-six, encompassing 3,800 students. Vocational yeshiva high schools received particular encouragement from JDC, and were especially advocated by Rabbi Dr. Leo Jung, chairman of the JDC board's Committee on Religious-Cultural Affairs. For a while, JDC covered 60 percent of the costs incurred for vocational programs. Three postsecondary technical training yeshivot that had been established by the early 1970s also received JDC support.

By the early 1970s, JDC was contributing to the support of 157 various yeshivot, with an enrollment of 25,110. They included students at the secondary level and beyond, married students up to the age of twenty-nine, students combining their religious studies with army service and those combining them with vocational studies.

JDC's support of the yeshivot augmented the institutions' limited budgets, which depended on modest grants from the government, fundraising, and fees from those who could afford it. The students of yeshiva high schools of all kinds were mainly from needy families, so beyond being unable to pay for their tuition and board, the meals offered in the yeshivot were an important part of their basic nutrition, and the boarding facilities were often an attraction for those whose families could not always take care of them.

With this in mind, JDC support included food programs. These were based on capitation allowances and — as in JDC's programs in northern Africa — in part on USDA (United States Department of Agriculture) supplies. However, these supplies were terminated in the late 1970s, when the US government determined that Israel was no longer an area of priority for such provisions. In the 1980s, the Swiss government donated milk powder in quantities that sufficed for the manufacture and distribution to yeshivot of many tons of cheese. To this day, I meet yeshiva rectors who recall with great appreciation the remarkable quantities of grain, rice, oil, and other commodities their institutions received through JDC.

With the overall needs of the yeshivot in mind, JDC's yeshiva budget was also designed to address various other aspects of the institutions' operations. A large percentage of the budget was allocated to capitation (per capita) grants, which were made to institutions on the basis of enrollment. Other funds were used to help yeshivot buy kitchen equipment, dormitory furniture, solar water-heating systems, and other physical necessities, and to facilitate yeshiva management (such as providing administrators with training in food management). Between 1948 and 1970, JDC guided and assisted in remodeling and/or furnishing 120 yeshiva kitchens and dining halls. JDC also made sure that the study halls were well illuminated and that each and every student had a bookstand and a seat.

Yeshiva building construction and renovation were not JDC's focus, but occasionally grants for this purpose were provided. During the 1967 Six-Day War, a few of the yeshivot in Jerusalem were damaged by Jordanian fire and JDC provided help in repairing or rebuilding these institutions. Also following the Six-Day War, JDC provided support for the founding of Yeshivat Hakotel in Jerusalem's Old City.[8]

Unable and unwilling to turn a blind eye to the general needs and wellbeing of JDC's yeshiva beneficiaries and their families, some of the organization's activities branched from the narrow definition of yeshiva support. In its earlier days, the Yeshiva Program assisted refugee rabbis who had found their way to Israel after Word War II and met with hard times. At its peak in 1960, this part of the program assisted more than 500 refugee rabbis through JDC-supported organizations. Their numbers declined over time as recipients

8.   Dr. Sara Kadosh, "JDC in Jerusalem 1914–2004" (presentation based on archival material in the JDC Archives in Jerusalem, JDC-New York, February 8, 2006).

became established in Israel, others passed away, and fewer and fewer Jews reached Israel as refugee rabbis.

Three convalescent homes run by Vaad Hayeshivot for the benefit of yeshiva rabbis and students — one in Jerusalem, one in Ramat Gan, and one in Netanya — also received JDC assistance. Unfortunately, these homes were closed over the years as the Vaad did not have sufficient funds for repairs and maintenance and their buildings deteriorated.

JDC developed a comprehensive health insurance program for yeshiva students and dependents, working through the Mifal Hatorah organization. Mifal Hatorah[9] was a parallel organization to Vaad Hayeshivot, established in Israel in 1950 for the distribution of funds for so-called "Zionist" yeshivot, such as Bnei Akiva, Noam, and similar institutions. With our health insurance program, yeshiva students and their families were able to benefit from the health services, including dental care, that Mifal Hatorah then provided. In this way, we assisted 18,000 individuals by 1974. This JDC program slowly decreased thereafter, as Mifal Hatorah experienced financial difficulties and as national health maintenance organizations replaced the need for separate and private health insurance. (The entire population in Israel belonged to one or another of these national health organizations, known as *kupot holim*.)

Helping Overseas Communities

Though Israel-based, the Yeshiva Program also undertook activities in the Diaspora that were related to the Jewish calendar and lifecycle events. It provided communities in Europe, as well as South America, India, and the Far East, with religious necessities and services, including scholarships for students who wished to become rabbis, ritual slaughterers, circumcisers, and scribes, or fill other religious functions in their respective communities. For communities too small to provide scholarship candidates, rabbis from Israel were posted for general duties or short-term service on the High Holidays and for communal Pesach seders.

Locating Funds

In 1971, the Yeshiva Department began to administer the Rothschild

---

9.   The Mifal Hatorah organization no longer functions.

Foundation ("Yad Hanadiv") Free Loan Fund.[10] It provided loans for various emergency needs of individuals, such as health care, home renovation, and aid for young couples settling down after marriage. Other funds for yeshivot in Israel were raised from the Central Funds for Traditional Institutions — individual Jewish community chests in Cleveland, Detroit, and Toronto. Cooperation with these Central Funds became long term as the JDC Yeshiva Department was asked to administer their annual allocations.

Friendship and Skills: Rabbi Dr. Aaron Greenbaum

The astounding scope of activity within JDC's Yeshiva Program was due to Rabbi Greenbaum's appreciable management skills. In fact, every superlative lavished on him was deserved. Our personal friendship had begun in Iran and Morocco, when together we visited schools, Talmud Torahs, and yeshivot in those communities during my tenures as education director. After moving to Israel, I likewise often accompanied him on his visits to yeshivot.

A Talmudic scholar who loved to research old manuscripts, Rabbi Greenbaum was able to enter any classroom and immediately participate in the Talmudic discussion that was taking place. He would pose questions on the Talmud sections being studied and occasionally made the principals and the teachers ill at ease when the students had difficulties in answering his questions. The yeshiva staff and students gladly looked upon his visits as an occasion to discuss their financial and material needs.

Rabbi Greenbaum was a wonderful, kind, and very wise person. I consider my acquaintance with him a privilege and a pleasure. Working together we became more than coworkers. We were friends.

Taking Over the Program

JDC and its education programs in the North African countries and Europe had reached milestones and achievements that made it possible for me to disengage gradually from my responsibilities in those regions. Late in 1982, JDC offered me the post that Dr. Judah Shapiro had originally suggested when I arrived in Paris in 1952, and which I had turned down: management of the

---

10. After Rabbi Greenbaum died in 1987, the fund was renamed — at Yad Hanadiv's suggestion — the Aaron Greenbaum Memorial Free Loan Fund.

Yeshiva Program in Israel. This time, I accepted the assignment. It was agreed that Rabbi Greenbaum would retire at the end of 1982, at age seventy, and that I would take over on January 1, 1983.

The usual lack of prior briefing for this program was of no serious consequence. I had been living in Israel for over ten years by then and knew the Yeshiva Program well. Besides being a yeshiva alumnus myself, I had felt drawn toward the Yeshiva Program that Rabbi Greenbaum was directing, and the time I spent with him visiting yeshivot had familiarized me with the institutions and the personalities involved. That said, I was, at this point, still an outsider, having accompanied Rabbi Greenbaum more as a colleague and a friend than in any official capacity. In late 1982, Rabbi Greenbaum and I coordinated a period of transition to enable me to assume the position with relative ease.

Part of the duties of my new position involved budgeting and long-term planning. I would now be entrusted with controlling and disbursing a budget, something I had not done since leaving Iran thirty years earlier. In the 1980s, the annual JDC yeshiva allocation from New York headquarters was $1 million-$1.5 million, to be disbursed, in the main part, in consultation with Rabbi Leo Jung and the Committee on Religious-Cultural Affairs that he chaired. In fact, all matters concerning the department answered directly to the Committee on Religious-Cultural Affairs in New York.

Unlike all my previous experiences with JDC — the DP camps, Iran, North Africa, and Europe — the unstated fourth 'R' in the JDC slogan "Rescue, Relief, Rehabilitation, and *Retreat* (phaseout)" did not apply to the Yeshiva Program at that time. Those who fashioned the program intended the JDC support of yeshivot to be long lasting. Support of Torah institutions was considered a lifelong task, not a gesture or a limited undertaking. Few, if any, Torah establishments could maintain themselves without outside help. The yeshivot in Israel were not different in this respect from such institutions in prewar Europe or in other parts of the Jewish world.

Practicality in the Service of Creed

The Yeshiva Program was as much a one-man operation as JDC ever allowed. I had two secretaries and an accountant, but no assistant. Leonard Rosenfeld, a former head of the New York Board of Jewish Education, and a close friend, helped out with consultations on a voluntary basis. Although the department had its offices in Jerusalem, at the headquarters of JDC-Israel,[11] it was independent of this part of the JDC organization and I was, administratively, a member of JDC's New York staff. Nevertheless, the Yeshiva Department could call on JDC-Israel in a friendly way if needed.

I took over the program with an "attitude," a sense of mission that transcended my previous appointments. Several years into the position, in the midst of a budget crunch, I explained my perspective to the JDC leadership:[12]

> The survival of Jewry as a distinct and identifiable people should be the concern of every Jew and surely of responsible Jewish communal leadership. Conversely, assimilation, or the disappearance of Jewry as a visible distinct group is the major threat facing Jewish individuals and communities everywhere.
>
> Assimilation takes on many forms. Its gross manifestations are religious conversion and intermarriage ... But there is a more subtle form of assimilation that has been equally virulent ... Its key ingredients are ignorance, alienation and abandonment of the cultural heritage and mores of Jewry and Judaism ... This loss of Jewish identity also spells assimilation and "exodus." It is often more "final" than conversion or intermarriage ...
>
> In Israel ... there are significant population groups ... who, out of ignorance or abandonment do not identify with the mainstream of the Jewish people ... with its history or with its destiny ... with its religion, with its culture, with its practices and with its mores ...
>
> An aggressive and an all-pervading program of formal and informal education plus collateral communal action can stamp out Jewish ignorance and non-involvement ... But to succeed, the education ... cannot be merely objectively informational ... It must be rich in Jewish culture, rich in Jewish ideals and rich in Jewish aspirations.
>
> Its aims must be not only to make us wiser but also better, not only more knowledgeable but totally committed — committed to

---

11. JDC-Israel is the arm of JDC that works in partnership with the country's government and non-profit agencies to enhance the social services that Israel provides to its vulnerable citizens.

12. Stanley Abramovitch, *Annual Report 1989–1990 of the Educational Religious Cultural Department* (Jerusalem: The American Jewish Joint Distribution Committee, December 1990), 5–7.

our country, committed to our people, committed to our Torah and committed to our God; committed to our history and committed to our future ...

This is the big "plus" of Yeshiva education as compared to general education. Its entire curriculum focuses on a single goal: uncompromising commitment to our land — Israel, to our people — Israel and to the Torah of Israel.

This is the key ingredient for the total survival of Jewry and Judaism — everywhere.

... The contemporary growing threat of assimilatory forces, therefore, dictates a greater vigilance, dictates a more aggressive approach and dictates an expansion of JDC educational programs in Israel and in the Diaspora.

Ideals aside, the JDC Yeshiva Program was a practical one that demanded practical attention. For the most part, I gladly adopted the administrative system that my predecessor had so efficiently constructed. But I was also able to implement my own ideas and strategies.

Hands-on Yeshiva Visits

As the program director, I took it upon myself to visit as many yeshivot as I could each year to keep abreast of developments in the field. These visits were ideal, combining pleasure with utility. With each visit, one learns something not only about the yeshiva but also about Jewish life and tradition. Since it is customary for the yeshiva rector to inaugurate such a visit with a *d'var Torah* (a brief Torah insight), the visitor inevitably learns a little more about the interpretation of a Biblical verse, a Talmudic dictum, or a slice of Jewish wisdom.

A personal pleasure that I gained from these visits was to run across, every once in a while, former students of the schools in Morocco that I had supervised while JDC's education consultant there. These encounters always brought me great surprise and gratification. A number of these students had managed to attain prominent positions in the Israeli yeshiva world. By now, the timid boys whom I had once tested in Jewish knowledge were grown family men, unrecognizable beneath their thick, dark beards. Of course, they were the ones to approach me on my yeshiva visits, reminding me of their backgrounds, and telling me with a chuckle how they had shuddered with apprehension when their school teachers informed them that the "inspector" was coming to test them.

From the professional standpoint, the challenges lay in helping to adjust administrative practices in yeshivot where necessary. As Orthodox institutions, yeshivot concentrated on learning and spiritual aspects, all the while relegating physical needs and facilities to a secondary position in their priorities. Thus, we insisted that attention be given to physical facilities in the kitchens, dining rooms, dormitories, and bathrooms. The introduction of computers under JDC's financing and guidance was to help yeshivot to keep up-to-date lists of students and to improve the level of bookkeeping, records of donors, and the details of income from different sources.

Despite our different focus on the administrative and physical facilities of the yeshivot, we were able to work with the yeshivot in a way that retained their trust. Indeed, JDC's success in working with the Orthodox — even today — lies in the ability it has displayed since the 1920s to maintain its bona fides with yeshivot of almost all kinds and to introduce necessary adjustments and advancement without arousing strong opposition or problems. Importantly, *hakarat hatov* — recognizing the good — is a quality that yeshiva study instills, and the rectors, both before and during my tenure, in Europe and in Israel, consistently expressed appreciation of any new ideas that were put forth.

Funds and Fundraising

Over the years, the government increased its support of the yeshivot in Israel. At one time it covered 25–70 percent of yeshiva expenses, depending on the type of institution. Those associated with government programs, such as yeshiva high schools and *hesder* yeshivot, would receive a higher percentage. The yeshivot still had to raise the remainder on their own.

Fundraising trips abroad are regular and often unpleasant events in most yeshiva rectors' lives. This necessity, I recognized, was not new to many of the yeshiva representatives. In fact, I heard an amusing story from Rabbi Avraham Kalmanovitch of the Mir Yeshiva in New York about his fundraising efforts before the war. It was his custom then to travel once a year from Mir in Poland to the United States to raise funds for his yeshiva. On one such occasion, he took with him a group photograph of the yeshiva students to show the JDC leadership and other potential donors. One of the JDC board members remarked with a raised eyebrow that the yeshiva boys seemed to be very well dressed in new suits. Rabbi Kalmanovitch answered with some embarrassment that in fact they had only a couple of these suits at the yeshiva. Now more eyebrows were raised in question. Each boy, the rabbi explained, had donned one of the suits for an individual photograph and then passed it on to the next student. Once all the students had been photographed, the yeshiva carefully combined all of the individual photographs to form the group image that was set before the board.

In the 1990s, as the economic situation in Israel improved, yeshivot began to engage in local fundraising as well. In order to assist in this task, a consultant was appointed by my department to give guidance and encouragement for this fundraising activity, with promising results.

Most of the time, though, encouragement of fundraising activities was not enough. The Yeshiva Department needed to continue supplying funds to the yeshiva institutions on a regular basis, since government support and fundraising still did not cover all the needs. The Yeshiva Department continued to administer the Free Loan Fund that had come under its wing in 1971, and which by the year 2005 had furnished more than 16,000 loans for married yeshiva students. The department also continued to receive grants from the Cleveland, Detroit, and Toronto Central Funds for Traditional Institutions. From New York, Rabbi Jung forwarded sums that he had raised through channels of his own.

For a number of years, the author Herman Wouk, as founder and administrator of the Abe Wouk Foundation, entrusted the Yeshiva Department with substantial funds for loans to married yeshiva students who faced serious emergencies. Although disbursing these particular funds was not formally part of my JDC responsibilities and although it put my secretary and the accounting staff to considerable work, the department did so willingly, with the knowledge that it was necessary for its client population.

Servicing the Diaspora

Being a division of an international organization, I considered it essential from the outset that the Yeshiva Department continue providing services in the Diaspora. JDC offices in different countries and key persons in communities were reminded that they could contact the Yeshiva Department for referrals if or when they required the services of religious personnel. Receiving such requests, I would call appropriate yeshivot in Israel and ask them to canvas their students for candidates. When a request included financial help for communities of the Diaspora, I could sometimes arrange it through other sources.

In this manner, the Yeshiva Department was able to continue assisting other JDC overseas programs. Since the 1970s, the Yeshiva Department had provided cantors and prayer books for Soviet Jews in transit in Italy. Likewise, in the 1980s, we arranged the same for Jewish refugees in Vienna and Rome. We sent out ritual slaughterers for the communities of Cairo and Alexandria. We organized religious supplies, such as matzoth and wine, prayer books and Bibles, for communities in Romania, Hungary, and Poland — and more recently in the former Soviet Union — just as I had done during the period of my responsibilities in these countries.

Controversy and Change

As the years passed, JDC's support of yeshivot became a topic of dispute within the organization. A new generation had joined the JDC board, and some of the new members, unlike their predecessors, could not comprehend why JDC should support yeshivot at all. After all, the original task of assisting the reestablishment of destroyed institutions had been fully accomplished. With other major challenges emerging, they asked, might the funds not be better used elsewhere? To my regret, headquarters agreed that the time for phaseout had come. The praiseworthy guiding principle of lifelong commitment to yeshiva support was already being contested.

Firm in my belief that the Yeshiva Department remained a necessary branch of JDC, I made it my personal challenge to sustain the program and demonstrate its effectiveness to the organization. I knew that any support that the Yeshiva Department desired — whether with the encouragement of Rabbi Jung or directly from JDC headquarters — would not be forthcoming if I limited myself to the existing activities of the Yeshiva Department. New ideas and a different approach were the order of the day.

Project-Focused Yeshiva Support

First of all, I decided to abolish the capitation grants, a funding method that the lay leaders found particularly objectionable. Over the years, domestic inflation, declining purchasing power of the dollar, an increase in the number of yeshivot in Israel, and a large uptrend in yeshiva enrollment meant that the same amount of JDC funding had to be stretched over an ever-growing population. JDC support thus became far less significant to each individual yeshiva. Without capitation, the budget would indeed stretch further and enhance the department's impact. However, instead of fomenting confrontations with yeshiva administrators by terminating the grants in one stroke, the program phased them out gradually and replaced them with a purely project-focused orientation.

Outreach

The first new project was outreach, initiated in 1992. The Yeshiva Department forwarded funds to institutions and organizations that would encourage yeshiva students and graduates to organize learning groups for people — especially immigrants, who were arriving in vast numbers, mostly from the former Soviet Union — who wished to learn more about their tradition. This step was taken with two goals in mind. First, it would provide yeshiva graduates with an opportunity to contribute to the community at large while earning some keep from the grants. Second, it would increase accessibility to religious study in Israel for the general public.

The idea proved successful; the outreach programs that JDC initiated and supported grew to include tens of thousands of part-time students. The benefits to Israeli society were outstanding too. To this day, every officer-training course in the Israel Defense Forces allots time for study of Jewish tradition. The most famous army units have regular study sessions. Several nonreligious kibbutzim, where this type of learning was unknown in the past, started study groups. In all kinds of localities — towns, moshavim, and kibbutzim — one can find regular study of Jewish tradition that began with encouragement from JDC.

A fine example is in Eilat. This resort town on the Red Sea, at Israel's southern tip, is certainly not known as a center of traditional Jewish study. However, when a group of fourteen young yeshiva families, graduates of Jerusalem's Yeshivat Merkaz Harav, settled there in the late 1970s and early 1980s with support and cooperation from the municipal religious and secular authorities, JDC stepped in with financial support for their effort. Over the years, the young families developed programs that attracted wide sections of the town's population, earning the municipality's commendation as an important enhancement of local life.

In Eilat today, *kollel* students teach in the town's general (nonreligious) schools. Their wives teach, give lectures, and offer tours of the area that emphasize the history of and Jewish connection to Eilat and its environs. Nonreligious kibbutzim near Eilat, including one affiliated with the American Reform movement, have invited *kollel* members to preside over weekly study sessions. Moreover, the group, known as Orot Eilat, set up (also with JDC's support) a central exhibition of Jewish religious items, demonstrating the method of their production. The exhibition has attracted tens of thousands of school students and is visited frequently by all the schools in Eilat.

Other yeshiva outreach programs across the country arrange day, weekend, or weeklong seminars on Jewish festivals, which are attended by all sections of the population, including those with rudimentary knowledge of Jewish tradition. Every year these programs continue to reach 25,000–30,000 people on a more or less regular basis. JDC also provided support for a program that arranges for underprivileged children to be tutored by *kollel* students.

Immigrants

A particular yeshiva outreach program that has been supported by JDC has targeted new immigrants. Under the management of a movement called Arachim ("Values"), a number of past yeshiva students and other scholars are in touch with thousands of immigrants in a countrywide program that offers religious instruction, lectures, and experiences. Focus has been placed on two immigrant groups: the hundreds of thousands of Jews from the former Soviet Union whose severe lack of Jewish knowledge has barred them from meaningful participation in Israeli Jewish life; and those from Ethiopia, whose religious background is so different from Jewish tradition in Israel that it further complicates their integration into Israeli society. Arachim runs informal weekends, Pesach celebrations, and other holiday gatherings, all of which provide immigrant participants with traditional Jewish family experiences.

Yedidim ("Friends"), another outreach program that JDC supported, enables yeshiva high school students to mentor students in primary schools. The high school students help the youngsters with homework, and together they participate in organized Shabbat programs. Several thousand immigrant and nonimmigrant youngsters participate in this program.

Another JDC-supported program, called Ahi ("My Brother"), organized groups of Israeli students from yeshiva high schools and general yeshivot to spend weekends in new settlements and communities that have large Russian-immigrant populations. A student group would share the entire Shabbat with the immigrant children, teenagers, and parents, providing them with a weekend filled with Jewish atmosphere. This helped to develop an interest in Jewish tradition and life among the immigrant population.

Other similar programs intended to help bridge the religious-cultural gaps between immigrants and veteran Israelis were, with JDC's encouragement and financial support, added to these over the years.

Prisoner Rehabilitation

Another type of yeshiva outreach that JDC assisted aimed to rehabilitate prisoners by encouraging them to begin studying Jewish tradition and imbibe its moral lessons. The Israel Prison Service had been making efforts to combat recidivism by working in conjunction with kibbutzim, small settlements, and other parts of the community where prisoners could be placed on work-release and in halfway houses. This sparked a yeshiva initiative to draw the prisoners toward the religious segment by setting up study groups in prisons and absorbing graduates of these study circles in yeshivot.

The activity began at Beersheba Prison, the country's largest, where the project was given a separate building. There, as in the other facilities that replicated the program, volunteer instructors from yeshivot served as teachers. The students, once they completed their sentences, were encouraged to enroll in yeshivot to reinforce what they had learned and to prevent the recidivism that would probably occur if they returned to their former lifestyles. The host yeshivot then provided the requisite new environment by arranging the resettlement of participating ex-prisoners and, if they were married, their families in places where their past was unknown. The yeshivot found the prisoners part-time work so that they would be able to support themselves while continuing to study part-time.

The program brought unique challenges; its success was impeded by a few participants who brought drug addictions to their new lives. Rabbi Avraham Chazan, whom I had known from earlier years in Casablanca where he had functioned as a teacher for Alliance and the École Normale Hébraïque, became chaplain of Israel Police and set up a program called Teshuva ("Repentance") that included a halfway house in Jerusalem for ex-convicts who wished to start anew. This program received JDC support, and other yeshivot emulated its approach. Some of these institutions failed, however, reporting that the former prisoners used their freedom to steal in order to buy drugs.

Even so, some students at several yeshivot — former convicts who had served lengthy prison terms and who were once heavy drug abusers — became indistinguishable from their fellow yeshiva students. In one very successful case, a former prisoner became a learned Talmudic scholar and went on to open his own yeshiva. By 2005, hundreds of prisoners had been rehabilitated thanks to such prisoner rehabilitation programs and the intervention of the yeshiva students, teachers, and administrators who carry out this challenging and praiseworthy work.

On the whole, this model of rehabilitation-through-religion and yeshivot proved much more successful than any other similar rehabilitation program and more than justified the support JDC provided for it over the years.

Learning Disabilities

Yeshivot, like other learning institutions, have underachievers and others who fall to the wayside because of learning disabilities. In part, this reflects liberal yeshiva admission policies; it also expresses the yeshiva world's reluctant recognition that no form of schooling offers a solution that can help each and every learning-disabled student.

We at JDC encouraged the opening of yeshivot for underachievers and the learning disabled. One such outstanding institution is a vocational yeshiva high school, Nachlat Har Chabad (established by Lubavitch) in Kiryat Malakhi, a northern Negev "development town"[13] that was settled largely with disadvantaged immigrants from northern Africa. There are about seventy students in this yeshiva, most of whom were referred by the Ministry of Labor and Social Affairs. The yeshiva gives these boys, many of whom have already been in other institutions and failed to progress academically or emotionally, the attention, care, and love that they need. Although all the students there are hard-core cases, they are managing to embark on steady vocational learning tracks and prepare for constructive future lives.

JDC's contribution in this case, and for eight other such institutions across the country, lay in its ability to persuade the yeshivot to hire professional

---

13. The Israeli government established some thirty "development towns" in the 1950s to be populated with newly landed immigrants, mostly from Muslim countries. Some of these towns did well but many remain underprivileged to this day.

personnel (psychologists, special educators, social workers, etc.) to help the rectors and teaching staff in handling this type of student population. Initially, JDC also participated in the costs of hiring the professional staff, who in the majority of cases have succeeded in helping handicapped students.

Women's Institutions

For years, JDC gave its backing to a range of yeshivot, but did not support girls' and women's institutions that provided similar learning opportunities. Indeed, many such institutions applied to JDC, but were turned down. By the 1990s, I found the exclusion of women's institutions out of step in an era when such gender distinctions had become untenable.

In 1993/94, a review of the yeshivot carried out by board members recommended that JDC change this policy. I had hoped that such a recommendation would mean additional funds for the Yeshiva Department, but only a small increase in the budget resulted. Nevertheless, the program adjusted its budgeting to benefit women's institutions and in the late 1990s provided financial and advisory support to as many as twenty such institutions in Israel, including several for underachieving and learning-disabled girls.

Preparatory Yeshivot

Beginning in the late 1980s, major developments occurred in the field of preparatory institutions for army service. Such institutions have included yeshivot offering educational and physical reinforcement for those who wished to join specific army units. Some religious students who face army induction wish to enhance their Jewish knowledge before they embark on their lengthy military service. The preparatory yeshivot that came into being in response to this interest and which multiplied to more than a dozen by 2005, immerse students in Jewish subjects for up to eighteen months, readying them to face the challenges of army service with strengthened religious identities. Considering these yeshivot worthy of additional support and encouragement, JDC's Yeshiva Department accorded them grants.

Skills Enhancement

In 1998 we introduced a one-time year-long course for yeshiva administrators that included guidance in office computerization and administrative efficiency. It was run with the assistance of JDC-ELKA — the Association for the Development and Advancement of Manpower in the Social Services in Israel. This association had been established in 1984 by JDC-Israel and the Government of Israel to provide senior government and other officials with training in management skills, with the ultimate goal of enhancing the quality and responsiveness of the services the public receives. Course graduates received certification from ELKA attesting to their participation in its courses, which assisted their professional advancement as well as their institutions' management.

In 2001, the Ministry of Labor and Social Affairs (Ministry of Welfare) came under the control of a Haredi (ultra-Orthodox) political party, Agudath Israel. The new minister invited a yeshiva administrator, whom he knew well, to become director general of the ministry — but the appointment required the approval of the Civil Service Commissioner, who requested evidence of the candidate's qualification for the position. The candidate produced the certificate he had received from ELKA as evidence of his administrative capabilities. His appointment was approved, and I later received a visit from the proud new director-general to thank JDC and ELKA for their assistance in preparing him for his important and prestigious appointment.

Ongoing Programs

In addition to the new projects that I initiated and which became a major focus in my work in the Yeshiva Department, several worthy projects already existing were further implemented and developed with JDC support. These included nutrition and health programs, which I proceeded to remodel in such a way that they would in fact help to stretch the yeshiva budgets.

Nutrition and Administration

In 1985, the Yeshiva Department organized seminars to guide yeshiva administrators and staff in providing balanced nutrition at minimum cost. Noting that the kibbutz movements had been buying in bulk for decades, it became clear to me that yeshivot could do the same if they pooled their needs. JDC was not positioned to engage itself in actual bulk buying and distribution for these institutions, so I contacted Gad Wilman of Kibbutz Ma'agan, whose book on nutrition and knowledge on bulk purchasing had come to my attention, and invited him to lecture and guide yeshiva personnel about food preparation, storage, and purchasing.

Gad Wilman became deeply committed to assisting the yeshivot with his knowledge and advice, and visited up to fifty institutions each year for many years to advise them on bulk purchasing and on running kitchens for groups. JDC conditioned further feeding support on implementation of his recommendations. What is more, we persuaded the yeshiva leaders to discuss the matter of bulk purchasing with Tnuva, Israel's mammoth cooperative that controls most of the country's produce market.

The fruits of these efforts soon became apparent. In 1990, the first group of yeshivot to undertake bulk purchasing had a combined purchasing power of $650,000 per month. Initially, the yeshivot elected to buy vegetables, insurance, haulage services, and banking services collectively at enormous savings.

Within a few years, even without a coherent program, these yeshivot were saving hundreds of thousands of dollars per year. JDC had given this purchasing activity a subvention at first, to cover the cost of coordinating the undertaking, but was able to phase out the support later on, when the yeshivot agreed — and became able — to cover their share. By 1995, the project costs were covered by a small commission deducted from the resulting savings. This project still has the greatest money-saving potential of all the projects supported by the Yeshiva Department. In fact, this program became one of the most significant in the material achievements of JDC's later involvement in the yeshivot. I owe tremendous gratitude for this advancement to Gad Wilman of Kibbutz Ma'agan.

Health Programs

In the 1960s and 1970s, JDC had supported health programs for yeshiva students and faculty — mainly clinics and maternity homes. Additional initiatives in this field were taken in the mid-1980s. At that time, the Yeshiva Department began a program that would promote dental care and oral hygiene, a much neglected area in Israel generally. Our Yeshiva Department recruited several dentists to volunteer half a day a week in the program. They would visit yeshivot and perform free examinations of students' teeth. Additionally, we arranged periodic lectures in yeshivot on dental hygiene. Since Israel has public dental clinics to which needy students may be referred, the goal was not to provide or arrange actual treatment but to enhance yeshiva administrators' awareness of the importance of their students' dental health.

Optical care is understandably of greater necessity among yeshiva students than the population at large. These students spend many hours each day intently bent over their books and analyzing the smallest of fonts. Yet optical care was neglected in this environment too. As with dentistry, it was awareness rather than insurance coverage that was the issue. In 1995, JDC — again in search of solutions that would require little or no budget — asked the head of ophthalmology at Shaare Zedek Medical Center in Jerusalem to devise a simple vision test that could be administered by yeshiva staff. For a number of years, the JDC Yeshiva Department did its best to encourage the yeshivot to make use of this test on a regular basis.

The Yeshiva Department Preserved

A Jubilee Milestone

In November 1995, the yeshivot joined forces to express their appreciation of JDC's work for them by organizing an evening to mark my fiftieth anniversary as a staff member of JDC. The event was attended by about 120 yeshiva rectors of all backgrounds — Ashkenazi, Lithuanian, Hasidic, *hesder* and Bnei Akiva (National-Religious), and Sephardi. All of them sat together, which was itself a remarkable scene given the realities of the Israeli Orthodox world. On that occasion, I received rabbinical ordination from a former chief rabbi of Israel, Rabbi Mordechai Eliyahu, and separate ordination from the chief rabbis of Jerusalem, Rabbi Shalom Messas and Rabbi Yitzhak Kolitz. Rabbi Simha Kook, chief rabbi of Rehovot, and Rabbi Ovadia Yossef, former Sephardic chief rabbi, added their own endorsements of these ordinations. All are towering scholars and I cannot fail to acknowledge the great personal honor that their action represented. However, I had to deny one notion that various participants held at that dinner; I had to make it clear that the occasion did not mark my retirement. This, I explained, was a jubilee milestone and not a parting call.

Downscaling the Program

Despite these plaudits for JDC's work and the efforts I and my department made to prove the necessity and benefits of the Yeshiva Program, our budget was cut. And as a growing number of board members pressed for available funds to be reallocated for other urgent needs in the Jewish world, such as those in the former Soviet Union, JDC board support for the Yeshiva Program continued to wane

I had often counted on support "from above" — from Rabbi Jung's Committee on Religious-Cultural Affairs and the board to which it answered. But through the late 1990s, with Rabbi Jung's advancing age and the shift in the organization's priorities to more dire material needs, even his influence and that of his committee was diminishing.

The results were inevitable. While continuing to develop and adjust programs to suit limited budgets, struggling to maintain the budget itself became a regular part of my job; I did not find it pleasurable.

We had to become tougher in weeding out non-qualifying yeshivot. For one thing, I discontinued — at the request of JDC headquarters in New York — support for anti-Israel institutions. We hardly accepted new institutions of any kind. Occasional exceptions were made for "yeshiva-plus" institutions — those that combine traditional study with vocational training, army service, community service, or other communal activities. We stopped providing funds for construction or renovation and eliminated the discretionary fund for emergencies. By the late 1990s, JDC no longer sponsored feeding programs extensively. Having less and less to offer those we had been helping, I gradually scaled down my visits to yeshivot.

The program's statistical records reflected this decline. Those statistics had once differentiated between yeshivot that received JDC support and those that didn't. In 1986, for example, the count was 170 of the former versus 97 of the latter. By 1992, financial support of yeshivot had already diminished to such an extent that the reports counted yeshivot that were merely "in contact" with JDC, i.e., not necessarily receiving any financial support from the organization, as well as those still receiving some financial backing. By 1997/98, when the Yeshiva Department issued its last annual report, the overall number of listed yeshivot had declined to 135, including 65 in "occasional contact" only.

The Yeshiva Program became an organizational anomaly and its continued existence, even on a drastically reduced scale, was itself in question. At the height of a JDC budget crisis in the 1990s, one important lay leader told me, "You know very well that if you were not sitting in this particular seat, JDC would have closed the Yeshiva Program long ago." This statement reflected the feeling among board members that JDC had fulfilled its mission to help restore yeshivot in Israel. As with many of our programs in Europe, the very fact that JDC had accomplished so much for the yeshivot made it legitimate to ask over again why we should continue.

JDC has always tried to avoid acting on the basis of political consider-ations and to stick to objective and professional needs. However, the political constellation in Israel in the 1990s, including intolerant and unwise attacks by Orthodox politicians on non-Orthodox Judaism, certainly did nothing to bolster support for the program within JDC. Furthermore, the Government of Israel, because of its internal political considerations, became increasingly willing to fund the yeshiva world by itself, and the country's growing affluence has endowed it with greater resources than JDC alone could marshal under any set of priorities.

In 2002, the annual JDC grant for the Yeshiva Program was stopped. Part of the funding that was once allocated for the yeshivot was instead redirected to a major vocational training program for married yeshiva students, a pro-gram undertaken by JDC-Israel in partnership with the Israeli government. This program provides an opportunity for these yeshiva students — many of them with large families to support — to obtain marketable skills, integrate into the workforce, and enjoy, as the program's name, Parnassa Bechavod, suggests, an honorable living.

Despite the official closure of the Yeshiva Program, I was left with some residual funds — a little that was unspent from previous years, interest income on endowments established to support the program's mission, and occa-sional donations, particularly from the Central Fund of Toronto. With these funds, JDC has been able to continue making one-time grants, with a focus on those institutions with which the Yeshiva Department had longstanding relationships.

It has remained my conviction that JDC, as an institution embracing all of Jewry, should not set its yeshiva support budget at zero. Still, I understand and accept the wider perspective of JDC board members who have an overall responsibility for Jewish requirements in more than sixty countries and must allocate limited JDC funds among many urgent and competing needs.

A Program to be Proud of

All said, JDC has made a major contribution to the rebuilding, development, and growth of the Torah institutions in Israel, and before that in Eastern Europe between the two world wars. The fact that the Yeshiva Program was an integral part of JDC activities for over eighty years has reflected the deep understanding of JDC board members for the need of rescuing not only Jewish lives, but also Jewish tradition and learning, which is a true foundation of Jewish life. That understanding remains deeply ingrained in the organization and continues to be strongly reflected in its work.

I take great pride in my connection with this aspect of JDC's work over many years.

The Former Soviet Union — Reconnecting Communities

Reentering the USSR — Through the Front Door

JDC was but a few months old when it first entered Russia to help Jews who had fallen into distress during World War I. First it helped those who were forcibly uprooted from their homes in Russia's border regions and driven eastward. Later it assisted those afflicted by the fallout from the Russian revolution and the savage pogroms that accompanied the Polish-Russian War of 1919–1921.

The terrible physical oppression of these years was a harbinger of another, no less relentless, oppression yet to come. The Bolsheviks who established the Union of Soviet Socialist Republics (USSR or the Soviet Union) opposed the religious, national, and community aspects of the Jewish people and so sought to destroy them. Gradually, they dissolved Jewish community administrations, banned religious institutions, confiscated well over 1,000 synagogues, targeted religious functionaries as enemies of the state, enforced Sabbath labor, banned study of the Hebrew language, and forbade the publication of religious or ethnic literature.

As the Soviet regime brutally collectivized the country, JDC's Agro-Joint program set up cooperatives and kolkhozy (collective farms) to help Jews survive and fit into the Communist economy. When Stalin's cruelties caused the kolkhoz policy to fail amidst famine, JDC food packages sustained masses of Jews in Ukraine and elsewhere.

JDC was officially forced to leave the Soviet Union in 1938, when Agro-Joint was wound up and its top professionals arrested, many never to be heard from again. JDC became known as "the Zionist spy organization" accused by the Kremlin of responsibility for the infamous Doctors' Plot of 1953. This was an alleged conspiracy of doctors, most of them Jews, to eliminate Soviet leadership by poisoning its members.

Until the late 1980s, overt manifestations of Jewishness verged on the criminal in the state's eyes, except where the state itself sponsored them through a weak and servile set of vestigial institutions.[1] By then, there were no more than a dozen ordained rabbis in the Soviet Union. Synagogues were attended by elderly Jews who had nothing further to lose. Younger Jews who dared to challenge the authorities did so, at most, by congregating outside synagogues on the Sabbath and Jewish festivals.

Despite its banishment, JDC managed to effect the distribution of cultural and religious items into the USSR throughout the years of the Communist rule. With the massive resources of the Soviet Union committed to obliterating Jewish life as we know it, these JDC activities were a vital lifeline for several tens of thousands of Jews who benefited from them. But they should not be mistaken for a massive and structured program of support for all Soviet Jews. Such a program became thinkable only after 1985, when Mikhail Gorbachev[2] launched the interrelated processes of glasnost ("openness") and perestroika (economic and governmental restructuring) that, as we know today, foretold the disintegration of the Soviet system in 1990–1991.[3]

Gorbachev's government chose JDC as the first vehicle for the official reconnection of Soviet Jews with the wider Jewish world. JDC had been overtly active in several Eastern European countries for several years, but the Soviet Union was in another league altogether — the object of five decades of dreaming.

Please Come In

In December 1987, Konstantin Kharchev, Chairman of the Council of Religious Affairs in the USSR, wrote officially to invite a JDC delegation to come to discuss the provision of religious services for the country's Jews. The six-member

---

1. As late as 1987, Jewish students were expelled from universities if discovered with Hebrew textbooks in their briefcases.
2. Mikhail Gorbachev was elected General Secretary of the Communist Party of the Soviet Union in 1985. He held his position as leader of the Soviet Union until 1991.
3. This chapter speaks mainly of the former Soviet Union (FSU); references to the USSR pertain to the period preceding the dissolution of the Union.

deputation — JDC board members Heinz Eppler and Manuel Dupkin II and their wives Ruthie and Carol; Michael Schneider, executive vice president of JDC at the time; and honorary executive vice president Ralph Goldman[4] — visited Moscow in January 1988. An agreement was reached for JDC to renew its activities in the Soviet Union, beginning with religious supplies and support for synagogues.

Later that year, the Soviet ambassador to Washington granted the official invitation for JDC to return to the USSR and work among the Jews of the Soviet Union, as we were doing in other countries. Now formally and publicly recognized by the regime, the front door to the USSR was officially open to JDC.

Joining the Team

In October 1989, Michael Schneider convened a team of JDC staff members to work in the USSR. The group — known as the Soviet Union Team (SUT) — was composed of six senior JDC representatives, including myself,[5] and was charged with determining an overarching goal and useful programs for JDC's activities in the USSR.

It was an honor to be asked to contribute to the revitalization of this concentration of Jewish masses in Eurasia following the seven decades of Communist abuse they had endured. More than forty years had now passed since my first endeavor with JDC, helping Jews to recover from the Holocaust, the greatest tyranny and devastation inflicted on their people in our time, if not ever. At that time, in the DP camps, I had been a novice, a volunteer in an organization straining to cope with the effects of disaster.

Now we faced the effects of the disaster Communism had wrought. Millions of Jews in the Soviet Union were now, at last, becoming accessible for an eleventh-hour venture in "Rescue, Relief, and Rehabilitation" that, at day's end, would become one of JDC's largest-ever endeavors. JDC did not appoint itself as the savior of Soviet Jews. It was the situation itself, and the

---

4. For more on Ralph Goldman, see Tom Shachtman, *I Seek My Brethren: Ralph Goldman and "The Joint."* (New York: Newmarket Press, 2001).
5. The members of the original SUT, chaired by Michael Schneider, were Ralph Goldman, Seymour "Epi" Epstein, David Harman, Asher Ostrin, Stuart Saffer, and myself.

surprising willingness of the Soviet authorities to allow us back in, that led us to undertake such a critical role.

❖ ❖ ❖

The SUT held its first meeting in London in November 1989 in a state of euphoria. Gazing at a huge map of the USSR on the wall, we divided the Soviet empire. Each member of the team would be a country director for one of the divisions. My designated "country" was North Caucasus and Central Asia. This region included the entire southern tier of the Soviet Union — the Asian republics of Kazakhstan, Kyrgyzstan, Uzbekistan, Tajikistan, Turkmenistan, and Azerbaijan, as well as Georgia, and the Russian republics in the northern Caucasus, from the Caspian Sea, through Chechnya and Nal'chik, to the Black Sea at Rostov. Together, these areas comprised a region larger than all my previous assignments combined.

One reason for this assignment was my service in Iran four decades earlier, which had given me exposure to Jews of Central Asian extraction, as well as some fluency in Farsi, which we thought might come in handy in "my" region. I also had extensive experience in working with "difficult regimes." That said, I felt that if I could work with some Ashkenazi communities too, it would give me a sense of comfort and familiarity. Therefore, I also took on some European territory, in the vicinity of Lviv (formerly Lvov) and Chernivtsi (which used to be known as Czernowitz) in western Ukraine.

We had a preconceived suspicion of what the USSR was. Glasnost or not, we were all conscious of the risks involved in entering "enemy territory." We would be tailed. We might be arrested or expelled. Or worse.

We began to gather whatever information we could about Soviet Jewry. As the 1980s were drawing to a close, the Jewish population was "estimated" at between 1.5 million (according to Soviet census data) and 4 million. It was more a guess than a hard, reliable number.[6]

By this time in 1989, the number of synagogues in the USSR had increased to 114 — yet they were not community institutions in the Western sense. Regular congregations, systematic religious instruction for the young, rabbinical training, a Jewishly educated class of householders, and the manufacture of religious articles: none of these existed. A locality might have a synagogue,

---

6.   Thus, all Jewish population figures in this chapter are approximations.

and/or sporadic volunteer welfare activities, but little more. Still, as we would discover, many surprises awaited us.

Perestroika had given rise to a cluster of interested novices who had emerged from the underground to establish rudimentary Jewish cultural centers. Their surreptitious origins were still apparent and their links to Jewish tradition were tenuous at best. After all, Soviet Jews had been trained for decades to view their identity as a cause of discrimination, if not of persecution, and their religion as something shameful and benighted in the atheist culture of the "Soviet Paradise."

Therefore, this initial eruption of Jewish activity under perestroika circumvented institutional religion. It also involved only a small minority of Soviet Jewry. In fact, much of the Jewish population was an undifferentiated and severely assimilated mass. The Soviets had labored for seven decades to accomplish this. A few decades more and they might have succeeded completely.

Getting Started

The SUT fashioned a vague-sounding yet meaningful mission statement: to reconnect Soviet Jewry with the Jewish people. The lifting of Soviet impediments on Jewish emigration in the late 1980s led throngs of Jews to leave for Israel, the United States, and other countries. Our reconnection mission would focus on those who would stay behind.

At this early stage, we chose to take responsibility for community-related activities that corresponded with our mission statement, as initially spelled out by Konstantin Kharchev in his invitation to enter the USSR. Hence these would be synagogue-based programs, including Jewish libraries, training of personnel for community functions (rabbis, ritual animal slaughterers, circumcisers, cantors, and spiritual leaders), production of books, and liaison with other Jewish organizations.

We thought that our target population would lean in numbers to the upper end of the wildly varying estimates, especially since we had decided to accept as Jews almost all people who approached us as such. While intermarriage was rampant, assimilation severe, and the fear among Jews of disclosing their Jewishness still lingering, our intended clients were now free to declare their Jewishness, organize, emigrate, or assimilate.

We were to work in cooperation with other Jewish and governmental entities. The Jewish Agency, which was also officially invited to reenter the USSR in the late 1980s, would be in charge of emigration and programs related to it. JDC was to cooperate with the Liaison Bureau,[7] which would run a Jewish festivals program in addition to its work in setting up and running Jewish schools. Eventually, we "ceded" most aspects of formal education to these two agencies, for reasons including the sizable Israeli resources in education staff and materials to which they had access. We would also work in many locations alongside Chabad-Lubavitch, Israeli consulates, and locally initiated Jewish organizations.

Our First Foray

In January 1990, I and the other SUT members prepared to explore the Soviet Union, just in time to bid it farewell. We agreed that each of us would visit his respective region, acquaint himself with its Jews, assess their needs, find people with whom he could work, and plan programs. We arranged to reconvene periodically to keep each other informed.

I first set foot on Soviet soil toward the end of that winter, as the members of the SUT arrived collectively in Moscow. The great metropolis would be the best starting point for us — a place to make contacts before visiting our assigned territories. At the time, the Jews in Moscow were at a loss to understand what awaited them in the future — though no more so than were we or, for that matter, the rest of the world. They saw the existing structure around them crumbling. The shops were empty. Food supplies were limited and inflation, previously unknown, was becoming a serious factor. Many had begun looking for a way to leave.

During the visit, I personally was afraid of doing anything that might provoke suspicion from the authorities. I imagine that my colleagues felt the same. We assumed that our hotel rooms were bugged, and that we may be followed and watched to see with whom we would meet. Indeed, I was "advised" by the security guard at the hotel to be cautious regarding whom I met and to stay in the hotel in the evenings. Local people could only visit me in the hotel lobby, in places where we could be seen, and certainly not in my hotel room.

---

7.   JDC literature usually refers to the Bureau by its Hebrew name, Lishkat ha-Kesher, or, simply, the Lishka.

It being JDC's standard policy to base its endeavors on local players, we took advantage of our time in the Soviet capital to begin building a network of such activists. Among them were Lubavitch rabbis, whose organization we learned already had representatives in many places. In fact, long before perestroika, the Lubavitcher Rebbe's emissaries had been traveling from town to town, trying to keep Jewish education and religious life alive. For this, many were sent to Siberian prisons, never to return.

We also took an active part in a conference of representatives of Jewish communities where cultural centers had been set up. The intention and accomplishment of the conference was the creation of a central body of Jewish communities in the FSU, the Association of Jewish Organizations and Communities in the USSR, also known as the Vaad.

The establishment of the Vaad was an important development. It represented the first attempt by Soviet Jews to organize themselves beyond the synagogues and cultural groups that existed at the local level. As the first attempt by Soviet Jews to establish their own central organization, the Vaad would receive financial support from JDC. For us there were immediate benefits, since the Vaad provided an invaluable service by acquainting us with hundreds of Jewish activists who in turn furnished us with lists of additional contacts in scores of localities.

The week that I spent in Moscow was helpful, but offered the barest orientation. To begin my introductory visits to these areas, I packed a modest amount of US dollars, drawn from a discretionary fund I had been given for local initiatives such as alleviating some immediate distress or jump-starting a program. I also took some slaughterer's knives,[8] prayer books, and shofars, knowing that these articles might be appreciated as basic necessities for Jewish observance. Finally, with no expectation of finding kosher food, I took a supply of canned provisions.

The total Jewish population of the areas for which I was now "country director" was over 200,000, spread across a region whose geography encompasses sizzling deserts and towering mountains. The increasingly fluid political affairs at that time resulted in shifting, unstable, or downright impassable borders. I realized that both factors would impede the sort of inter-community coalescence that we knew in the West.

---

8. These were special knives authorized for *shehita*, ritual slaughtering.

I also suspected that in these areas I would not often find anything like the Jewish hospitality and eagerness to study that I had experienced in Iran during my tenure there. Nor would I be likely to find the vibrant and proud traditions of the North African and Yemenite Jews that had unfolded before me in their countries.

Yet beneath the dulled exterior and crushed community pride that Communism had left behind, as I pried into the lives of Jewish individuals in my region, I would discover sparks of color and hope. The potential for reconnected and active Jewish life in these areas would soon become evident.

With such an enormous area to cover, my initial tours of the region under my responsibility were spread over a period of two years, starting in January 1990. In each and every location, I examined whatever existing Jewish collective infrastructures I could find to see how we could build upon them and with whom we could work. Where no hint of infrastructure existed, I explored the needs and wishes of the dispersed Jewish populations.

Programs that I started up on these first visits included those we had determined at the outset: establishing or supporting Jewish libraries, providing basic religious items such as prayer books, *shehita* knives, and shofars, organizing synagogue and Pesach seder services, arranging training for community functionaries, and providing seed funding for small welfare needs. These steps were not universal; at first they were made only where interest and foresight were evident.

Although I found that most Jews were located in larger cities, many were settled in provincial towns and peripheral settlements. During World War II, when refugees were moving from the west, the Soviet authorities had discouraged them from settling in main towns, where accommodation and employment opportunities were lacking. Instead, they were directed to the provinces, where they could be placed in kolkhozy to live and work. In some peripheral locations, I would find just a handful of families; in others they would number as many as a few thousand.

Tajikistan

My first introductory visit began in Dushanbe, capital of Tajikistan, on a Friday morning in January 1990. From my hotel I headed for the synagogue, where I found a young man slaughtering chickens. I addressed him first in Hebrew and then in Farsi. He stared uncomprehendingly and suspiciously. Conclusion number one: contrary to our earlier assumptions, neither language would be of much use to me in this part of the world.

The young man was dubious. He stepped into the synagogue, returned with a prayer book, and made me read from it to make sure that I was Jewish. This led me to my second conclusion: Soviet Jews at that time remained deeply suspicious, if not fearful, of outsiders. Glasnost may have moderated the Soviet practice of hounding people who made contact with foreigners, but the recriminations of the recent past were still fresh in Jews' minds.

Dushanbe had a second, older slaughterer. He was a man well into his eighties and when I went to meet him, he told me in very poor Hebrew that an undeserved prison term at the Soviets' hands had driven him into retirement. He recalled that there had been two ritual slaughterers in Dushanbe in the early days too. He had served those he called Bukharan Jews, while another served the Ashkenazim — Russian Jews who had settled in Tajikistan mainly during the war years. Both had been imprisoned for eight years.

He had been living in trepidation and fear since his prison experience and therefore asked me not to mention his name or story anywhere. To allay his fears, I tore up my notes and threw them away as he looked on. Hence my third conclusion: The Jews in these areas had maintained religious services of sorts throughout the Soviet era but tended to do so on an ethnically separate basis.

I took interest in the ethnic divide and familiarized myself with the history of the Bukharan Jews whom I would meet in various Asian areas. Since Tajikistan and Uzbekistan had once been part of the Emirate of Bukhara, the Jews of the region became known as Bukharan. Their origins, it is believed, date back to the exiled Jews of Babylon, today Iraq, who later moved to Iran. Hence their use of a Persian dialect, Bukhari. However, this dialect of the Persian language was completely different from the Iranian Farsi that I was familiar with. Over 2,000 years these Jews have maintained Jewish traditions, wherever they have settled.

Of the 11,500 Jews in Dushanbe in 1990, 9,500 were Bukharan and the remainder Ashkenazi. The Bukharans were businesspeople and merchants, with some petty artisans — cobblers and hairdressers. Most Ashkenazim were government officials, intellectuals, and university-trained professionals. Neither had any form of central organization, besides an Ashkenazi Cultural

Committee headed by a Dr. Dakhtayef, a professor of medicine at the local university who was shortly to leave for the United States.

The Bukharan Jews and the Ashkenazim had little to do with each other. The former tended to look down on the latter as Johnny-come-latelies, or worse, shared the stereotype that the Ashkenazim had accepted Soviet evacuation from European areas instead of standing and fighting. Hence I arrived at another conclusion: In order to build one community in places like Dushanbe, it was in practice necessary to first build two.

I attended Sabbath prayer services that were conducted by Bukharan Jews. Even during the most difficult periods of Communist rule, the Bukharan Jews, I found, had not abandoned their traditional orientation. However, few could read the prayers in Hebrew; most relied on a Russian transliteration. Even the synagogue officers had little knowledge of Jewish laws and practices. Many of these Bukharan Jews were planning to move to Israel or other destinations abroad.

The Ashkenazim made do with a small room next door for their services. A few older men recited prayers as best they could, though no one actually knew how to conduct the service. Their *gabbai*, they told me, was well versed in Jewish tradition and could read from the Torah. However, he had left for Israel, taking their only scroll with him. The one they were now using had been borrowed from the Bukharan Jews.

Kyrgyzstan[9]

Small populations of Jews lived scattered in different areas across Kyrgyzstan, but my visits in the area have been limited to the core Jewish collective of Frunze (Bishkek before the Soviet era and reverting to that name later, with independence). My wife, Noemi, and I first visited the city with the telephone number of a Dr. Sergei Bernstein, who was able to introduce us to the other active Jews in the city. One of them was his mother, a woman in her seventies who had attended a Hebrew high school in Riga, Latvia. Now she organized Hebrew classes for children and adults, and arranged Jewish cultural activities. This one person was a godsend to the Jews of her city.

During my stay I met a couple who asked me to officiate at their wedding

---

9.   The order of my introductory visits as they appear from here on is primarily of geographical rather than chronological sequence.

that was to take place a few days later. It had been a very long time since a fully Jewish marriage had taken place in Frunze. The couple would be leaving for Israel soon after the wedding.

There were 4,000–5,000 Jews in Frunze in 1990, mainly Ashkenazi but also some Bukharan. The administrator of the only synagogue in town at that time was Mendel Berkovitz. He was originally from Moldova — but not originally a Berkovitz or a Mendel.

After surviving the war, he had settled in Kishinev and set up a metalwork shop with two non-Jewish partners. In spite of the strict Communist regime, Mendel and his associates managed to bribe their way to prosperity. They did well until someone informed the KGB that the enterprise was buying metal scrap on the black market. His partners blamed the Jew and the authorities willingly concurred.

Facing the prospect of years in the gulag, Mendel amassed as much cash as he could and fled eastward by train, eventually arriving in Tashkent as an undocumented alien. Several days later, Mendel spotted a man in the street who looked Jewish. With trepidation he approached him and asked him if he was Jewish. Mendel was fortunate; the man directed him to the synagogue. By carefully establishing contacts in Tashkent, he bought a new internal passport, changed his name to Mendel Berkovitz, and found employment there. Soon he married and moved to Frunze, where he was completely unknown. There he became active in the synagogue and observed Shabbat and Jewish holidays. The couple had a daughter, Rosa, in whom Mendel invested all his Jewish consciousness. He made a good living and felt content.

When his only daughter grew up, he sent her to university. There, to her parents' utter dismay, she met a Tartar, fell in love, and decided to marry him. Her parents' pleas to reconsider fell on deaf ears. Heartbroken, Mendel severed relations with his daughter. He had lost his only child, he said. His wife fell ill. Quietly he prepared to leave for Israel, leaving his daughter and, by then, his granddaughter behind. He and his ailing wife left in 1992 to spend the rest of their days among their people.

During this first visit to Bishkek, I was able to initiate a welfare program to help the elderly whose pensions had recently lost their value and who therefore could no longer survive on government support.

In searching for a suitable local resident to manage the program, we came across Rosa Fish. She had already organized a group of women volunteers to visit the lonely and occasionally bring them food packages and medications. This was done on a limited scale, solely and only with local support, so the women were more than happy to extend their activities to include JDC's welfare. Now they would be able to increase the number of food packages and medications and provide for more needy Jews than they could before.

Kazakhstan

There are at present thirteen substantial Jewish communities in Kazakhstan, a country larger than all of Europe that has arbitrary borders and a population of diverse nationalities and tribes. The people of Kazakhstan, like those of other republics in the region, eke out a living on top of vast natural resources that the country has not yet fully exploited.

Many Jews in this republic descend from political prisoners whom Stalin had banished to the gulags along with their wives. With hundreds of miles of prairie surrounding each camp, the prisoners did not even have to be guarded. During the Khrushchev era of 1958–1964, additional Jews came to the region, drawn by government incentives under a program to turn Kazakhstan into Russia's breadbasket. The discovery of large mineral deposits lured still more. Thus, over the years, Jewish collectives — mainly of Ashkenazim — came into being.

Synagogues, Jewish institutions, and Jewish knowledge were very scanty in these localities when I arrived there for the first time. Jews in the provincial communities told me that they had never seen a religious Jew or any Jewish religious items. At the most, they had heard about the shofar or matzoth. Here was a place where reconnection would have to start from the very foundations.

I recall my first visit to Kazakhstan for the exceptional warmth and hospitality that I received wherever I went. My first stop in 1990 was in the capital, Almaty, accompanied by Noemi. Since the Jewish Agency had already posted a representative there, we turned to him to introduce us to the Jews of the city.

Almaty then had an estimated Jewish population of 12,000–14,000, but little sense of Jewish community. It did, however, have a Jewish cultural committee, chaired by an electrical engineer named Emil Kagan. I found his telephone number and asked to meet with him. Afraid to meet us at our hotel,

Berber Jews in southern Morocco, living in mud huts.

Berber Jewish woman and children in Tafilalet, southeast Morocco.

Girls infected with trachoma in southern Morocco, 1952.

A schoolboy at the heder in Rissani, southern Morocco, once home to the Baba Sali. Many boys displayed on their heads a front patch of hair left uncut, based on a belief that a person would be rescued from hell by this lock.

A schoolgirl reading out loud from her Hebrew primer at a JDC-supported school in Sefrou.

At a reception marking the end of a school year in Casablanca, 1975. Second from left: Rabbi Shalom Eidelman, Lubavitch representative in Morocco; Right: Rabbi Aaron Monsonego, director of Ozar Hatorah schools in Morocco and, since the late 1990s, chief rabbi of Morocco.

Jewish schoolgirls receiving lunch at a JDC-
supported feeding
program in Medenine,
between Gabes and
Tataouine in southern
Tunisia.

Visiting the girls' section of the Torah v'Chinuch (formerly Daber Ivrit) school in
Djerba in the early 1970s.

Lag b'Omer celebration in Djerba, outside the El Ghriba synagogue. The Torah scroll case is decorated with silk scarves and carried to a synagogue in the Hara Srira Jewish community of Djerba amid song and dance.

Students of the Daber Ivrit girls' school in Djerba. Sitting with a brown coat is the late Evelyn Peters, who was JDC director of Tunisia and India for over twenty-five years. On the right are David and Tzvia Kidushin.

A *mori* (rabbi) in Raida, northern Yemen, 1996.

We came across this Jewish boy in Saada, Yemen, 1996, working the bellows in his family's metal workshop.

Rabbi Eliezer Shach addressing a farewell reception on the retirement of Rabbi Dr. Aaron Greenbaum, director of JDC's Education-Religious-Cultural ("Yeshiva") Department in Israel, 1982. Other rabbis, from left to right: Rabbi Markovitch, chief rabbi of Ramat Gan; Rabbi Shlomo Zalman Auerbach; Rabbi Meir Chodosh; Rabbi Shach; Rabbi Greenbaum. I sit beside Rabbi Greenbaum.

Hesder yeshiva — combining Torah studies and military service.

Ethiopian students performing at the Bnei Akiva Tikvat Yaakov yeshiva high school in Moshav Sde Yaakov.

Officiating at one of the first Jewish weddings in Bishkek, Kyrgyzstan, after glasnost, 1990.

Unloading packages of clothing donated by JDC to the Jewish community of Oni, Georgia, after the 1991 earthquake.

The matzo factory in Tbilisi, Georgia.

Making a home visit to a housebound elderly woman in Rustavi, near Tbilisi, Georgia, accompanied by the local Hesed director.

The synagogue of the Mountain Jews in Baku, Azerbaijan.

Affixing a mezuzah at the opening ceremony of the new Hesed building in Nal'chik, southern Russia, 2000.

With Svetlana Danielova, member of the local parliament in Nal'chik (southern Russia), an activist for the advancement of women, and a leading member of the Jewish community, 2002.

Bringing a new Torah scroll, donated by Lubavitch, into a synagogue in Almaty, Kazakhstan, 2004.

Abramovitch family, 2007.

Receiving rabbinical ordination from Chief Rabbi Mordechai Eliyahu on my comple-
tion of fifty years of service with JDC, including directorship of the JDC Yeshiva
Program, November 1995.

JDC President Ambassador Milton Wolf presenting a gift marking fifty years of service with the organization, 1995.

Receiving an honorary doctorate from Bar-Ilan University for fifty years' contribution to Jewish education, 1995.

Kagan suggested that we wait outside, whence someone would lead us to a nearby park.

Our conversation was slow, strained, and distrustful at first. I knew no Russian at the time, but I did speak German, so Emil's wife, who also did, translated. After describing local Jewish life, the activities of the cultural center, and his own work, Emil's confidence grew and he informed us that he and his family, including his elderly mother, would be leaving for Israel within the next two weeks. Then he told his family's story, one that seemed to encapsulate the entire Soviet Jewish experience.

Even before the Bolshevik Revolution, Emil's grandfather, Yakolev, had been a committed and active Communist. During the revolution, he was tasked with occupying the Zhitomir area of Ukraine, a mission he accomplished with just a few men. His services earned him the rank of general, and appointment as governor of the area. He ruled fairly but with iron discipline. As a faithful executor of Communist Party policies, for example, he "collected" gold from the Jews and non-Jews of Zhitomir and turned it over to the party for the needs of its central committee. No one doubted his faith in and devotion to Communism and the party — or so it seemed.

After several years, he was inexplicably accused of dishonesty, profiteering, and embezzling government funds. Neither his arguments nor his evidence were believed. Convicted and executed, all his property was confiscated, leaving his widow and children destitute: as the family of a "traitor," they had neither pension rights nor income. Yet somehow they survived.

Yakolev's daughter — Emil's mother — was an officer in the Red Army during World War II. She met and married another Jewish officer and the two of them fought all the way to Berlin, where her husband became a commander in a section of the German capital. Eventually, the family landed in Almaty, where Emil's father was appointed to teach at a military academy. It was there that their two sons were born.

Emil's wife, Marina, was from Ukraine. Her father, from the town of Uman, was also a devoted Communist who volunteered whenever his country wished to colonize a new area. His service included a stay in Birobidzhan when the Soviet authorities declared it a Jewish autonomous region. After World War II, he spent time on several Japanese islands that the Soviets had occupied, again as a colonization volunteer. Eventually, however, he became disillusioned with his life of unrequited toil and moved back to the USSR proper, ending up in Kazakhstan. Marina told us that his name was Nachman, but did not know why, since none of her ancestors had had that name. I told Marina the story of Rebbe Nachman of Breslav, the famed Hasidic leader who was buried in Uman. This was a revelation for Marina, whose Soviet education had blinded her even to the acclaimed Jewish history of her own family's origins.

After our walk in the park, the Kagans felt secure enough to invite us to their home, where we met Emil's aging mother, whose hands shook uncontrollably. Once we were sitting in their living room, Emil explained why they did not wish to be seen with foreigners, believing that this might cause problems before their departure. The secret police, Emil explained, had an office in our hotel. Thankfully, his fears were not realized and the family left for Israel and settled successfully in Haifa.

With my usual interest in Jewish education, I asked some locals in Almaty whether there was anyone who could teach children and start up some Jewish classes. I was told to visit a Reb Leib.

He lived on the fourth floor of an old, rundown building. Reb Leib opened the door slowly and warily. I peered inside. The apartment was strewn with boxes and crates. An open tractate of the Talmud rested on a simple table in the cramped kitchen. I stepped in. Reb Leib, who must have been close to ninety, greeted me with a loud complaint: How could a Jew enter a dwelling without kissing the mezuzah? I quickly corrected my oversight. Then we sat down and he told me about his life.

He had been born in Belarus and had attended a yeshiva in his hometown before becoming a follower of the Chabad-Lubavitch movement. Then came the Revolution. All yeshiva studies were interrupted and Reb Leib, like many others, was swept away by the torrential enthusiasm of the new order.

"You must not ask me about those years," he said of the seven decades that followed. "They do not exist. They were wasted."

Other members of the community later filled in the holes in his story. He had gone on to study geology, worked in his field, and put his origins and religion out of sight and out of mind. Now, in his old age, he had rediscovered the pleasure of Jewish study and had resolved to devote the rest of his life to the study of the Talmud.

Unfortunately, though, Reb Leib was too advanced in years to teach the Jewish children or hold classes. So JDC, with the help of other local Jews, stepped in to initiate courses in Hebrew for adults and celebrations of the Jewish holidays.

The area of Karaganda, north of Almaty, had been used for a number of gulags, one of them just for mothers with children. When I first visited Karaganda, it had a community of 4,000 Jews, Kazakhstan's largest provincial Jewish community at that time. The coal mines provided work for the local population, but most of the Jews occupied professional positions.

The head of the Jewish community was the deputy director of the mines. He received me in his spacious and well-furnished office. We discussed the Jewish community and how JDC could provide assistance for its elderly and needy. After our discussion, he invited me to join him in his private swimming pool and sauna. Towels, soap, and shampoo were laid out for us. Lunch was served after our swim. Caviar, chicken, meat, and cooked vegetables were part of the vast menu. My host, as well as the waitresses, were quite surprised and disappointed at my insistence on declining — for reasons of kashruth — the sumptuous but non-kosher meal prepared in my honor.

The disparity between the wealth and comfort of this official and the poverty that I witnessed among the Jews of the community was immense. Yet it became evident that no questions could be asked. Under Soviet rule, the privileges of a deputy director of mines in Karaganda had been the accepted norm.

During that first visit I was already able to initiate a program of food distribution for the needy and medical examinations for the sick. My wealthy host and head of the community was able to locate a reliable member of the community to oversee the package distribution as well as volunteer doctors to carry out the medical services.

Uzbekistan

The Jewish population of Uzbekistan is made up of Ashkenazi and Bukharan Jews. The Ashkenazi Jews had arrived from other parts of the Soviet Union in the nineteenth and twentieth centuries, the majority arriving during World War II. Many fled the Holocaust; others were evacuated by the Soviet government when key industries were relocated to the area. Most had lost all ties to Jewish life after decades of enforced atheism.

On the other hand, the Bukharan Jews, who trace their roots in the region back many centuries, clung tenaciously to Judaism and to Jewish communal life, even during the Soviet era. These two Jewish groups live separate yet harmonious lives in Uzbekistan, both enjoying cordial relations with their Muslim neighbors.

In the capital, Tashkent, I gained further insights on the ethnic divide and the vestiges of Jewish practices. Here the Ashkenazim were by far the majority, at 45,000 versus 12,000 Bukharans in 1990. This ratio was primarily due to the importance of the city as a destination for Russian and Polish Jewish refugees during World War II.

Still, in 1990, of Tashkent's four synagogues three were Bukharan and one Ashkenazi. Again, there was no central organization besides a Jewish cultural center. The Ashkenazi synagogue supported itself by manufacturing matzo. The vast majority of Ashkenazi Jews never attended services, even on the High Holidays, and besides Jewish burial were not interested in Jewish life at all. In fact, many denied their Jewishness outright. This, I learned, was quite common among Jews under Communist rule, the purpose being to gain access to the many professional and academic opportunities that were not available to Jews.

The Bukharan Jews in Tashkent, however, did not mask their Jewish nationality. They attended synagogues whenever possible, and attempted to practice the faith as they knew best. The younger generation of Bukharan Jews, like everywhere in the Soviet Union, was ignorant of Hebrew and Jewish tradition because the Communist regime had rendered the teaching of religion and Hebrew nearly impossible.

I met the Bukharan rabbi of Tashkent, Avrech Katziev, who was about to leave for Canada. No fitting successor was available. I also visited the Ashkenazi synagogue, where a few Russian Jews told me that the *gabbai* of their synagogue, Reb Shimon Giltz, lived nearby and, behold, was also preparing to leave for Israel the very next day.

I decided to pay a visit to Reb Giltz before he left. He was reluctant to let me into his home until I identified myself as an official of the JDC, the "Joint." Hearing this, he flung the door open and invited me in. I found his home in turmoil. It was strewn with broken cups and fragments of unidentifiable objects. With a haggard look on his face, he was packing kosher food for his trip. Reb Giltz insisted on making me a cup of tea. Then he told his story. Originally from Ukraine, he had fled to the east and southeast during World War II, eventually settling in Tashkent, where he had been living ever since. His familiarity with JDC dated from the 1920s, when Communists created a famine in Ukraine in order to break the resistance of peasants. Had it not been for JDC food parcels, he concluded, the Jews there would have starved. Our meeting, he told me, was the first time he had encountered a JDC representative since then, and he was glad to host me to give belated thanks for JDC's lifesaving service.

His initial reluctance to admit me was due to a more recent tragedy. Locals who heard that he and his wife were about to emigrate assumed that they had a stash of cash somewhere in their house. Construction workers from a nearby building eventually broke into their home and brutally murdered his wife because she could not give them the money they demanded. Now Reb Giltz was fearful for his own life and wary of anyone knocking on his door.

The Jews of Tashkent who had maintained their Jewish identity had already developed several potential settings for JDC programs. The Jewish cultural center was located in rented quarters and provided Hebrew instruction in the afternoons to about 1,000 participants under Jewish Agency auspices. The afternoon school was quite rudimentary, run by a few teachers who knew a bit of Hebrew, having acquired the language surreptitiously during the time when studying Hebrew was dangerous. Only a few textbooks were being used. Those who participated in the Hebrew courses did so primarily in preparation for emigration to Israel. Jews also visited the center on Sundays to meet other Jews, learn about emigration possibilities, and hear the latest news from Israel. In a nutshell, the center was already doing the job that JDC intended.

During my first visit I was already able to help to rectify the lack of learning materials. I immediately arranged for a shipment of books and audiocassettes to supplement what the center already had, and used my discretionary funds to furnish the center with audiocassette players.

During that first visit to Tashkent, I observed that the numbers of needy elderly Jews was disproportionately high. This was because many of the refugees from the European parts of the Soviet Union who had been evacuated during the war to Uzbekistan — and to Tashkent in particular — were older, beyond the age of army mobilization. These refugees had difficulty integrating in the local economy. Their financial independence worsened as the years passed and as they became more and more elderly. I took it upon myself to initiate basic welfare activities there and then by allocating funding for food parcels.

Southwest of Tashkent is Samarkand, a city on the silk route from China that had once been an important trading and business center. My first contact there was a Mr. Chodosh, an Ashkenazi Lubavitch Hasid. There were 14,000 Jews in Samarkand in 1990, Mr. Chodosh told me, including 2,000 of European origin who did not interact with the Bukharan majority. Most Jews lived in a self-imposed ghetto that carried the Farsi name *mahaleh* that I had known from Iran. Jewish life in the ghetto centered on the one synagogue — of an original fourteen — that the Soviets had allowed to remain in service.

The intensity of Jewish life in Samarkand took me by surprise. All the Bukharan Jews, it seemed, were conscious of tradition if not actually observant. Even Uzbeki peasants in the area knew about the Jewish Sabbath and brought their produce to the *mahaleh* market for sale on Fridays. Those outside the ghetto, too, tried to maintain Jewish communal life as much as possible and were engendering a renaissance that was impressive by the standards of the region.

I found Hebrew classes were already set up and regular synagogue services were being held. Jewish kindergartens and afternoon schools were being opened. Lubavitch had brought in several young men from Israel who had started a yeshiva. There were Jewish youth clubs, student groups, and a cultural center operated by a local cultural committee.

Mr. Chodosh introduced me to Rabbi Emanuel Shimonov, the dynamic young man whom everybody in the neighborhood adored. He was the moving spirit of Jewish life in the city. Besides organizing most of the Jewish activities, he was also the local *shohet* (ritual slaughterer) and *mohel* (ritual circumciser). He had proved himself just the sort of person around whom one could build a strong community — and so I would consider him until he emigrated to the United States a few years later.

The Jewish families in Samarkand seemed close-knit, yet I came across a trend there that proved to be widespread in the entire region: a combination of rampant intermarriage (mainly among the Ashkenazi Jews), easy divorce, spouse abandonment, and children of broken homes in need of care. When these circumstances combined with the mass emigration movement, problematic situations arose. For example, when women whose husbands had disappeared wished to leave for Israel, as many did, the authorities did not allow them to take their children with because their husbands had not given permission to remove them from the country.

I met one such woman, Irena, a teacher whose husband had left her and her son for a Tartar woman. Irena fell in love with another young Jewish teacher from Lithuania and they decided to make aliyah with her five-year-old son, without her husband's permission. In order to do so, Irena went to Moscow for a visit, for which she needed no permit. While in Moscow, she obtained tourist visas for Israel and thus took her son with her without requiring her husband's consent. Once in Israel, she applied for and received immigrant status and married her beau. The three of them live happily in Israel today.

On my first visit to the city of Bukhara, west of Samarkand, I did not have the name or number of any contact person. But a young lady was waiting for me at the hotel when I arrived — a friend of Irena, the teacher I had met in Samarkand. Here, in Bukhara, I found a vibrant Jewish community of about 2,000 Bukharan Jews. Yitzhak Abramov, a local Jew, played a leading role in the community. He ran a synagogue that he had restored and was accepted as the local rabbi. There was also a community organization, headed by a Jewish businessman. I made a note that JDC would be able to augment the existing infrastructure and boost the services already existing in welfare, education, and Jewish cultural activities. Most Jews in Bukhara lived in a ghetto, but here too, did so due to tradition, not coercion. My escort introduced me to others in the community, including the community president and the *shohet*, who was an old, ailing rabbi.

About fifty miles south of Samarkand lies the small town of Shakhrisabz. Once again, with no name of a contact person in hand, I searched for a cobbler on the main street. I knew that in this region this trade was practiced mainly by Jews. Indeed, the first cobbler I happened upon was able to guide me to the Jewish section of the town and gave me the name of the head of the Jewish community there. I discovered that quite recently half of the 4,000 Jews who had inhabited the town had already emigrated. But the community leader claimed he had no such intention. He showed me his spacious sitting room with great pride. Rooms in Israel are small, he had heard, and he doubted that he could enjoy such a large sitting room anywhere else.

My host took me to the synagogue to meet the rabbi-*shohet*. I asked the rabbi where he had learned *shehita*. He explained how the previous *shohet* left for Israel but visited him before his departure. The man handed over the *shehita* knife to the rabbi and with that appointed him the next *shohet* for the community.

Despite some material comfort in the Jewish area of Shakhrisabz, the remainder of the community would leave for Israel over the following years, rendering JDC's involvement unnecessary.

Turkmenistan

I first visited Turkmenistan in 1992, in the company of Israel Szyf, who had by then taken up a position as JDC's resident representative in Uzbekistan. This was a pleasurable reunion with my friend Israel, whom I had first met in Germany where he was working with the DPs as a Jewish Agency emissary. Later, in 1950, I had invited him to help in the education program in Iran. He accepted and later took over the Ozar Hatorah program in Iran. Following that, Israel continued his Ozar Hatorah activities in Paris, maintaining those responsibilities until arriving in Uzbekistan, where he would remain based for almost ten years.

Most of the 2,000 Jews of Turkmenistan lived in the capital, Ashkhabad, and had come there during World War II from western Russia. They had businesses or practiced liberal professions.

A few poor Jewish families received assistance from some of those who were better-off. There was no synagogue, no Sunday school, no religious services, and no central committee. Jews occasionally met on Jewish festivals. Intermarriage was rife.

Many planned to emigrate and were in touch with the Jewish Agency, which had started to move Jews out of the capital. At our first meeting with a small group of Jewish representatives, the participants were primarily interested in hearing about Israel and Jewish life in the United States and elsewhere, and less interested in discussing the needs of its elderly or poor community members.

Presently, the Jewish Agency moved close to half of the Jews from Ashkhabad to Israel. Over 1,000 of them remained, along with those intermarried Jews who lived in smaller settlements surrounding the capital who had decided to remain. JDC would need to find a way to provide for the needy of the Ashkhabad community.

Southern Russia

On the foothills of the northern Caucasus, a mountain range that stretches practically from the Caspian Sea to the Black Sea, is the southwestern leg of Russia. This area is inhabited by various agrarian tribes, including the

Chechens. Jews have lived among these tribes for centuries, working as crafts-men and artisans. They are known as "Mountain Jews" and speak a distant dialect of Persian. They have steered clear of most tribal wars and, when nec-essary, defended themselves vigorously. The Mountain Jews maintain strong community customs, including arranged marriages of young girls, avoidance of higher schooling, and — in an anomaly in that part of the world — com-munity philanthropy.

At the time of my first arrival in this region, one of the largest Jewish com-munities was in Nal'chik, the capital of Kabardino-Balkaria. The city then had 10,000–12,000 Mountain Jews who were in one area of the city called Kolonka and who led a normal community life by regional standards.

I met a woman in Nal'chik named Svetlana Danielova, a young grand-mother, a member of the local parliament, an activist on behalf of women's rights, and a Jewish community leader. Svetlana had already opened a Jewish youth club in Kolonka where young people enjoyed music, formed an orches-tra, engaged in plastic arts, and learned Israeli dances and songs. I assumed — and was correct — that in Nal'chik JDC would be able to develop a welfare program of food distribution and a central kitchen for the needy in coopera-tion with this vital community leader.

But finding a basis for JDC programs would be harder than I had bargained for. With the disintegration of the Soviet Union, local Muslims took control of Nal'chik and its government, dismissing some Jewish officials. Eventually, Svetlana Danielova was also voted out of parliament, because the depleted Jewish community could no longer ensure her reelection. When I met her a few years later, Svetlana was leaving for the United States.

Mountain Jews also lived in Dagestan, east of Chechnya, on the Caspian Sea. I visited Buynaksk, where in 1990 about seventy Jewish families lived among members of the Kalmiki tribe. The synagogue in Buynaksk was 100 years old, and the building next door had once belonged to the Jewish community but had been confiscated during the Soviet era. I was greeted by the town's ritual slaughterer-rabbi. He opened the synagogue and showed me around. His dream, he said, was to obtain a new *shehita* knife to better serve his com-munity. When I handed one to him, he pronounced it a genuine miracle, which we celebrated with a *l'chaim*, a small toast.

My introductory visit to Makhachkala, the capital of Dagestan, was in 1992. By that time, we had a resident representative in the area, Menachem Elazar. Menachem accompanied me on this visit and we began at the synagogue, where we met the local rabbi, Daniel, who also served as the *shohet* and was busy slaughtering chickens for Shabbat. Observing his efforts, he too was clearly in need of a new *shehita* knife. As I had just done in Buynaksk, I presented the rabbi with a new and kosher knife.

We discovered that Daniel knew a little Hebrew. In conversing with him briefly, he told us about his community of Mountain Jews, about his definite plans to move to Israel in the near future, and about the community's unelected yet most powerful leader, a man named Shimmi, who owned a garage and dabbled in other businesses.

It was not long before Shimmi himself appeared. A short, stocky man with small, sharp eyes, he asked relevant questions about us, the purpose of our visit, and how long we would stay. Then he ruled that we were not to stay at the hotel that we had booked into. It was too dangerous; the hotel management worked hand-in-hand with one of the town's many organized-crime gangs. No, we would stay with him. He insisted.

That evening we went to his house, a small fortress guarded by dogs and tough servants. A kosher fish dinner did full credit to the hospitality of the Mountain Jews, each course welcomed with a generous toast of vodka. Hours later, we were led to our room, the quantity of vodka consumed making sleep welcome and immediate. The next morning, we woke up to find that we had slept in an armory. Under the beds, hanging on the walls, and sticking out of the cupboard were hand grenades and all manner of guns. Shimmi was at a loss to understand the shock on our faces.

"You are in Makhachkala," he said. "In Makhachkala you must be prepared for anything. It is part of life in this area."

Our dedicated host insisted on accompanying us all the way to my next stop — all the way to Derbent. It was local custom, he explained.

Derbent, a city that claims to be 5,000 years old, was the main Jewish community in Dagestan in the early 1990s. Many centuries ago, the Khazari kingdom, famed in Rabbi Yehuda Halevi's work *The Kuzari*, ruled here, and as far north as Volgograd and east to the Black Sea. The first Jews who settled in Kiev over 1,000 years ago came from this area.

Prior to perestroika, the city had 25,000 Mountain Jews, but by the time

I arrived in 1990, the population had already dwindled to 16,000. I found an unusually solid community, well versed in and proud of their long history. It had two synagogues, a ninety-three-year-old rabbi called Nachman Gadilov, and a community chairman, a young man named David Davidoff. A Jewish Agency emissary was already stationed there and a Jewish education center offered Hebrew classes.

Spending one evening in the company of local Jews, I asked them how they made a living. One of the men present explained that as the person responsible for entertainment programs in municipal parks, he charged three rubles to enter the park — two for the municipality, and one for him. Another, a music teacher, ran the local conservatory and received a government salary. He explained that when a mother arrived to enroll her child he told her that the youngster would have to pass an exam. After testing the child, he informed the mother that the child lacked the skill to be admitted. The mother would then slip 100 rubles into his hand, whereupon the child's musical talent suddenly improved. Many of those present told similar stories, each also knowing exactly how the other swindled his way to solvency.

Nevertheless, Derbent had a significant number of poor and elderly. JDC would need to implement its programs here too in order to provide assistance for them.

In Pyatigorsk in the Stavropol region, Jews who had felt uncomfortable in Muslim areas increased the community's numbers from about 4,500 to 10,000 by 1990. There I met a builder and businessman in his fifties named Roman Gavrielov. He was the Jewish potentate who seemed to own half the city and had great influence with the local authorities. Soon after I first met him he even started an airline that transported Jews from nearby Mineralnye Vody to Israel and back. Among his many ventures, Gavrielov patronized a full-time Jewish day school. He owned the school building and another that served as a library and a venue for Hebrew classes.

When I first reached Rostov-on-Don in southern Russia, I found some 12,000 Ashkenazi Jews who had replaced a much larger indigenous Jewish presence that the Nazis had devastated in their drive to the oil wells in the Caspian Sea. Fortunately, the Nazi advance was halted in the Caucasus and never reached its target. Of the four synagogues in Rostov-on-Don, the post-Soviet government had restored only one to the community's control. Few Jews used it, though.

During that very first visit I brought together a group of Jews to create a Jewish welfare committee, through which JDC could channel relief to those in need. It led to the opening of a soup kitchen in the synagogue that would eventually serve Jews throughout the city.

Georgia

My wife and I first visited Georgia in April 1990. Unlike the localities I had visited up to that point, this one was in utter disarray. Even though it was Stalin's birthplace, local nationalism and resistance to Soviet rule had always been strong there; Georgia is culturally unique, with a language and script quite different from others in the area. With the disintegration of rule from Moscow, the conflicting factions that populated the republic entered several years of civil strife, rampant organized crime, and economic decline. This beautiful land that once boasted fine wine and popular tourist resorts would become, with Moldova, the poorest of the former Soviet republics.

The history of Georgian Jews is not well known even to the country's Jews themselves, and no one could explain to me when they came to Georgia or from where. Some claimed that Jews arrived in Georgia long before the advent of Christianity. This tradition has sheltered them from anti-Semitism, the Christians recognizing that Jews who had arrived in Georgia long before the crucifixion could not be held accountable for it.

I arrived in the capital, Tbilisi, with the address and telephone number of Rabbi Ariel Levine, a self-taught Orthodox Jew, born in Tbilisi to nonreligious Ashkenazi parents. I had previously met Rabbi Levine on my initial trip to Moscow in 1990. Now he introduced me to other key members of the Tbilisi Jewish community.

The Jews of Tbilisi — 15,000 Georgians and 2,000 Ashkenazim at that time — were a feisty group who had weathered the Soviet era with an uncommon degree of cohesion. Many of the prominent Jews made a respectable living in business and the professions. Others, though, were poor. There was a Jewish quarter with two active synagogues that were attended regularly by hundreds of Georgian Jews and a handful of Ashkenazim.

The first attrition of Jewish leadership in Tbilisi had occurred in the 1970s, when détente enabled many Georgian community leaders, intellectuals, and officials to emigrate, while others moved to Moscow. Nevertheless, many Jewish organizations were still functioning in the city when I arrived. There was Derech Yehudi, which engaged primarily in running Hebrew classes; a Maccabi sports organization; a students' union, which later became a JDC-supported Hillel chapter; children's and adults' choirs; a theater group; and a Georgia-Israel friendship league. However, there was no umbrella organization and little inclination to form one. This was where JDC would be able to step in and centralize Georgia's community activities.

At this early stage in 1990, I met with the synagogue committee. The man in charge, Abram Shvilli, was not interested in starting a Jewish school or a Talmud Torah. What he wanted most was a feather-plucking machine so that the chickens slaughtered on the synagogue premises could be easily prepared for sale. The synagogue also baked eighty tons of matzo in advance of Pesach.

I visited Hebrew classes in a school building rented for Sundays and saw between 100 and 150 young people and as many adults attending. The Sunday school was run by Rivka Krupnick, an Ashkenazi who taught Russian literature during the week in a government school. She had devoted much of her time to starting these classes and developing a Jewish women's group called Rahamim ("Mercy") that provided assistance to the needy and home visits to the ill. Although they acknowledged her contribution to Jewish life in Tbilisi, the Georgian Jews never accepted the Ashkenazi Rivka as one of their own. Here too, I saw that JDC could augment the existing welfare activities.

Kutaisi, a smaller town in central Georgia, once had a thriving community of about 5,000 Jews. At one time, the community built a factory for the manufacture of cloth, suits, and dresses, thereby ensuring employment for the Jews. These Georgian Jews kept their traditions and had a well organized community structure. There were three large synagogue buildings and a small welfare program for the most needy, who received some aid before the Jewish festivals.

JDC would expand these activities by supplementing the food provisions. The closing of the factory and the departure of the more comfortable members of the community in time decreased local resources and increased the number of the needy who became dependent on JDC help.

Azerbaijan

My first tour of Azerbaijan took place in 1992 amid the civil strife between Azeris and Armenians that had turned more than a million Azeris — in a country that had only seven million inhabitants all told — into refugees. The Jews of Azerbaijan were observing the turmoil anxiously, fearing that the xenophobia toward the Armenians might spill over to them too.

The Ashkenazim and Mountain Jews had separate synagogues and separate institutions. The Ashkenazim were mainly intellectuals and professionals. The Mountain Jews had migrated from the northern Caucasus centuries earlier and most had businesses.

The Jewish Agency and the Liaison Bureau had preceded my visit in Azerbaijan, so when I arrived in Baku, the capital, I saw Hebrew classes and Jewish Sunday schools already running. But JDC already had some involvement: as part of our earliest programs in the USSR, JDC had created a lending library in a Jewish Agency-sponsored youth club called Aleph. Now I hoped to expand this to include community development by working alongside the leading Jewish personality in that city, a well-connected lawyer named Mark Haikin.

Unfortunately, Mark was killed in a car accident several months after my first visit. In an uncommon development in this conservative region, a women's committee known as Chava stepped into the breach. This committee came to focus on single-mother families to whom it would provide some vocational training to enable the mothers to enter the workforce and support their families. JDC would provide additional welfare and cultural support for the Jews of Baku.

I also visited Kuba, about 120 miles north of Baku and home to a community of about 5,000 Mountain Jews. Jews had settled in the area in the eighteenth century at the invitation of the local Muslim ruler who wanted to develop the entire region. Until the Soviet era, the community maintained its traditions strictly and built over a dozen synagogues. These Jews, who live in a Jewish area called Krasnaya Sloboda, traditionally married their children at the very young age of twelve or thirteen — a practice they preserve to this day.

Most Jewish men in Kuba spend their time in Moscow, where they have taken over a local market and sell clothing imported from China. Some of them have become wealthy from this business, enabling them to renovate their Kuba homes into luxurious dwellings. The menfolk return to their families for the Jewish holidays, these days being the main focus of their Jewish family lives.

When I first arrived in Kuba, the community had a *shohet* and a *mohel* but no rabbi or teacher. The Soviets had confiscated all but one of the synagogues in the Jewish area.

Western Ukraine

Given my wish to deal with some communities in European areas of the Soviet Union, I was also assigned responsibility for western Ukraine, even though it was disconnected from my other areas.

These were communities that had suffered successive massacres. The notorious Chmielnicki pogroms of 1648–1649 claimed the lives of some 250,000 Jews. Pogroms returned in the 1880s and again after 1917 during the Russian Civil War. Further massacres of Jews took place during the subsequent Polish-Russian War, in the course of which two JDC workers — Israel Friedlaender and Bernard Cantor — were shot by Red Army troops after being mistaken for Polish officers. Later, during World War II, many Ukrainians collaborated with the Nazis in exterminating Jews in their thousands.

During my introductory visit there, I saw places that once had well-known, thriving, and strongly religious communities — including villages and shtetls that gave rise to some of today's most famous Hasidic dynasties. From places such as Berditchev, Belz, Viznitz, Uman, and Breslav, *tzaddikim* (righteous individuals) provided spiritual leadership to masses of Jews in far-flung countries and left an enduring imprint on Jewish history and culture.

Signs of the vibrant, creative, and powerful Jewish life of the past were (and are) still evident, but the spiritual heights achieved by their residents are not. Old single-story wooden huts still stand in Jewish quarters no longer inhabited by Jews. Some Jewish cemeteries remain. Berditchev's is overgrown with weeds, and shortly before my visit the grave of Rabbi Levi Yitzhak of Berditchev (1740–1810) had been set afire. The Jewish cemetery of Chortkiv is an empty field; that of Belz is vacant but for a few tombstones recalling the Hasidic greats who hailed from there. In other cemeteries, one can see the lonely grave of a *tzaddik*, restored by his devotees.

As I traveled from place to place, familiar place names brought to mind great chapters in our past, as well as that last, horrific chapter, in which a millennium of Jewish civilization was virtually obliterated. For me, this emphasized the importance of JDC's mission to restore those communities wherever Jews remained.

Lviv was part of Poland before World War II. It had had a Jewish population of about 70,000 — one-third of the total — and was a renowned Jewish center with thirty synagogues and a full range of cultural institutions. Very few Jews and very few Jewish institutions survived the Nazi occupation of 1941. At the end of the war, Lviv was annexed to the Soviet Union and then became a gathering place for the vestiges of the region's Jewish population. When the Soviet Union disintegrated, Lviv was included in the independent Ukraine.

When I first visited Lviv, it was still the main Jewish locality of western Ukraine with an Ashkenazi population of 12,000–14,000 Jews and a lone synagogue. I found a spectrum of agencies that had taken an interest in helping to rebuild the Jewish community. The one that involved itself most in Lviv's religious life was the Karlin-Stolin Hasidic group, which has performed many of the religious community functions that JDC helped to instill elsewhere.

The second main Jewish center of western Ukraine was Chernivtsi, southeast of Lviv. Before World War II, its Jewish community of 50,000 was well established and had a lengthy history of achievements in all areas of Jewish culture. The German occupation treated the Jews of Chernivtsi and the vicinity as it did Jews elsewhere. The community's many buildings survived, but to this day the authorities have agreed to make restitution of only one synagogue to serve the city's Jews.

On my first visit, I found a city with some 7,000 Jews. Few were originally from Chernivtsi; most were survivors from other parts of the area. The hub of Jewish life was a central cultural organization known as the Cultural Fund, established at the onset of perestroika.

The Fund was housed in two rooms assigned to the community in a building that had once been the center for the Jewish community's organizations and that still boasts a Magen David on its façade that survived the Soviet regime. Inside, however, banisters, once also decorated with metal Stars of David, had not been so fortunate: the Soviets had severed the top and bottom points of every single star from the ground floor to the top so as to destroy any semblance to the Jewish symbol.

Determining Characteristics and Needs

My eye-opening introductory visits enabled me to draw initial conclusions for JDC action in the area assigned to me. First and foremost, any JDC programs would have to validate and support the traditions of each ethnic Jewish group in my region — Ashkenazim, Bukharan, Georgian, and Mountain Jews — each with its own lengthy history, usually wrapped in layers of legend and tradition.

One of my most important discoveries was that the Soviet policies of religious control and suppression had been much less severe in the Asian republics than elsewhere. Even during the worst of Stalinist oppression, regular worship, *shehita*, and *milah* continued in most of these areas. Of the thirty-five synagogues that had remained functional in the Soviet Union, twenty were in the Asian republics and the Caucasus. Thus, my region was singular in that Soviet rule had not totally denuded its Jews of their identity and traditions. Indeed, their thirst for reconnection focused on tradition.

The trust and respect for religious guidance that endured in these areas — unlike the situation in most other areas in the FSU — provided a platform upon which a community could be developed. As I saw it, religious functionaries in these areas took their duties seriously even when they lacked the knowledge and tools to perform them properly. Their communities expected them to do so.

Furthermore, the large non-Ashkenazi Jewish population had a centuries-long tradition of *tzedaka* (organized charity as a Jewish value) and communal responsibility. Hence, being more philanthropic and community-oriented, Jews in these regions had an advantage over others in countering the wretched condition of the government services. Where this tradition was not practiced, it would be JDC's job to provide a link with the past. Where the local resources could not suffice to counter the poverty and provide the welfare needs of fellow Jews, JDC would step in with support.

Jewish emigration affected these republics just as it did the entire FSU in the late 1980s and early 1990s. Many Ashkenazim feared retribution in newly independent Muslim republics where local populations supposed, perhaps with some justification, that the former Soviet regime had sent the Jews to help "Russify" these areas. Although nowhere were Jews targeted in local strife, they left in large numbers — Ashkenazim, Bukharans, Georgians, and Mountain Jews alike.

As elsewhere, the cultural-committee leaders with whom JDC had hoped to work tended to make aliyah most quickly. Those who remained included needy Jews, businesspeople, and young members of the Jewish intelligentsia who were well placed in public life.

The Jews who remained, though, craved reconnection. They were enthralled with the idea of a Jew from far away coming to help them. They seemed to take well to me and my Orthodox bearing — something that might have aroused suspicion of political or KGB involvement had I worked in Belarus or Moscow.

Although emigration slowed in 1992, it continued at significant levels. In some locations in my region, Jewish populations would vanish, or nearly so, even before communities could form.

There would be some demographic replenishment. "Archeological Jews," as we called them, emerged from the underground as confidence grew that the new freedoms across the region would prove durable. While JDC developed programs to reach these and other Jews, Jewish life received a new legitimacy that accelerated this process. Paradoxically, therefore, the FSU's Jewish population in the mid-1990s showed a marked increase over that estimated in 1989/1990 — even though hundreds of thousands had emigrated in the intervening years.

JDC Programs Develop in Growing Circles

First Efforts and Findings

All of us SUT members came away from our exploratory journeys with a mass of facts, impressions, and anecdotes. Vast though the Soviet Union was, only a few regional differences came up as we compared notes — the persistence of Jewish life in the Asian republics being one of the most important.

Our initial contacts or synagogue visits unwrapped before us — at times with extreme suspicion or caution — the Jewish setting of each location. Jews lived not only in major cities but in all manner of localities, large and small, from the Pacific coast and the farthest reaches of Siberia to the European areas of Russia, Belarus, and Ukraine. Some cities, such as Moscow, Saint Petersburg, and Kiev, had Jewish populations in the hundreds of thousands. Others had smaller populations, and in some places the Jews could almost be counted on one hand. The more remote and smaller the locations were, the needier we found the Jews to be — and the harder they would be to serve.

"Community leadership" often consisted of one spirited individual per town. Many localities lacked even this. Those who had community conscious- ness were usually the first to emigrate, and once they were gone it was not easy to find a second echelon that could step in. Secular Jewish activities, such as women's committees and cultural projects, were as porous as the religious ones.

The poor were everywhere and their numbers and proportions mounted amidst the collapse of the Soviet "classless" economy and the emigration of the young and healthy. The old were completely neglected as rampant infla- tion eroded the value of their pensions week by week. The housebound and the bedridden were left without organized care, and were reliant on good neighbors for survival. These findings had daunting implications for JDC, for its mission statement, and for the SUT members.

To our amazement, however, seventy years of Soviet brutalities had not managed to destroy Jewish identity and consciousness completely. Soviet (soon to become "FSU") Jewry was still alive, populous, and quietly vibrant. It greeted JDC with genuine warmth and welcomed those activities that we were able to initiate. It was now up to us to jumpstart community develop- ment. Where to begin was a different question.

Steps Toward Infrastructure

The initial contacts and the haphazard nature of our first efforts, we concluded, needed some focus. If we wanted to help these Jews live Jewish lives of their choosing, it would not suffice to provide community-oriented services as we had begun doing. We would have to help in developing Jewish communities. The future of FSU Jewry, as well as the future of aliyah, depended on the exis- tence of a solid community structure. Developing a systematic infrastructure of our own, we figured, would gradually forge a mass of individuals into a community.

This was a novel approach for JDC. Rarely in the past had it needed to define community development, let alone community creation, as a primary activity. Even after the Holocaust, survivors emerged with their Jewish iden- tities and community orientation intact. Similarly, in North Africa, Israel, and elsewhere, the basic human building blocks of Jewish life endured, even amidst the grimmest hardship and poverty. Our community-building work in the FSU would be more groundbreaking than we had ever imagined.

As a preliminary, the SUT devised a working concept of community for its work: a collective of Jews within reasonable geographical proximity who have common interests and who could make use of common religious, social, and cultural services. To attain our goal, we focused on involving local players as much as possible. All programs, be they in religious services, welfare, education, meals, or culture, would be undertaken in conjunction with local Jews, for the purpose of achieving community fusion. Wherever we found fragments of communities, they would be our cornerstone. Elsewhere, we would attempt to create them. On their shoulders we would develop programs to the limits of our ability and theirs.

My future field visits — several per year — would follow an appropriate and standard modus operandi that our eager clients would find effective. At seminars that local players organized, I would hear everyone out and deliver summarizing remarks to keen ears. When synagogues hosted the seminars, I would deliver a brief speech on some point of Torah. These words, too, would be taken in wholeheartedly by my audiences. All the while, I would encourage people to think in community terms and to work actively in putting JDC's programs into service wherever possible.

To organize itself for its immense task, JDC established a separate FSU Department in 1990. This department, based in Israel, was directed initially by Michael Schneider, and later by Asher Ostrin.

From 1992 the FSU Department allocated field representatives to each SUT member. Each representative takes responsibility for a particular region, overseeing JDC's programs and working hand-in-hand with the country director and local players in order to implement JDC policy and create empowerment. The representatives spend most of their time in their FSU locations, returning to SUT headquarters in Jerusalem for consultations from time to time. Over the years, I have been allocated five representatives to accompany my work in the Asian areas.[10]

---

10. At present, Zvika Timberg and Max Wiesel are the representatives for my areas of the FSU. Menachem Elazer, Israel Szyf, and Meir Zissov were resident representatives in the past.

Initial Progress: Community Building

The extensive emigration of the late 1980s brought to the fore a large stratum of Jews in need of welfare services. The welfare needs were obvious to all of us. But when we added up the numbers of Jews in distress and gauged the extremity of their woes, we doubted whether JDC could or should tackle welfare in a large way at all. None of us thought at that time that welfare would or should be the linchpin of our entire enterprise. We feared that JDC did not have the financial means to handle such a large undertaking. We felt that government support and local efforts ought to be the primary resources for the needy.

At this early stage, our attempts to tackle the matter were only sporadic. We set up offices and welfare committees in some major towns, where we recruited and trained local Jews to run basic welfare programs. The first of these welfare programs were modest and included the establishment of canteens, food-parcel distribution, and some activities for the homebound. We saw our job as financing and overseeing the systemization of these activities. By doing so, we hoped to encourage local players to think in community terms, anticipating that we could build on them later.

We soon realized, however, that much more was needed. There was no way that JDC could turn its back on so much Jewish misery.

Until we reached that realization, though, it was our intention to cleave to our original mission statement: Jewish reconnection via community development. We concentrated on the religious, cultural, and educational aspects of community building. If we could succeed in building viable Jewish communities in this way, they would eventually have the capacity for programs of their own. My work in this respect was very similar in its development and implementation to that of my other SUT colleagues.

One of our first major programs was the distribution of books — tens of thousands of Jewish religious and secular volumes — to individuals and libraries. We wanted to enable the region's highly literate Jews to educate themselves about their people and heritage. Every item, every shipment, vanished upon arrival. Had this happened in a settled community, one would call it theft. Here though, we saw it as the absorption of water in parched soil. In 1990, JDC allocated half of its USSR budget to libraries. Before long, Soviet Jews knew of JDC as "the library people." Some still do.

As for religious activities, JDC considered them part of the renewal and maintenance of Jewish life. In fact, we discovered a surprising interest in traditional life-cycle and festival activities among Jews at large. Jews who normally could not connect to religion in the classic sense found these celebrations historically and socially meaningful.

Pesach seders in particular soon became a central feature of FSU Jewish life and identity. The Pesach story of freedom resonated strongly with the Soviet Jewish experience — "Let my people go."[11] JDC's seder program developed so that over time outlying localities benefited from it too. Over the years we began to move away from carrying out large communal celebrations and began distributing family seder kits, Pesach videocassettes in Russian, audiocassettes of Pesach songs, and packages of relevant books for smaller communities.

For the High Holidays, we sent emissaries, mostly young yeshiva graduates, to twenty-seven localities in the summer of 1990 and thirty-eight the next year to run services and celebrations. In advance of each round, we sent tons of supplies to the Choral Synagogue in Moscow for distribution. The experience opened our eyes to the need to train local leaders to organize the celebrations and to decentralize our distribution methods, since the Moscow-based system was not able to handle perishable festival items. And thus the program evolved.

Since synagogue attendance peaked at festival times, we distributed books related to the festivals in thousands of copies. For the rest of the year, JDC published a prayer book and distributed it where needed. JDC also published a book in Russian, titled *Guide for the Living*, on how to conduct a Jewish burial ceremony. The very arrival of all these precious objects whetted the Jews' appetite for more.

For the older participants, the ritual events marked a return to an almost forgotten childhood and an occasion for pride, dignity, poignancy, and hope — especially since the experiences have allowed the young and the old to intermingle. For us, they have given evidence of the damage caused by the decades of Soviet hostility toward Jewish practice, of the trampled traditions that Communism attempted to vanquish. Notwithstanding the impressive progress since those years, the tormented Jewry is still a long way from full recovery.

---

11. Exodus 5:1. This phrase was used in Israel and Western Europe as a slogan in campaigns for the freedom of Jews in the Soviet Union.

Thus, JDC quickly became a mass purveyor of Jewish religious services and supplies in the FSU. As demand spiraled, however, matters threatened to get out of hand. Our supplies were being distributed to large numbers of individuals who snapped them up spontaneously but had no practical use for them. Consequently, in June 1992, the distribution of religious articles was merged with other ongoing JDC activities.

The supply of religious articles facilitated a training program for community functionaries, which ballooned into an enormous enterprise that did have reconnection implications. The supplies also benefited JDC-inaugurated bar and bat mitzvah programs, regional seminars for religious development, and a cantorial seminary in Moscow.

In the course of these and other advanced programs, we sent promising candidates to Israel for further training. Returning to the FSU, these trainees usually benefited their communities significantly with their enhanced knowledge and capabilities in religious functions.

We established brief rabbinical seminars, financed rabbis' positions in some localities, subsidized Yeshivat Ohalei Yaakov at the Moscow Choral Synagogue (the first yeshiva in the FSU that no one could accuse of being a government tool), and for a time posted Israeli rabbis to the FSU for year-long service.

Despite these efforts, local communities continued to lack a systematic ability to provide life-cycle services as a matter of course — services that were more in demand than we had imagined. This was brought to my attention many times during my visits to Jewish collectives in the FSU.

On one of my early trips to Ust-Kamenogorsk in Kazakhstan, the leading figure among the few Jews there took me one day to see an old, bedridden woman. After sharing her history and her war stories with me, the woman said, "You're a Jew; you've got everything you need. But I want a Jewish burial." She begged for this and, when the time came, we arranged it through the local community. This and many other personal exchanges have given evidence of the eternal Jewish spark — the *pintele yid* in Hasidic thought.

To enhance the provision of such services, JDC-FSU strengthened its religious activities in the mid-1990s by hiring Rabbi Meir Schlesinger[12] of Jerusalem and tasking him with investing all JDC operations, including

---

12. Rabbi Meir Schlesinger founded the Sha'alvim *hesder* yeshiva near Jerusalem in 1961 and headed it until 1994. He continues to run seminars in the FSU.

general ones such as welfare and nutrition programs, with a non-coercive but perceptible Jewish complexion. Rabbi Schlesinger's seminars would teach the local Jewish leaders the Jewish dimension of welfare, charity, medical ethics, community structure, education, and the importance of Jewish renewal. Seminars would also provide the leadership with the understanding and practicalities of Jewish life-cycle rituals, such as *milah* (circumcision), bar mitzvah, marriage, and burial. With the help of this religious training, JDC aspires to give the communities the tools, the knowledge, and particularly the values to become self-sufficient in their community lives.

These initial programs for Soviet/FSU Jews stirred and suited our clients' yearnings and served our overarching goal. At the same time, other programs were being initiated or fortified. They included assisting communities in reclaiming previously confiscated community properties, involvement in various levels of Jewish education, and cultural enhancement.

After the Soviet Jews had endured decades of state-sponsored assaults on institutions, communities, and ownership of property, the renewal of Jewish communal activity was crippled by a sheer lack of places to meet. We first discussed the need to reclaim confiscated buildings from the government in early 1990, when restitution requests and initiatives in several cities came to our attention. With community coalescence as our prime objective, JDC resolved to play a proactive role in encouraging communities to reclaim property.

Under the laws, recipient entities had to be religious communities. As a result, we became active in reclaiming, restoring, and equipping synagogues, and also in training local community leaders in archival research and in how most effectively to use and renovate the properties once they were reclaimed. In the early 1990s, more than eighty synagogues were reclaimed, refurbished, and tailored to community needs with JDC assistance. Of these, thirty-three were in the Asian areas.

In Lviv, western Ukraine, JDC provided assistance and financial support in renovating a reclaimed synagogue and equipping it with a modern kitchen and dining room. The Nazis had used the building as a stable; the Communists as a warehouse.

The old synagogue in Chernivtsi, southeast of Lviv, was also reclaimed from the authorities and restored for religious services. Soon after its restoration, non-Jewish women from the area began to come to the synagogue.

They wanted blessings from the rabbi to solve family problems. This unusual tradition dates back to the times when Jewish life was well known and revered by the peasantry of Ukraine, who wished to take part in the blessings offered by Hasidic rabbis.

Reclamation of communal property, however, was of no use to communities that had no prior claim to assert, or where — as in Baku in Azerbaijan — the authorities steadfastly refused to consider restitution. Jews in such situations struggled to set up embryonic services in scattered locations. In response, we swayed from JDC's longstanding policy not to consign funds to real-estate acquisition and purchased premises to house community institutions — principally the welfare and Jewish community centers that would become a central vehicle for JDC's community-building programs.

From 2001 and over the following years, we were able to acquire buildings that became the central address of the Jewish communities. With the help of a generous benefactor, the Posner family of Pittsburgh, such acquisitions took place in three localities in my areas, namely Baku in Azerbaijan, Tashkent in Uzbekistan, and Tbilisi in Georgia.

Formal and Nonformal Education

JDC's niche in the field of education in the FSU tapped into those elements necessary for fulfilling our community development and reconnection mandate and in which Israeli agencies were not active.

The stereotyped pre-perestroika Soviet Jew — the refusenik whose Russian haute couture and advanced academic degrees typified his Jewishness more than they did his "Russianness" — prompted JDC to identify higher education as a fulcrum for community reconnection. The initiative in this matter, as in many others, was taken by Ralph Goldman, who recognized the importance of intelligentsia in the FSU. The Open University of Russia established relations with the Open University of Israel, and the Soviet Academy of Sciences established a Jewish section. Consequently, Sefer, the Moscow Center for University Teaching of Jewish Civilization, was opened in 1994 with JDC support to coordinate and strengthen the academic study of Judaism that burgeoned across the FSU.

Indeed, one of our outstanding achievements in the realm of education has been in the academic field. In my region alone, JDC's financial and technical support enabled Jewish academics to open five university-level Jewish studies centers — in Tbilisi (Georgia), Almaty (Kazakhstan), Bishkek (Kyrgyzstan), and two in Baku (Azerbaijan). All are active today and have attracted hundreds of students.

JDC also added a vital dimension to Jewish school education. At one time we provided each school child with a basic set of books, including a Bible, a prayer book, a history book, a volume on Jewish festivals, and a Hebrew primer. The number of books distributed in this fashion probably reached the million mark by 2003. We have helped upgrade kindergartens and provided schools with occasional assistance in equipment and repairs. JDC has held seminars on Jewish knowledge for the schools' qualified Jewish teachers.

In Tbilisi, Georgia, Rabbi Levine obtained funding from a group in the United States that placed him in charge of the Jewish education program in the city. He used the funds not only to maintain the first Jewish day school in Tbilisi but also to help some of the needy by distributing medicine and money. In addition, he began a Sunday school for about ninety boys and girls and a *kollel* (yeshiva for married students). JDC helped by providing the schools with books, a library, and teaching aids.

Rabbi Levine, who became chief rabbi of Tbilisi in 1993, had to leave his position in the city suddenly in 2002, when he was threatened by local criminal elements who wanted a share of the money he was supposedly receiving from abroad. He took his young family to Israel but has continued to visit Tbilisi from time to time to direct the school, the *kollel*, and his other activities.

To give JDC's material assistance a more lasting effect, we assisted in teacher training. Again our methods mirrored those that we had used in other countries: providing manuals, running workshops, and offering consultations on curriculum development, teaching techniques, and Jewish tradition. In these activities, we tried to use the direct goal — preparing classroom teachers — as leverage for a higher purpose: creating a communal leadership that would eventually become self-sufficient.

Dr. Seymour "Epi" Epstein, one of the original SUT members who was now heading the education project for the FSU,[13] assisted in the formation of

---

13. Epi was also the country director for Siberia and the Baltic states, in addition to serving as JDC's director of Jewish education in Europe and North Africa.

a Jewish Principals' Association that was reminiscent of the association that I had helped to set up in Europe.

Aspiring to extend community awareness to all generations in the FSU, voluntarism has been taught to youth under a program developed by JDC. Across the FSU, welfare and community centers and Hillel groups enlisted students to visit senior citizens, help them in their homes, read for them, and run errands for them. Without doubt, by including this facet of Jewish ethics in FSU Jewish education, the path toward reconnecting the young Jews to the Jewish people was widened.

In informal education, JDC found three useful long-term vehicles of community development and reconnection: Jewish community centers (JCCs), Jewish summer and winter camps, and the Hillel movement. Foremost among them were Jewish community centers. In no way resembling the American Jewish institutions that go by this name, they are homegrown offshoots of the cultural centers developed during perestroika as places where Jews could gather.

JDC saw FSU-style JCCs as catalysts in fostering community development, community coalescence, and the formation of autonomous leadership. Where such centers did not exist, therefore, we helped to develop them. Where awareness of the potential of a JCC was lacking, we stimulated it. To achieve this, JDC arranged seminars to train local leaders in the functions of a Jewish community and in ways in which they might best develop their own communal programs. These seminars were well received, and the communities sent representatives to attend, often at their own expense.

To formalize our commitment to the long-term viability of the JCCs, our Jewish Renewal Department in Jerusalem, directed by Sara Bogen,[14] researched and recommended several community-center models and interacted with other Jewish organizations to exert more effective influence in implementing these models. Eventually, that department took upon itself to coordinate the FSU Jewish community centers and related activities.

---

14. Sara Bogen was then a JDC staff member based in Jerusalem responsible for JCC activities and informal education in the FSU. Like other senior staff members of the FSU Department at the time, she also carried a "country director" assignment, overseeing programs in Saint Petersburg and northeastern Russia.

The JDC-supported Jewish library program found its home at the JCCs and other similar institutions. JDC sponsorship also plays a role in the JCC menu of dance and music groups, art exhibitions, concerts, lectures, and Jewish history courses. An FSU-wide annual Jewish book week called Ofek has become a regular feature in most larger Jewish communities, serving not only as a celebration for those already involved in Jewish life but as a magnet for the unaffiliated and as a way for the wider population to gain insight into Jewish life and heritage. Since JDC's early years in the FSU it has coordinated and co-financed this event in collaboration with the JCCs.

Other programs organized in cooperation with the JCCs have included child-oriented Jewish outreach. While JDC understood that Jewish knowledge is a path to a Jewishly connected child, it also saw cultural activities as ways of cultivating Jewish identity. Arranging bar mitzvah and bat mitzvah celebrations at the JCCs might connect children with their Jewish roots. At the same time, arranging and subsidizing a gifted child's musical training could also serve this purpose, since many FSU Jews considered high culture a manifestation of Jewishness.

Jewish summer and winter camps became our second vehicle in informal education. JDC's goal in operating or financing such camps focused on the building blocks of community development: education, socialization, and welfare.

Where local players organized summer or winter camps, JDC provided financial support, trained counselors, and almost always distributed books and learning materials. In some locations, JDC-FSU organized camps through JCCs and welfare centers.

We also began sending children to the Ronald S. Lauder AJJDC International Jewish Summer Camp in Szarvas, Hungary, which was established in 1990 to provide first-time exposure to Judaism to Jewish children from the unraveling Communist bloc. Sending children to Szarvas not only immersed them in a Jewish experience that they had never had, it helped strengthen the bonds among the children from a particular region. Furthermore, their introduction to Jewish youngsters from other countries has proven immensely effective in deepening their Jewish identities.

The very process of selecting children to attend the camp in Hungary was an exercise in community coalescence. Community leaders were involved in selecting children for the camp and the parents' interest in sending their children to a camp in another country automatically involved them in a Jewish group dynamic, and hence communal involvement.

With community-building in mind, we viewed the camps, like the schools, as appropriate settings for the inculcation of Jewish values, foremost *tzedaka* (charity). Our educational materials made this clear and encouraged camp operators to apply the principles in the innumerable opportunities that came about. An innovative family camp was also targeted to this end. It was devised by the SUT in 1993 to thwart generation-gap alienation between Jewishly informed children and less-informed adults. The time at the camps was used for lectures, learning about the Jewish calendar, and basics of the Bible. Overall, the camp experience welded the participants into a group, strengthened the families' Jewish identity and knowledge, and influenced the parents to become active in communal life after their return home.

JDC involvement in camps peaked in the 1990s with annual enrollment of about 30,000 youngsters across the FSU, including many such camps in my region. From that point on, though, it diminished, largely due to emigration.

The Hillel movement was our third main informal education vehicle. Instigated in Moscow in 1993/1994 by Jonathan Porath of the FSU Department and Yossie Goldman of Hillel International, it is a partnership with the Charles and Lynn Schusterman Family Foundation. Hillel chapters gradually spread across the FSU. JDC supports the Hillel venture by providing part of its budget and managing the rest, which comes from American Jewish philanthropies.

Hillel in the FSU bears little resemblance to its American namesake. Chapters are off-campus and their target age group, from late teens to late twenties, oversteps the student population by far. They have a permanent cadre of counselors that is largely made up of former students who verge on the age of thirty.

Hillel has two broad goals: to cultivate young Jewish leaders and leverage them for community service and outreach, and to give young FSU Jews a chance to deflect assimilation dangers by furnishing them with Jewish social surroundings and content in their daily lives.

The focus on community service encourages Hillel members to give support to the weaker members of society. They are sent on Jewish welfare missions. In outlying areas, they conduct Pesach seders and distribute food parcels. In their hometowns, they mentor children of single-parent families. Thus, the 500 participants of five Hillel chapters and a few dozen youth clubs in my areas play an active role in JDC Jewish renewal, culture, and welfare programs.

Welfare: A Challenge Too Great to Ignore

Despite our initial belief that welfare needs were beyond our writ, 1991 brought an event that made this position untenable. An abortive coup in Moscow led to a higher scale of disorder and disintegration throughout the region. Government medical and other services slumped further; food supplies declined, and conditions of near starvation among the elderly increased in various areas.

The needs of the elderly Jewish poor became epidemic. While we feared that meeting them would exhaust our financial and human resources, render other activities impossible, and make only a minor dent in the hardships, we inevitably came around to a dialectic way of thinking. True, welfare is beyond us. But at the same time we have no choice but to confront it.

No other course of action was conscionable. JDC history is a history of helping people, which means, among other things, welfare. Never had we sacrificed this responsibility in favor of reconnection ("rehabilitation" in the classic JDC terminology). We owed it to vast numbers of elderly Jews to help them live out their lives in dignity.

Once it was decided to undertake a welfare program, JDC set aside the necessary budget for the FSU and appointed Dr. Amos Avgar, then country director in Saint Petersburg, as welfare coordinator for the entire region. As he settled into his position, an unusually fierce winter set in. Avgar's first task, a monumental one, was to initiate a winter relief program, a package of emergency welfare programs that JDC put together in response to the acute distress.

Within a period of six months, Avgar and the SUT staff found themselves administering massive feeding efforts in the FSU. Since the supplies included 500,000 packages from the United States Department of Agriculture, JDC's actions represented both world Jewry and the American government. By agreement, we distributed 10 percent of the packages to Jews and the rest to hospitals and miscellaneous local non-Jewish organizations.

In the midst of this operation, senior JDC officials fanned out across the region to participate in the effort. In addition to helping the needy elderly

Jews, we used the opportunity to gain access to Jewish homes, open more doors for JDC, and acquaint ourselves with more FSU Jews and their needs.

I went to Kiev, the Ukrainian capital, on a two-week assignment and personally distributed about fifty parcels to Jews there. One elderly woman whom I visited ordered me to remove some newspapers from a cupboard. The papers told an amazing story, of how during World War II she had been a top pilot and squadron commander and downed numerous German planes. Now she was living on an army pension, which was comparatively high, but she still lacked funds to take care of all her basic needs.

Then the woman asked me to bring her an object from a corner in her room. It looked like a piece of stone.

"Look," she said, "it's a piece of matzo that has become fossilized. I don't keep Pesach, but every year I put it on my table as I take my normal meals."

Such was the state of Jewish commitment that I encountered: a faint but persistent flicker in a firmament of physical and spiritual darkness.

The Hesed Network

In 1992, after establishing the winter relief program, we estimated that our primary welfare beneficiaries in the FSU — Jews aged sixty-plus — numbered well over half a million. We also anticipated that within a few years that population would account for about one-third of FSU Jewry. With that in mind, Amos Avgar and his Jerusalem-based welfare team began to develop and pilot a more comprehensive strategy for JDC welfare activities in the FSU, one that could be long-term and replicated on a massive scale.

An initial target was to concentrate our assistance on systematic and affordable programs as opposed to improvised responses to individual crises. Yet community-level welfare action was unknown in the USSR. Our decision to develop it committed us to training its practitioners. We dispatched "roving experts" throughout the FSU to visit and train local welfare organizers, and to develop an approach that we hoped could be applied across the region.

A unique welfare initiative was started in Kiev. JDC, in cooperation with the community's committee, developed a multi-service welfare center to fund shopping and housecleaning assistance, home visits for shut-ins, distribution of second-hand clothing, a library and video center, and a regular "ask the doctor" program. JDC provided financial support and training. Observing this center's initial success, JDC began to view it as a model that could be applied across the FSU.

The model was tested, adapted, and codified in Saint Petersburg in 1993. It was termed a Hesed welfare center (in the plural: Hasadim). Variously translated as "kindness" or "loving-kindness," *hesed* denotes care for others' needs. Once Hesed Avraham, the model developed in Saint Petersburg, proved itself, we moved to open similar centers across the FSU. As expected, each has met its primary goal: alleviating welfare distress. These centers, frequently alongside JCCs, quickly became prime agents of Jewish reconnection in the FSU.

The expansion of the Hesed network was a dramatic tale. At first, Hesed centers were opened with the help of a "Hesed Commando," staffed by local medical and welfare professionals and volunteers. The Hesed Commando would visit communities for several weeks at a time, helping local people open locally differentiated centers. Some locations would require JDC's help and guidance at all stages of assessing needs and then financing, establishing, staffing, organizing, and activating a Hesed center. Others — those with existing and stronger community infrastructures — would suffice with financial backing and would implement a Hesed center with JDC's guidelines. To serve very small Jewish populations, JDC opened hundreds of smaller centers and developed a Hesed-on-wheels model, the HesedMobile.

The widespread Hesed network could not have been formed as it was without JDC's undertaking, where necessary, to provide appropriate community premises. JDC ensured that either reclaimed, rented, or purchased buildings were secured to house Hesed centers.

A key to the success of Hesed centers and their activities has been professional local management. Realizing that a major long-term effort to achieve this was at hand, JDC established the William Rosenwald Institute for Communal and Welfare Workers in Saint Petersburg in 1994. Local Hesed directors and other staff continue to receive organized training through the institute. Later, the Rosenwald Institute's work would be supplemented by that of nine regional training institutes.

JDC's formulated goal was to assure that each Hesed center encompass the three key principles of *hesed* — community, voluntarism, and *Yiddishkeit* — which are constants in JDC programs.

Community relates to the involvement and responsibility of the empowered community at large.

Voluntarism entails the creation of volunteer consciousness — a novelty in the FSU — in order to give the community the additional manpower that it needs to run Hesed programs. Each Hesed board is composed of local community leaders, businesspeople, and relevant professionals. Over time, the decision-making prerogatives in welfare, initially held by SUT members and their field representatives, were shifted to these locally-operated Hesed boards.

Yiddishkeit brings JDC back to its mission statement in the FSU: Jewish reconnection. That Hesed centers would celebrate Jewish festivals was taken for granted. However, we took this a step further. Everything offered by a Hesed should be infused with a Jewish spirit.

The *socialization* aspect of community-building also became a leading element of the Hesed centers. The Hesed-based social activities and clubs bring Jews — elderly and young — together. Volunteers of all ages, including Hillel members, interact through Hesed programs. Caregivers visiting the housebound provide desperately sought companionship. Disparate welfare organizations work together. Moreover, in 2002 we began to pair Hasadim with Jewish federations and benefactors worldwide — giving the concept of reconnection a new twist.

The Hesed centers developed their activities as each Hesed learned to cater to the particular needs of its clients. Organized distribution of food parcels led to the development of regular kitchens and meals on wheels for the housebound. In response to the social isolation many Jewish elderly face, Hasadim adopted a program called Warm Homes, referring lonely seniors to gatherings at people's apartments for social companionship. In a later development, some Hasadim began to organize delivery of fresh food to elderly Jews who can no longer shop or travel to a communal dining hall but can cook for themselves.

Hasadim also host JDC's medical and therapy programs, which are run by Jewish volunteer doctors. In 1995, to meet the needs of Hesed clients, JDC established a Medical Equipment Employment and Production Center in Saint Petersburg that uses volunteer labor to manufacture wheelchairs, walkers, canes, crutches, and other aids. The Hesed centers that receive this equipment lend it to tens of thousands free of charge. Some of the Hesed loan programs for medical equipment have been augmented with emergency centers and telephone hotlines for the elderly.

Hesed Success: My Areas

By 2006, JDC had established or supported the establishment of some 200 permanent Hasadim and more than 80 HesedMobiles in the FSU.

In Kazakhstan alone, I oversaw the establishment of thirteen main Hasadim — one for each of the republic's regions. Branching out of the thirteen Hasadim are small operations in over ninety localities in these regions of Kazakhstan. Despite the fact that by the mid-1990s fewer Jews remained in all of Kazakhstan than had been in its capital, Almaty, six or seven years earlier, Jews still live in over 100 localities — and through the Hasadim and their offshoots, JDC was able to reach almost all of them.

The Hesed in Almaty is a fine example of the program's evolution. At first, we ran a JDC office in the center of the city in an apartment that we purchased. Soon after, we opened a Hesed that was operated from the office and directed by two local officials whom I hired. The first, Dr. Sasha Bar-On, gave up his medical practice to work for JDC full-time. The second, a social worker, was an older, unmarried Jewish woman. During one of my visits, this social worker was found dead in her apartment after having been murdered, apparently by a burglar in search of money. Hers was the first grave in the new all-Jewish cemetery that the Almaty municipality had provided for the community.

JDC later purchased additional apartments adjoining its office in Almaty to house the community's Hesed and JCC. A local group called Mitzvah took upon itself to run this combined JCC/Hesed center. With JDC funds, it has provided food parcels, meals for the needy, talks, lectures, a place for students to gather, a lending library, and a meeting place for Jewish war veterans. Over time, this center became the hub of Jewish life for Almaty's 7,000 remaining Jews.

One of those Jews was Grigoriy, a man in his fifties whom I met on one of my later visits to Almaty. He was born in Rovno, Ukraine, and raised as a Soviet war orphan. Given basic needs but no love, warmth, or smiles, Grigoriy had learned from other boys how to fight, swear, steal, and cheat. At the age of fourteen, he was enrolled in a vocational school that trained him to become a certified electrician. Then he was told to fend for himself. After his military service, he migrated alone from factory to factory, from republic to republic.

Then he was diagnosed with diabetes. Unwilling to adhere to the dietary restrictions the disease demands, his condition deteriorated until he lost first one leg, then the other. By this time, he was living in a tiny apartment in Almaty and getting by on a paltry disability benefit. Although able to move about on a board with wheels, he could not reach the top of his gas stove to cook. It was in this terrible state that a volunteer from the Hesed in Almaty found him.

The Hesed provided him with a special wheelchair and had his bathroom rebuilt for his needs. A homecare worker visited him daily and provided him with food appropriate to his condition. Above all, he was given loving care for the first time in his life. The attention made him weep like a child.

Grigoriy knew that he had been born Jewish but had never been with Jews and had never seen a synagogue in his life. "Show me a synagogue," he begged of the Hesed nurse. That was a challenge in itself. A heavy man, he had to be lowered to street level and placed in an ambulance. The Hesed arranged it all. He was taken to synagogue for a Hanukkah service.

Entering the prayer house, Grigoriy was engulfed in emotions of wonder, astonishment, and boundless gratitude. The crowd of worshippers, the happy children, the large menorah, the traditional potato pancakes that were given out after the service — tears streamed down his cheeks as he took it all in. For Grigoriy, the miracle of Hanukkah occurred not 2,200 years ago, but right then, on the day that the Hesed took him to the synagogue.

The Hesed that we established in Taganrog, Russia, in 2000 has become one of the finest examples of the model's grand strategy. As soon as its activities began, the Hesed attracted the city's disconnected Jews like a magnet. A large group of volunteers came together. A food distribution center was opened for the needy. Mass celebrations of Jewish festivals were organized. Young people were drawn to the center as a place to meet and dance. A women's committee came together. Suddenly, as we had hoped, the dispersed Jews of Taganrog became a community. In 2006, the Taganrog Hesed had 500 clients, about a quarter of the city's estimated Jewish population.

In some places, local communities were able to develop welfare services with less intensive involvement from JDC. Having begun basic JDC welfare activities in Tashkent, Uzbekistan, during my very first visit, within a short time a unique welfare program was developed for the Jewish needy of the city. Along with JDC's resident representative in Uzbekistan, Israel Szyf, we organized cooperation between the local Jewish cultural committee, the officers of the Ashkenazi synagogue, and the Bukharan committee to distribute food packages to the needy several times a year. We also used this mechanism to hand out schoolbooks and religious necessities and to provide the especially destitute with extra help.

The array of locally directed programs in Tashkent rendered the establishment of a Hesed there less necessary for some time. Eventually, however, we established a Hesed and JCC together in a "Jewish House," to enable coordination of all JDC activities in the city. By 2006, these institutions were available to serve all the needy among the 10,000 Jews who remained in Tashkent.

A similar development of JDC activities took place in Tbilisi, Georgia. The JDC library and kindergarten in Tbilisi gradually grew to include the whole gamut of JCC programs and a framework for the diverse groups within the community. From 1990 we began implementing welfare activities alongside those of the the local Jewish women's group, Rahamim. The latter preferred to continue in its small-scale programs apart from the all-embracing JDC program. JDC began making a significant investment in organizing long-term welfare work for the very needy Jews who had regularly spent winters without heat, light, and fuel for cooking. By 1996/97, when the Hesed in this city was opened, some 750 people were receiving food parcels and 50–60 people were given daily hot meals. These figures have increased considerably since then.

The Tbilisi Hesed soon became the central Hesed of Georgia, the other five provincial Hasadim remaining smaller and less active. In 2003, with the help of the Posner family of Pittsburgh, we purchased a building to house the community's institutions, and it became home to the Hesed and JCC, and by 2006 had become one of the largest in scope in my region. It sponsors a golden-age club, a doctors' service including loaning of medical equipment, nurses to care for the elderly, the ill, and the bedridden, and a well-functioning library.

This large program, developed at first by Menachem Elazar, the long-serving JDC resident representative in Georgia, and later by Meir Zissov who succeeded him, is a matter of life or death for many Jews. In fact, I was told that the guardian of the Jewish cemetery in Tbilisi testified that burials dwindled at the same time as the city's Hesed began providing for the sick, needy, and elderly.

The Baku Hesed is the only one in all of Azerbaijan, the republic's compact size allowing all programs for the periphery to be directed from there. What was fascinating in this case was how the Hesed induced rival groups to cooperate. It also began to augment a food distribution program that the Chava women's organization had initiated in the city, and it supported a medical clinic that JDC helped to open on the basis of volunteer Jewish doctors.

Exceptional Cases

Despite the keenness of local Jews in my areas to reconnect with their roots, and in spite of the needs of the poor and elderly, JDC's work has been restricted in some Asian areas where distances, poor roads, and political instability have limited our reach. As in other areas in the FSU, there are peripheral areas that do have Hasadim, while others have small branches belonging to a central Hesed in the nearest main city. Where neither has been possible, we send out food parcels, medicines, and religious items by HesedMobile a few times a year.

Over the years in Tajikistan, for example, the collapse of law and order and violent tribal conflict prompted all but about 350 Jews in Dushanbe and 100 Jews in the Leninabad area to emigrate as soon as they could. For those who remained, conditions prevented JDC from running its full range of programs in the region. Nevertheless, in 2004 we opened an office in Dushanbe, run by a local person, to provide basic assistance for needy Jews.

A less common difficulty faced us in Turkmenistan, where most of the 2,000 Jews of the capital city, Ashkhabad, emigrated while the few who remained did not join forces to assist the Jewish needy. Thus, it became virtually impossible to find a foothold for JDC activity in Turkmenistan. In the end, we located a local Jewish woman willing to help in distributing JDC assistance. JDC transfers money to her and she arranges food packages for the needy Jews who remained there. The JDC resident representative in Tashkent also sends supplies such as matzo for Pesach and other items for the Jewish holidays.

Out-of-the-ordinary events sometimes dictate the need for non-routine attention. In April 1991, for example, the provincial town of Oni in Georgia was devastated by an earthquake. To assist the 350 Jewish families in the town, JDC arranged a large shipment of new clothing that they could use or barter for other necessities. I informed Georgian officials that I wished to deliver the clothing personally. Itzik Moshe, the Jewish Agency representative in Georgia, cleared the shipment through customs and arranged for a helicopter from the government. We loaded the parcels into the chopper and flew to Oni, where the mayor, government officials, the Jewish community committee, and various non-Jews gave us a very warm welcome. We handed the consignment to the community committee, which undertook to distribute it equitably. For the next few years, Oni was a *cause celebre* for foreign relief agencies and Georgian officials, and some of JDC's highest officers attended ceremonies there. The synagogue, damaged in the earthquake, has since been renovated and the country's president, Eduard Shevardnadze,[15] attended its reopening.

After an earthquake in 2001 that affected the population of Tbilisi, Georgia, local Jewish businesspeople donated $50,000 to rebuild the homes of the needy. JDC added a substantial one-time donation of its own, tendering it to a relief committee established by the central synagogue.

Also in Georgia, in Kutaisi, JDC's Hesed was temporarily closed in 2002. This highly unusual step occurred when members of the local underworld had threatened dire consequences for the Hesed director unless the Hesed turned over a cut of the funds received from JDC. The director refused to divert the funds for any other purposes than he had received them. Soon after, his home was robbed of all his valuables. JDC immediately spirited the Hesed director and his family out of the country. After a short time, a replacement was found, who continues to manage the JDC-supported Hesed program.

Thus JDC's extensive Hesed and additional welfare activities have come to reach as many Jews as it can across the FSU, as communities and as individuals. The Hesed network gives support for the unique needs of each community and attempts to ensure that no Jew remain wanting for the basic necessities of life.

Feeling the Budgetary Pinch

At first, JDC provided a small budget for its FSU activities. Minor amounts of foreign currency did wonders in the economic straits of the time.

---

15. Eduard Shevardnadze was president of the Republic of Georgia from 1992 until he was overthrown by the popular and peaceful "Rose Revolution" of 2003.

Managing finances in the FSU, JDC encountered government norms and regulations that were convoluted and difficult to fulfill if we wished to develop our activities efficiently. Nevertheless, JDC's policy was to remain aboveboard. We paid a high price for this, since differences in official and black-market currency exchange rates alone could add up to 50–70 percent. We were not saints; in a vacuum, we might have turned a blind eye here and there. But the importance of our mission would not permit JDC to risk its activities in the FSU by ignoring government regulations.

After a brief period in which operating costs were low, prices throughout the region rose steeply. Furthermore, the intensity and scale of material needs increasingly strained JDC's FSU budget. America's Jewish Federations responded to these needs with a special hunger campaign to supplement the regular allocations they made to JDC's activities. But funding this massive relief enterprise while maintaining adequate budgets for our non-welfare activities would pose ever more complex challenges for the organization at large, as well as for us country directors.

In the mid-1990s, restitution funding began to play a critical role in our welfare program. Beginning in 1995, JDC and the Claims Conference[16] joined in a partnership to support welfare programs for elderly Jews who were considered to have been victims of Nazi persecution. Later, two other major sources of restitution funds — the Swiss Banks Settlement and the International Conference for Holocaust Era Insurance Claims (ICHEIC) — also entrusted JDC to deliver relief to those who had suffered at the Nazis' hands.

These restitution funds were earmarked for Nazi victims. Yet overall, Nazi victims made up little more than half of JDC's total welfare client population. In my areas, non-Nazi victims constituted the large majority of welfare clients, the German army having never reached these countries. This distinguished elements of my work from the JDC work in other areas of the FSU, non-Nazi victims not being entitled to assistance paid for by restitution funds.

---

16. Since 1951, the Conference on Jewish Material Claims Against Germany, also known as the Claims Conference, has secured and distributed reparations for Holocaust survivors and their heirs. Some 70 percent of the annual allocations were forwarded to JDC for use in meeting the welfare needs of Jewish communities and individual Jews in Europe. See also the section on the Claims Conference in the "Back to Europe" chapter of this book.

Therefore my work has been further challenged by the need for funds to enable the provision of welfare and Jewish renewal services for all those who needed or wanted them. In my particular regions, we have had to be largely dependent on allocations of unrestricted funds provided to JDC by the American Jewish Federation system, or on designated gifts from Federations and from individual donors and foundations, notable among them the Harry and Jeanette Weinberg Foundation and the International Fellowship of Christians and Jews (IFCJ). With support from these sources, I was able to build up the range of JDC programs for the entire Jewish population in my area.

Still, funding the care for these "non-Nazi victims" has remained a major concern. Such needy Jewish elderly are by no means limited to my region: tens of thousands are scattered across the FSU. Inevitably, over the years the urgency of meeting the basic human needs of these impoverished Jews took its toll on our other activities. Until the JDC board launched an initiative to reinvigorate our "Jewish renewal" programming in 2006, funding for these programs was increasingly scarce.

At times, the FSU country directors have sought additional financial assistance for particular cases and needs. One such case followed a visit that I made in Tbilisi. There I met a destitute pensioner who papered the windows in his dilapidated house to keep winter at bay. After his son died tragically, the old man saved every penny, depriving himself of everything, to buy a tombstone with Jewish markings. It was very important to him. When I mentioned this particular case at a JDC board meeting in New York, a member of the JDC board contacted me with a $500 donation — enough to erect the stone and to improve the man's living conditions.

The Children's Initiative

While JDC strained to ensure that poverty among the elderly was addressed effectively, another concern emerged: needs among Jewish children and their families. Masked for a while by the tendency of parents to keep their material needs private, it was only in the late 1990s that this problem attracted JDC's attention as being more than just anecdotal.

In 1999, however, the once sporadic reports about poverty among the younger generation were reaching JDC professionals with sufficient frequency for the FSU Department to launch a new program. Dubbed "Mazel Tov," this combined Hesed/JCC program helped new parents by loaning baby equipment such as cribs and strollers, provided the poorest among them with diapers and vitamins, and all the while drew the families into Jewish community life through parenting classes and Jewish activities.

Mazel Tov grew steadily and took hold in sixty-nine locations. But it was also clear that the program was only a partial solution. JDC was receiving reports of elderly clients passing food to their grandchildren in Hesed dining rooms; of disabled children unable to leave their homes; of children living without heat or electricity.

As a result, a formal study of the situation was spearheaded by JDC board member Spencer Foreman, the head of one of New York City's largest hospitals, and involving the Myers-JDC-Brookdale Institute in Jerusalem. The results confirmed the need for a more systematic response. In 2003, JDC acted upon a suggestion made by Steve Schwager, JDC executive vice president, and launched a Children's Initiative for children at risk.

With its introduction, our eyes were opened to the large numbers of children in need of support. They include children living in poverty or in broken homes; those abused, orphaned, sick or physically disabled, socially excluded, educationally challenged, and more. The Children's Initiative led to programs that could address those needs through welfare (including provision of food, clothing, medical assistance, and other basic needs), family support, early childhood education, school tuition support, and recreation.

A short time after embarking on the Children's Initiative programs, we found that there were even greater needs than we had assumed. To be effective, help had to be extended to the entire family of the child at risk. Rabbi Yechiel Eckstein, founder and president of the International Fellowship of Christians and Jews, offered substantial financial aid, enabling JDC to expand the program, include many more children at risk, and run summer camps for the entire family over a number of years.

The Children's Initiative programs also sought to strengthen the children's and their families' ties with their communities and build their Jewish identities. JDC encourages children and their families to take part in community activities, including Jewish holiday celebrations, cultural programs, the summer and winter camps, and youth clubs.

To ensure that the programs respond to local needs, JDC has supported training for hundreds of local Jewish professionals and volunteers through seminars that provide the knowledge and skills to work effectively in early childhood programs. Many of the coordinators and professionals involved in Children's Initiative activities study for second degrees, focusing on psychology and social work.

I welcomed the opportunity to implement the Children's Initiative in my region, enabling us to reach out to some 6,300 children by 2006. The programs — tailored to the situation in each location — focused on the needs and wishes of the children and their families.

One program of particular note is in the Kazakhstan region. Its goal is to provide assistance to those children affected by Soviet nuclear testing that took place there. Radiation had affected both the parents and the children. The proportion of handicapped and malformed children born in this area is higher than in any other area of the FSU. Moreover, medical problems that are much less common in other areas often appear in these children. Our help includes medical and therapeutic care according to the needs of the children and their parents.

A Shift in my Assignment

In 2002, I handed over responsibility for the Lviv and Chernivtsi areas and the programs that I had initiated there to the country director of western Ukraine, Itzik Averbuch. In its place, I took on Armenia, geographically a more logical allocation in the midst of my areas.

The main concentration of Jews in Armenia is in the capital, Yerevan. There is a clear view of Mount Ararat from this city. Located just across the Armenian border with Turkey, this is the mountain on which Noah's ark landed at the end of the Flood, according to tradition and as it is written in the Bible.[17] No one knows how many Jews live in Yerevan today. Estimates ran between 350 and 700 in 2006. The rate of intermarriage with Armenians and Russians is very high.

Armenia is also home to a small community of *gerim* — Russians who converted to Judaism two and a half centuries ago. These Jews still maintain, to some extent, Jewish tradition and separateness from the rest of the Russian population. Most of Jewish law has been forgotten over the years, but what they do remember they keep strictly, such as *mikve*, Jewish burial, occasional

---

17. Genesis 8:4.

synagogue services when a quorum can be found, and reading from the Torah scroll. The children of this community have emigrated to other areas, so JDC assistance is primarily for the fifty elderly members. This comes in the form of food packages and other medical and welfare assistance as needed.

In Yerevan itself, the local rabbi, a Lubavitch follower, takes care of the synagogue, where regular services are held. With our help, he opened a small Hesed in the synagogue building to provide for welfare programs, including food packages for forty needy families. A cultural program, run by the local cultural committee independently of the synagogue, is also supported by JDC and provides lectures, Hebrew and history study groups, and regular meetings on current events. Festival celebrations are arranged for the entire community by the rabbi.

Regrettably, in a pattern often repeated across the region as, indeed, in Jewish communities around the world, the synagogue-based programs and those of the cultural committee do not combine forces. While these separate ventures ensure diversity of activities, in small communities the division can be counterproductive. This, though, is one of the great — and ongoing — challenges of the community building that is the essence of our work.

JDC in the FSU Today

The Vast and Ongoing Program

JDC's program in the FSU remains one of the largest JDC has ever undertaken. As of December 2006, JDC had some 220,000 elderly welfare clients and 22,000 children in children's programs, in close to 3,000 locations across the FSU. It supports a gamut of initiatives designed to renew Jewish life after Communism's decades-long assault on the soul of Soviet Jewry. Our program in the FSU today, indeed, is comparable in scale to the organization's work in post-World War II Europe, when JDC was involved in helping Holocaust survivors and reconstruction in Europe.

Although funding challenges remain, we continue to be fully involved in the Hesed network, one of the largest and most logistically complex relief efforts ever mounted by Jews for Jews. As a result, no FSU locality with a Jewish population of consequence lacks basic welfare services today. As a matter of fact, we reach far beyond even these centers to bring succor to thousands of individuals who are even more isolated.

We fund the hiring of local homecare workers for the bedridden and the housebound. We distribute food parcels, run soup kitchens, and encourage the development of formal and informal education. Smaller and outlying localities that have nonviable Jewish communities receive visits by HesedMobiles or financial support from JDC to pay for food parcels or other care.

That said, the Hesed program continues to evolve as conditions in the region change. The soup kitchens and food packages in a number of communities have been replaced by a debit card that enables the Hesed client to purchase the food items that he or she prefers from a list of goods agreed upon with a supermarket and within an allocated budget. While the clients gain control to enjoy their personal choices, this new system also checks waste and saves funds. The homecare program for the home- and bed-bound has also been adjusted in many locations. A program called SABA encompasses examination of each individual case and molds the service provided to the individual's needs and economic situation. These improvements strengthen the self-respect of the client and ameliorate the Hesed services.

For some, JDC's provisions are lifesavers. About 30 percent of our clients in 2006 are over the age of seventy-five. This is remarkable given that the life expectancy of a non-Jewish Russian male is fifty-nine years (and declining!). Thus, it is assumed that Hesed's services are keeping Jews alive longer than neighbors who do not benefit from comparable services. For all that, enough remains to be done to sustain the Hesed effort in the FSU. In the Asian republics, this effort remains a great challenge and priority.

The JCCs and their activities, which today commonly include libraries, have acquired prime importance in our reconnection mission. The provision of religious supplies continues through focused JDC community programs and services that are delivered to local religious leaders.

Since 2003, the FSU-wide Children's Initiative program has been targeting children at risk. Much of the material welfare and social support for these thousands of children is provided through the Hasadim and JCCs, though increasingly a new Jewish Family Outreach Service model is taking root in locations where the Initiative is implemented. It is expected that the budding Children's Initiative will evolve further as the needs require it to.

Having entered the FSU's southern-tier republics to find what seemed a fumbling Jewish infrastructure — albeit generally stronger in its Jewish identity and community cohesion than in the other parts of the FSU — the rainbow of communal activities and services that we have been able to develop there is dramatic. What has made this all possible has been the partnership of local participants in each and every location. These local partners of JDC, with so many of whom I have worked personally, have made a grand mark in the renewal of their respective community's lives.

In all, we have opened sixty JCCs and other Jewish renewal organizations in the Asian areas and northern Caucasus, providing Jewish religious and cultural services for Jewish renewal for some 27,000 people. We have incorporated in these institutions the training for religious functionaries, under the direction of Rabbi Meir Schlesinger, and the seminars on community leadership that JDC made available to Jewish communities across the FSU.

With the assistance of JDC's representatives in this region, we have overseen the establishment of forty-two Hasadim, serving 20,000 needy elderly Jews in 2006. Many of the Hasadim augmented or incorporated previously existing welfare programs.

Most of the Hasadim in my areas eventually combined with other community cultural programs in integrated Jewish community service centers known as *Evreiski Dom*s ("Jewish Houses"). They successfully and variously merge Jewish activities, usually including a JCC and Hesed welfare center. Other activities might include a Sunday school, a synagogue, or a day center for the elderly. The Hasadim strive to attract young people — no easy matter because young Jews in most places have alternative leisure and entertainment options. That they are generally free of charge, as all JDC welfare services have been, is an attraction.

Every Hesed and JCC in my areas has a board or committee of local lay leaders. These committees are involved in all policy decisions as well as the daily running of their programs. They constitute the central body of the local communities and therefore play a crucial role in our joint mission to build viable, autonomous, self-sufficient communities.

Behind the staggering scope of JDC's activities in the FSU remain the goals that comprise JDC's FSU mission: to reconnect disengaged Jews with their heritage, to create community cohesion and consciousness, to ensure that Jewish material needs are met; and, ultimately, to develop self-sufficiency. We have made energetic progress toward the first three of these goals. We have also progressed toward the fourth, although its financial component remains elusive, due mainly to economic conditions in the FSU.

It is this last hurdle that has become a focus of JDC's efforts in recent years. During the first decade or so of our involvement in the post-Soviet republics, JDC focused its reconnection efforts on developing the human and physical infrastructures necessary to run the programs needed to reach out to and engage Jews in Jewish life. Now, these efforts are seeking to ensure that these programs are financially viable — that they are structured and organized in a way that is sustainable.

Like my colleagues elsewhere, therefore, I have encouraged the directors of the community centers to take a "business approach" to their maintenance. This means introducing some Western concepts of fundraising, such as soliciting donations from more affluent community members and, where the law allows, charging for some of their services. These steps generate income that help offset the budget cuts that JDC has had to implement, but also reinforce the awareness among local Jews that, ultimately, the communities and the services they enjoy are theirs to shape, and theirs to support.

All told, the process of achieving local financial participation is still in its early stages. Yet ultimately its success will determine whether and when JDC is able to "go out of business" in the FSU by handing over the programs it has helped develop to communities that can truly sustain themselves.

Great Expectations

In many localities across the FSU, community depletion has leveled off. Yet, while the region's Jewish population is expected to remain stable overall, we are witnessing an internal shift of Jews from peripheral localities to major cities. This, of course, has implications for the infrastructure that we have put in place — requiring that Hesed centers and JCCs serving smaller populations be closed and that fewer resources be invested in cities whose Jewish futures seem assured.

In some of my areas, centralized services are provided from main towns to communities in the periphery. Kyrgyzstan is a case in point. Most of the Jews of the area left by 1998 and fewer than 1,500 remained in Bishkek in 2006. The Bishkek Hesed, established in 1997, was and continues to be the only one in all of Kyrgyzstan, functioning as a central address for peripheral Jewish collectives. JDC was able to purchase adjoining apartments to house this Hesed and a JCC to run their welfare and cultural programs.

Wherever possible, JDC maintains its services in communities still justified by their numbers. In Bukhara (Uzbekistan), JDC established a Hesed center with local assistance and in a separate building runs JCC activities. A Jewish day school has more than 100 children populating its classrooms each year. These services continue and are greatly appreciated by the now relatively small community — 1,000 Jews in 2006.

In Georgia, most Jews in provincial towns left in two phases: from towns to cities and thence to destinations abroad. The remaining Jewish population in this area was prominently of the intelligentsia. There were about 11,000 Jews in Georgia in 2006 and JDC provides welfare and cultural services to Jewish collectives in six main towns and to individuals in peripheral areas.

JDC remains a presence in smaller locations, too. Karaganda (Kazakhstan), Samarkand (Uzbekistan), Kutaisi (Georgia), Nal'chik (southern Russia), and Makhachkala (southern Russia) had only 1,000–2,000 Jews in 2006, a fraction of the numbers that had been in these places in the early 1990s. Most of these Jews now have no plans for emigration and hence JDC's Hasadim or regular aid remain constants in their Jewish welfare.

Larger communities, some of them self-sufficient, continue to benefit from JDC services and support as necessary. This is the case, for example, in Kuba, Azerbaijan, whose 4,000 Jews continuously help their own needy, JDC providing supplemental food packages, medicines, and winter relief wherever necessary.

In 2006, the children's program and the Hesed center in southern Russia's Rostov-on-Don are sufficiently well organized to serve the relatively large Jewish population of 12,000–15,000, and to supervise programs in smaller communities in southern Russia. Here, in fact, the Jewish population has grown over the years and doesn't seem to have been affected by mass emigration as elsewhere. JDC continues to oversee the community programs in Rostov.

Questions to Ponder; Challenges to Meet

As JDC approaches almost two decades of renewed involvement in the region, we still face questions, whose answers we cannot provide with certainty, and challenges that keep us deeply involved in programs in the FSU.

Have the FSU's populations of Jews truly become Jewish communities? This is perhaps the most difficult question. A Jewish community is a mosaic composed of various aspects of religion, welfare, and culture. We laid some of those foundation stones and cemented them in place by means of Hasadim and Jewish community centers. However, the cement is weak and many stones are still missing.

Elsewhere in the Jewish world, communities build institutions. In the FSU, it is the other way around. In this respect, the FSU has no Jewish communities in the Western sense.

And yet it has a great deal of Jewish activity that bespeaks community. First and foremost, nearly all FSU Jews today know that they are Jewish and all have a community of some kind with which they may affiliate if they wish it — and many of them wish it. Gone is the fear of declaring and the need to hide one's Jewishness. Much of the credit for this goes to political changes and to the confidence built up over the years.

The concepts of leadership, leadership succession, and community stability, though, have not yet jelled, even though the programs JDC and others have put in place are building generational links. Enough activists have chosen to build their lives in the FSU that a semblance of leadership continuity has evolved. Several localities have begun to do their own fundraising and develop local leaders.

In all these respects, the Jews of the FSU wish it; we facilitate it. JDC imparts vigorous assistance by continuously offering courses in management, fundraising, and working with volunteers. These programs attract good people, some of whom will become tomorrow's leaders.

So have we really succeeded in laying the foundation of future strong communities? When we reflect on the issue, we ask ourselves several key questions: Has a commonwealth of interest groups taken shape? Has a "solar system" paradigm formed, with planets and asteroids revolving around a hub? Do individuals feel themselves to be part of a community? We have made great progress, but there is still a long way to go.

In spite of today's financial strains, JDC remains committed to a two-part mission in the FSU: "advocating, supporting, and creating opportunities for FSU Jews to reconnect with the Jewish People; and fostering the development of Jewish communities capable of responding to the needs of its members in distress."

JDC expects to remain involved in all of these — easing problems where they arise and facilitating favorable trends wherever they come into sight. We expect Jewish consciousness, identity, and sense of community to continue growing. We expect the Jewish cultural revival to continue to flourish.

As the generation that lived through the Nazi horror continues to slip away, the proportion of "non-Nazi victims" among our welfare client base will expand, reducing the role restitution funds play in supporting our Hesed programs. At the same time, we anticipate that our roster of needy cases may diminish with the improvement of the economic situation, although those who remain in need will require more substantial assistance as restitution funds for their aid will continue to shrink.

We encourage and mobilize local Jewish philanthropists to take up some of the slack. The community institutions that receive this philanthropy will, we hope, assume increasing responsibility for planning and operations. We will do our best to improve the management skills, governance capabilities, and self-sufficiency of local leaders. We will create new and improved partnerships with Israeli, Diaspora, and nongovernmental agencies, mainly in the hope that they can contribute financially to the program. Yet the purpose of the latter is not exclusively to raise more money. We expect to be viewed by these outside agencies — and of course to actually be — as partners, mentors, mediators, consultants, organizational models, and advocates of communal integration.

Theoretically, it remains JDC's goal in the FSU, as everywhere, to disengage after it deems its enterprise to have yielded permanent, sustainable improvements. The six executives who, in 1989, peered through the crumbling Iron Curtain and wondered if Soviet Jewry remained viable can now glimpse preliminary signs of a permanent reconnection of FSU Jewry with the Jewish people. But for now, the grand exit strategy remains a distant hope.

Phenomenal Organizational and Personal Satisfaction

If and when JDC tells the full story of its endeavors in the FSU, it will testify to triumph. This is among the grandest chapters in JDC's history, and probably the last and greatest chapter in the many decades of my JDC life.

As a member of the original SUT — the Soviet Union Team — and as a country director and senior member of JDC's FSU staff, for me this has been an ongoing story of an ongoing endeavor. It marks not only a high point of my career but the opportunity to perform one of the greatest services a Jew can render for his people — to help revive the Jewish lives of thousands of people and to do whatever I could to alleviate the hardships of my Jewish brothers and sisters.

The experiences of my past postings came into use in the FSU and were enhanced by those I gained in this region. My sensitivity to the needs of others developed as I learned to be more objective, more patient, more considerate of different opinions. These values have served me well as I have worked with local players and with my JDC colleagues to forge cooperation in the face of enormous, unprecedented challenges.

My enthusiasm has carried me through more than sixty years with JDC. How privileged I am — personally and professionally — to have been part of this magnificent endeavor to reclaim the great Jewry of the FSU for the Jewish people, my people.

Epilogue: Reflections on a Lifetime

The Talmud teaches that all marriages are made in heaven. It is clear to me that this extends to my long-term relationship with JDC: like a marriage, it transcends mere happenstance.

My career with the Joint began in the aftermath of the greatest horror inflicted on our people in modern times: the near-destruction of European Jewry. Having lost both parents and two siblings to Nazi excesses, I felt a need to do something for the war survivors. My sense of Jewish identity, strong to begin with, became much stronger in the course of my five years as a youth in yeshiva and subsequent five years of rabbinic training at Jews' College in London. Working with JDC gave me an opportunity to put my innermost convictions into practice. So I joined the organization as the youngest novice in its ranks and traveled to the American zone in Germany armed only with a charge to "start programs" for the Jews in distress there, even as I nursed my own forlorn, personal hope of finding a relative — close or distant — among the displaced persons.

It was my duty and privilege to help the survivors pick up the pieces. Almost imperceptibly, that first encounter with Jews in need transformed into my life's work. I witnessed and shared in historic developments across Europe and North Africa where Jews who faced misfortune — physically, spiritually, culturally, economically, or socially — required help. Later, I was able to contribute to the miraculous revival of Jewish sovereignty and Jewish study in our homeland. Finally, my work brought me almost full circle, involving me in helping the Jews of the former Soviet Union pick up the pieces in the wake of the second greatest calamity inflicted on our people in modern times: Communism's assault on and near-destruction of Soviet Jewry.

I have been fortunate to work with an organization whose operating approach emphasizes warm interpersonal interaction. I consider my ability for such interaction something of a forte. Combined with the sense of common cause with my fellow Jews that is rooted in my identity, this helps explain why I have enjoyed relationships with JDC colleagues and beneficiaries that surpass basic working relations. It also explains one of the most treasured phenomena in my life: that I have remained in touch with many whom I first came to know professionally for years, and often decades, after the professional relationship ended.

I have had the honor over the years to work alongside many dedicated and talented JDC staff. Some, including a few mentioned in this book, continued to be associated with JDC decades after their retirement. Among them is JDC's legendary former chief executive, Ralph Goldman, who retired initially at age seventy but returned for a second stint in this role on an interim basis. It was during this second tenure that he made the amazing breakthrough in the Soviet Union. Today, at over ninety, in recognition of his vision, intellect, and continuing contribution to JDC and to the Jewish people he so loves, Ralph remains honorary executive vice president of JDC and a daily presence in the life of our organization.

There are others too whom I cannot fail to mention. Ted Feder, a senior staff member who had served in Germany, Europe, and Israel, had a corner of his own at New York headquarters until 2003, nearly twenty years after his retirement. He credited this work with having kept him alive. He passed away aged eighty-nine in January 2004. Herbert Katzki, whom I first came to know well in the late 1940s and early 1950s in Germany and Iran, served JDC from 1936. After his retirement, he continued to perform various duties on a voluntary basis at JDC until he passed away in September 1997, aged eighty-nine. Abe Loskove, who succeeded me as country director in Iran, began his JDC career in 1945 in Germany. He went on to serve in Libya, Italy, Iran, Morocco, and Europe, until his retirement in the mid-1990s.

But the organization's attention to personal relationships yielded benefits far beyond JDC's internal environment. It has helped foster an atmosphere of cooperation and a foundation of trust with local community members that have contributed immeasurably to my work. Thus, in Europe and northern Africa I was able to influence Jewish education with personal involvement in teachers' skills and qualifications and in programs revolving around them.

The same mutual confidence guided me in my relationships with the yeshiva deans and the Jews in the FSU.

Wherever I have been, I have encountered Jews who, even as recipients of relief, have shared JDC's sense of "jointness," of the universal fraternity of the Jewish people. However, even the smallest JDC program could only succeed if its intended beneficiaries and JDC's representatives shared the same basic goals and joined forces in achieving them. We were able to aid the displaced persons in the camps in postwar Germany, the school principals in Europe, the destitute communities in North Africa, yeshiva students in Israel, and above all the renascent communities' leaders in the FSU because all of us — staff, local leaders, and beneficiaries — shared a common cause. Wherever we have been, we have located Jews who wanted to persevere as Jews; and linked to them was our own drive to persevere.

Wherever JDC has come onto the scene, we have found community leaders and rabbis already collecting and distributing aid. More often than not, however, the needs have been far greater than the funds available from local resources. With its own staff, know-how, and funds, JDC has made it possible to expand local efforts, to offer help to as many needy Jews as possible, to assure continuity and to initiate new programs. With limited resources, one had to learn not only to distribute them judiciously but also how to refuse when necessary. My guiding principle has been that, when in doubt, one should always decide in favor of the applicant. It has always proved wiser and more charitable to err on the side of generosity. I have also learned that often all a person requires is a kind word, a listening ear, and patience. To talk about one's problems can often be a partial solution in itself; sometimes, indeed, it is the only one that is required.

This sort of approach cannot be rigidly programmed into an organizational culture. It must spring from the ability of those involved to identify with the people whom they serve, an ability perpetuated as much by careful selection of staff as by any training regimen. Whenever I entered a community or any collective of Jews, I was mindful to apply this sensitivity and considerateness through conduct and actions that broadcast a message of "us together" as opposed to "us and you," let alone "us versus you."

For me, this began with my position in the Föhrenwald DP camp, where I took my meals with the camp residents and spent time with every patient at the camp hospital. Later on, my custom when entering a community was to visit the synagogue and take up a position as a member of the congregation and, if asked, occasionally as the prayer leader. If the congregants sat on the floor to eat their meals, so did I. When they invited me to their homes, I accepted. Moreover, I made a point of learning their languages to be able to communicate directly with my fellow Jews, be they in Iran, France, Morocco, or the Soviet Union.

Among my most rewarding encounters have been those with former schoolchildren, scholarship recipients, or beneficiaries of JDC programs. I relish seeing and hearing of the good achieved by the modest help given many years previously. It has indeed been my good fortune to be with JDC for so many years and thereby to meet many of our former "clients." I have heard from them about successful careers in worthy professions, about their families, and about the roles they have come to play. So many individuals have recalled with gratitude what JDC had done for them years back when they were in need of a helping hand.

A Changed World

As I look back over sixty-plus years, I marvel at the resilience, tenacity, and perseverance of those battered by abusive regimes or by grinding poverty and am reminded of the promise in *I Samuel* 15:29: "The Eternal One of Israel will never fail us."

I recall the Jewish world soon after World War II and look at it now. The changes are enormous. In 1946, European Jewry — so recently the heart of the Jewish world — lay in ruins. More than 250,000 Jews were in limbo, as DPs in Germany, Austria, and Italy. There were only a few survivors in Poland, most of them still afraid to declare their Jewishness. Most communities in the Baltic states and in the Balkans had been practically obliterated, those surviving also fearful of asserting their religion under the new yoke of Communism. Behind the newly established Iron Curtain, only Hungary with 250,000 Jews and Romania with 450,000 could claim a substantial Jewish presence.

Beyond Soviet control, the Belgian, Dutch, Italian, and Greek communities were decimated. So was France's, although enough had survived for the French community to become an anchor of Jewish life on the Continent. The small Jewish communities of Switzerland, Spain, and Portugal — neutral countries during World War II — survived the war intact. They hosted significant numbers of refugees, but reverted to their prewar condition at its conclusion.

At the same time, in the immediate postwar years, the communities of North Africa and the Middle East had yet to begin their precipitous decline. As they had been for centuries, these communities were still home to a million Sephardic and "eastern" Jews.

How different the map of the Jewish world is today. After the war, Jews in search of new communities and new lives began migrating between countries across Europe and other continents, further eliminating some communities while strengthening others. The creation of the Jewish State in 1948 set in immediate motion waves of aliyah from all countries where Jews lived. The 600,000 Jews who lived in Israel when the state was created increased almost tenfold by the turn of the millennium, as large influxes of Jews from Muslim countries, Europe, the former Soviet Union, and other countries swelled its population.

JDC, and I as a staff member, have given our all to enable the wellbeing of communities that have diminished and to aid the continuity and Jewish connectivity of those that have survived or been reborn. Looking back over the years, I feel more privileged than words can express to have taken part in these historic events of the Jewish people.

❖ ❖ ❖

As a young man who trained for a career in rabbinics and education among the Jews of Great Britain, I changed course in a providential way. I am reminded of an anecdote related by Rabbi Abraham Joshua Heschel: Two Jews are arguing. One states that the commandment of dwelling in a sukkah (tabernacle) on the festival of Sukkoth is the greatest mitzvah of all, because one immerses oneself in the sukkah "boots and all." The other Jew argues that Shabbat is a greater mitzvah. Once one leaves the sukkah, he explained, one leaves the mitzvah behind. The mitzvah of Shabbat, in contrast, envelops one wherever one goes and in whatever one does.

So it has been for me for over sixty years. I have been enveloped by the atmosphere of JDC, surrounded by the mitzvah of loving-kindness, of helping, of caring for fellow Jews, of viewing every Jew I encountered as my brother. For that, I am deeply grateful to God Almighty and His many emissaries in this world.

I could never have done my job without the encouragement of my family. Whatever I have achieved in my life could not have been accomplished without the understanding and support of my wife, Noemi, who practically raised our children alone and only occasionally joined me on my travels. Those periods of time that I was away from my family came at a great sacrifice for my wife, for me, and for our children. Those many months of absence from home as our children were growing up can never be recaptured. This is especially so in the case of our dear son Moshe who drowned while a yeshiva student in 1978 when he was only eighteen years old. I was away in Iran at the time, but took the first flight back to mourn and be with my family.

My children knew many things about my work but they had never joined me on any working trips. Finally, in the summer of 2003 I took my son Yossi and his oldest son Moshe with me on a working visit to Georgia. At last, they would actually experience something of what I had been doing those many years.

Our surviving children — Edna Adele, named after my mother, and Joseph Zvi, named for my youngest brother — have given us grandchildren and great-grandchildren. All live in Israel.

❖   ❖   ❖

Elsewhere — in another world, one whose existence I accept on faith — there is a family that has surely known and followed my career. In that world is my family who perished in desperation and agony. Among them were my mother, two brothers, uncles, aunts, and cousins.

My mother accompanied me to the train that would take me from Poland to England as a young teenager. With tears in her eyes she blessed me and said, "My child, be a good Jew." Those words, my mother's parting wish for me, still reverberate. I hope and pray that I have honored them.

✐ Glossary

aliyah. (Hebrew) Jewish immigration to Israel.

Aliyah Bet. Organized illegal immigration to Palestine at the time when the British mandate restricted such immigration, 1934–1948.

beit midrash. (Hebrew) Study center; Jewish house of study.

Bnei Akiva. Zionist youth movement established in Israel in 1929 and that subsequently spread to countries worldwide. Based on the ideology of "*Torah v'avodah*," Torah study and work.

Bricha. An illegal Jewish immigration movement enabling Jewish displaced persons to flee Eastern Europe across the occupied zones and board Aliyah Bet ships bound for Israel, 1945–1946.

Chabad. (Hebrew Acronym: *Chochma, Bina v'Da'at* — "wisdom, understanding, and knowledge"); The movement of the Lubavitch Hasidim.

cholent. (Yiddish) An Ashkenazi traditional stew, served at the Shabbat morning meal.

dhimmi. (Arabic) A non-Muslim subject of an Islam-governed state.

d'var Torah. (Hebrew) Sermon; Religious discourse; A brief Torah insight.

Eretz Yisrael. (Hebrew) The Land of Israel.

eruv. (Hebrew) In Jewish law, a boundary that is determined in order to enable a Jew to carry on Shabbat beyond the walls of private property.

Evreiski Dom. (Russian) Jewish House; In the FSU (former Soviet Union), physical centers established by JDC for Jewish community gatherings and activities.

gabbai. (Hebrew) Person who assists and coordinates the running of synagogue services.

ger. (Hebrew; pl. *gerim*) Convert to Judaism.

grush. (Polish) Smallest coin in Poland.

Haggada. (Hebrew) Book containing the order of the Pesach seder, including the retelling of the Exodus from Egypt.

hakarat hatov. (Hebrew) Recognizing the good that is done.

hakham. (Hebrew; pl. *hakhamim*) Sage (term used in Muslim countries).

hakim. (Arabic) Term used for a Jewish doctor in Iran.

Hasid. (Hebrew; pl. Hasidim; adj. Hasidic) Member of the Hasidic ultra-Orthodox movement established in Eastern Europe in the eighteenth century.

havdalah. (Hebrew) Ceremony marking the end of Shabbat and festivals.

havruta. (Aramaic) A study partner.

heder. (Hebrew) Literally, room; See **Talmud Torah**.

hesder **yeshivot.** (Hebrew) Yeshivot in which students spend three years at study, within a five-year commitment to the Israel Defense Forces.

Hesed. (Hebrew) Literally, loving kindness; General title of the JDC community-based welfare centers in the FSU.

hilula. (Aramaic) Literally, festivity; In Muslim countries, the commemoration of the death of a sage, marked by feasts, prayers, and dance.

hiluq. (Hebrew) In Morocco, a Jewish community's distribution of funds to its needy.

Kapo. Jewish inmates of concentration camps forced by the Nazis to carry out tasks in the camps, often brutally, against their fellow Jews.

kashruth. (Hebrew) Jewish dietary laws.

kehilla. (Hebrew) Jewish community, community administration, or communal organization.

kibbutz. (Hebrew) A communal agricultural settlement in Israel.

kiddush. (Hebrew) Blessing over wine on Shabbat and festivals; refreshments following synagogue services that are introduced by such a blessing.

Kindertransport. An organized rescue operation that transported children from Nazi-occupied Europe to safety in England, 1938–1940.

kolkhoz. (Russian; pl. kolkhozy) A collective agricultural farm in the Soviet Union.

kollel. (Hebrew) Jewish academy of religious study for married men.

l'chaim. (Hebrew) "To Life"; A toast.

Lubavitch. Hasidic movement, also known as Chabad, founded in the late eighteenth century by Shneur Zalman of Liadi (1745–1812).

mellah. (Arabic) A city's Jewish quarter in Morocco.

mullah. (Arabic) Muslim religious leader.

ma'abarot. (Hebrew; sing. *ma'abarah*) Transit camps for immigrants in Israel in the 1950s.

Magen David. Star of David; Jewish six-pointed star symbol.

mahaleh. (Farsi) Jewish ghetto or quarter.

matzo. (or **matza**; Hebrew; pl. matzoth) Unleavened bread, eaten on Pesach to symbolize the bread that did not have time to rise as the Jewish people fled Egypt in haste.

Midrash. (Hebrew; adj. Midrashic) A compilation of homiletic writings on the Jewish scriptures.

mikve. (Hebrew) Ritual bath

Mimouna. (Hebrew/Aramaic) Holiday celebrated by Moroccan Jews at the close of Pesach.

minyan. (Hebrew) Quorum of ten men necessary to hold a prayer service.

Mishnah. The first written compilation of Judaism's oral law, codified around 200 CE by Yehuda HaNasi.

mitzvah. (Hebrew; pl. mitzvoth) Commandments in Judaism.

mohel. (Hebrew; pl. *mohalim*) Jewish ritual circumciser.

mori. (Hebrew/Yemenite) Teachers for young boys in Yemen.

Musar **movement.** An ethical movement of Lithuanian Jewish origin, developed in the nineteenth century.

olim. (Hebrew) Jewish immigrants to Israel.

paytan. (Hebrew; pl. *paytanim*) One who performs *piyyutim*, liturgical songs.

Pesach. (Hebrew) Passover.

peyot. (Hebrew) Sidelocks.

pieds-noirs. (French) Term given for the European inhabitants of Algeria.

pintele yid. (Yiddish) "Jewish spark."

piyyut. (Hebrew; pl. *piyyutim*) A liturgical song.

Rebbe. (Yiddish) Teacher; Hasidic leader; Rabbi.

rebbetzin. (Yiddish) The wife of a rabbi.

Rosh Hashanah. (Hebrew) Jewish New Year.

Rosh Yeshiva. (Hebrew) Dean of a yeshiva.

Shabbat. (Hebrew) Sabbath.

shehita. (Hebrew) Jewish ritual slaughter.

shohet. (Hebrew; pl. *shohtim*) Jewish ritual slaughterer.

shtetl. (Yiddish) Small Jewish town or village in Eastern Europe.

shtibl. (Yiddish) Small synagogue.

simanim. (Hebrew) Literally, signs; The term used in Yemen for *peyot* (sidelocks).

skhina. (Hebrew/Aramaic) Moroccan Jewish dish, equivalent to the Ashkenazi "*cholent.*"

tallit. Fringed shawl used by Jewish men during the morning and other particular prayer services.

Talmud. (Hebrew; adj. Talmudic) A large compilation of rabbinic discussion of Jewish law, primarily based on and including the Mishnah.

Talmudist. One who is well versed and dedicated to Talmud study.

Talmud Torah. (Hebrew; pl. Talmudei Torah). Religious school for boys, also known as heder.

tefillin. The two phylacteries, worn by Jewish men during the morning weekday prayer services.

tefina. (Hebrew/Moroccan) Moroccan Jewish dish, equivalent to the Ashkenazi "*cholent.*"

Tikkun Hatzot. (Hebrew) Midnight Service; Lamentations and psalms recited at midnight in mourning over the destruction of the Temple and the exile of the Jewish people.

Torah im derekh eretz. (Hebrew) Literally, "Torah with the way of the land"; Coined by Rabbi Samson Raphael Hirsch (1808–1888) and denoting the integration of religious life with the secular world.

tzaddik. (Hebrew; pl. *tzaddikim*) A righteous person.

tzedaka. (Hebrew) Charity.

tzitzit. (Hebrew). Fringed garment, worn by observant Jewish men under or over a shirt.

yahrzeit. (Yiddish) Jewish commemoration of the anniversary of a death.

yeshiva. (Hebrew; pl. yeshivot) A Jewish institute of higher religious study.

Yiddishkeit. (Yiddish) Jewish way of life.

yizkor. (Hebrew) Jewish memorial service for the deceased.

Yom Kippur. (Hebrew) Day of Atonement.

~ Maps

Germany after World War II

Iran in the 1950s

Europe before 1989

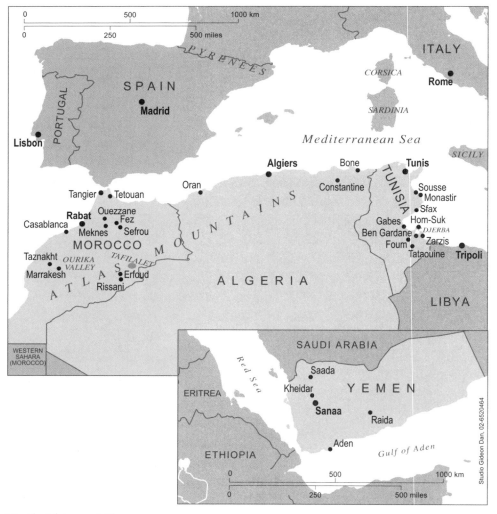

North Africa and Yemen

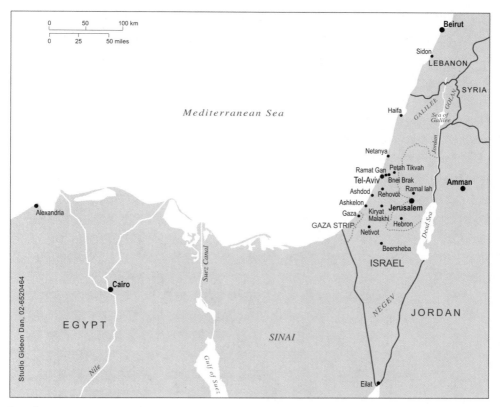

Israel

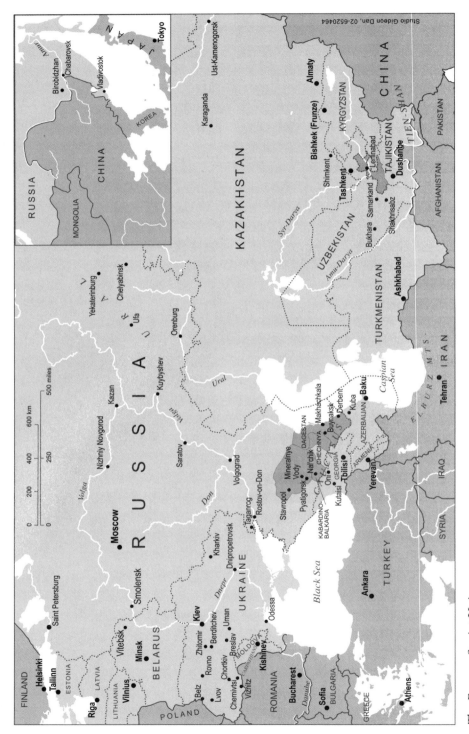

The Former Soviet Union

⌁ Index

A

Abe Wouk Foundation 176
Abuhatzeira, Israel. *See* Baba Sali
Abuhatzeira, Rabbi Meir 115
academies, religious 29. *See also kollel*
Aden 32, 55, 154
Agro-Joint 189
Agudath Israel 168
Ahi ("My Brother") 179–80
airlift
   from Aden 32, 32 n. 3, 154, 156
   from Tehran 66
Akiva school (Strasbourg) 93
Aleph youth club 214
Alexandria (Egypt) 152, 177
Algeria 88, 98, 101, 148–51
Algerian Jewish Cultural Commission 149
Algerian Zionist Federation 149
Algiers 148, 149, 150, 151
aliyah xxiii, 5, 25, 30, 32, 35, 36, 37, 53, 64, 65, 66–67, 79, 89, 95, 111, 134, 207, 218, 219, 255
   and broken homes 156, 295
   from Europe 105
   from Frunze 199
   from the FSU 205, 208
   from Iran 53, 66, 67, 68, 70, 71
   from Libya 75, 89
   from Morocco 105, 110–11, 114, 128, 134
   from the Soviet Union 106
   from Tashkent 204
   from Tunisia 136
   from Yemen 153, 156

Aliyah Bet 25
Alliance Israelite Universelle 70, 87, 88, 89, 90
   Constantine 149
   Hamadan 42
   Iran 34, 41, 56, 57–58, 76
   Isfahan 43, 71
   Kashan 45
   Lebanon 159
   Marrakesh 116
   Morocco 120–21, 122, 123–24, 126–27, 130, 131–32, 133, 134, 135, 180
   Paris administration 123
   Tehran 55, 56, 59, 60, 63–64
   Tunisia 141–42
   Yazd 45
Allied forces xix, xx-xxi, 3, 5, 13
Almaty 200–202, 226, 234–235
American-British Commission on Palestine 20
American Jewish Federation 240
American Jews xxii, xxiii, 33, 68, 96, 109, 227, 229
American Occupation Zone 5, 18, 20, 22, 25, 251
American Reform movement 179
Amman 154, 158
Amsterdam 85
Annaba. *See* Bone
anti-Semitism 4, 20, 212
Antwerp 21, 93
Arachim ("Values") 179
Arafat, Yasser 146

Arendt, Professor Moshe 94
Armenia 37, 214, 242
army service. *See* Israel Defense Forces
Ashkenazi Cultural Committee 197–98
Ashkenazi Jews 46, 56, 63, 103, 113, 115, 139
    n. 4, 146, 164 n. 1, 168, 185, 192, 197–98, 199,
    200, 203, 204, 206, 211, 212, 213, 214, 216,
    217, 236
Ashkhabad 208, 237
assimilation xv, 33, 150, 157, 173–74, 193,
    229. *See also* conversion, religious;
    intermarriage
Association of Jewish Day School Principals
    (European) 101, 108
Association of Jewish Organizations and
    Communities in the USSR (the Vaad)
    195
Association of Jewish School Principals
    (France) 101
Atlas mountains 116
Auschwitz xv, xviii, xxi, 17, 18
Australia 20, 105
Austria xxi, 4, 7, 81, 84, 94, 98, 100, 105–6,
    254
Averbuch, Itzik 242
Avgar, Amos 230
Avicenna 46
Azerbaijan 192, 214–15, 225, 226, 237

B
Baba Sali 116
Babylon 37, 197
Bachad xiii
Bachrach, Dr. 45–46, 73
Bad Windsheim 22–23, 23n, 24–25, 26, 27,
    28, 29
Baerwald School. *See* Paul Baerwald School
    of Social Work
Baku 214, 225, 226, 237
Balkans 254
Baltic states 4, 226 n. 13, 254
Bamberger, Mr. 87
bar mitzvah 106, 117, 149, 223, 224, 228
Baranovitch 165

Barcelona 85
Bar-On, Sasha 234
bat mitzvah 223, 228
Bayswater Synagogue xvii
Beckelman, Moses (Moe) 34, 36, 75, 130
Becker, Lavy 30
Beersheba Prison 180
Beirut 159–60
Beit Avraham yeshiva (Jerusalem) 165
Belarus 164, 202, 218
Belgium 21, 84, 103, 105, 254
Belz 165, 215
Ben Ezra synagogue (Cairo) 153
Ben Gardane (Tunisia) 139, 143
Ben-Gurion, David 6 n. 4, 35, 65, 167
ben Hensh, Rabbi Shlomo 119–20
Berditchev 215
Berdugo, Joseph 115
Bergen-Belsen xxi, 33
Bergman, Ami 153
Berkovitz, Mendel 199
Bernstein, Sergei 198
Bibles xvi, 41, 94, 100, 142, 146, 229, 242
    printing and distribution 22, 91, 121, 177,
    226
Birobidzhan 201
Bishkek. *See* Frunze
Black Sea 192, 208, 210
Blass, Abraham 61–62
Bnei Akiva xviii, xx, xxi, 31
    yeshivot 170, 185
Bnei Brak 8, 165
Bobov 168
Bogen, Sara 227
Bolshevik Revolution 201
Bolsheviks 189
Bone (Annaba) 149, 150
books 16, 91, 102, 185, 205, 226
    printing 22, 59, 91, 121
    production and distribution 11, 22, 28, 57,
        91, 93, 121, 127, 132, 143, 193, 221, 222, 226,
        228, 236
    publication 93, 100, 136, 222
books (types)

Hebrew 91, 121, 127, 190 n. 1, 205, 227
history 91, 100, 226
prayer 2, 100, 177, 195, 196, 197, 222, 226
primers 59, 121, 226
religious 22, 221, 222, 226
See also Bibles
borders (geographical) 5, 7, 10, 88, 195, 200
Bortniker, Elijah (Eli) 96, 98, 99
Bourguiba, Habib 137
Bouskila, Rabbi Yaakov 118
boys' schools 119, 128, 130, 131, 132, 142, 143, 144, 149. *See also* Talmud Torah
Braunschvig, Jules 127
Breslav 122, 215
Bricha 25
Brisk, Yeshiva 168
Britain. *See* England
British government 5
British Occupation Zone xxi, 5
broken homes 156, 206, 241
Brown, Maurice 55, 59–60, 67, 70
Brussels xv, 21, 87
Buchenwald (DP camp) 2
Budan 48
budget 35, 36, 52, 56, 58, 62, 75, 81, 82, 90, 92, 99, 105, 120, 125, 130, 131, 133, 149, 167, 168, 169, 172, 173, 178, 182, 183, 185–86, 187, 221, 229, 230, 238–39, 244, 246
building reclamation 82, 169, 216, 224, 232
Bukhara 197, 207, 247
Bukharan Jews 168, 197–98, 199, 203–4, 206, 207, 217, 236
Bushehr 67
Buynaksk 209

C
Cairo 152, 153, 177
camp, family 229
camps, death and extermination 4, 16–17, 136
camps, displaced persons. *See* DP camps
camps, labor. *See* labor camps
camps, refugee. *See* refugee camps
camps, summer/winter xvii, xx, xxi, 31,
122, 134–35, 227, 228, 241. *See also* Ronald S. Lauder AJJDC International Jewish Summer Camp (Szarvas, Hungary)
camps, transit 71
Canada 109, 110, 127, 133
Cantor, Bernard 215
Carthage (Tarshish) 135, 136
Casablanca 112–13, 114–15, 116, 119, 124–25, 127, 128, 129, 130–31, 134, 135, 142, 154, 180
Caspian Sea 192, 208, 209, 211
Caucasus 192, 208, 211, 214, 217, 245
Cazes-Bénatar, Hélène 111–12
CBF. *See* Central British Fund for Jewish Relief
cemeteries 61, 66, 67, 76, 136, 151, 215, 234, 236
Central Asia 39, 192
Central British Fund for Jewish Relief (CBF) xx, xxi, 26
Central Committee of Jews of the American Zone 24
Central Committee of the Liberated Jews in Bavaria 5, 16
Central Funds for Traditional Institutions 171, 176
Chabad-Lubavitch. *See* Lubavitch
charity. *See* tzedaka
Charles and Lynn Schusterman Family Foundation 229
Chava (women's committee) 214, 237
Chazan, Rabbi Avraham 180
Chechnya 192
Chernivtsi 192, 216, 225, 242
children xi, xii, xiii, xviii, 1, 13, 82, 91, 92, 146, 254
Amsterdam 85
Armenia 243
Austria 106
Azerbaijan 214
France 82, 93
FSU 228–29, 235, 243, 247
Georgia 213
Holocaust survivor 2

Iran 34, 38, 39, 40, 41, 43, 44, 45, 47, 48, 49, 50, 52–53, 54, 57–61, 64, 65, 71–73, 74
Israel 179, 180
Italy 93, 106
Kazakhstan 201, 202, 203
Kyrgyzstan 198
Morocco 113, 114, 116, 121–23, 126–28, 129–33, 135, 149
North Africa 109
outreach program 228
reclaiming 18
refugee xx, xxi, 2, 31
Tunisia 140, 142–44, 145, 157
Uzbekistan 206, 247
Yemen 155, 156, 157
See also Children's Initiative; Mazel Tov program
Children's Aid Society. See OSE
Children's Initiative
  FSU 240–42, 244
  Kazakhstan 242
China 5, 205, 214
Chmielnicki pogroms (1648–1649) 215
Chodosh, Mr. 206
Choral Synagogue (Moscow) 222, 223
Chortkiv 239
circumcision 40, 117, 217, 224. See also mohel
Claims Conference 91–94, 102, 103, 105, 108, 239n
Cleveland 171, 176
clinics 40, 43, 44, 60, 62, 64–65, 66, 72, 73, 74–75, 92, 149, 163, 184, 237. See also polyclinics
clothing and footwear xiii, xxiii, 9, 14, 19, 22, 40, 43, 44, 49, 52, 61, 114, 155, 176, 214, 237–38
clothing programs 34, 46, 47, 67, 112, 231, 237–38
  school 40, 43, 44, 52, 54, 59, 61, 71, 74, 140, 241
Cohanim, Aziz 44, 71
Cohen Sedeq, Mr. 70
Cohen, Henry 19

Cohn, Louis 98
Cold War 80
Columbia University 96
Comite de Gestion 164–65
commandments, religious. See mitzvoth
Committee on Religious-Cultural Affairs (JDC) 168, 172, 186
communal leaders, training of. See training: communal functionaries and leaders
Communism, Communists 149–50, 189, 190, 191, 196, 198, 199, 201, 204, 222, 224, 228, 243, 251, 254
community development 195, 214, 219, 220, 221–225, 227, 228, 229, 233, 243
community leadership 102, 117, 125, 150, 173, 212, 219, 224, 226, 227, 245, 248
community organizations 90, 207. See also individual organizations
community reconnection (FSU) 190, 192, 200, 217, 218, 220, 221, 223, 225, 227, 229, 230, 232, 233, 244, 246, 249
community schools 55, 121
  Tunis 140, 143–45
concentration camp 17, 85
Conference on Jewish Material Claims Against Germany. See Claims Conference
Constantine 149, 150
Continental Europe 80, 81
conversion, religious 38, 157, 173
Copenhagen 87
Council of Religious Affairs in the USSR 190
Cremieux Law 148
Cuenca, Andre 41, 56, 63–64, 70
Cuenca, Batya 63–64
Cultural Fund (Chernivtsi) 216
culture
  French 56, 123
  Georgian 212
culture, Jewish 180, 214, 215, 216, 221, 224, 228, 247, 249, 251
  activities and programs xxii, 19, 61, 82, 86, 92–93, 163, 198, 207, 219, 220, 228, 230, 241, 243, 245, 246

centers 193, 195, 201, 204, 205, 206, 227 (*see also* JCC)
committees 149, 197–98, 206, 218, 236, 243
heritage 164, 173
services 220, 245, 247
supplies 22, 190
curriculum
in Alliance schools 56–57, 90, 123, 127
in Föhrenwald 11
France 90, 91
FSU 226
Iran 45, 57, 58, 72
JDC Yeshiva Program 174
Morocco 123, 124, 127
ORT 87
Ozar Hatorah 90, 124
Tunisia 142
customs. *See* Jewish tradition
Czernowitz. *See* Chernivtsi

D

Daber Ivrit school (Djerba) 144–45, 147
Dachau 13
Dagestan 209–10
Dakhtayef, Dr. 198
Danielova, Svetlana 209
Davidoff, David 211
daycare programs 43, 74, 122
day schools xxii, 11, 12, 19, 85–94, 101, 108, 141, 150, 211, 226, 247
De Gaulle, Charles 151
Denmark 105
dental aid and care programs 74, 170, 184–85
dentists 18, 47, 72–73, 184
Departement Educatif de la Jeunesse Juive au Maroc (DEJJ) 122
Derbent 210–11
Derech Yehudi school (Tbilisi) 213
détente 106, 213
Detroit 171, 176
Deutsch, Rabbi Abraham 85–86
dhimmi 37, 39, 46, 110

Diaspora, the Yeshiva Department and 170–71, 176–77, 178
diphtheria 14, 60
Dispensaire Polyvalent clinic 149
Displaced Persons. *See* DPs
distribution
food 28, 40, 166, 168, 203, 209, 221, 229, 235, 236, 237, 244 (*see also* food packages)
milk 60, 61, 73, 114
packages 203, 222, 230
supplies 6, 9–10, 23–24, 28, 60, 66, 152, 177, 222–23, 237
Divan, Rabbi Amram 119
divorce 40, 41, 206
Djerba 136, 137–40, 141, 142, 143–45, 147
doctors 3, 14, 18, 43, 44, 47–48, 53, 55, 59–60, 65, 67, 117, 137, 189–90, 203, 231, 233, 236, 237
Doctors' Plot 189–90
DP camps (Germany) xx, 2, 3–12, 18–26, 74, 81, 82, 84, 98, 112, 163, 164, 172, 191
residents' committee 14
DP committees 14, 24
DPs xxi, xxiii, 2–3, 4–5, 6–8, 9, 10, 11, 12–13, 14, 15–19, 20, 22, 23–25, 26, 27–29, 34, 81, 83, 84, 208, 254
Dupkin, Carol 191
Dupkin, Manuel, II 191
Dushanbe 196–98, 237

E

Eastern Europe xxii, xxiii, 5, 25, 31n, 32, 36, 80, 81, 83, 84, 89, 161, 166–67, 188, 190
Eastern European Jews xxii, xxiii, 5, 25, 32, 80, 84, 89, 103, 161, 166, 167
Eckstein, Rabbi Yechiel 241
École Normale Hébraïque 127, 180
École Normale Israélite Orientale (ENIO) 88
École Populaire 56, 60
Education Department (JDC) 79, 96, 167
education 33, 56, 71, 72, 73, 74, 123, 126, 131, 149, 181, 209. *See also* schools; teachers
academic 225

conference 95–96

formal 19, 89, 173, 194, 244

girls' 29, 71, 74, 121, 142, 144, 147, 209, 226 (*see also* girls' schools)

Hebrew 45, 58, 124, 127 (*see also* Hebrew; "Hebrew in Hebrew" teaching; Hebrew teachers)

informal xx, 19, 83, 89, 122, 152, 170, 173, 244 (*see also* camps, summer/winter; Hillel; JCC)

Jewish xv, 29, 45, 56–59, 64, 79, 80, 84, 86, 87, 92, 93, 95–96, 97, 98, 100–103, 104, 106, 107–8, 109, 121–35, 140–45, 149, 159, 195, 202, 211, 224, 226–27, 252–53

materials 11, 90, 91, 94, 100, 102, 141, 143, 150, 194, 205, 228, 229 (*see also* curriculum)

Morocco 112, 121–35

programs 19, 22, 28, 34, 43, 52, 58–59, 74, 79, 93, 95, 96, 98, 99, 104, 108, 113, 114, 120, 124, 125, 127, 130–31, 134, 135, 142, 143, 144, 150, 179, 187, 208, 226 (*see also* Yeshiva Program)

secular 33, 52, 71, 130, 144

teaching materials 11, 90, 91, 92, 100, 102, 141, 143, 150, 194, 229 (*see also* Hamoré)

education, nonformal. *See* education: informal

Education-Religious-Cultural Department, JDC 167. *See also* Yeshiva Department (JDC)

Egypt 46, 56, 148, 151–53

Egyptian government 153

Eidelman, Rabbi Shalom 134–35

Eilat 178–79

Eisenberg, Azriel 95–96, 97, 100

Eisenhower, Dwight David 3, 6, 20

Elazar, Menachem 210, 236

elderly 82, 83, 92, 112, 117, 134, 140, 147, 151, 163, 190, 199, 203, 205, 208, 211, 230, 231, 233, 236, 237, 239, 240, 241, 243, 244, 245

elementary schools. *See* primary schools

Elghanayan (family) 77

Elghanayan, David 35, 62, 64

Elghanayan, Habib 35, 62, 64, 77

El Ghriba synagogue (Djerba) 139

Eliav, Aryeh "Lova". *See* Lewine, Lova

Eliyahu, Rabbi Mordechai 185

ELKA. *See* JDC-ELKA

Em Habanim schools (Morocco) 115, 117, 132

emigration xiv, xx, 12, 16, 38, 48, 52, 77, 105, 114, 115

from Algeria 88

from the FSU 193–94, 205, 206, 207, 208, 213, 217, 218, 219, 221, 229, 237, 246, 247

to Israel (see aliyah)

from Morocco 126, 130, 133

from Tunisia 141, 145, 146, 148, 151, 152

from Yemen 154, 157, 158

See also immigration

England, xi,xiii, xvi-xix, xx, 1, 16, 17, 21, 25, 26, 30, 31, 32, 40, 57, 79, 81, 96, 101, 125, 141, 157, 255, 256. *See also* London

Enoch, Hanoch 94, 100

Eppler, Heinz 191

Eppler, Ruthie 191

Epstein, Seymour "Epi" 134, 191 n. 5, 226–27

Erfoud 115

eruv 138

Ethiopia 179

Etz Chaim Yeshiva (London) xiv, xvi, xviii

Etz Haim Yeshiva (Israel) 164

Europe xx-xxi, xxii, xxiii, 1, 5, 6 n. 3, 7, 8, 24, 25, 29, 31, 34, 73, 79–108, 109, 112, 120, 122, 127, 130, 131, 133, 134, 136, 146, 159, 164, 165, 166–67, 170, 171, 172, 175, 187, 188, 222 n. 11, 226, 227, 239n, 243, 251, 252, 253, 255. *See also* Eastern Europe

European Association of Jewish Day School Principals. *See* Association of Jewish Day School Principals

European Council of Jewish Communities 108

European Jews xxii, xxiii, 3, 5, 6, 29, 32, 33, 79, 80, 81–83, 84–85, 86–90, 92, 94–95, 105, 107, 251, 254

F

facilities (kitchens, dining room, dormitories, bathroom, etc.) 3, 54, 67, 73, 175, 145, 168, 169, 175, 224, 233, 241. *See also* kitchens

Far East 159, 170

Farsi 36, 38, 40, 51, 69, 71–72, 192, 197, 206

Feder, Ted 98–99, 252

Federation of Jewish Communities (Algeria) 149, 150

feeding 52, 53, 54, 184, 230

    canteens 10, 82, 132, 140, 149, 221

    center 49

    meals 113, 117, 133, 140, 149, 168, 220, 233, 234, 236

    milk 60, 61, 73, 113, 114, 169

    programs xxii-xxiii, 34, 40, 43, 45, 46, 47, 59, 60–61, 67, 71, 73, 82, 186

    See also food; food packages; schools: lunch programs

Feldafing (DP camp) 3, 7

Fez 114, 116, 117, 121, 132

financial assistance 80n, 81–82, 87, 88, 89, 90, 97, 121, 123–24, 130, 131, 132, 140, 144, 152, 166, 177, 178, 180, 182, 186, 195, 224, 225–26, 228, 231, 232, 240, 241, 244, 248

Finkel, Rabbi Eliezer 164

Finland 105

First World War. *See* World War I

Fish, Rosa 199–200

Föhrenwald (DP camp) 3, 5–9, 10, 11, 14–16, 17, 18, 19–22, 23, 27, 28, 29, 30, 253

Fonds Social Juif Unifié (FSJU) 82, 98, 105, 151

food 1, 9, 10, 19, 27, 40, 42, 44, 45, 49, 50, 52, 59, 71, 72, 112, 119, 133, 184, 194, 195, 204, 230, 235, 241

    delivery of fresh 233

    distribution programs 168–69, 203, 209, 230, 237

food packages 9, 22, 24, 42, 44, 112, 152, 165, 189, 200, 205, 213, 221, 229, 231, 233, 234, 236, 237, 243, 244, 247

distribution 28, 40, 166, 203, 209, 221, 229, 235, 236, 244

footwear. *See* clothing and footwear

Foreman, Spencer 241

Forgotten Million, The 33

former Soviet Union (FSU) 108, 153, 177, 178, 179, 186, 189–250, 255

    outreach programs 228, 229

Foum Tataouine 139, 143

Fraenckel, Andre 120

France xii, xiv, 29, 56, 81, 82, 84, 85, 87–89, 90, 98, 101, 103, 105, 109, 110, 111, 112, 115, 127, 129, 130, 133, 136, 146, 150–51, 160, 254

Frankfurt 26–28, 83

Free Loan Fund. *See* Rothschild Foundation

French Occupation Zone 5

Friedlaender, Israel 215

Friedman, Nathan Zvi 7, 8, 13

Frunze (Bishkek) 198–200, 226, 246

FSU. *See* former Soviet Union

FSU Department (JDC) 220, 227n, 229, 240–41

G

Gabes 139, 143, 146

Gadilov, Nachman 211

Gavrielov, Roman 211

Gemorman, Menachem 8–9

Geneva 97, 99, 106, 107, 109, 120, 140, 159

Georgia 192, 212–13, 217, 225, 226, 236, 237–38, 247, 256

Georgian Jews 168, 212–13, 217

Ger Hasidim xii, 165

German government 24, 92

ghetto xv, xviii, xxii, 16, 40, 44, 71, 74, 112, 137, 206, 207. *See also* Jewish quarter; *mahaleh*; *mellah*

Giltz, Reb Shimon 204–5

girls' schools 44, 45, 88, 126, 128, 129, 130, 142, 143 146. *See also* women's institutions

glasnost 190

Goldman, Gad 11–12, 22, 27

Goldman, Ralph 191, 225, 252

Goldman, Rabbi Yaakov 166
Goldman, Yossie 229
Goldmann, Nachum 92
Golpayegan 47, 67
Gorbachev, Mikhail 190
Gorodetsky, Rabbi Benyamin 116
Great Britain. *See* England
Greece 84, 105, 254
Greenbaum, Rabbi Dr. Aaron 167–68, 171–72
Greenspan, Rabbi Nahman xvii
Grodzinski, Rabbi Chaim Ozer 166
Gugenheim, Rabbi Ernest 99
Gugenheim, Madame 99
gulags 153, 199, 200, 203
Gymnasium (Poland) xiii, xiv, xv, 16

H

Haber, Sam 24, 30, 107
Haggada 111
Haikin, Mark 214
Haji Abdallah 57, 63
Haji Aziz synagogue (Tehran) 56
hakham 41, 47, 71, 72
Hakham Netanel 69, 70
hakim 47–48, 53. *See also* doctors
Halberstam, Rabbi Jekutiel Judah 6–7, 12, 13
Halevi, Rabbi Yehuda 210
Halperin, Rabbi Zev 115
Hamadan 38, 42, 46, 64
Hamoré (teachers' journal) 98, 99–100, 101, 102, 105, 107–8, 141
Hanukkah 61, 235
Haredim 183
Harrison, Earl 6
Harry and Jeanette Weinberg Foundation 240
Hasadim. *See* Hesed centers
Hashid 32, 154
Hasidim, Hasidism xii, xv, 7, 12–13, 88, 128, 157, 165, 166, 168, 185, 202, 206, 215, 216, 223, 225
Hassan II, King (Morocco) 111, 134

health 36, 40, 59, 60, 67, 72, 83, 112, 113, 170, 171
health care programs 59, 113, 183, 184–85
health centers 113, 114. *See also* clinics; hospitals; polyclinics
Hebrew
    books 91, 121, 127, 190 n. 1, 205, 227
    classes 45, 122, 140, 144, 198, 202, 205, 206, 211, 213, 214, 243
    language xv, xvii, 33, 43, 48, 52, 57, 58, 59, 65, 98, 106, 121, 122, 124, 127, 136, 139, 141, 144, 145, 146, 156, 189, 196, 197, 198, 204, 205, 210
"Hebrew in Hebrew" teaching 102–3
Hebrew teachers xix, 58–59, 71, 72, 103, 127, 140
Hebron Yeshiva (Israel) 164, 165, 168
heder. *See* Talmud Torah
Heidelberg 26–27
Hekmat, Mrs. 62
Henshaw, Jean 3, 8, 19
Herman, Meyer 70, 72–73
Herzog, Rabbi Isaac 20, 166
Heschel, Rabbi Abraham Joshua 122
hesder 168, 175, 185, 223n
Hesed centers 232–34, 236, 237, 244, 245, 246, 247, 248
    Almaty 234
    Baku 237
    Bukhara 236
    FSU 195, 196, 217, 218, 220, 222, 224
    Kazakhstan 234
    Mitzvah 234
    Oni 238
    Saint Petersburg 232
    Taganrog 235
    Tashkent 236
    Tbilisi 236, 238
    Uzbekistan 236
    Yerevan 243
"Hesed Commando" 232
HesedMobile 232, 234, 237, 244
High Holidays 152, 170, 204, 222. *See also* Rosh Hashanah; Sukkoth; Yom Kippur

Hillel 152, 170, 204, 213, 227, 229, 233
hilula 119, 139
Hirsch, Rabbi Shimshon Raphael 33
Hobrat Hatalmud rabbinical academy 143
Hoffman (Yahil), Chaim 30
Holland xxi, 105, 254
Holocaust xxii, 2, 13, 16–17, 18, 22n, 23, 29, 32, 63, 80, 85, 86, 92, 108, 164, 191, 203, 219, 239, 243
Holy Land 65, 157
hospitals 3, 14, 40, 75, 92, 152, 163
    maternity 74, 75, 185
    pediatric 60–61, 75
    See also clinics; polyclinics
Hungarian Jews 4, 105, 114, 254
Hungary xxiii, 7, 114, 125, 177, 228–29
    Communist 105, 254
Hurwitz, Sylvia 55, 60, 67
hygiene 39, 40, 42, 53, 54, 184
    programs 60, 74

I

Ibrahim, Ali 42, 55, 64
immigrants, outreach programs for 178, 179–80
immigration xiii, xvii, 179–80
    to France 88–89
    to Israel 34, 67, 71, 85, 111, 163, 178, 181, 199, 207 (*see also* aliyah)
    to Palestine 5, 30
    to Spain 85
    to United States 18, 106
    See also emigration
independence
    Algeria (1962) 88, 148, 151
    Israel (1948) 34, 152, 153, 161, 166
    Morocco (1956) 85, 110–11, 120, 123, 126, 133
    Tunisia (1956) 136, 137, 141
independence, community 82, 105, 224, 245, 247
India 140
informal education. *See* education: informal

Intergovernmental Committee on Refugees (IGCR) 6
intermarriage 64, 134, 152, 157, 173 193, 199, 206, 208, 242. *See also* assimilation
International Conference for Holocaust Era Insurance Claims (ICHEIC) 239
International Fellowship of Christians and Jews (IFCJ) 240, 241
International School of Geneva 106
Iran 32–77, 79, 80, 84, 90, 112, 114, 117, 120, 121, 123, 124, 127, 171, 172, 192, 196, 197, 206, 208, 252, 254, 256
Iraq 35, 70, 88, 197
Iraqi Jews 37, 38, 54–55, 56, 57, 63, 66, 69
Iron Curtain xxiii, 80, 83, 102, 108, 249, 254
Isfahan 38, 42, 43–44, 47, 48, 60, 65, 66, 67, 71
Israel, State of xxiii-xiv, xxiii n. 2, 29, 35, 65, 67, 110, 136, 152, 153, 163, 166, 255
    creation of 109, 152, 255
    government of 95, 163, 181n, 187
    See also Palestine
Israel Defense Forces 166 n. 7, 168, 178, 182, 186
    hesder 168, 175, 185, 223n
    preparatory yeshivot 183
Israelitische Kultusgemeinde (IKG) 83
Israel Prison Service 180
Italy 7, 16, 75, 81, 84, 85, 105, 106, 177, 252, 254
Ittihad-Maroc (Moroccan Alliance) 124, 133, 135
JAFI. *See* Jewish Agency
Jaleh school 56, 60, 63
Japan 164, 201

J

JCC (Jewish community center; FSU) 227–28, 232, 234, 236, 241, 244–45, 246–47
JDC Scholarship Fund. *See* Scholarship Fund
JDC-ELKA 183

JDC-Israel xiii, 173, 183, 187

Jerusalem xxii, xxiii n. 2, 48, 65, 83 n. 4, 110, 115, 138, 139, 144, 164, 165, 166, 169, 170, 173, 178, 180, 185, 220, 223, 227

Jesode-Hatora school (Antwerp) 93

Jewish Agency (Jewish Agency for Israel; JAFI) 52, 55, 65, 66, 67, 70, 76, 87, 89, 111, 114, 144, 149, 151, 163, 194, 200, 205, 208, 211, 214, 237

    Torah Education Department 89

Jewish Agency for Palestine 6, 19, 25, 27, 28, 30

Jewish Brigade 8, 21

Jewish burial 40, 204, 222, 223, 224, 236, 242

Jewish festivals 59, 139, 190, 208, 213, 222, 226, 233. See also High Holidays

Jewish festivals program 179, 194

"Jewish House" 236, 245

Jewish movements xvii, xviii, 1, 5

Jewish Principals' Association (FSU) 227

Jewish quarter 137, 138, 141, 212, 215. See also ghetto; mahale; mellah

Jewish Relief Unit (JRU) xx-xxi

Jewish renewal 224, 230, 240, 245

Jewish Renewal Department (JDC) 227

Jewish Restitution Successor Organization. See JRSO

Jewish symbols 216

Jewish tradition xvi, 23, 33, 40, 41, 45, 48, 63, 109, 112, 117–20, 121, 123, 134, 138, 139–40, 141, 146, 147, 153, 155, 157, 165, 174, 178, 179, 180, 188, 193, 196, 197, 198, 204, 206, 207, 209, 212, 213, 214, 217, 222, 226, 235, 242

Jews. See American Jews; Ashkenazi Jews; Bukharan Jews; Eastern European Jews; European Jews; Georgian Jews; Hungarian Jews; Iraqi Jews; Kurdish Jews; Lebanese Jews; Mashhadi Jews; Mountain Jews; North African Jews; Polish Jews; Russian Jews; Sephardic Jews; Syrian Jews; Tunisian Jews; Yemenite Jews

Jews' College xviii, xix, 251

Jonah 135

Jordan 158, 169

Jordan, Charlie 96, 99

JRSO (Jewish Restitution Successor Organization) 166

Jubareh (Isfahan) 43

Jung, Rabbi Leo 168, 172, 176, 177

K

Kabardino-Balkaria 209

Kagan, Emil 200–202

Kahaneman, Rabbi Yossef Shlomo 165

Kalisz xi-xiii, xiv, xv, xviii, 11, 16

Kalmanovitch, Rabbi Avraham 164, 175–76

Kanoune Kheyr Khah clinic (Iran) 40, 62

Kapo 11

Karaganda 203, 247

Karlin-Stolin Hasidic group 240

Kashan 42, 44–45, 64

Kashfi, Mrs. 62

kashruth xvii, 9, 10, 27, 106, 119, 131, 135, 152, 195, 203, 204, 210

Kassel 27

Katziev, Avrech 214

Katzki, Herbert 30, 34, 75, 252

Kazakhstan 192, 200–203, 223, 226, 234, 247

    children's program 242

Kerman 42, 45–46, 54, 57, 64, 72, 73

Kermanshah 38, 42, 46, 49, 69

KGB 199, 218

Kharchev, Konstantin 193

Khazari kingdom 210

Kheidar 156

Khomani, Shalom 50

Khomein 67

Khomeini, Ayatollah 64, 77

Khonsar 47–48, 67

Khorramabad 48–49

Khrushchev 200

kibbutzim (collective agricultural settlements) 178, 179, 180, 183

Kibbutz Ma'agan 183, 184

kiddush 50, 117–18

Kidushin, David 144–45, 146

Kidushin, Tzvia 145, 156
Kielce pogrom 5, 25. *See also* pogroms
Kiev 210, 218, 231
kindergarten 43, 62, 92, 104, 113, 122, 128, 140, 147, 206, 226, 236
Kindertransport xx, 31
Kiryat Malakhi 181
Kiryat Sanz 13
Kishinev 199
kitchens xi, 9, 10, 50, 54, 169, 175, 184, 202, 224, 257. *See also* facilities; soup kitchens
Klausenberger Rebbe. *See* Halberstam, Rabbi Jekutiel Judah
Klausner, Abraham (Abe) 8
Kolitz, Rabbi Yitzhak 185
kolkhozy 189, 196
kollel 126, 135, 167, 179, 226
Kollel Hasidei Gur 168
Kolonka (Nal'chik) 209
Kook, Rabbi Avraham Yitzhak Hacohen 164
Kook, Rabbi Simha 185
Kopnivsky, David 87
kosher food. *See* kashruth
Kowsar school 44, 59, 71
Krasnaya Sloboda (Kuba) 214
Krupnick, Rivka 213
Kuba 214–15, 247
Kuku (family) 63
Kurdish Jews 49, 50, 65, 66
Kurdistan 49, 65
Kuresh school 55
Kutaisi 213, 238, 247
Kyrgyzstan 192, 198–200, 226, 246
labor camps 13, 129

L
Ladino 38
Ladispoli (Italy) 106
Lag b'Omer 119, 139
Lake Urmia 51
Land of Israel xviiin, 65
Landsberg (DP camp) 2–3, 12
Latin America 35, 127

Latvia 198
Lazare, Lucien 99
learning disabilities, programs for 134, 181–82
Leavitt, Moe 167
Lebanese Jews 157–60
Lebanon 33, 56, 124, 146, 156–60
Leib, Reb 226
Le Refuge yeshiva 29
Levinas, Emmanuel 88
Levine, Rabbi Ariel 212, 226
Levi Yitzhak of Berditchev, Rabbi 215
Lewi, Rabbi Isaac Meir 33–34, 35, 36, 41, 43, 44, 49, 51, 55, 64, 69
Lewine, Lova 36
Liaison Bureau 194, 214
liberation xx–xxi, 3, 4, 5, 9, 17, 25, 28
Liberov, Rabbi Sa'adia 129–30
libraries 91, 102, 193, 196, 211, 214, 221, 226, 228, 231, 234, 236, 244
Libya 35, 74, 75, 148, 252
Liebman, Rabbi Gershon 28–29, 85, 86
Lipsker, Rabbi Michael 114–15, 128, 130
Lithuania 12, 16, 88, 166, 207
Lithuanian yeshivot xvi, 165, 166, 168, 185
London xiii, xiv, xvi, xvii–xix, xxi, 8, 14, 21, 31, 32, 46, 157, 192, 251
Lopian, Rabbi Eliyahu xvi, xviii, 8
Lorestan 48
Loskove, Abe 54, 75–76
Loskove, Ruth 76
Lubavitch 87, 90, 101, 146, 165, 181, 194, 195, 202, 206, 243
    Morocco 114, 115, 116, 118–19, 121, 122, 128–31, 132, 133, 134–35
    Tunisia 140, 141, 142–43, 144, 145, 146, 147
Lubavitcher Rebbe 1, 118–19, 128, 129, 130, 143, 146, 195
Lviv 192, 216, 224, 242
Lvov. *See* Lviv
Lyon 86, 88

M

Maccabi (Tbilisi) 213

Madrid 85

Magen David (symbol) 216

Magnes, Judah 20

mahaleh 40, 43, 44, 49, 54, 56, 65, 66, 68, 74–75, 84, 117, 206

Maimonides 117

Maimonides school (Algiers) 150, 151

Majlis 37, 38

Makhachkala 210, 247

MALBEN 163

Mantoux 60

Marrakesh 116, 120

marriage 10, 12, 18, 40, 147, 171, 199, 209, 224

  and wedding parcels 12, 19

  Yemenite 156

  See also kollel

Marseille 86, 88, 115

Marshall, Louis xxiii

Mashhad 38, 75

Mashhadi Jews 38, 55, 108

massacres. *See* pogroms

Matusof, Rabbi Shlomo 114, 115, 116, 128–29, 134

Mayer, Astorre 85

Mazel Tov program (Children's Initiative; FSU) 240–42, 243

medical care 40, 49, 52, 59, 60, 66, 67, 155, 163, 236, 241, 242

  examinations 184, 203

  first aid 111

  inoculations 60, 67

  medications 114, 200

  optical care 185

  services 203

  See also dental aid

Medical Equipment Employment and Production Center (Saint Petersburg) 233

medical programs 34, 40, 52, 53, 82, 117

  therapeutic 233

  yeshivot health 184–85

See also health care programs

Meir, Golda 20

Meknes 114, 115, 128, 132

Melchior, Rabbi 87

mellah 112, 113, 114, 116–17, 122, 126, 128, 132, 134, 135

Memorial Foundation for Jewish Culture 92–93, 108

Merkaz ha'Hinukh ha'Atzma'i 168

Merkaz Harav Yeshiva (Israel) 164, 178

Messas, Rabbi Shalom 115, 118, 185

Miandoab 49, 51

Mifal Hatorah 170

mikve (ritual bath) 8, 130, 242

milah. See circumcision

Milan 85, 87, 93

milk-bottling plant (Casablanca) 113

Mimouna 41

Mineralnye Vody 211

Mir Yeshiva (New York) 164 n. 2

Mir Yeshiva (Poland/Israel) 164, 168, 175

mitzvoth 13, 38, 40–41, 48, 99, 110, 119, 173, 198, 204, 222, 224, 255

Mohammed VI, King (Morocco) 134

mohel 146, 206, 215

Moldova 199, 212

Monsonego, Rabbi Aaron 119, 124, 125

Montreal 30, 110, 133

Morgenthau, Henry xxii

Moroccan Alliance. *See* Ittihad-Maroc

Morocco 33, 35, 41, 56, 88, 107, 109–35, 140, 141, 143, 148, 149, 171, 174, 252, 254

Moscow 36, 191, 194, 195, 207, 212, 213, 214, 218, 222, 223, 229, 230

moshavim 178

Moshe, Itzik 237–38

Mossadeq, Muhammad 68

Mountain Jews 209–11, 214, 217

Munich 2, 3, 5, 6, 8, 9, 10, 14, 16, 17, 18, 21, 23, 24, 28, 29, 30

musar movement xvi, 28

Myers-JDC-Brookdale Institute 241

N

Nachlat Har Chabad 181
Nachman of Breslav, Rebbe 202
Nal'chik 192, 209, 247
Namurdi, Nahman 63
Nazi Germany xv, xvii, xx, 4, 29
Nazis xviii, xx, 4, 6, 7, 11, 16, 17, 63, 79, 85, 86, 98, 136, 147, 211, 216, 249, 251
Nazi victims 239
    "non-nazi victims" 240, 249
Nebuchadnezzar 37
Negev 181
Nehavand 49
Netanya 13, 170
Netiv Binyamin Afghanistan 168
New York xxii, 1, 22 n.7, 33, 56, 59, 62, 63, 68, 87, 92, 96, 97, 98, 103, 120, 123, 124, 125, 126, 129, 131, 143, 154, 157, 159, 164, 167, 172, 173, 175, 176, 186, 240, 241, 252
    Board of Jewish Education 172
    Committee for Jewish Education 95
Nimrodi (family) 63
Noam yeshivot 170
nonformal education. *See* education: informal
North Africa 79–80, 92, 100, 107, 109–51, 160, 161, 171, 172, 196, 219, 226 n. 13, 251, 253, 255. *See also* Algeria; Egypt; Morocco; Tunisia
North African Jews, relocation to France of 88–89, 105. *See also individual countries*
Norway 105
Nuremberg 22
nutrition 112, 113, 168, 183, 184
nutrition programs 132–33
    yeshiva 224
    See also feeding: programs

O

occupation zones xviii, xxi, 5, 18
Ofek (FSU book week) 228
Oleisky, Yaakov 12
Oni (Georgia) 237
Open University 225

Operation Magic Carpet 32, 153–54
Oran 148, 150, 151
Orot Eilat 179
ORT 12, 19, 28, 44, 55, 61–62, 69, 70, 71, 87, 125
    Algiers 135
    Morocco 131–32, 135
OSE (Children's Aid Society)
    France 92
    Morocco 113
    Tunisia 164
Ostersetzer, Rabbi Shmuel 93
Ostrin, Asher 191 n. 5, 220
Ozar Hatorah 87
    France 88–89, 90
    Iran 33, 34, 36, 41, 43, 44, 47, 57–59, 69, 70, 73, 76, 208
    Lebanon 159
    Morocco 115, 117, 119, 122, 124–27, 130, 132, 133, 134
    New York 159
    Tunisia 140
Ouezzane 119
Ourika Valley 120
outreach programs 178–81, 228, 229

P

Pahlevi, Mohammad Reza Shah 37, 39, 46, 56, 63, 68, 76–77
Pahlevi, Reza Shah 37, 39, 56
Pakistan 45, 77
Palestine xviii, xxii, 2, 5, 6 n. 4, 8, 20, 25, 27, 28, 29, 30, 33, 153, 163, 164–65, 166 n. 6, 167. *See also* Israel, State of
Paris xiii, xiv, xvi, xxi, 1, 3, 18, 28, 32, 34, 43, 52, 56, 57, 59, 64, 69, 70, 75, 79–80, 82n, 83, 86, 88, 91, 94, 95, 96, 97, 98, 99, 100, 101, 109, 112, 113, 120, 123, 130, 137, 140, 151, 167, 171, 208
Parnassa Bechavod program 187
Passman, Charles 30, 165–66
Paul Baerwald School of Social Work 83
peddling 40, 47, 126
perestroika 190, 193, 211, 216, 227

Pesach 40, 99, 111, 119, 179
    matzo 152, 213, 231, 237
    seder 170, 196, 222, 229
Petah Tikvah (Lomza) yeshiva 165
Peters, Evelyn 140
physicians. *See* doctors
Pinson, Rebbetzin Leah 142, 145–56, 147
Pinson, Rabbi Nisson 141, 142, 143, 145–46,
    147
PLO 146
pogroms 5, 25, 38, 164, 189, 215
Polacco school (Rome) 85, 93
Poland xi-xiv, xv-xvi, xviii, xxiii, 4–5, 16, 17,
    18, 21, 81, 88, 115, 164, 165, 175, 177, 216, 254,
    256
policy, JDC 1, 6, 10, 24, 101, 144, 182, 195,
    220, 225, 239
Polish Jews xii, xiii, xiv, 4, 16, 17–18, 81, 254
Polish-Russian War (1919–1921) 189, 215
polyclinics 49, 60–61, 74–75. *See also*
    clinics
Ponevez yeshiva (Lithuania/Israel) 165, 168
Porath, Jonathan 229
Portugal 81, 254
Posner family (Pittsburgh) 225, 236
postnatal care 60
practices, religious. *See* mitzvoth
prayer books. *See* religious supplies: prayer
    books
prayer services xvii, xix, 1, 7, 8, 41, 56, 117,
    139, 198, 204, 206, 217, 222, 243
    leaders of 56, 222
    quorum for 152, 243
    See also synagogues; *yizkor*
prayers, teaching of 51, 94, 121
primary schools xiii, 74, 85, 114, 117, 126, 128,
    135, 142, 147, 159, 168, 179
prison xiv, 11, 180–81, 195, 197. *See also*
    gulags
prisoner rehabilitation, outreach program
    for 180–81
programs. *See* Ahi; Arachim; Children's
    Initiative; clothing programs; culture,
    Jewish: activities and programs; daycare
programs; dental aid and care programs;
    education: programs; feeding: programs;
    food: distribution programs; health care
    programs; hygiene: programs; Jewish
    festivals program; learning disabilities;
    Mazel Tov program; medical programs;
    nutrition programs; outreach programs;
    Parnassa Bechavod program; prisoner
    rehabilitation; schools: lunch programs;
    welfare: programs; welfare: school pro-
    grams; Yedidim; yeshiva outreach pro-
    gram; Yeshiva Program
property, confiscated 82, 152, 189, 201, 209,
    215, 224
property, reclamation 5, 89, 153, 207, 212,
    224, 225
Pyatigorsk 211

R
Rabat 114, 116–17
rabbinical academies. *See* yeshivot
rabbis, training of. *See* training: rabbis
Rafsanjan 47, 72
Rahamim ("Mercy") (women's group) 213,
    236
Raida 154, 155
Ramat Gan 107, 170
Ramsgate College 141
Raskin, Rabbi Yehuda 134–35
rations 7, 9, 10, 19, 22, 27, 28
reconstruction, cultural 86, 224
reconstruction, of communities in Europe
    6, 80–83, 84–106, 107–8, 109, 243
Red Army 4, 201, 215
refugee camps (Iran) 66, 67–68, 74, 76. *See
    also* DP camps
refugees 6, 151, 164
    European 81, 83, 84, 105, 115, 255
    German xx
    Hungarian 105
    Iran 54, 65–68
    Iraq 37
    Muslim world xxiii
    Polish 33, 88, 115, 204

Soviet 177, 196, 204, 205
See also DPs
Rehovot 64, 185
relatives xvi, xviii, 5, 10, 16, 20, 21
religious activities 221, 223
religious supplies 22, 170, 177, 179, 190, 191, 192, 196, 200, 223, 236, 237, 244
  Bibles xvi, 41, 94, 100, 142, 146, 229, 242
  prayer books 2, 100, 177, 195, 196, 197, 222, 226
  religious books 22, 221, 222, 226
  shofar 195, 196
religious suppression 189, 190, 191, 195, 203, 204, 209, 215, 216, 217, 219, 222, 224, 243, 251
"Rescue, Relief, and Rehabilitation" xxii, 172, 191
restitution 216, 224, 225, 239, 249. *See also* Claims Conference; International Conference for Holocaust Era Insurance Claims; JRSO; Swiss Banks Settlement
reunification 17, 18, 21
Rezayeh 49, 51, 65
Riga 46, 198
Righteous Gentiles 18, 26
Rissani 116
ritual slaughter. *See shehita*
Rock, Eli 6, 9, 30
Romania xxiii, 12, 80, 177, 254
Rome 68, 85, 87, 93, 177
Ronald S. Lauder AJJDC International Jewish Summer Camp (Szarvas, Hungary) 228
Rosenfeld, Leonard 172
Rosh Hashanah xix, 1, 2, 129. *See also* High Holidays
Rostov-on-Don 192, 211–12, 247
Rothschild Foundation ("Yad Hanadiv") Free Loan Fund 170–71, 176
Russia xviii, 18, 36, 56, 65, 82n, 106, 128, 189, 192, 200, 208, 209–12, 218, 235, 247. *See also* former Soviet Union
Russian Jews 106, 180, 189–250. *See also* former Soviet Union

S
Saada 154, 155–56
Saadya brothers 43
SABA 244
Sadoun, Bughid 136
Saint Petersburg 93, 218, 227n, 230, 232, 233
Sally Mayer day school (Milan) 93
Samarkand 205–7, 247
Sanaa 154–55
Sanandaj 49, 65
Saqqez 49, 50, 65
Sarcelles 88
Satmar 157, 168
Scandinavia 81, 83, 84, 101
Schauman, Dr. 87
Schiff, Jacob H. xxii
Schleissheim 23, 24–25
Schlesinger, Rabbi Meir 223–24, 245
Schneerson, Rabbi 1
Schneerson, Yosef Yitzchak 115
Schneider, Michael 191
Scholarship Fund, JDC 103–4, 105, 107
scholarships 83, 92–93, 103, 104, 170. *See also* Scholarship Fund
school provisions 22, 28
schooling. *See* education
schools xii, xvii, 11, 12, 19, 33, 40, 43, 44, 45, 46, 48, 49, 51, 53, 54, 57, 59, 60, 61, 63, 71, 73, 74, 83, 85, 86, 87, 88–89, 91, 93–94, 101, 102, 104, 105, 106, 107, 115, 116–17, 119, 121–35, 140, 142, 143, 144–45, 146, 147, 149, 150, 151, 159, 160, 181, 198, 211, 213, 226, 241, 247, 253
  administration 89, 102
  afternoon 85, 205 206
  lunch programs 40, 73, 74, 105, 133
  Sunday 208, 213, 226, 245
  See also boys' schools; day schools; education; girls' schools; secondary schools; vocational schools; yeshiva high schools
Schwartz, Joseph J. ("Joe") 1, 2, 34, 35, 36, 66, 68, 165
Schwartz, Leo 30

Scouts, Jewish 122

Second World War. *See* World War II

secondary schools xiii, 74, 126, 143, 168

Sefer — Moscow Center for University Teaching of Jewish Civilization 225

Sefrou 115, 124, 130, 132

seminars 83, 90, 220
    cantorial seminary 223
    community fuctionaries 223
    Jewish festivals 179
    local leaders 223–24, 227, 245
    rabbinic 223
    religious development 223
    teacher training 59, 70, 71, 89, 91, 94–96, 102, 105, 108, 122, 123, 127, 134, 140, 226, 241
    yeshiva administration 183
    See also vocational workshops

Sephardic Jews 34, 63, 88, 89, 103, 124, 157n, 166, 185, 255

Sfax 137, 140, 143, 146–47

Sha'ar Hashamayim synagogue (Cairo) 153

Shaare Zedek Medical Center 185

Shabbat xviii, 7, 10, 27, 36, 41, 50, 72, 106, 117, 118, 128, 130, 138, 139, 146, 149, 179, 180, 199, 210, 255

Shah. *See* Pahlevi

Shakhrisabz 207–8

Shalom, Isaac 33, 124–25, 159

Shanghai 112, 164

Shapiro, Judah 28, 79, 84, 85, 91–92, 93, 167, 171

Shavuot 119

Shebabo, Isaac 141, 144

shehita 10, 47, 49, 50, 118, 119, 128, 131, 143, 166, 170, 177, 193, 195, 196–97, 206, 207, 209, 210, 213, 215

Shereshevsky, Ezra 98–99

Shimonov, Rabbi Emanuel 206

Shiraz 38, 42, 43, 44, 49, 57, 59, 60, 62, 66, 71–72

shofar 138, 195, 196, 200

Shoshani, Avraham 59, 74

Shvilli, Abram 213

Siberia 128, 129, 164, 195, 218, 226

Sidon (Saida) 159, 160

Siebold, Janet xx, 26

Six-Day War (1967) 111, 136, 145, 159, 160, 169

Slobodka (Hebron) yeshiva 165

Slonim 165

smallpox inoculations 60

social work xxi, 22, 83, 112, 182, 234, 242

Sonderkommando 17

Sorotzkin, Rabbi Zalman 166

soup kitchens xxii, 82, 209, 212, 244

Sousse 137, 143, 146, 147

South Africa 2, 20

South America 2, 81, 170

Southern Russia 208–12

Soviet Academy of Sciences 225

Soviet Occuption Zone 5

Soviet Union xii, 33, 36, 69, 80, 87, 115, 130, 189, 190–91, 192–95, 201, 203, 204, 205, 209, 214, 215, 216, 217, 218, 221, 222, 231, 251, 252, 254

Soviet Union Team (SUT) 59, 191, 193, 194, 218–19, 220, 221, 226, 229, 230, 233, 249

Spain 84, 85, 88, 109, 110, 151, 254

Stalin 128, 189, 200, 212, 217

Stavropol 211

Stockholm 87

Strasbourg 85, 86, 88, 93, 99, 120

students' union xviii, 213. *See also* Hillel

Sukkoth 255. *See also* High Holidays

supplies, distribution
    clothing 40, 43, 61, 231
    by debit card 244
    food 28, 40, 166, 168–69, 203, 209, 221, 229, 230, 235, 236, 237, 244
    meals on wheels 233
    packages and parcels 9, 12, 19, 24, 33, 189, 200, 203, 221, 222, 229, 230, 231, 233, 234, 236, 237, 238, 243, 244, 247

survivors (Holocaust) xviii, xx, 2, 3, 4, 5, 6, 7, 8, 12, 13, 15, 16, 17, 18, 20, 21, 25, 28, 29, 33, 81, 83, 84, 85, 129, 164, 165, 199, 216, 219, 239n, 243, 251, 254

SUT. *See* Soviet Union Team
Sweden 105
Swiss Banks Settlement 239
Switzerland 24, 81, 94, 95, 96, 102, 106, 254
synagogues xii, 235, 245, 254
  Algeria 151
  Armenia 243
  Azerbaijan 214
  Bukhara 207
  Buynaksk 209
  Caucasus 217
  Chernivtsi 216, 224–25
  Choral Synagogue (Moscow) 222, 223
  Derbent 211
  Djerba 138–39, 143, 145
  Egypt 152, 153
  El Ghriba synagogue 139
synagogue restoration 153, 207, 212, 224
Syria 56, 88, 124
Syrian Jews 33, 124, 159
Szyf, Israel 58, 59, 70, 71, 72, 73, 74, 120, 208, 220 n. 10, 235

T
Tachkemoni school (Antwerp) 93
Tafilalet 116
Taganrog (Russia), 259
Tajikistan 192, 196–98, 237
Talmud xiv, xvi, 8, 10, 22, 71, 91, 115, 118, 171, 202
Talmud Torah xii, xvii, 85, 114, 115, 116, 117, 121, 124, 125, 128, 130, 131, 132, 140, 143, 144, 145, 149, 171. *See also* boys' schools
Tangier 110, 113–14, 119, 125–26
Tarshansky, Rabbi Shlomo 167
Tashkent 199, 204, 205, 225, 235, 236, 237
Taznakht 118
TB tests 60
Tbilisi 212–13, 225, 226, 236, 238, 240
teacher training xxii, 34, 44, 53, 59, 70, 71, 89, 91, 103, 123, 124, 126, 127, 130, 140, 226, 242
  training center 126
  See also seminars

teachers 45, 47, 94, 95, 102, 121, 127, 139, 144, 149, 180, 206, 207, 215
teachers' journal. See *Hamoré*
teaching aids xxii, 86, 89, 91, 226
teaching materials 11, 90, 91, 92, 100, 102, 141, 143, 150, 194, 205, 228, 229
technical training yeshivot 168. *See also* training
Tehran 32, 33, 34, 35–36, 37, 38, 39, 41, 43, 47, 48, 50, 51, 52, 53, 54–56, 57, 58–68, 70, 71, 73, 74–75, 76–77, 84
Tel Aviv xxiii n. 2, 8, 107
Ten Lost Tribes 49
Tetouan 123, 132
textbooks 45, 53, 57, 59, 86, 89, 91, 102, 131, 132, 143, 190, 205, 226
Timberg, Zvika 220 n. 10
Tnuva 184
Toaff, Rabbi Elio 85, 87
Toledano, Rabbi Baruch 115, 128, 132
Toledano, Samuel 125
Torah scroll 8, 28, 139, 198, 243
Torah studies 114, 129, 139, 166, 167, 172, 188, 222
Torat Hesed yeshiva (Baranovitch) 165
Toronto 171, 176, 187
tradition. *See* Jewish tradition
training
  communal functionaries and leaders 82–83, 103, 183, 193, 196, 222, 223, 224, 225, 226, 227, 248, 249
  rabbis 131, 150, 192, 251
  teacher xxii, 34, 44, 53, 59, 70, 71, 89, 91, 103, 123, 124, 126, 127, 130, 140, 226, 242
  technical 168
  vocational xx, 19, 22, 26, 27, 28, 52, 53, 62, 74, 76, 84, 87, 132, 142, 166, 168, 186, 187, 214
  welfare and community workers xx, 1, 2, 3, 6, 22–23, 83, 231, 232
transit camps 71
Transylvania 12, 13
Tripoli 74, 148
Truman, Harry S 5–6

Tunis 135, 136, 137, 140, 141, 142, 143, 145, 146, 147, 154
Tunisia 135–47
Tunisian Jews 35, 109, 135–40, 141, 146–47, 148
Turkey xxii, 56, 77, 88
Turkmenistan 192, 208, 237
typhoid 60, 67, 74
tzedaka (charity) 77, 119, 217, 229, 224

U
UJA (United Jewish Appeal) 68, 92, 120
Ukraine 189, 201, 204, 218, 225, 234. *See also* western Ukraine
Uman 201, 202, 215
Unite Populaire 122
United Nations 29. *See also* UNRRA
United States xxii, 2, 10, 12, 18, 20, 23, 55, 57, 68, 77, 80, 91, 98, 99, 105, 106, 112, 128, 131, 133, 157, 159, 160, 167, 175, 193, 198, 206, 208, 209, 226
United States Department of Agriculture (USDA) 112, 113, 169, 230
UNRRA (United Nations Relief and Rehabilitation Administration) 2, 3, 4, 6, 7, 8, 9, 10, 19, 22, 23
USDA. *See* United States Department of Agriculture
USSR. *See* Soviet Union
Ust-Kamenogorsk 223
Uzbekistan 192, 197, 203–8, 225, 235–36, 247, 248

V
Vaad, the. *See* Association of Jewish Organizations and Communities in the USSR
Vaad Hatzala 22, 33
Vaad Hayeshivot (Yeshiva Council) 166, 170
Versailles 83
Vienna 77, 83, 106, 177
Viteles, Harry 20, 21, 32, 34
Viznitz 165, 215

vocational schools 12, 29, 61, 85, 131–32, 135
vocational training. *See* training: vocational
vocational workshops 19, 22, 26–27, 187
vocational yeshiva high schools 168, 181
vocational yeshivot 166
Volgograd 210
voluntarism 227, 232, 233–34
volunteering xx, xxi, 9, 12, 21, 26, 31, 47, 99, 173, 180, 184, 191, 193, 199–200, 203, 232, 233, 235, 237, 241, 248, 252
Vynnikov, A. 65

W
Waltner, Rabbi Zushe 125–26
War of Independence (1948) 34, 152, 166
Warburg Scholarship Fund 103
Warburg, Miriam xxi, 1, 14
Warhaftig, Zerach 20
Warm Home 233
Warsaw Ghetto xv, xviii, xxi, 15
Warsaw xiv-xv, 15, 17, 85, 167
Wehrmacht 3
Weizmann, Chaim 65
welfare 43, 52, 53, 112, 147, 200, 203, 205, 208, 209, 213, 219, 221, 226, 230–31, 234, 235–36, 237, 238, 240, 243, 245, 247, 249, 253
    for housebound 219, 221, 223, 227, 231, 233, 235, 236, 244
    programs 43–44, 46, 70, 71, 73, 76, 79, 83, 112, 116, 133, 140, 147, 199, 200, 207, 209, 212, 213, 214, 220, 221, 224, 225, 230, 231, 236, 238, 239, 241, 243, 245, 246
    school programs 40, 44, 53, 59, 133, 150
    workers 84, 232
    See also Hesed centers; social work
Western Europe 73, 80, 81, 83, 89, 90, 101, 105, 106, 108, 109, 127, 222n
western Ukraine 192, 215–18, 224, 242. *See also* Ukraine
Wiesel, Max 220n
Wiley, John C. 36–37, 55
William Rosenwald Institute for Communal and Welfare Workers (Saint Petersburg) 232

Wilman, Gad 183–84

Windsheim (DP camp) 21, 22–23, 24, 25, 26, 27, 28, 29

winter relief 230, 231, 247

WIZO (Women's International Zionist Organization) 149

Wolfrathshausen 3

women's committee 62, 146
    Chava (Baku) 214
    FSU 219
    Kashfi (Iran) 50
    Morocco 115
    Rahamim (Tbilisi) 212, 236
    Taganrog 235

women's institutions 182

World Health Organization 60

World Jewish Relief 26

World War I xvi, xxii, 163, 189

World War II xxii, 80n, 96, 109, 110, 111, 129, 164, 165, 166 n. 6, 196, 201, 203, 204, 208, 215, 216, 231, 254

Wouk, Herman 176

Y

Yahil, Chaim. See Hoffman, Chaim

Yazd 42, 45, 63, 64, 72

Yedidim ("Friends") 179

Yemen 153–58, 160

Yemenite Jews 32, 153, 154–58, 196

Yerevan 242, 243

yeshiva, girls' 126

Yeshiva Department (JDC) 167–68, 170–71, 173–174, 176–77, 178, 182–88

yeshiva high schools 168, 175, 179, 180

yeshiva outreach program, immigrants 178–80

Yeshiva Program (JDC) 131, 144, 163–88

Yeshivat Hakotel (Jerusalem) 169

Yeshivat Meah She'arim 168

Yeshivat Ohalei Yaakov 223

Yeshivat Sanz 168

Yeshivat Toldot Aharon 168

yeshivot xiv, xvi, xviii, 29, 143, 164, 165, 166, 168, 169, 170, 175, 185, 223
    feeding program in 224
    Haredi 168
    preparatory 182
    See also hesder; kollel; vocational yeshivot; Yeshiva Department; yeshiva high schools; Yeshiva Program

Yiddish xiv, 38, 103, 115

Yiddishkeit 223, 231, 233. See also religious activities; religious supplies; religious suppression

yizkor 2

Yom Kippur xix, 2. See also High Holidays

Yossef, Rabbi Ovadia 185

youth xviii, xxi, 3, 6, 11, 26, 53, 61, 83, 92, 104, 122, 128, 133, 227–30, 241

youth activities. See education: informal

Youth Aliyah xxi, 14, 31

youth club 206, 209, 214

youth movement xviii, xx, 152

Z

Zargan 48, 67

Zarzis 139, 143

Zeilsheim 28, 85

Zerbib, Rabbi 149

Zhitomir 201

Zionism xvii, 5, 89, 111, 122, 136, 149, 167, 170, 189

Zissov, Meir 220 n. 10, 236

Zoroastrians 37

Zrubavli 45